LINKS OF HEAVEN

When he isn't writing about golf,
RICHARD PHINNEY
is a radio and television documentary maker whose
work appears on the BBC and Channel 4, and in North
America. He has also hosted a series of television
programmes on golf in Ireland. He now lives in
Montrose, Scotland, where he plays over the second
oldest golfing ground in the world.

A former sports broadcaster,
SCOTT WHITLEY
is a lawyer and writer in Toronto, Canada. An
acknowledged expert on real ale and the malts of
Scotland and Ireland, he also teaches business law to
aspiring golf club professionals.

LINKS
of HEAVEN

A COMPLETE GUIDE TO
GOLF JOURNEYS
IN IRELAND

**Richard Phinney
and Scott Whitley**

In memory of Eddie Hackett, the soul of Irish golf.

First published 2007 by
Aurum Press Limited
7 Greenland Street
London NW1 0ND
www.aurumpress.co.uk

First published in the United States of America by Baltray Books, 1996

A catalogue record for this book is available from the British Library.

ISBN-10: 1 84513 227 0
ISBN-13: 978 1 84513 227 9

10 9 8 7 6 5 4 3 2 1
2011 2010 2009 2008 2007

Illustrations by Bill Russell
Map by Stephen Dew

Design: bluegumdesigners.com
Typeset in Simoncini Garamond

Printed and bound in Great Britain by MPG Books, Bodmin

Contents

CONTENTS

Golfer's map of Ireland

Preface to the second edition

WHEN WE PRODUCED the first edition of *Links of Heaven*, we were driven by the desire to tell a story that we felt had not been told. That is still our objective in this much expanded and completely updated volume, almost a decade in the making.

There are thirty-one new chapters, and we now cover every full-length links in Ireland, as well as just about any other course you would likely want to play. Together they tell the saga of the fascinating rise and fall, and rise again, of golf in Ireland. It is a tale set largely on the most fabulous linksland on earth, peopled with extraordinary characters, and full of examples of the community spirit that makes golf in Ireland so unique.

In researching the new edition, we have been sustained by the generous praise the original book received from reviewers (the warm reception in the Irish press has been especially gratifying), and from some of our own heroes in the golf world.

We were moved, in particular, by notes of support received from legendary golf writers Peter Dobereiner and Herbert Warren Wind, and by the broadcaster (and former PGA champion) Dave Marr. As we discovered later, all were in failing health, but they took the time to look at the manuscript and offer ringing endorsements. There were similar messages from the likes of Ken Venturi, Raymond Floyd, Ben Wright and David Owen – people who didn't know us, but who were touched by what we had written, or at least what we had written about.

But most of all we were inspired by the enthusiasm of our readers. A remarkable number took the time to write or e-mail us, often at great length, to thank us for enhancing what had clearly become more than a golf trip. Many talked of a journey of discovery, taken with a father, son or brother, or a band of close friends, an experience they would obviously remember for the rest of their lives. And for some the journey was best taken alone. A reader from California reported:

> At Portsalon we met a lone figure wandering around on the fifteenth fairway with his golf bag and Links of Heaven in his hand like a person on a pilgrimage. He was looking for the sixteenth tee. He arrived the day before and was awestruck by the surroundings, all of which he credited directly to you. His seven days were to be spent chasing locations you had mentioned. We told him he was in good hands.

With feedback like that we felt a responsibility to bring *Links of Heaven* up to date. A huge amount has happened in golf in Ireland over the last ten years, and we wanted to document the changes, and try our hand at sorting out the good from the bad. It is a presumptuous task, but twenty years of exploring courses in the hidden corners of Ireland have only reinforced our views about what makes Irish golf so special.

It is most definitely not the luxurious parkland courses, the playgrounds for the very wealthy, which have sprung up around Ireland in recent years. The aim of this book is to encourage and equip you to seek out places where you will find much better golf, better value, better *craic*, and a far more satisfying sense of being connected to the extraordinary sporting and social phenomenon that is golf in Ireland.

INTRODUCTION

INTRODUCTION

Some of the Irish links, I was about to write, stand comparison with the greatest courses in the world. They don't. They are the greatest courses in the world, not only in layout but in scenery and 'atmosphere' and that indefinable something which makes you relive again and again the day you played there.

HENRY LONGHURST

A man would think that the game of golf originated here.

TOM WATSON, ABOUT BALLYBUNION

THE MAGNIFICENT SEASIDE LINKS of Ireland have stirred the imagination of the golfing traveller since Old Tom Morris, in 1894, pronounced Lahinch to be the greatest course of all. In the twilight of Queen Victoria's reign, the well-heeled golfing world flocked to Ireland – by boat, train, and horse and carriage – to taste the golfing pleasures offered at the golf resorts at Lahinch, Portrush, Portsalon and Rosapenna. The famous Triumvirate of professionals – Vardon, Taylor and Braid – were regular visitors, and the membership at Portrush included the two best women golfers in the world.

In the first quarter of the twentieth century everything began to change. The British aristocracy declined, the locus of the golf world moved to America, and Ireland entered a period of civil strife, partial independence and reconstruction. Golf travel to Ireland dwindled and remained dormant for more than half a century, although the reputation of its courses was fervently defended by a line of influential writers that stretched from Bernard Darwin to Henry Longhurst to Herbert Warren Wind.

Only in the 1970s and 1980s did golf travellers return in substantial numbers, encouraged by the ease of jet travel and the ringing endorsements of a new generation of golf celebrities such as Tom Watson. What they found was an unbeatable combination of breathtaking natural scenery, thrilling links golf and unparalleled hospitality. With the beginnings of a peace process in Ulster, the number of visiting golfers from North America, Britain and Europe has reached unprecedented levels. Benefitting from the prosperity that has at last blessed their island, the Irish are also golfing as never before. With a little effort, however, it is still possible to enjoy some of the finest courses on the planet in blessed tranquillity.

There is, quite simply, no better place to play golf.

One obvious reason is that Ireland is blessed with the finest stretches of true, natural linksland in the world. To golf along Ireland's rugged coastline is to encounter a succession of spectacular views, each more astounding than the last. And it doesn't hurt that nature's gifts have been refashioned by some of golf's most distinguished architects. Old Tom Morris, Alister Mackenzie, Tom Simpson (and his assistant Molly Gourlay), H. S. Colt, Robert Trent Jones and Jack Nicklaus have all left their signature on Irish soil. And the Irish golf architects Eddie Hackett and Pat Ruddy have added a stirring string of seaside courses of the highest calibre.

Just as intriguing are the mysterious origins of the great links of Portmarnock, Royal County Down and the incomparable Ballybunion. Like St Andrews, they just evolved, caressed and moulded by club members who spent a lifetime playing on their sandy soil. These courses – of no one age, and of no one hand – convey a sense of timelessness that cannot be recreated by bulldozers carrying out an architect's plan.

But there is a further dimension to the Irish golf experience that would make a golf holiday in Ireland worthwhile even if the courses were as flat and unappealing as day-old stout. Scratch the surface of even the most exclusive Irish golf club and you will find a genuine spirit of hospitality, and an eagerness to share (over a whiskey or a Guinness) tales about the game that the Irish have come to love with a passion equalled only in Scotland. Clubhouses in smaller communities are as friendly and egalitarian as any Irish pub.

It was not always so. Ireland's most famous courses were founded by the ancestors of British aristocrats who supplanted Irish peasants on their own land. It was well after the Second World War before golf became, by any definition, a sport of the people. The transformation has been remarkable. What were once the playgrounds of the gentry are now lovingly managed by the descendants of tenant farmers. Golf courses have even been built to provide jobs for the poor. It is a transformation not only of class, but also of race – the proud use of Irish at the Ceann Sibéal golf club on the Dingle Peninsula was unthinkable a century ago.

Politically, Ireland remains divided, but the Golfing Union of Ireland governs the game in all thirty-two counties and the all-Ireland inter-club competitions have always been pursued with an intensity that has no match in any other golfing country. The popularity of golf has exploded in Northern Ireland and in the Republic, ignited by television coverage and the rapidly increasing affluence of an island where income levels were, until recently, about half the European average. Today more than 400,000 Irish men and women play golf, twice the number of only a few years ago, and thousands more compete for their Christmas turkeys on the pitch-and-putt courses that dot the island.

The last fifteen years have also seen an explosion of golf course construction unknown in Ireland since the 1890s. Play has begun on more than one hundred new courses, and dozens of established clubs have undertaken major renovations. The worldwide publicity garnered from Ireland's successful hosting of the Ryder Cup in 2006 can only add to this momentum. The bad news is that green fees have gone up, and it would no longer be true to say that golf in Ireland is a bargain. But the sheer quality and depth of the roster of links courses in Ireland means that it still offers unbeatable value to those willing to divert from the itinerary of the standard Irish golf tour.

It would be a travesty, of course, to think of Ireland – North and South – as merely a golf destination. It is a place with an ancient and complex culture, its own language, and a tumultuous and often tragic history. Although Ireland is changing rapidly, the rooted quality of Irish life can still be startling (accents can be different in towns only a few miles apart). Each time you play golf in Ireland you encounter a new community with its own way of speaking and thinking about the world, and its own story. It is these encounters that make a golf journey to Ireland so fascinating. You will be sifting through layers of time as you marvel at unspoiled countryside, experience the charm of a village pub, and sample the attractions of vibrant and historic cities. And you will be collecting a bouquet of memories that will linger for a lifetime, and perhaps even help you face the challenges you left behind at home.

We hope that this book will assist anyone who is embarking on the journey for the first time, rekindle the memories of those who have already been, and be of interest to anyone with a love for the game of golf.

Acknowledgements

This book has been made possible by the generosity of scores of Irish golfers who offered us so much of their time and good humour. We would also like to thank Tony Boner, Maurice Buckley, Bob Byrne, Frank and Hilary Casey, William Condon, Jay Connolly, Noel Cronin, Sean Coyne, John Dalzell, Ivan Dickson, Paul Diver, Trey Fouché, Hugh Gillespie, Dr Edwin Holland, Michael Howard, Mary Huggard, Paul Hughes, Denis Kane, Mike Kearney, William Kelly, Joseph Kennedy, Jack Magowan, Michael Mangan, Liam McAndrew, Sean McCormack, Hugh McDermott, Hal McElroy, Jim McKenna, Alison Metcalfe, Bob Mulholland, Michael O'Brien, Jim O'Regan, Gary Partington, Tom Prendergast, John Quigley, Alan Reardon, William Rocke, Pat Ruddy, Cathal Toland, Simon Tormey, Pat Turvey and Mike Walker.

We are also indebted to the dozens of historians, writers and club members who have produced the many exceptional club centenary books that have appeared during the last twenty years. Taken together they represent a remarkable record of the social history of Ireland, as well as the development of some of the golf world's great treasures (they also make handsome mementos). We have benefited greatly as well from William Gibson's *Early Irish Golf* and from the histories of the *Golfing Union of Ireland* (by William Merton) and of the *Irish Ladies' Golf Union* (by Dermot Gilleece and John Redmond).

Thanks also to Kevin Friend of BCN Productions, who invited Richard to host a series of television documentaries on golf in Ireland, exposing his golf swing to the world, but also contributing to our research. We would also like to thank our informal team of unpaid reviewers. While the authors have played every course profiled in this book, Jerry Lee, Alain Roy, Mark Whitley and Alain Wilson provided valuable second opinions and made our own journeys to Ireland as memorable as we expect yours will be.

Finally, we'd like to thank our long-suffering wives and children, Julia and Huw, and Maureen, Jamie and Katie, for putting up with our numerous absences with unfailing good humour.

This second edition has been made better by everyone who wrote to us to share their Irish golfing experiences, often getting in touch at www.irishgolf.com. We always love to hear from you.

About this book

The core of the book is divided into four geographic sections – the Southwest, the Northwest, the East and Northern Ireland – corresponding to Ireland's great golfing regions. Each section begins with in-depth chapters on every full-length (6,000 yards or more) links course in the region. That is followed by 'Other Courses of Interest', which include some shorter links and parkland courses that we feel merit consideration because of their quality, importance or because (especially in the case of Northern Ireland) they represent good value in an area a little short on links. As always, we have described the distinct qualities of each course and club, and filled in any historical background that we think will enrich your experience.

In case you do not wish to golf every day on your journey, we have also provided a summary of outstanding sightseeing 'Diversions' that are available near Ireland's major golfing regions. These chapters may also be a source of ideas for the non-golfing spouse or friend. More detailed tourist information can be obtained from the resources listed at the back of the book.

The 'Contexts' section has chapters on the fascinating saga of women and golf in Ireland, the overall historical context, and Irish food and drink.

There is also an entire section entitled 'Planning Your Journey', which will help you get the most out of limited time and budgets. Here you will find suggested day-by-day trip schedules, information about how to book starting times, what to take and what to expect during your journey. There is also an accommodation guide geared to the golf destinations we have recommended.

Finally, we offer an annotated listing of one hundred and fifty more golf courses. While not all are of championship calibre, a visit to any of these courses will rarely go unrewarded, and if the club is off the beaten track the welcome will be doubly warm.

A note about authorship

While this book has been a joint effort in terms of conception, research and editing, the bulk of the narrative has been written by Richard Phinney, and he must therefore take the bulk of the responsibility for any shortcomings, errors and omissions. He is also the 'I' in first-person narratives. Exceptions include the chapters on 'Diversions', 'The Nineteenth Hole', and the 'Planning Your Journey' section, which Scott Whitley has written. Ireland's finest eighteen holes were decided jointly and scientifically over several pints of Guinness, none of which, in Scott's view, were quite warm enough.

The Joy of Links

On a links there is so much that is natural, and it has taken centuries to get that look and feel, so you'd be a lunatic to tamper with it more than is necessary.

PAT RUDDY, IRISH WRITER AND GOLF ARCHITECT

ALTHOUGH IRELAND HAS more than four hundred golf courses of all descriptions, its great legacy to the sport is the forty seaside *links* that form a bracelet of dazzling golfing gems along the island's craggy coastline. These courses are found on the same type of treeless, fiercely undulating terrain, linking the sea and farmland, which inspired the game's inventors. As the sandy soil was of no use save for grazing sheep, the ingenious Scots created a game that could be played on this unproductive ground. All golf courses built since are imitations, however abstract, of these original layouts and the natural features they incorporated – the sand pits where sheep sheltered against the wind, the dunes, and the areas of heather and fescue grass that came to be known as 'rough.'

To play a classic links is to play the genuine article, and return to the origins of the game. For some the combination of stunning coastal scenery, bracing natural elements, and the scent of history can make it something of a spiritual journey. (Michael Murphy's *Golf in the Kingdom*, a mystical voyage to an ancient links in Scotland, remains one of the best-selling golf books of all time.)

Another reason links golf is so special is that there isn't very much of it. Less than one half of one per cent of golf courses are links, almost all of them in the British Isles, and virtually all of the world's linksland has been used up for golf courses and human settlement. During the last forty years only Ireland has seen a significant number of new links created, and European Community conservation laws may prevent the building of any more.

The eminent American golf writer Herbert Warren Wind described the unique qualities of a true links with his usual precision and grace:

> At first glance, even the most distinguished linksland courses look utterly ordinary to the man who has never played them before. If a golfer stands on the terrace at the Augusta National Club, say, and takes in the wide panorama of lush fairways

swinging through tall pines, he senses at once that an authentic championship layout awaits him – an experience that also occurs at most of the world's renowned inland courses. But let him stand on the first tee at St Andrews or Ballybunion, and all he sees is a treeless sweep of billowing pale-green land with a few dun-colored sand hills in the distance – a most unpromising vista. A fragment of fairway is visible here and another fragment there, and a few numbered flags are blowing in the breeze, so what he is looking at is evidently a golf course, but it might as easily be pasture land. It is only when the golfer gets out onto a linksland course that he discovers, to his amazement, that it is filled with great golf holes, all the more appealing since their strategic features were molded by nature instead of by the bulldozer.

One of the most common misconceptions about links courses is that they are all the same. At Ballybunion, centuries of erosion and silting have pushed the linksland together, creating huge dunes and dramatic plateau greens which to many people represent Irish links. But the gently rolling terrain at Portmarnock – an equally great links – is entirely different.

On a links, the architect's job is less to create something new than to tease out the golf holes that are already there. When Tom Simpson advised the members at County Louth on how they could improve the course in the 1930s, he scolded the original designers for failing 'to observe and/or take advantage of the glorious possibilities that the ground afforded'.

For all its rewards, links golf can take some getting used to. Bobby Jones stomped off St Andrews in frustration halfway through his first tournament there, in 1921, though he later came to love the world's oldest course with a passion.

The classic links courses were not, of course, designed for 'target golf' – the high, precise and spinning shots, made easier with improvements in equipment, which can make hazards obsolete. Anyone who has watched the British Open on television knows that wind and hard greens can be a great equalizer, forcing competitors to use the imaginative low shots of an earlier time. But on a fine day, the great subtleties of even St Andrews are lost in the relentless aerial attack of the top professionals.

But for the average player – who drives the ball something less than 250 yards and whose long irons do not soar to the heavens – links golf is a wondrous, fascinating challenge every day of the week, and one in which brute strength is not the imperative it is on many inland courses. The absence of trees, the rollicking fairways, the unimpeded ocean winds, and the unpredictable placement of deep fairway bunkers mean that holes can be played any number of different ways. The corners of doglegs can be breached (or not) and a variety of lines of approach to the greens are possible. The ever-changeable wind adds more complexity. Depending on the wind's direction and velocity, even Bobby Jones had three different ways to play the Long Hole (the fourteenth) at St Andrews. For the mere mortal there are countless more.

Some survival tips

It has become a cliché to say that one needs to master a pitch-and-run shot to survive on a links. This used to be the case in the old days, when the sandy soil on links greens would dry out quickly in the summer and become as hard as a bowling alley. With the widespread introduction of watering systems, however, greens are much more receptive to high pitch shots, except on days that are extremely windy.

For the average player it is the *drive* that requires the most severe revision of thinking. Because of the absence of trees, there is an entirely misleading sense of space on links courses. Golfers who would retreat to a long iron off the tee on narrow, tree-lined fairways at home can be found whaling away on Royal County Down, which has some of the most exacting rough in the world. On a breezy summer day in Ireland, when the rough is at its fiercest and the fairways their hardest, there is an enormous premium to be gained from staying out of the rough. Not only do you avoid losing your ball in a gorse bush, you have the enjoyment of seeing your drive bound unexpected distances.

Links golf is not primarily about strength. On inland courses, it is often necessary to drive the ball a considerable distance in order to make the rest of the hole playable. The alternative is an embarrassing lay-up in front of the lake that the designer wants you to fly with a towering Vijay Singh three iron, or an irritating wedge to get around the neck of a dogleg. On links courses, indignities are more likely caused by miscalculation than a lack of strength. Disaster strikes because you have let the wind carry your ball like a kite into the deep gorse, or bounced your chip clear over the green, or tried to be more ambitious than you should have out of a pot bunker.

'Without the wind, it would be like playing snooker,' is how an Irish playing companion describes golf. Far from considering wind a nuisance, he thinks of it as the spice that brings out the full flavour of a links course, and the game.

It's an attitude worth cultivating, for a links course demands the skills of a sailor. You have to find ways to let the wind help you when it can, and resist the urge to fight it when it can't. There is no more helpless feeling than seeing your ball snatched by an Atlantic breeze and deposited into a great field of gorse. On extremely windy days you feel out of control and disoriented. Even putting is a new experience.

The wind can make par a very abstract term. Getting a six on an upwind par 4 can be more difficult than on a downwind par 5. The wise approach is to forget about par and concentrate on each stroke. Sometimes even par 3s are better played as two-shot holes. In the 1951 British Open at Royal Portrush, defending champion Bobby Locke refused to aim for the green at the famous Calamity hole, preferring the safety of a hollow to the left of the putting surface, which is perched on the edge of a great chasm.

Finally, there are the unpredictable lies. Tom Morris and other nineteenth-century Scots would be appalled at the thought of flat, immaculate fairways. The essence of links golf was to take the good bounce with the bad.

'We have been so anxious, in the sacred name of fair play, to take all the element of luck out of the game, that we have to a proportionate extent destroyed its value as a test of each man's ability to stand up to bad luck,' lamented the golf historian Robert Browning in 1955. 'Modern golf is a stiffer test of a player's skill, but it has robbed the game of something of its charm as an adventure of the spirit.'

The adventure of the spirit is still very much alive on Irish links.

'Anything that is in nature is not wrong,' said the late Irish golf architect Eddie Hackett of the sometimes frustrating swales found on the fairways and greens of his best courses. Hackett rarely inserted artificial mounds, but he also hated taking out natural ones.

In the end, playing links golf is not about changing one's game, but about changing one's *attitude*. When Bobby Jones stomped off St Andrews, it wasn't because he didn't have the game for the strange new conditions (he was the greatest player of his age by far). He just wasn't in the right frame of mind. Jones came to love links golf, as did the likes of Arnold Palmer, Tom Watson and Tiger Woods after him. Chances are you will too. Soon you will be disappointed when the weather is too calm, critical when the rough is too benign, and positively insulted when sand traps around the green are too shallow. You will discover that there are few greater thrills than making a good recovery out of a deep pot bunker, belting a blind tee shot directly over the exact sand hill you were aiming at, fashioning just the right pitch-and-run over undulating terrain, or playing the wind perfectly on an approach to the green.

At its best, links golf is both charmingly old-fashioned and thoroughly modern. For some it is addictive, an intoxicating mixture of elemental surroundings and multi-faceted strategy that no other kind of golf can duplicate. At the very least it is likely you will find the experience of golfing on the timeless links of Ireland to be a provocative and arousing departure from your normal routine, and one that will enrich your appreciation of the sport wherever you may play it.

Kings of the Links

It is a numbingly cold November morning, and we are stumbling our way through a rough field along the sea wall near the tiny village of Ballyconneely on the west coast of Ireland. I cannot recall when I have ventured out of doors on a nastier day. It is no more than forty-five degrees and I am being thrashed by rain whipping off the ocean. The wind is deafening and the raindrops feel like ice pellets on my cheek.

We have reached a sturdy barbed-wire fence, and my companion, a frail eighty-five-year-old man in rubber boots and a heap of black rain gear, has taken it into his head that we need to roll *underneath* it. The bottom wire can't be more than a foot from the ground. But Eddie Hackett is already on his hands and knees before I have a chance to suggest an alternative course of action.

'Jack Nicklaus wouldn't do this, would he?' shouts the dean of Irish golf architects, as he lies flat on his back and begins to squirm his way under the dangerous-looking wire. There is a gleam in his eye and just a hint of mischief in his lilting Irish voice. 'Maybe he would design the course from an aer-o-plane.'

Frankly, at that moment the inside of an aeroplane sounded pretty good to me. So did a hot whiskey in front of a blazing fire. I didn't fancy rolling under that fence. Or three others like it. I didn't feel like wading through a creek, or stomping through heaps of seaweed. I have never been so wet, or so cold. But it was a once-in-a-lifetime chance to see the greatest links designer of our generation in action.

◆ ◆ ◆

'I tried being a priest once, but I believed too much in golf,' says Pat Ruddy, pausing just long enough to make you wonder whether he is pulling your leg. Then his face bursts into a big amiable smile that makes laughter irresistible.

Later, Pat Ruddy drives me around the European Club, the magnificent links he designed, built and still operates south of Dublin, in a beat-up station wagon. There's a pile of magazines in the back seat from one of Ruddy's publishing enterprises.

'I try to work on cinematic principles,' he says as he stops the car next to the second green. 'It's not just a pretty thing, you are trying to disorient the guy, the optics are changing all the time.'

Ruddy grabs a golf club out of the boot, and gestures to a high dune next to the green.

'Come up here to the third tee, the one we use for state occasions,' he says. Eschewing the path, he climbs up the grassy dune in his leather dress shoes, leaning on the golf club.

As it often is at the European Club, the view from the tee is exhilarating, the challenge laid out thrillingly before you.

'The two gathering bunkers over here are pretty small but they are gathering balls all right,' says Ruddy, pointing his club at the hazards. 'And we have this one there for the son of a bitch who tries to get away from that idea!'

In some ways, Eddie Hackett and Pat Ruddy couldn't be more different. Hackett was the mild-mannered professional, good enough to play in the British Open, who went to Mass every day. Ruddy is a garrulous and sometimes profane ex-newspaper man who never threatens par on the golf course.

But it is the attributes they share that make them Ireland's greatest golf architects, and important figures for anyone who cares about the special kind of golf that can only be played on the planet's precious and limited supply of linksland.

Eddie Hackett died in 1996, and Pat Ruddy has entered a period of active semi-retirement. Yet their legacy in Ireland will last as long as golf is played. It is not just that they have designed more genuine links courses than anyone else in the last seventy-five years. In many cases, their vision, persistence, generosity and passion for the game actually made them happen.

Here, then, are the stories of the Kings of the Links.

Saint Eddie

Don't be embarrassed if you've never heard of Eddie Hackett. Almost nobody has outside his native Ireland.

'I find that nature is the best architect!' he shouted to me on that frigid November morning in 1995, as he trudged through knee-high grass, pacing the width of a fairway that at this point existed only in his mind.

'I just try to dress up what the Good Lord provides. Of course, He gave us a lot in this place.'

Two decades beyond Ireland's official retirement age, Hackett was designing an additional nine holes for the Connemara Golf Club. He had laid out the original course in 1970 for a local community group that believed a golf course might spur economic development in a region devastated by unemployment and emigration. The holes weave through a stark landscape of exposed slabs of rock, and on a fair day the course is hauntingly beautiful, swallowed up by the natural elements.

'They had no money, you know,' Hackett said as he hitched up his rain suit. 'I told them if you're that keen on golf, I'll go down and I'll put a stone in for a tee and a pin in for a green, and you can pay me when you can.

'The only thing I insisted on is that the course be laid out according to the play on the best possible lines.'

Connemara is only one of a string of magnificent seaside courses along Ireland's rugged western coastline that have earned Hackett a permanent and unique place in golf history. They are not only beautiful and challenging tests of golf, they will be among the last links courses ever built.

The fantastic linksland found in Ireland is in a class of its own. It is not only the historic and world-famous links of Ballybunion, Lahinch, Portmarnock, Royal County Down and Royal Portrush that set the Emerald Isle apart. It is that Ireland also has new links. Until recently, the west coast of Ireland was the last place on earth with large stretches of undeveloped linksland. Much of this potentially priceless golfing ground was found on commonages: grazing land owned jointly by several local farmers. While better known designers jetted around the world, producing luxury resorts from Morocco to Bali, Eddie Hackett worked patiently with communities that wanted to turn these largely unproductive lands into golf courses.

'Eddie is the unsung hero of Irish golf,' says Pat Ruddy 'At a time when there was no money, [he] travelled the highways and byways of Ireland. Half the people playing golf in Ireland are doing so because of Eddie

Hackett. And I don't know anyone who has said the slightest bad word about him.'

Father Peter Waldron, an avid golfer who spearheaded the development of Connemara, goes further.

'Oh Eddie Hackett is a saint, you know,' Waldron told me when Hackett was still alive. 'He is totally self-effacing, and he has more integrity than almost anybody I have ever come across. And he works for pennies.'

Hackett's best-known creation is probably Waterville, a severe but breathtaking test of golf on the picturesque Ring of Kerry. But if you travel north up the thinly populated coast from Waterville, you will encounter a string of hauntingly beautiful links with lyrical names that are every bit as memorable. All were designed by Eddie Hackett, often on shoestring budgets, and all are accessible and relatively inexpensive for the visiting golfer.

The first stop is Ceann Sibéal – an undiscovered gem thrust out on the farthest extremities of the Dingle Peninsula. Connemara is next, followed by Carne, a course built in the early 1990s as a non-profit community project on the remote and economically depressed Belmullet Peninsula. Whereas Connemara is relatively flat, Carne is a breathtaking ride through some of golf's most imposing sand dunes, a kind of Ballybunion on steroids.

Although tamer and less exposed to the Atlantic winds, Enniscrone, in County Sligo, is one of the most popular links among Irish golfers, with thrilling elevated tees, superb par 3s, and a series of exquisite short par 4s through wonderfully contorted terrain. Further up the coast is Donegal, a sweeping, stately layout that many consider Hackett's finest achievement. Finally, at the northern tip of Ireland, Hackett also designed St Patrick's, a spectacular but barely maintained links that will soon be torn up by Jack Nicklaus.

Hackett's graceful and natural designs are the perfect complement to the much older west-coast links of Ballybunion, Lahinch and Rosses Point. And they are an integral part of what is arguably the most stunning stretch of seaside golf in the world.

So why is Eddie Hackett not better known? The remoteness of his best courses has certainly played a part, as has the fact that Hackett stayed so close to home throughout his life. In a design career that spanned thirty years, he designed or remodelled all or part of eighty-five courses, a remarkable total for a man with no partner and no employees. However, every last one of them was in Ireland (Robert Trent Jones, by contrast, built courses in at least twenty-three countries).

But the main reason for Hackett's relative obscurity was surely his striking reluctance to blow his own horn. I asked him about it when I met him again in the relative calm of his cluttered Dublin house shortly before his death (a widower, he lived alone, though his children lived nearby).

'We Irish had a terrible inferiority complex, with the English occupation and the way we were terrorized and savaged,' he explained. 'It's only starting to go with the new generation.'

Hackett's gentlemanly manners were very much in evidence during my visit. A teetotaller, he kept lifting himself out of his ancient easy chair to fill up my glass of Jameson's. He wore a cardigan over a shirt and tie, and as he told his life story, with the aid of yellowed newspaper clippings and faded photographs, it struck me that Hackett was one of golf's most important connections to an earlier, golden age. At the time, he must surely have been the last man alive who could say that he had lunch with James Braid, Harry Vardon, and J. H. Taylor – the Great Triumvirate that dominated golf at the turn of century. It happened at the British Open at Hoylake in 1936 and was one of Hackett's most cherished memories.

Born in a Dublin pub in 1910, twelve years before Irish independence, Hackett survived a Dickensian childhood of periodic penury and grave illness (he spent long stretches in hospital with tuberculosis). One of the brighter moments of his youth came the day his father announced proudly that he had become one of the first Catholic tradesmen to be allowed into a golf club in Ireland. Young Eddie took to the game too, the one sport his doctors would allow him to play.

His father went bankrupt while Eddie was still a teenager, so Hackett was thankful to get a job as a clubmaker, working with hickory shafts, at the Royal Dublin Golf Club. He worked on his game, and was offered a job as an assistant professional in South Africa.

'I'd never been out of Ireland. When I left Royal Dublin to go, I took one tram with my clubs on my back, and then another to [the port at] Dun Laoghaire. And I got on a boat to Liverpool, a train to London and Southampton. I booked on the Carnarvon Castle [a liner], as there were no aeroplanes in those days. Then I was on the Blue Train through the desert.'

Hackett returned to Ireland a few years later, and in 1939 landed a job as the head professional at the exclusive Portmarnock Golf Club for the princely sum of £10 a week (though it went down to £2 a week during the war years).

'As the professional I was never allowed into the clubhouse,' Hackett told me. 'I'm an honorary member now, and I still don't go into the clubhouse. It's just the way I am.'

Hackett left Portmarnock in 1950 to take part in an ill-advised business venture. The next few years turned out to be the worst of his life, and he spent another nine months in bed in a near-fatal battle with meningitis. Hackett returned to golf almost by chance in the early 1960s when the Golfing Union of Ireland asked him to give teaching clinics across the country. One of the clubs was looking for someone to design a golf course (one of the first full-length courses to be built in thirty years) and Hackett's name was recommended. He stumbled his way through the job and suddenly he was an expert. For all intents and purposes he was Ireland's only golf architect.

'In those years, there was no one else to go to,' said Hackett, 'unless you went to an English architect, but they were expensive. All my life I've been charging too little, but at that time, you see, I wouldn't have the confidence in my abilities.'

On occasion, Hackett even tried to convince clubs not to hire him.

'I told them that if I was in your position, and I wanted to make some money, I wouldn't use Hackett, I'd use a Nicklaus or a Palmer or a Trent Jones.'

In two notable cases, clubs followed his advice, and hired Arnold Palmer (Tralee) and Robert Trent Jones (Ballybunion Cashen). Both are worthy efforts, built on spectacular terrain, but they have a theatricality that is out of sync with the great Irish and British links. The consensus in Ireland is that they don't rank with Hackett's best, which have an air of maturity and grace rare in young courses of any kind.

Hackett's courses tend to be long from the back tees, with clearly visible landing areas, large greens and spectacular elevated tees. Despite his great love for the classic links of Ireland and Scotland (which he played as a young professional), Hackett eschews two of their most common features – blind tee shots and hidden hazards – and prefers to make a hole's challenges clearly visible in the modern style. Every one of his links courses is enormously enjoyable, even thrilling to play, with at least a half-dozen holes that will stop you dead in your tracks in admiration.

The admiration is always as much for Mother Nature as for the architect, however. Hackett never draws attention to himself. There are no bizarre sand traps, ostentatious ledges, artificial mounds or strangely shaped greens so common in modern design. One of his most beautiful holes in Ireland is the eleventh at Waterville, which tumbles entirely naturally through a long channel of majestic dunes. The very next hole, called 'The Mass', plays over a valley that sheltered Catholics as they worshipped in secret during periods of religious repression at the hands of the English.

'When I made that hole the contractors, local men, came to me and they said: "Eddie, we're not going to dig up or touch this ground for you. Because Mass was celebrated in the hollow." I said "You needn't be worried."

'And we never touched it. It's a plateau green, it's natural. And there's not a bunker on it either. It doesn't need one and that's the best tribute you can pay a hole.' (Alas, Tom Fazio has since introduced a bunker in front of the green.)

Because Hackett's layouts are so sensitive to the natural terrain, there is always a consistent style and rhythm to his links that takes its theme from the specific natural surroundings. Nothing seems artificial or imposed. Hackett would have been horrified to think his courses looked like one another – he didn't want to leave his signature about. He didn't talk so much about designing golf holes as finding them, and he was proudest when he could point to a hole and say 'it's just as nature.'

'I could never break up the earth the way they tell me Jack [Nicklaus] and Arnold [Palmer] do,' he said. 'You disrupt the soil profile and anyway, it's unnatural. I use what's there within reason. You're only as good as what the Lord gives you in features. And you can never do with trees what you can do with sand dunes.'

Hackett also made a virtue of necessity. Many of his clients couldn't afford bulldozers. But in the process he touched the lives of ordinary people in a way that few architects have.

'Looking back it was a growing and achievement point, and a self-believing point for the community,' says Father Peter Waldron of the original golf development at Connemara in 1970. 'And economically it turned the key to a whole new area of opportunities for the entire region.'

Built for perhaps £70,000 with almost entirely local labour ('We never had to move a rock,' Hackett said proudly), the golf course is now responsible for pumping millions of euros each year into the local community, from overseas and Irish visitors.

Hackett had been seriously ill not long before my visit to his home. Near the end of our conversation I asked him about his faith. Religion can be a delicate subject in Ireland, and at first Hackett seemed reluctant to talk about it, as if he could be misinterpreted.

'You could say I would be religious, yes, but that doesn't mean I can't be friendly with others,' he said finally. 'I'm not narrow. But my own faith is very strong. There's one prayer from *The Imitation of Christ* that I read every night: "Dear Lord, give me grace to be meek and humble of heart, to be glad when people think little of me."

'I've been very lucky in my life. Most people never get to design a links. I've done ten. When I'm out [on the course] I pray to the Lord to give me the light to do what's right.'

Pat Ruddy – the dreamer

'I'm on a high going to any golf course,' says Pat Ruddy with the boyish enthusiasm that has never left him. 'But going to special ones like Augusta [National], it's just where you want to be. To be there, and to look at the scenery and flowers and the goddamn grass. If it's in really good shape you want to get down and roll on the bloody thing. You know, the way a kid rolls down a hill.'

There have been obstacles and disappointments along the way, but to hear Pat Ruddy tell it, his life has been one long roll on the grass. He is the kid who never had to grow up, who still can't quite believe that he has been able to make a living by immersing himself in the sport he loves so passionately. He has been a golf reporter, golf editor, golf promoter, golf publisher, golf architect and golf course developer. And he remains the owner of what may well be the last truly great championship links that will ever be built.

Golf in Ireland hit its nadir during the early 1950s. The Protestant merchants, military officers and aristocrats who had started the game in Ireland had declined in numbers and wealth, and the sport held few attractions for the average farmer or working man. In the small market town of Ballymote, County Sligo, it was a struggle just to maintain a nine-hole golf course.

'There would have been thirty golfers max at good times, a hard core of ten addicts,' remembers Ruddy, whose family moved to Ballymote when he was ten. Ruddy is a loquacious man who likes a good laugh and who tends to look at the bright side of life. His memories of childhood have a glow about them – a lovely non-stop adventure with golf at its centre.

'Dad used to come and pull me out of school when they were stuck for someone to play the fourball,' he says. 'And I found it a wonderful substitute for mathematics or English or Irish or Latin. The clubhouse was made of corrugated iron, no toilets, just hang up your coat and go golfing. They stacked up a bit of dirt in little rectangles two feet high to make a tee.

'They talk now about the rough being tough, but back then the fairway would be fifteen paces wide and the only way you could find the ball when it went into the rough was to watch it like a hawk and line up the fourball and scuffle up and down with your feet.'

As an adult, Pat Ruddy would become a one-man writing and publishing machine, so it is little surprise that books had a special place for him as a youth.

'Henry Cotton's golfing album, a beautiful book, influenced me a lot in my life. He took a camera and wrote little essays pertaining to the pictures showing the King of Belgium swinging the club, and down in Monte Carlo hitting balls into the sea. And I thought: "God almighty, if only I had a dozen balls – and here they are hitting them into the sea." Amazing stuff!

'So I started to carry a camera, started to write. I used to sit in the back seat at school drawing plans of golf courses. On the side of all of the books I had written "Pat Ruddy, Master Golfer".'

After deciding against pursuing a playing career, Ruddy bought a typewriter and wrote to the *Evening Herald* in Dublin. He was only nineteen, but he had an instinct for promotion.

'Dublin seemed a million miles away. I'd been there once or twice ever. So I wrote to this paper and said I was a genius and knew everything about golf, and they said they would give me a guinea a week for a column on golf in the west of Ireland. That was riches to me.'

Before long, Ruddy had married, joined the staff of the *Herald*, and was writing more words about golf than just about any man alive. At one point, he wrote a full broadsheet page *a day* on golf for the *Evening Herald*, and freelanced for magazines around the world. One of Ruddy's proudest moments at the *Herald* was his role in spearheading the movement to build a publicly funded golf course. Using the paper to relentlessly publicize the plight of what he coined the 'Homeless Golfers', Ruddy helped shame politicians into allocating the necessary funds. The golf course proved an immediate success.

Working for others was never going to satisfy the irrepressible Ruddy, and in 1973 he quit his job to found and write his own golf magazine. He was often engaged to promote tournaments, and one of his favourite tactics involved attempts to get into the Guinness Book of World Records.

'I wanted Liam Higgins [an Irish professional] to hit the longest drive down an airport runway. So I got a couple of hundred Spalding balls – they were the sponsor of the tournament – and looked for a runway. I thought you could rent one just like that by phoning Dublin airport. But I was wrong. Luckily the minister of defence was a golfer and he got a military airport, and Liam managed to make the record hit!'

There is an Irish twinkle in Ruddy's eyes when he finishes such a story, and the laughter that ensues is often punctuated by exclamations of 'Do you like it? Do you like it?' One of his most fondly remembered stunts was cancelled at the last moment.

'I was going to do the longest par 3, you see. I had Liam Higgins training parachute jumping, and we were going to fly over Royal Dublin, putt the ball out of the aeroplane, and then jump out and putt out.'

For the next ten years Ruddy continued to be a publisher, writer and general golfing impresario ('in one little corner of the planet roaring my head off about golf'). He got to travel to Augusta and other famous golf shrines and inevitably began to wonder how he might turn his childhood dream of building a golf course into reality. He bought some land near Ballymote but the project was a disaster.

'I went to the University of Stupidity and got an honours degree,' says Ruddy with a huge grin. 'It was the wrong ground, there wasn't enough money, people were stealing machinery when I was away. So I backed off.'

A few years later, however, Ruddy and Tom Craddock (a well known golfer in Ireland at the time) won the chance to design a new parkland course near the Dublin airport. St Margaret's was well received, and other assignments followed; Ruddy's publishing enterprise continued to thrive, and he had a little money in the bank again.

Then, in 1987, Ruddy spotted an advertisement in the property section of a Dublin newspaper that would change his life.

I first met Ruddy eight years later in his living room in the Dublin suburb of Dun Laoghaire. There was a lively fire going, and his wife Bernadine had spread out some tea, and ham sandwiches. The day when Ruddy first showed up at Brittas Bay with a couple of shovels to begin work seemed like ancient history. Golfers were flocking to the European Club, and Pat Ruddy could afford to see the humour in the obstacles he had to overcome.

The main problem was that he had no idea what he was doing. He didn't even know how to grow grass on links terrain.

'I seeded half of Wales,' he told me. 'And the first night it all blew away. There was serious learning going on.'

Then someone showed him a photograph of the Cashen Course at Ballybunion, while it was under construction.

'It blew my mind wide open. It showed what the bulldozers had done. It looked like the Sahara. And I said to myself: "Holy Jesus, am I going to have to do that?"'

'You have to shape it. You have to take up the turf, shape it and put it back. On a parkland [course] it takes a year to grow in, but on a links it takes two years or longer. You just have to wait. It cost me an arm and a leg, but it seemed I was destined to do it because money kept coming in at the right time. And it wasn't about the money anyway, it was the achievement.'

Ruddy's rambling house, built next to a golf course, is an entertaining place in its own right. It is part suburban home, part office (Ruddy edits his own golf magazines in the basement) and part golf museum, crammed full of amusing golf knick-knacks, musty golf books, old photographs and memorabilia. Although some of the golf antiques are undoubtedly quite valuable (they include a club with a wooden shaft and a tiny spoon-shaped head used to flick a putt over stymies) there is something engagingly artless about the house. Its contents seem to be an extension of Ruddy's personality, a three-dimensional expression of his overwhelming enthusiasm for the game.

'I've always tried to infect people with golf,' he says. 'I have a funny bent of mind, a mix of wild imagination but I'm an awful simple person as well. And I have a pretty analytical mind that can dissect situations.'

Ruddy disguises his ambitions for the European Club in humour and self-deprecation, but he is constantly searching for those 'intangibles' that will set his course apart. He has rejected the idea of constructing houses or another nine holes on the extra land that he has. Either option would make him a lot of money, but would jeopardize the sense of seclusion that Ruddy feels is the mark of most great courses.

'You can't build a golf course with a set square; it's an art form moulding the thing into the landscape,' he explains. 'The developer who wants to fit in lots of roads and houses is thinking different. It's like asking me to run a four-minute mile shackled, trying to put in houses. It just can't frigging be done in my opinion.

'I remember this place in the beginning was almost frightening in the loneliness you would feel. I don't want to lose that.'

In retrospect it seems that every road in Ruddy's life has been leading to the European Club, from the time he doodled course plans in his notebooks at school. But his success at Brittas Bay led to another chapter in his career that may be just as important to his legacy.

In 1992, he was asked to take a look at some unused linksland at Ballyliffin. Amazed at what he saw, he persuaded the club to embark on a much more ambitious expansion than they had been contemplating. Three years later, Ruddy's Glashedy Links opened to wide acclaim.

'Ballyliffin shook the country up,' says Ruddy. 'It showed what a little village could do.'

That was followed by what may be an even better links at Rosapenna (Sandy Hills), a major overhaul of Portsalon, and an update to the Eddie Hackett layout at Murvagh.

'I was very fortunate that County Donegal adopted me in the 1990s and allowed me to do links work at four venues. They trusted me with land and money. I would hope I worked with passion on their behalf. And I firmly believe the aggregate outcome is that we have revitalised that area, which used to be the Riviera of British golf and brought it back to the fore of golf.'

If there were any doubts that Ruddy's pioneering work had put Donegal back on the golf map, they were dispelled in 2006 by the announcement that Jack Nicklaus would design a thirty-six hole complex at St Patrick's, adjacent to Ruddy's Sandy Hills (and digging up the work of Eddie Hackett in the process).

Ruddy has also shown himself to be a superb designer of parkland courses. And unlike Eddie Hackett, he has had a chance to show what he could do on the other side of the pond.

The location of his only North American project, a former refuse tip in Montreal, is fodder for Ruddy's ever-present sense of the ridiculous.

'They [threw] their filth in there for thirty years, and [then] they wanted a course built that is environmentally sensitive,' he says with the expectant grin he uses when there is a punch line looming.

'Usually you have to say, it's a God-given site, so I was delighted to be able to say: "Your site is a dump!"'

Le Club de Golf de l'Ile de Montreal is a spectacular thirty-six holes of golf on treeless terrain, full of obvious references to the links courses of Ireland.

Since Ruddy, like Hackett before him, has never had full-time employees in his design operation, the Montreal project took him away from home for long periods. It also seems to have shown him that he has nothing left to prove.

'I made a resolution to organize myself differently,' he says. 'I had done a number of courses I liked, and I could go on, but the only motivation would be money. So I stopped to go golfing!'

It means, of course, that Ruddy now has even more time to spend on his beloved European Club.

'I have no doubt that it's a great piece of golf ground. I have no doubt I have done a reasonable job to start with. I have a committee of one, so I have the freedom to sit here and to think, and the freedom to do.

'You know when you get an examination paper you would always get a higher mark if you rework it. So there are more marks to be gained at Brittas Bay and that gives me great pleasure. All I have to do is live a while.'

Pat Ruddy and Eddie Hackett never collaborated on a design project, but at Donegal Golf Club their work is happily intertwined. Hackett laid out the original course in 1973, and thirty years later Ruddy was hired to update some of its features.

The President of the club, Derek Whaley, is perhaps the only person who saw both Ruddy and Hackett work on the same piece of ground.

'Eddie was very much about giving a lot of consideration to the land, the lie of the land, the things that exist in it,' says Whaley. 'He tended to leave it as nature presented it.'

Those who dissect golf course architecture call that approach minimalism, and it is very much in vogue today. Eddie Hackett has always been the ultimate minimalist. Bunkers and other man-made hazards are almost an irrelevancy on Hackett's links courses. For Hackett, strategy was fundamentally something that nature should determine.

'I like anything where nature dictates the way you make the hole,' he told me. 'I very seldom put it in if it's not there.'

It is a reticence that Pat Ruddy could never be comfortable with.

'Pat sets up the course that, yes, will play comfortably if you do it his way,' says Whaley.

For Ruddy, there is usually a right and wrong way to play every hole, and spacious fairways that allow multiple landing areas are not often a favoured feature on his courses. At Donegal, Ruddy has introduced two winding streams (something Hackett would not have considered) to penalize indifferent shots, knocked down a hill to eliminate a blind tee shot and, in his usual way, has agonized over the placement of every bunker.

'It is very easy to get them aesthetically right, but to get them strategically right is different,' Ruddy says. 'Designing a links course is like a big chessboard. There's the climate, the topography, the different people who play it. It is complex. Best thought out slowly.'

At the end of the day, it is not so much a style of design that Pat Ruddy and Eddie Hackett have in common, but a reverence for the game. For these self-taught architects, designing courses on scarce links terrain was not so much a gigantic thrill, as a gigantic responsibility.

'Every links is stressful in that you can leave things behind,' says Ruddy. 'You could reverse the golf course, put it sideways, there are umpteen options. You are always worried about what you are leaving out there.'

We'll give the last word to the man to which Irish golf owes so much.

'You see Richard, I don't look for a legacy of posterity,' Eddie Hackett told me in the last year of his life. 'I just want to do what I'm paid to do, not even so much what I'm paid because sometimes I do courses for nothing. People say "you don't have to worry Eddie, you've done great courses", but it's the course you're at [that counts]. I always have a sense of apprehension, of responsibility.

'A sense of inspiration, too, because suddenly you get the feel. There's always one way that's better than all of the others. There must be no better way of doing it as far as I'd be concerned.'

THE CLASSICS

(and more)

Golf on the rugged coast of Counties Kerry and Clare is a uniquely Irish experience, with huge dunes, crashing sea and remote, hospitable communities. The Southwest offers Ireland's most magnificent coastal scenery – including the famed Ring of Kerry and Dingle Peninsula – and the golf courses share in the splendour. While it was Old Tom Morris's original layout at Lahinch that first brought golfers to the region, it is now Ballybunion that quite rightly defines Irish golf in foreign eyes. But there is much more to admire in the Southwest, including the only links courses designed by Arnold Palmer, Robert Trent Jones and Greg Norman, and the superlative work of Irish architect Eddie Hackett at Waterville. There are also a handful of less well-known but enchanting courses that on a sunny day will have you looking at local real estate prices. And to top it all off there is Killarney – as different to Ballybunion as it is possible to be – and yet just as intensely Irish.

BALLYBUNION (Old)

Founded: 1893

Designed by: Unknown (refined by William McCarthy, Tom Simpson, Molly Gourlay and Tom Watson)

To put it simply, Ballybunion revealed itself to be nothing less than the finest seaside course I have ever seen.

HERBERT WARREN WIND

Almost unknown forty years ago, Ballybunion is now a legend, receiving almost as many visitors as St Andrews. They don't come for the history or the luxurious surroundings – you wouldn't want to send anyone a postcard of the clubhouse. The attractions of Ballybunion are found entirely on the links, which weaves its way through some of golf's most stirring terrain. It is not just the size or the wild look of the famous Ballybunion sand dunes, nor the beauty of the seaside holes – it is the way the links fits so superbly into what nature has provided. Many golf courses are blessed with fine natural settings, but at Ballybunion one feels that the gods have also designed the holes.

✦ ✦ ✦

Preparing to tee off at the first hole of Ballybunion Old can be a bit disheartening. In the high season, you may be herded into foursomes by staff whose ingrained Irish hospitality has developed a veneer of officiousness. Despite the not inconsiderable green fee you have paid, you may be forced to play the forward tees, and the new clubhouse (architecturally a cross between Star Trek and Stalin) will cast a less than graceful shadow. But somehow the graveyard changes everything.

Not a metaphorical graveyard mind you, as in 'Rae's Creek at Augusta National is the graveyard of many a golfer's hopes.' No sir, this is the real thing.

It doesn't matter if you've already heard about it, or played Ballybunion before, there is still something deliciously unsettling about navigating around the remains of departed souls on your opening drive. Make no mistake about it, the tombstones do come into play. Next to St Andrews, the mystique of Ballybunion may cause more nervous shanks off the first tee than any course in the world.

Who on earth would have the nerve to place a tee so close to a cemetery? At Ballybunion no one knows for sure. We like to think the answer will turn up in the Old Testament somewhere. Okay, Ballybunion isn't *that* old. But its much commented-on sense of timelessness is wonderful to experience first hand just the same. At Ballybunion, one feels that one is playing the primordial links, that this is *Golf Before Man*.

The Ballybunion legend was for a long time embellished by the course's role as golf's archetypal *undiscovered* treasure. Due to its isolation in a poor and inaccessible part of Ireland, Ballybunion was known to few foreigners, save for a handful of intrepid golf writers. Like some seventeenth-century Spanish explorer, they would periodically send word back to the 'civilized' golf world of the amazing riches they had found.

It started as early as 1934. 'Never have I been more surprised,' wrote Viscount Castlerosse (who would later design the celebrated course at Killarney) in his widely read London newspaper column. 'Ballybunion is the best course I have ever played on. It is better than St George's or Princes or Rye. I except St Andrews, but then that is not a golf course. It is a miracle.'

Despite the occasional journalistic raptures, Ballybunion remained obscure. As late as 1971, Herbert Warren Wind, the greatest of American golf writers, could proceed almost by accident to Ballybunion and be astonished by what he discovered.

'To put it simply, Ballybunion revealed itself to be nothing less than the finest seaside course I have ever seen,' he wrote in the *New Yorker*.

Not everyone reads the *New Yorker*, of course, and it was not until Tom Watson took up the torch in the early 1980s that visitors began arriving in great numbers.

Today Ballybunion is no longer a secret. In the summer it seems that *everyone* – at least in New Jersey and Florida – has heard of it. Foursomes tee off every ten minutes, and the club has built an enormous fortress/clubhouse to accommodate them. To recapture the thrill of discovery that the early 'explorers' must have experienced you will have to visit Ballybunion in the off-season. On a weekday in November the course reclaims its splendid isolation.

Though Ballybunion may look ancient, it is not in fact so very old. But its mystique isn't hurt by the fact that its origins are oddly unclear. No one really knows who created the links; the theories run from Old Tom Morris, to James Braid, to a local hotel owner. It is known that the original eighteen holes were laid out by someone hired by the local railway company, which thought a golf course would attract more passengers. The links later shrank to nine holes and then was extended once more in 1927. Again, no one is sure who was responsible. Everyone does agree that Tom Simpson – one of the best designers of the period – was engaged to make renovations in 1936.

Simpson was shocked by what he saw. 'The beauty of the terrain surpasses that of any golf course we know, not excepting Pine Valley in America,' he wrote in his report to the club. 'Never for one moment did we imagine, or expect to find, such a really great course or such a glorious piece of golfing ground.'

Simpson was perceptive enough to leave well enough alone. He and his associate Molly Gourlay, one of golf's few female architects, replaced two greens, inserted a few bunkers, and went home. (In recent years, Tom Watson has shown similar restraint in remodelling a few bunkers and changing the sight lines on the last hole).

It could well be that the most important architects were the club members themselves, especially Patrick McCarthy (who worked for the railway) and his two sons, William and Paddy. Between them they filled the position of secretary at Ballybunion almost continuously from 1897 to 1952.

That such a famous club can trace its history with such little certainty may seem strange, until one realizes that for half a century the members of Ballybunion could fit comfortably into the tin shed that served as a clubhouse. There were no more than fifty full members (almost half of them women) when Simpson and Gourlay made their finishing touches.

The course

If the cemetery is the first signal that Ballybunion is not your average track, the second hole confirms it. A quintessential Ballybunion hole, it is a ferocious par 4 into shaggy sand dunes that requires a perfectly played second to a green set high on an exquisite natural plateau. It's the kind of heroic shot you rarely find on the more subdued links of Scotland and England. Ballybunion is full of them.

What is amazing is that the dramatic golf one finds at Ballybunion evolved entirely without the benefit of bulldozers – every pathway through these magnificent hills was put there by nature. It is a fantastic and inspiring place to play.

Not all the holes are as good as the second. The following three holes – a par 3 and two par 5s – are solid links holes, but rather out of character with the rest of the course (they used to be the finishing holes, until a new clubhouse necessitated a much better routing). Although also on relatively flat land, the sixth is a terrific, nerve-racking par 4 that challenges you to bite off the corner of a dogleg, then tantalizes you with a humpy green that backs right onto the edge of a seaside cliff. In recent years, coastal erosion had forced the par-4 seventh inland, but an international fundraising campaign has helped the club restore the thrilling cliff-side green that had originally been introduced by Tom Simpson (both greens are still used).

The very short eighth is Ballybunion's 'postage stamp'. It seems simple on first glance, but the skinny green, set charmingly in a bowl of dunes, is plagued by violent undulations and fierce pot bunkers. The ninth is a long par 4 that, like the second, requires a difficult approach shot to an elevated green.

It is all very wonderful, yet what sets the course apart are the holes still to come. The front nine flirts with the most rugged stretch of linksland, but the back nine is swallowed up by it.

As Herbert Warren Wind said, in his famous piece in the *New Yorker* that helped put Ballybunion on the golfing map, the secret of Ballybunion's charm is that 'sand-hill ridges do not run parallel to the shore but at a decided traverse. This opens all sorts of possibilities – dogleg holes of every description sculptured through the choppy land, and straightaway holes where the sand hills patrol the entrance to the green like the Pillars of Hercules.'

Almost all of the holes on the back nine at Ballybunion are extraordinary, and to pick out individual holes is really beside the point. Suffice to say that you hit a variety of thrilling, often downhill tee shots through the dunes and precise approach shots to fabulously sited natural greens. Around each corner is a view more stunning than the last. At under 6,600 yards, Ballybunion is not extraordinarily long, but it is both difficult and fair. Despite the large number of heroic shots required, you never feel unjustly punished. And you always want another go. British journalist and television commentator Henry Longhurst summed up the feeling of playing

BALLYBUNION

Ballybunion very well, indeed:

> Its simple, elemental quality sweeps away the cobwebs of golfing theory and brings home to you once more the original fact that golf is a business not of pivots, hip turns, wrist formation and the rest but of grasping an implement firmly in two hands and banging the ball with it.

Appropriately enough, the course that begins with a cemetery ends with an archaeological site. According to the club, the massive sandtrap known as the 'Sahara' that lies across the eighteenth fairway contains a 'curious mixture of sand, shell, ashes, stones and bones, the source of which could date to the late Iron Age, around the fifth century A.D.' Apparently they hadn't invented the sand wedge back then.

Due to the tremendous number of visitors, you are restricted to eighteen holes per day on the Old Course. The positive side is that you are offered an opportunity to play Robert Trent Jones's Cashen Course, a fascinating if very different links on equally spectacular terrain.

Location: On Sandhill Road, just south of Ballybunion; 65 miles from Shannon Airport and 40 miles from Killarney

Green Fee: €150 (Old Course): €110 (Cashen); €200 (both courses, same day or consecutive days)

Restrictions: Weekdays only; write well in advance

Manager: Jim McKenna

Address: Sandhill Rd., Ballybunion, Co. Kerry; **tel:** (068) 27146; **fax:** (068) 27387; **e-mail:** bbgolfc@iol.ie; web: www.ballybuniongolfclub.ie

---

BALLYBUNION (Cashen)

Built: 1984

Designed by: Robert Trent Jones

This God given piece of land, with its tumbling undulating free flowing rhythm of line is beauty beyond description – a piece of land with the ocean on one side of it, river on the other... There are no weak holes on the course. Each is a spectacular gem.

ROBERT TRENT JONES

If you haven't a caddie it is a murderous thing.

JOHN MORIARITY, LONG-TIME MEMBER OF BALLYBUNION

The Cashen is not just a second course at Ballybunion, it is a theatrical event all its own, and a highlight of any golfing visit to Ireland. Considered by Trent Jones to be one of his masterpieces, the Cashen is like a daring film that is loved by some critics but less appreciated by the masses. It is the *Apocalypse Now* of links golf – controversial, occasionally self-indulgent, big budget (by Irish standards of the time) and full of splashy set pieces. But the overall effect is the opposite of what is conveyed by the magical Old Course next door. On the Cashen, the whole seems somehow less than the sum of its dazzling parts.

The merits of the Cashen course at Ballybunion have been hotly disputed since the day it opened in 1984, and the debate shows no sign of letting up. Things probably would have gone more smoothly had the club decided to go with the layout originally drawn up by Eddie Hackett, the Irish architect who had already designed several outstanding links courses on the west coast of Ireland. But instead the club approached Robert Trent Jones, the most celebrated and influential architect of his generation.

47

From the beginning Trent Jones saw Ballybunion New (as the course was then called) as his *pièce de résistance*, his chance to show what he could do on true linksland, and on a spectacular stretch at that.

'When I first saw the piece of land chosen for the new course at Ballybunion I was thrilled beyond words,' Trent Jones later wrote. 'It was the finest piece of linksland that I had ever seen, and perhaps the finest piece of linksland in the world.'

Trent Jones's design made few concessions to the difficulty of building a golf course on such steeply contoured terrain, and construction was something of a nightmare. But when the course finally opened, there were many instant admirers. The well-known golf writer Peter Dobereiner, for one, called it 'the greatest links course in the world.'

Others were considerably more cautious with their praise, though they had to admit that there was no links like it. Whereas an architect like Hackett would have been content to tap the fantastic natural contours of the land, Trent Jones went a step further. The course is very much in the links tradition, but the hand of the architect is everywhere in sight. It is obvious that Trent Jones felt that each hole had to have some element of high drama.

The result includes some of the most wondrous links holes in the world, especially the par 4s and 5s that tumble in, around and over the steepest of the sandhills. Whereas the Old Course has a natural charm, the Cashen has a surreal kind of beauty. The par-5 fifteenth, for example, requires a second shot played downhill through a narrow chute into a hollow that is almost encircled by gigantic dunes. There is an arresting hush even on the windiest of days as the dunes cut off the wind and all outside sound. The wild terrain and almost unearthly sense of solitude would make a good set for a science-fiction movie.

The par-4 fourth is an utterly different experience, marked by a drive from an elevated tee that seems to take in the whole world. Though only 350 yards, the hole uses up acres and acres of ground, as Trent Jones succeeds in creating an impression of almost unlimited space. The stunning panorama, which includes a river on the left and the ocean on the right, makes it difficult to find the correct line on the ill-defined fairway far below.

In between these extremes of seclusion and exposure are many arresting holes. What the Cashen course lacks in elegance it makes up for in variety.

Each hole seems to have a different theme, and the changes of pace are frequent and always dramatic.

It is also notoriously difficult to walk, which is a real constraint in Ireland, where electric carts were once considered sacrilegious and are still relatively rare by American standards. Not only are there steep climbs on many holes, but the trek between green and tee is often an exercise in mountain climbing. As interesting as many of the holes are, a round on the Cashen is always something of an ordeal. Some members flatly refuse to play it.

A few of the holes just haven't worked that well. The club has already eliminated one of the most spectacular – a right-angled par 4 in which the drive was taken from the top of one sand dune to a narrow strip of fairway and green on the top of another sand ridge, like hitting between the roofs of two skyscrapers. It has been replaced by a straightforward par 3 (the twelfth) that no one would confuse with a Trent Jones original. The elevated green on the fifth was replaced because it was deemed too hard to reach on foot. And the seventh hole, which runs tight along the seawall, has been untidily cut from a par 5 to a par 4 because no one has figured out how to grow grass on the first part of the fairway.

'When they were building the new course I walked it and met Trent Jones and he told me that he could grow grass on those areas by the sea,' recalled John Moriarty, a long-time trustee of the club. 'I told him "if you can, you should be out on the Sahara" because we had tried everything possible. We'd grow weeds if we could. He didn't listen but he learned the hard way.'

Less severe modifications have been made elsewhere to reduce the penal aspect of some of the holes, and Tom Watson – a great friend of Ballybunion's – may well be asked to make further changes at some time in the future.

It is to be hoped that the members don't go too far. For while the Cashen may have some flaws, it is ambitious and imaginative, an example of a great architect at the height of his creative powers.

Location: On Sandhill Road, just south of Ballybunion; 65 miles from Shannon Airport and 40 miles from Killarney

Green Fee: €150 (Old Course): €110 (Cashen); €200 (both courses, same day or consecutive days)

Restrictions: Weekdays only; write well in advance

Manager: Jim McKenna

Address: Sandhill Rd., Ballybunion, Co. Kerry; **tel:** (068) 27146; **fax:** (068) 27387; **e-mail:** bbgolfc@iol.ie; **web:** www.ballybuniongolfclub.ie

---

CEANN SIBÉAL

Founded: 1971; Extended: 1992

Designed by: Eddie Hackett and Christy O'Connor Jr

There is a strong cultural orientation here. We're the only club that is Irish speaking. Everyone that works here is Irish speaking and we try to create an atmosphere and an occasion for speaking it.

BERNARD O'SULLIVAN, FORMER CAPTAIN OF CEANN SIBÉAL

Set out like an afterthought on the western extremity of the Dingle peninsula, Golf Chumann Ceann Sibéal is a little-known but friendly enclave of Gaelic. The links by the stunning cliffs of Sybil Head are in one of the last remaining *Gaeltacht*, and so everything at Ceann Sibéal is in Irish, from the scorecard to the signs on the washrooms. The most westerly in Europe, the course itself is eloquent in any language, one of Eddie Hackett's most bewitching creations. The setting is mesmerizing, too, with the Three Sisters rock towering behind the course, and the sea crashing against the cliffs just below. If the legendary giants of Irish lore played golf, this might be where they would play.

For our money, just *driving* to Ceann Sibéal is one of golf's great experiences. Forget the drive into Augusta's Magnolia Lane (you'll need an invitation anyway). Try instead the three-hour spin from Killarney to the Irish-speaking village of Ballyferriter along the coast of Dingle Bay. It is an astonishing drive, as colossal cliffs push the road almost into the sea at times, and Macgillycuddy's Reeks look glorious in the distance across the bay. As the terrain becomes starker and more spectacular it becomes harder to believe that there is a golf course at the end of it.

Eventually, you arrive in Dingle, a remote fishing port that is also a base for sightseers and hikers. But the golf course is several miles farther west, past Ballyferriter, to a craggy spot called Sybil Head (or Ceann Sibéal in Irish). It is all cliffs and surf and haunting desolation. On a stormy day it feels as if you are at the end of the earth.

Of course this *was* the end of the earth for many centuries, at least as far as Europeans were concerned. The remains of ring forts of Irish kings dot the surrounding landscape. There are also several impressive Christian ruins dating back a millennium or so, a reminder that Irish monasteries were the last refuge of Christian learning during Europe's Dark Ages. Just off shore are the Blasket Islands. Though unpopulated today, these islands once produced some of the best writers of Gaelic literature.

On our first visit to Ceann Sibéal, we found that some people still consider the area a kind of refuge, a place apart from the pressures of modern life.

'The only things I miss really are hockey and baseball, especially the Red Sox,' Danny Mitchell told us in his Boston accent. It turned out that the thirty-year-old Mitchell spent a year here with some relatives following college, and decided to stay. Now he was one of five crew members on an eighty-five-foot fishing boat, and he was completing a course for aspiring skippers in Donegal.

'My family visit me *here*,' Mitchell said, clearly implying that he didn't travel to Boston. 'My father can't believe there's a golf course of this quality in the middle of nowhere. And that we have it to ourselves for most of the year.'

Our other playing partner was Mitchell's friend Paul Duffy, an artisan who moved his family to Dingle from Dublin because of his concern about crime. He purchased a piece of land near Ballyferriter and put up a trailer on the site. His wife and two young children loved it, he said, and his pottery business was working out just fine.

Although they had adapted well, Mitchell and Duffy were still outsiders in this tightly knit, ancient community. And in some ways, that's not so bad.

'People around here would call us *blow-ins*,' Mitchell said. 'So they don't expect so much of us, you can push the boundaries a bit as far as behaviour is concerned. You have to get used to the quiet, but people look after you. And it's quite cosmopolitan in the summertime.'

On this late October day the hurly-burly of the tourist trade had long subsided. Only a trickle of golfers were trying their luck on a gloriously sunny and windy day.

A good number of Dingle's members are blow-ins, including some of the Germans who are snapping up coastal properties on the peninsula. There are also several hundred 'country' members from Dublin and other cities, who travel to Dingle to play golf during their holidays.

This influx of golf-related tourism is what the founders of Ceann Sibéal had in mind when they asked Eddie Hackett to lay out an eighteen-hole course in 1969 (he was also designing Waterville at the time). The thirty original members found, however, that they had only enough money to build nine of the holes, with precious little left over for maintenance, let alone for building a clubhouse.

The club lay almost dormant for a decade, but the success of other community golf developments along the west coast of Ireland encouraged the members to organize a fundraising drive to finish the project and build a clubhouse. Fortunately, the stakes that Hackett had used to lay out the back nine were still lying in the ground – almost twenty years later!

The course

It is to the credit of Eddie Hackett and Christy O'Connor Jr (who finalized the design of the second nine using Hackett's basic layout) that the spell cast by Dingle's beautiful, elemental surroundings is not broken by the golf course itself. Ceann Sibéal is built on the side of a hill that slopes down to the sea, with the clubhouse at the top. You can see most of the course from the first tee, and at first it doesn't look like much. The fairways don't seem well-defined, and the huge sand ridges of Ballybunion or Waterville are conspicuously absent.

But what you can't appreciate without teeing off are the undulations that, in combination with the natural slope of the land, will severely test anyone's short game. Hackett has made use of every swale and hollow, and of a creek that winds through ten holes, without resorting to gimmicks (not that the club could have afforded them). As intriguing as the course is, it does not try to compete with the drama of the natural surroundings.

Faced with land that generally slopes only in one direction, Hackett has mixed difficult uphill holes with exciting downhill tee shots. Ceann Sibéal is particularly exposed to the wind, and when the fairways and greens are hard and fast, there is really no place to relax. If anything, its course rating of 71, from back tees of 6,700 yards, is too low.

There's something to rattle the nerves on just about every hole, even though few look difficult at first glance. The third, for example, is only 359 yards, but there is a small pot bunker smack in the middle of the fairway that causes alarm far in excess of its size. There is thick rough on the right to catch those who compensate too much, and an elevated and sloping green that makes pitch shots difficult.

The par-4 fourteenth, 342 yards straight downhill, is another illusion. It looks easy, but Hackett has left intact a strange mound just in front of the green that knocks pitch-and-run shots off course, and provides precious little room to stop the ball with a high pitch.

On other holes the natural undulations are used to provide the severest test of shotmaking. The tenth, at just under 200 yards, is one of the toughest par 3s in Ireland. Slightly uphill, the hole is visually intimidating, since you can't see the putting surface over the rugged expanse of rough. And the green slopes severely from front to back, making it extremely difficult to hold a long iron.

When we asked Eddie Hackett if the hole was perhaps a bit unfair, he looked perplexed, before replying: 'It is what was *there*, you see.'

At Ceann Sibéal, what is *there* is a heck of a lot of fun. The three excellent and utterly different par 5s on the back nine (which made up the original nine-hole course) are good examples. The eleventh starts from an exhilarating, elevated tee and then snakes over the creek to a well-guarded green. The thirteenth doglegs at right angles around the tiny village of Ballyloughtra (the brave will try to cut the corner by flying across the stone wall that marks the village's border). And the eighteenth is straight uphill to the clubhouse, which sits rather forlornly against the barren mountainside. After a tough round, the eighteenth looks menacing (and exhausting), but those who bear down and concentrate can end the round on a high note, and drink in the marvellous views with added enjoyment.

You will be tempted to play again, though perhaps not in the fashion of Ceann Sibéal members Vincent O'Connor and Richie Williams, who played again *six* times in a single day in August 1998. We're not sure who keeps track of such things, but their 126-hole marathon apparently set an Irish record.

Location: Sybil Head, west of Ballyferriter, western end of Dingle Peninsula. Follow signs for Ballyferriter, and then for the golf links, from Dingle Town

Restrictions: None

Green Fee: €65-75

Secretary: Steve Fahy

Address: Ballyferriter, Dingle, Co. Kerry; **tel:** (066) 915-6255; **fax:** (066) 915-6409; **e-mail:** dinglegc@iol.ie; **web:** www.dinglelinks.com

DOOKS

Founded: 1889

Designed by: Martin Hawtree and the Members

Lying on a promontory jutting out into Dingle Bay, the Dooks course commands as fine views of sea and blending mountains as one could desire. On a fine sunny day the vista is magnificent, and a yellow strip of sandhills stretching across the blue waters of Dingle Bay form a contrast to sea and purple mountain that is charming to the eye.

IRISH GOLF MAGAZINE, 1909

If there was a golf scene in *The Wizard of Oz*, it might have been shot at Dooks, an unconventional club that plays the game in a setting of almost surreal beauty, with picture-perfect sea and mountain views and fairways brimming with flowers. Even the ponds are special here, with their rare species of Natterjack toad. The links used to be dream-like too, with one green shaped like a saucer and another requiring a compass to find. However, Dooks's famous quirks are in the process of being ironed out in an aggressive redesign by Martin Hawtree. It may seem crazy for a club to rip up their much-praised course for something almost entirely new, but in the wonderful, unpredictable Land of Dooks, we expect that everyone will return from the adventure unscathed.

✦✦✦

If the adage 'too many chefs spoil the broth' normally applies to golf course design, then Dooks was perhaps the glorious exception that proved the rule. The club has always prided itself on its self-sufficiency (its motto is *Per ardua ad astra*, 'through hard work to the stars') but the members took the principle to an extreme in the early 1970s when they decided to expand their nine-hole course. Strapped for cash, the members decided to do it themselves. A committee of nine was struck, and each committee member was given the responsibility for designing one hole!

In any other place, this would surely be a recipe for disaster, but at Dooks, believe it or not, it was a great success. The new holes were, for the most part, terrific. The members did all of the construction work themselves as well, from shaping greens to digging bunkers, to finding sod from construction sites. They even managed the difficult task of building a couple of lovely seaside holes on what had been pure beach sand.

It took a few years, but they saved some money all right. The total cost of the nine-hole expansion, including design and construction, was about £2,500.

It is one of the ironies of Irish golf that this very success has given Dooks the financial wherewithal to dig up what they had worked so hard to create. This time the overhaul (not fully completed at the time of press) is costing *100 times more*, but in the over-heated Ireland of the twenty-first century even that seems a bargain.

'We were nearly €200,000 under budget over the first two phases [of the reconstruction],' says club secretary Declan Mangan. 'Of course, we're very frugal.'

It is only the latest of the many curious developments that pepper Dooks's colourful history.

The club's founders were ordinary enough, the usual group of upper-class Protestants bewitched by the new fad of golf then sweeping high society. Nor is it surprising that they were attracted to the beautiful setting on the shores of Dingle Bay.

Since then, however, life at Dooks has been decidedly unorthodox. For example:

■ Unusually for golf clubs of the time, Dooks attracted fervent Irish nationalists as members as early as 1908. However, club officials crossed out the names of signatures made in the Irish language from club records. The course was seriously damaged and temporarily closed during the political unrest of the early 1920s.

■ In 1921, the captain of the club was a woman (Lady Gordon), a situation all but unheard of in Ireland, before or since. Another woman (Lina Hickson) held the important post of Honorary Secretary for sixteen years.

■ In 1942, club members from the local area craftily held a meeting during a petrol shortage, and wrested control of the club from the wealthy vacationers who had run it since its inception.

■ In the 1960s, the club faced eviction at the end of its lease. The members launched a national media campaign, comparing the situation to the famine of the nineteenth century, when some absentee landlords let their tenants starve. A Fighting Fund was established, the landlord succumbed to rhetoric and public pressure, and the members bought the property outright for £7,000.

■ The tables were turned in 1981 when environmentalists complained to the media that the club planned to drain a vital breeding ground for the Natterjack toad. Turning the situation to their advantage, the members became the toad's great advocate, building new breeding sites for the amphibian and adopting it as their club logo.

The latest chapter in the club's history has not exactly followed a script either.

It all started simply enough. Something had to be done to a first hole that was far too close to a private residence. So Martin Hawtree, fresh from his excellent revisions up the coast at Lahinch, was asked to have a look around.

Hawtree felt that if the first was changed, the second hole needed to be modified. Which affected the third. And so on. The old holes fell like dominoes before the architect's enthusiastic eye. Before long Hawtree and his team were presenting a five-year redevelopment plan that, according to a local newspaper, envisioned Dooks becoming the equal of the greatest links in Ireland.

'He came back with a most wonderful plan,' says Mangan. '"We can do the first [hole]", he told us, "but there's way more to this".'

It all sounds a bit like calling someone in to fix a light bulb, and then being persuaded to rebuild your house. But everyone seems to be happy with the outcome.

'The new holes are beautiful – magic altogether,' says Mangan.

The project leader for Hawtree was Marc Westenborg.

'The club were fantastic to deal with,' he says. 'They put their complete trust in us.'

So much so that once the renovations are complete, the only holes that will not be touched are the tenth, a par 5 running along the beach, and the par 3 eleventh. The rest have all been significantly changed, so Dooks will soon be essentially the work of Hawtree and Westenborg.

'It was completely different to any other course we've worked on,' says Westenborg. 'Many Irish links have high dunes and don't have views. But Dooks is special in that all eighteen holes have the views of mountains and the countryside and the sea.

'And there is a much wider diversity in plant life, heather, gorse, wild roses, we even found a little herb called the pennyroyal that hadn't been seen in Ireland for years. Heather grows on the *fairway* there. Other places would kill for that.'

One of the chief stylistic changes to the course involved the greens.

'The putting surfaces were generally flat, so we introduced some undulations, nothing too much though,' says Westenborg.

One discarded green that certainly *did* have undulations was that of the old thirteenth, known throughout Ireland as The Saucer.

'If it was a papal issue, it would probably involve excommunication,' Mangan told veteran Irish golf writer Charlie Mulqueen in an interview. 'Some of the members were upset, others were delighted to see it go; they thought it was a crazy hole. Instead of playing into a saucer, you're [now] playing into an upturned bowl although Hawtree has kept a spine running up the middle of the green to remind people of the old days and it's wicked enough as it is.

'I was with Hawtree when he first saw the thirteenth and he turned to me and said: "I don't believe it, if I designed that, I'd be sacked on the spot." But he still said he wouldn't change an inch on it. It was an agronomist's call. The Sports Turf Research Institute told us the green was sinking bit by bit.'

Because the original eighteen holes at Dooks were made on the cheap there were few artificial touches, and the links had a natural, traditional feel to it. Westenborg told us the new course will retain those qualities, and it is one reason the designers put in fewer bunkers than they might have elsewhere.

We would be remiss not to pay our last respects to the old eighteenth hole, a thoroughly charming, if archaic par 5 with an invisible green. After hitting two good shots, first-time visitors to Dooks would find themselves on a fairway leading to nowhere. Some additional hunting would reveal the goal, set like some secret encampment in a depression just over a ridge. Yes, the approach shot was blind, but anyone with a sense of humour was thoroughly charmed.

The eighteenth is now a par 4, with the green plainly in site. While the renovations aren't quite finished, Declan Mangan is quite sure of the end result. And he doesn't care that Ballybunion, Waterville and Lahinch may continue to attract more overseas visitors.

'They can have the quality golfers, we'll have the quality course,' he predicts.

It is a preposterous claim, of course, that the links at Dooks could some day be spoken about on the same terms as its far more illustrious neighbours. And the comment was no doubt made with Irish tongue firmly in Irish cheek. But then again, sometimes at Dooks you get the feeling that anything is possible.

Location: Eight miles southwest of Killorglin off N70 (Ring of Kerry)

Restrictions: Tee times are set aside for visitors throughout the week from 10:00 a.m. to 1:00 p.m., and from 2:30 p.m. to 5:00 p.m.

Green Fee: €80

Secretary-Manager: Declan Mangan

Address: Glenbeigh, Co. Kerry; **tel:** (066) 976-8205; **fax:** (066) 976-8476; **e-mail:** office@dooks.com; **web:** www.dooks.com

---

DOONBEG

Founded: 2001

Designed by: Greg Norman

There is nothing like this left in America....The hardest thing in the world is to get on the dance card of people who are so affluent that they can go anywhere in the world.

Leonard Long, Kiawah Partners

Many wondered if Greg Norman was the right man to create one of the last links courses on the planet. So it is to Norman's credit that the verdict is still out on Doonbeg. Whether or not his vivid design is the best way to use this heaving piece of linksland on Doughmore Bay in County Clare, Doonbeg is without doubt an exciting and provocative course to play. We could do without the greeters and the forecaddies, the piles of range balls shaped like D's, and the needless and wasteful opulence of the facilities, designed to attract Americans with more money than they know what to do with. But against all expectations, it is the Irish who play the most golf here.

◆◆◆

If you are one of those who feel that the decision to plop down a luxurious American-style and American-run resort next to a sleepy Irish coastal village is at least questionable from a cultural, ethical or aesthetic standpoint, don't blame the Americans.

The idea was 100 per cent Irish, and are those responsible ever proud of it.

'This project is the single largest tourism project ever to have been undertaken in the west of Ireland,' crowed Kevin Thompstone of Shannon Development, a governmental agency meant to create jobs in the counties nearest to Shannon airport. 'The Doonbeg project is the equivalent of getting a major international industry such as Intel or Dell to set up in West Clare and Shannon Development is delighted to have played its part in bringing this about.'

The organization is no doubt more *relieved* than anything, for the project they invested so much energy getting off the ground was almost derailed any number of times.

The saga started in the early 1990s, when the agency arranged for the purchase of some little-used linksland near the village of Doonbeg from four local farmers, and then sought bids from developers to build a high-end golf resort. Part of the bait was a promised €2 million economic development subsidy from the European Union.

The American company Landmark National won the deal and engaged Greg Norman to do the work.

The project was plagued by environmental objections, including alleged threats to the Narrow-mouth Whorl, a tiny but rare snail. Things became so chaotic that the environmental agency established by the Irish government was suing two other governmental departments. Eventually, a compromise was reached, with fifty acres of the property declared off limits to the golf course.

By now, Landmark had handed over the project to Kiawah Development Partners, the enterprise responsible for turning a ten-thousand-acre island off the coast of South Carolina into a golfing paradise and upmarket residential community. The Ocean Course at Kiawah Island hosted the Ryder Cup in 1991.

As at Kiawah, the excellent golf at Doonbeg has been used as a lure to persuade the fantastically wealthy to purchase expensive holiday homes. Another strategy is to create an 'advisory board' of the rich and famous that includes Wayne Huizenga, the owner of the Miami Dolphins, American sports broadcaster Jim Nantz (the voice of The Masters), the BBC's Terry Wogan (who hails from Limerick), and the head of the PGA of America.

What the owners didn't expect was that the Irish themselves would be wealthy enough to take part in significant numbers. But with the GDP of Ireland almost doubling from the beginning of the project to today, over 150 have stumped up the price of a full membership: a refundable deposit of €60,000 with annual dues of €2,400. And naturally the Irish residents are able to play the course much more frequently than American members.

'With the boom in this country there's no shortage of dough,' says head professional Brian Shaw. 'The Irish have travelled now, to Dubai, to the States, all over the world. They realize they like the service element to it.'

If Dubai is your idea of cultural authenticity, then you may want to stay in the Lodge at Doonbeg. It boasts the normal sort of international 'five-star' luxury in which no sofa is too plush. An 'Irish atmosphere' is created by shipping in some building stones from Cork, hanging a bunch of prints from the local seaside, serving rare Irish whiskeys in the bar, and building a spa that somehow 'takes inspiration from the natural environment of the County Clare coastline.' It is, for all intents and purposes, a sophisticated Walt Disney World for grown-ups. If you want to move here, there are dozens of housing units on the site that sell for more than US$1 million each.

Time spent in the Doonbeg theme park is no doubt enlivened by meetings with some of the ordinary folk from the village of Doonbeg. The local parish was given a quota of 150 cut-rate golf memberships, and while the locals don't get all the perks of full members, the appeasement strategy seems to have worked.

'Anyone that had two arms and two legs joined up,' says Francis McInerney, a former Gaelic football star who is the vice-captain of the Doonbeg Golf Club that is affiliated with the Golfing Union of Ireland. He told us the cost of joining for him and his neighbours was €1,200, and that the annual dues were €440 a year, only about twice what a normal green fee costs at Doonbeg.

'Obviously we would like to play more [but] we have a good relationship [with the owners],' he said.

McInerney says local property prices have 'gone through the roof' because of the club, and with 200 full-time staff at the resort, most of them employed locally, the economic benefits to the local village are obvious enough. But if you want the numbers, Shannon Development will spell them out for you.

'It represents an investment of €150 million in the area, which will generate the same again in additional indirect tourism investment, giving an estimated total tourism investment of up to €300 million along the West Clare coast and surrounding area,' bellows Mr Thompstone in a press release.

All well and good. But if you have read the chapters on Carne, Donegal, Connemara and Enniscrone, you will know that small west-coast communities have built world-class links courses, and attracted thousands of visitors, without giving up ownership or control. You can't blame Greg Norman or the people at Kiawah, who have used their deep pockets, good sense, and genuine love of the place to make friends with almost everyone. They have set up the Doonbeg Foundation to support local charities, ensured the environmental regulators are kept happy, and diligently maintained rights of way across the golf course for the surfers who prize the beach here.

Nevertheless, an uneasy question will always linger unpleasantly over Doonbeg: Did the last linksland in Ireland really need to be turned into a playground for the world's richest people?

The course

Designed after years of environmental battles, Greg Norman's first and only links course does seem a bit squeezed in places, not quite spacious enough for his lofty ambitions (the Shark 'considers Doonbeg his design legacy', according to the club's slick promotional materials).

But we didn't mind the quirky routing and criss-crossing fairways, or even the pedestrian intersections where staff ensure that wet-suited surfers can cross the links safely. After the numbing perfectionism of the off-course facilities, these oddities and glitches are something of a relief, and give the place some much-needed charm.

'I told my guys when I first saw the site that we had to discover the golf course,' Norman has said. 'We had to keep looking until we found it.'

These kind of phrases have become a cliché of course, trotted out even when golf architects are building a course on a flat piece of desert, but in Doonbeg's case the rhetoric may well be true. By all accounts Norman visited the site at least twenty times. And while it is a little hard for us to believe the claim that fourteen of Doonbeg's greens and twelve of its fairways were 'simply mowed', there is no doubt that Norman found some very good holes indeed.

The first hole is a good example, and a great way to start a round. There are arresting views of the beach, and an exciting downhill tee shot to a beautiful fairway lined with low dunes. This is a relatively easy par 5, but a few deftly placed pot bunkers near the green make you earn your birdie. And it is a pure pleasure hitting into the green, which snuggles into the curve of a gigantic dune.

Most of the holes at Doonbeg are eye opening, including those less influenced by the duneland. Norman never lets you get bored, and when the winds sweep off the Atlantic, as they usually do, this is one lively place to play golf.

In order to meet environmental requirements, the course moves around the highest dunes, rather than through them, using them as backdrops for some terrific green sites.

It was not just the regulators who gave Norman hassles. After the course opened he had to contend with the high handicaps of Doonbeg's lifeblood – the middle-aged American executives willing to fork out the cash necessary to live out their Irish links fantasy.

Whereas Kiawah Island has five golf courses, Doonbeg only has one, and as one Kiawah partner put it when the course opened: 'I need to get middle-aged Americans around this course. And I need them to want to get back.'

A programme was gradually undertaken to soften the course's most uncompromising edges – removing the odd blind shot, widening a few landing areas to take into consideration the prevailing wind, and enlarging a few greens.

It's not clear how much Norman fought the changes to the course he had spent so much trouble on, but the alterations were not radical. Doonbeg is still a championship test.

There is a hiccup at the sixth, which forces an uninteresting lay-up off the tee, but the rest of the holes are always stimulating.

Indeed, Norman never lets up, perhaps feeling this would be the only eighteen holes of links golf he would ever get a chance to create. Even on the more natural holes, you can almost feel the Great White Shark staring down at the plans. The two-time Open champion has an eye for links golf holes all right.

When Norman shows the greatest restraint (as at the first) the holes are particularly fine, but his use of more aggressive bunkering on the plainer parts of the land is often effective as well. In Norman's hands, even the bunker in the middle of the twelfth green seems more intriguing than irritating.

The most consistent elements are perhaps the large, energetic greens. If fourteen of these are truly 100 per cent natural, then they have been brilliantly discovered and utilized. You can definitely be wrong-sided at Doonbeg, and different pin placements can transform the character of many holes.

The unusual routing of five par 5s and five par 3s also provides great enjoyment to the average golfer, and Doonbeg boasts what may be the best two very short holes you'll find on a single golf course. The ninth is played along the cliff's edge to a green angled around a high dune like an upside-down L. And the fourteenth, played to a cliff-side shelf perched only 111 yards from the back tees, is as close in spirit to Troon's postage stamp as we've come across. It doesn't look at all the same, but there is the same mixture of fear and anticipation. And because it is completely exposed to the fierce winds, those who have played it frequently say it never gets boring.

Many think the par-5 thirteenth is the best on the course, and it is a hole very much in the Irish links tradition. It requires a blind tee shot to a delightfully undulating fairway that narrows menacingly as you pursue the green, which is set high in the dunes, exposed to the sea winds. The fifteenth is apparently the designer's favourite, a stern par four that uses some of the sharpest dunes terrain on the course to excellent effect and ends with a fifty-yard-long green almost enclosed in dunes.

What is perhaps missing at Doonbeg is the sort of harmony that classic links have – the feeling that while every hole is gloriously different, they are somehow cut from the same cloth. Doonbeg is too much of a mixture of natural beauty and clever artifice for that. You feel that Norman set out to make a statement on every hole.

In terms of the great designers of Irish links golf, Norman's spiritual predecessor is not Harry Colt or Tom Simpson or Alexander Mackenzie, but Robert Trent Jones. As Jones did when designing Ballybunion's Cashen course, Norman sprinkles a collection of interesting ideas around Doonbeg that make us think of what a links can be in the modern era, and many of them work quite wonderfully. But we wonder how well it will age when the excitement of something a little new begins to fade.

To use a metaphor that may appeal to a well-heeled member of Doonbeg, sipping a special-edition Bushmills in The Lodge, the pleasures of the course here are designed to be drunk right away. Whether the links will seem as compelling as the whiskey in twenty years' time remains to be seen.

Location: On N67, about 4 miles north of Doonbeg village

Restrictions: None

Green Fee: €190

Reservations: Marie Collins

Address: Doonbeg, Co. Clare; **tel:** (065) 905-5602; **fax:** (065) 905-5247; **e-mail:** reservations@doonbeggolfclub.com; **web:** www.doonbeggolfclub.com

LAHINCH

Founded: 1892

Designed by: Dr Alister Mackenzie (with Old Tom Morris, Martin Hawtree and Charles Gibson)

I think that if my suggestions are carried out the course should not only compare favourably, as a test of golf, with any of the British Championship courses, but will become so interesting, exciting and popular that it will attract hundreds of visitors from overseas.

DR ALISTER MACKENZIE, 1927

Known widely, if somewhat misleadingly, as the St Andrews of Ireland, Lahinch is a marvellous place. There is no community in Ireland with a stronger sense of connection to the sport, and the club's evolution has in many ways paralleled the history of Ireland itself. The championship quality and classic feel of the links is the work of Alister Mackenzie (of Augusta National and Cypress Point fame), and his legacy here seems secure after a sympathetic 'restoration' by Martin Hawtree. But you also get a glorious whiff of Old Tom Morris at two of golf's most famous and exquisite anachronisms – the holes they call the Dell and Klondyke. Lahinch is an entirely successful blend of old and new, and when the greens and fairways are firm and fast there are few places that are more delightful to play.

◆◆◆

Symbolically at least, the turning point in the story of the Lahinch Golf Club came during the final of an important match-play tournament in September, 1920. As the finalists teed off, a large crowd of spectators were startled by the sight of a band of Irish Volunteers marching into the clubhouse. The revolutionaries removed the club flag, and raised the Irish tricolour. While the match progressed, British soldiers arrived from nearby Ennistymon with orders to remove and burn the nationalist flag and raise the club flag once again. Before the contest was over, the Volunteers had returned and put up another tricolour.

The game of musical flags seems amusing in retrospect, but the

65

backdrop was the deadly serious confrontation known in much of Ireland as the War of Independence. Only a few months earlier, the giant sand ridges on the Lahinch links had been a place of refuge after a British Army unit (the infamous 'Black and Tans') set fire to most of the town in revenge for the ambush killing of four soldiers by the IRA. Two people died in the blaze.

That the golf club should find itself embroiled in the independence struggle is no surprise, given its early associations with the privileged class. Founded in 1892 by a group of wealthy Limerick merchants with close ties to the army, the club's first quarter-century was dominated by the Protestant elite, descendants of those who were granted title to much of Ireland during the seventeenth century. There were no members from the Catholic village of perhaps 200 that lent its name to the links. However, it seems that most residents welcomed the golf course as a much-needed tourist attraction to complement the swimming that could be had on the fine Atlantic beaches. The impact of the golf club on the village's fortunes are evident from this excerpt from the *Clare Journal* in 1907:

> The interesting and rising little seaside resort of Lahinch is bête en fête this week as several golf championships are being played off. The Lahinch Links are regarded by golfers as not second to any other in the Kingdom. The otherwise quiet seaside place is, for the time being, transformed into a centre of passion and gaiety. Among those who arrived on Saturday was the Right Honourable Lord Chancellor of England with a distinguished Party.

With the building of a railway link from Dublin, Lahinch became Ireland's foremost golfing destination. Aristocrats in London could board the train at 6 p.m., and even with the ferry crossing be at Lahinch at noon the next day. They could then check-in to any one of a number of fine and newly built hotels and lodges.

The atmosphere at Lahinch changed quickly after the establishment of the Irish Free State in 1921. The First World War greatly depleted the ranks of the aristocracy, and the club finally began to admit local members. One of the first was John Burke, whose brother had been part of the volunteer brigade that burned the club flag. Burke became Ireland's best player after teaching himself the game through some lessons printed in an English newspaper.

It took time, but eventually the golf club became a genuinely local affair, though there are still a large number of members from Dublin and Limerick. There is a nice symmetry to the fact that in 1976 the club that was once a target of Irish nationalists had the honour of seeing one of its members (Dr P. J. Hillery) elected as President of an independent Ireland. Dr Hillery served as President for fourteen years, and it was with genuine pride that the members of Lahinch used to claim that he was the best golfer among all of the heads of state in the world!

The course

Lahinch's early fame must be credited to Old Tom Morris, who laid out the original course for one pound plus travel expenses and made no secret of the fact that he thought the links to be one of the best in the world. But the course was largely overhauled in 1907 by Charles Gibson, a professional from Westward Ho!, and then again, and in a more profound fashion, by Alister Mackenzie in 1927.

Mackenzie's influence on golf architecture continues to the present day, through the example of his work and the persuasiveness of his writings, which established many of the principles of modern design. In this context, it is interesting to note that in the same year he designed Cypress Point in California, Mackenzie decided to keep intact two of Lahinch's most famous holes – Klondyke and the Dell – which feature blind shots unthinkable today. The passage of time has only confirmed Mackenzie's wisdom. The charm of Lahinch remains its sense of timelessness, and these two holes bring back the ghost of Tom Morris and remind the golfer of the very roots of golf.

Mackenzie's work at Lahinch has itself not gone unaltered. Erosion swallowed up two seaside greens, but the most damage may well have been done by local star John Burke, who apparently spearheaded efforts (in about 1930) to flatten out the majority of Mackenzie's greens, many of which were multi-tiered.

'The suggestion was that John Burke couldn't putt on these greens, so they almost became table top,' says Martin Hawtree with a hint of a chuckle.

'I think the club felt they were trading under a false name, that the Mackenzie elements had been ploughed out. My task was to restore the Mackenzie course.'

In truth, Hawtree had no way of restoring Lahinch to the state Mackenzie left it in, as no plans or drawings had survived. Reading Mackenzie's books, examining photographs of other courses, and picking up shreds of evidence where he could find them, Hawtree used his imagination to rebuild green sites and renew the bunkering.

'The object was to restore the Mackenzie *spirit* of the course,' Hawtree says.

It was determined that only the greens at the ninth, eleventh and fourteenth were Mackenzie originals. Similarly strong contours were added to just about all the others. Hawtree also moved bunkers around, partly to take into account the effect of technology on the game, and he persuaded the club to keep the sand-faced bunkers that he believed Mackenzie intended (rather than adopting the revetted style seen on some other links courses).

'It took four years, and I made eighty or ninety visits, but I really came to love the work there,' says Hawtree. 'I was given the freedom to do what was right, and I received tremendous support from [the club's] committees, and that support grew and grew as years went by.'

The virtually unanimous verdict is that this care and attention has paid off. Lahinch has never looked or played better, and the excitement begins in earnest on the newly extended third hole. Here the reward for hitting a brave and accurate drive high into the dunes is an exciting second over a wild patch of grass to a green, framed by sky and sea, that falls off on all sides.

Then it is time for an unforgettable lesson in golf history.

'The Klondyke is one of the prettiest holes in Ireland,' reported *Irish Field* magazine in 1909. 'The drive [is] down a narrow valley where a perfect lie can be had. The second shot should be a good iron over the Klondyke, a formidable sandhill, to the green.'

Today, Old Tom Morris's famous hole has been lengthened to a par 5, meaning that the approach is only blind for long hitters going for the green in two. But the sense of entrapment after the first shot (the valley is surrounded by steep hills) and the feeling of escape in hitting the second over the wild, fescue-covered ridge, is perhaps unique in golf.

The next hole, the Dell, is even more famous – a blind par 3 over a large dune to a precious rectangle of green set between sand hills. The line is provided by a white stone that is shifted depending on the pin position, and the best shots often bounce off the hill behind the green. The Dell has been controversial since its inception, and has perhaps been saved by the childlike charm of its hidden putting surface. If you don't take the Dell too seriously, it is pure fun to play. It will be the shot you remember best after the round.

Not for the last time at Lahinch, we now experience a marvellous change of pace, with three holes that take us thrillingly right to the water's edge. These are Martin Hawtree's most visible contributions, as he has relocated two greens and introduced an entirely new par 3 at the eighth.

'Our brief was to use as much of the duneland as possible and get the value of coastal views,' Hawtree says. 'As it happened, the original Mackenzie layout did this, but one of [the greens] disappeared into the sea.'

The ninth and tenth are Mackenzie originals, par 4s with strategy and intrigue galore, and the twelfth, a lovely dogleg hugging the beach, has been rather nicely lengthened into a par 5.

The variety of holes at Lahinch is remarkable. A series of punishing par 4s is now on the horizon, but not before the tantalizing, 279-yard thirteenth, with its rebuilt three-tier green and maddening undulations just in front of the putting surface.

There is no place to catch your breath at Lahinch, and the greenkeeper's habit of closely shaving the grass around the greens only adds to the exhilarating challenge, enabling you to use low running shots to your advantage, but also encouraging balls to slip off the green into deep hollows or bunkers. You will experience plenty of heartbreak at Lahinch, but you will spend less time floundering in deep rough than elsewhere in Ireland.

After several uphill and often blind drives on the front side, the final stretch is filled with dazzling downhill tee shots. Hawtree's division of the fourteenth and fifteenth fairways (they used to be joined in the middle) has been a success on safety and aesthetic grounds, and Lahinch's finish is as stern and demanding as it has always been.

Until, that is, you get to the eighteenth, a lacklustre par 5 that crosses the fourth fairway and runs too close to the road, and which is only partly redeemed by its charmingly undulating fairway. Though Hawtree has given the club some ideas, it is a hole no one quite knows what to do with.

The restoration has also meant some losses. The members, oddly enough, were apparently most disturbed by the demise of the old third, a formidable but unsubtle par 3 that John Burke had created to replace one of Mackenzie's eroded holes. One of the few greens easily viewed from the clubhouse, it had been the deciding hole (in playoffs presumably) of some historic match-play events.

And then there is the par-3 eleventh, with a small, sharply contoured green that Mackenzie aficionados considered one of the best he ever created.

'It is sharply contoured, very small and had to be abandoned in winter because there was not enough pin-able area,' says Hawtree. We introduced a parallel hole to that, but played further out to the sea. Now they can play either hole.'

It's a tribute to Hawtree that we were surprised to learn just how many changes he had made, as the essential character of Lahinch has not changed at all. Of course, that is even more a tribute to the membership, which has clearly accepted that it has responsibilities as stewards of one of golf's most historic links (even Hawtree admits he would have ditched the Dell and Klondyke given half a chance).

We sometimes think that Lahinch's famous goats call attention away from the merits of such a remarkable golf course, but they can hardly go unmentioned. In the clubhouse there is a broken barometer accompanied by a small notice that reads, 'See goats.' If the animals are huddled next to the clubhouse it apparently means that poor weather is approaching.

It is an original bit of local lore to be sure, but if you have only one day at Lahinch, it will take more than a little weather to keep you off its fairways for a second round.

Location: In town of Lahinch, 35 miles west of Shannon Airport

Restrictions: None

Green Fee: €145

Secretary/Manager: Alan Reardon

Address: Lahinch, Co. Clare; **tel:** (065) 708-1003; **fax:** (065) 708-1592; **e-mail:** info@lahinchgolf.com; **web:** www.lahinchgolf.com

TRALEE

Founded: 1896

Present course built: 1984

Designed by: Arnold Palmer and Ed Seay

Robert Louis Stevenson was wrong, and by a long chalk, when he described the Monterey Peninsula of California as the finest conjunction of land and sea that this earth has to offer. As a spectacle, Tralee is in a different class.

PETER DOBEREINER

If Tralee doesn't quite live up to its setting, that's hardly a criticism. The views of cliffs and beaches are mind-blowing, and constantly draw your attention away from the admirable efforts of Palmer and Seay. Tralee is certainly in the running for the most stunning seaside golf course in all the world, and film buffs will perhaps recognize the landscape for David Lean's *Ryan's Daughter*. There are some tremendous golf holes at Tralee, even if there are places where the American architects seem to be trying too hard. But, like a charging Arnold Palmer, it will sure get your adrenaline going.

In Ed Seay's opinion, it was no kind of weather in which to be laying out a golf course. He felt as if he was wearing every piece of clothing he owned, yet it was no defence against the ice-cold rain whipping off Tralee Bay. He had to admit, however, that Michael O'Brien didn't seem to be bothered. The two of them were choosing the final tee location for the sixteenth hole of the new course at the Tralee Golf Club – O'Brien was a member of the greens committee. The future sixteenth green was set up in the dunes next to a cliff, requiring a long carry over wasteland. There would be no place at all to bail out.

It is a moment Seay can remember as if it were yesterday.

'I turned to Michael and told him, "If we put the tee here you'd need a driver on a day like this,"' says Seay in his Florida drawl. '"And if you were short of the green you'd get a twelve."'

'I remember Michael O'Brien looking at me straight on and saying,

"What's wrong with that Ed? It beats a thirteen."'

For Ed Seay, the design partner of Arnold Palmer, it was another sign that this was no ordinary assignment. It was an introduction to an entirely different way of looking at golf, and at life.

'They taught me a great deal about what the true essence of golf is,' he says. 'We've lost it completely in the United States.'

Ed Seay was not the first architect to have adventures at the Tralee Golf Club.

'When I laid out the new course [at Tralee] times were difficult in this country,' wrote Lionel Hewson in *Irish Golf* about his experience in 1922. 'Laying out the course . . . was a little upsetting as men sat around on the demesne walls watching me measuring, and bullets used to fly in those days on little provocation.'

Hewson was, after all, laying out a golf course during a civil war. Just a year earlier, a government soldier was shot and killed while playing golf at the club, the only on-course fatality in Ireland that can be attributed to political violence.

Sixty years later, the members of Tralee were on the move again. Their nine-hole course near the town of Tralee was getting awfully crowded on weekends, and they had just purchased a much larger and spectacular property near the village of Barrow, eight miles away.

Though the club had precious little money in the bank, the members continued to think big. Only a famous architect would do, and that is how Ed Seay – ex-US Marine, noted golf course designer and partner to the most recognizable name in golf – found himself along the edge of a precipice, in the west of Ireland, in 1982.

'It was my first real observation of a European linksland,' Seay remembers, the excitement of that day still evident in his voice. 'It was magnificent! Set out on the cliffs and with these tremendous dunes – it was as pretty as any site I'd ever seen in the world.

'I called Arnold on the phone and said, "This place is dynamite. You don't get an opportunity like this every day."'

Unbeknown to Seay, the club had also asked four other architectural firms to bid on the project, and the greens committee was meeting that day to hear Seay's proposal.

The meeting took ten hours.

'I don't know if you have had any experience in a meeting at an Irish golf club,' Seay says. 'There is a lot of talking and drinking, I'll tell you that.

'They were as tough as ninepenny nails to begin with. And rightfully so, they had absolutely no money. They hoped to sell the land from the tiny nine-hole course – but, I mean, my back yard is bigger.

'So we offered them a deal. If they would put the money they would have paid us into the course then we'd do it [at a reduced rate].'

Eventually Seay and Palmer landed the contract. Seay did most of the day-to-day work, though his celebrated partner did fly in for a day, hold a press conference, and charm the pants off everyone. ('We were very impressed with Mr. Palmer,' Michael O'Brien told us. 'He is very down-to-earth and he answered all our questions.')

The culture shock that Seay experienced continued during the building process. The club couldn't afford to hire an outside contractor to construct the course, so Seay and Palmer agreed to fly in a supervisor from the United States. The club somehow came up with a bulldozer. Much to Seay's amazement, the club also decided not to install an irrigation system.

'They were sure that the Good Lord would provide the water,' he says. 'And I guess they were right.'

The Good Lord also provided plenty of wind, however, and the grass seed the club planted was blown away time and time again. O'Brien now thinks that it might have been better to use a different mix of soil, but the club didn't help matters by insisting that Seay create the most dramatic holes possible.

'On number three they wanted to move the green as far out [on the edge of a cliff] as they could,' Seay says. 'Because of the salt and the wind I told them they were going to have to rebuild it every year. They didn't care.'

The twelfth is Tralee's most famous and controversial hole, a vicious par 4 of 440 yards that requires a perfect approach shot to a green set high on a shallow plateau, surrounded by fierce links rough. 'They [the members] wanted no mercy. I told them that with the wind in your face it's going to take a one or a two iron. But they wouldn't hear of any changes.'

When Seay inquired who the superintendent was going to be, he was in for another surprise. There wasn't going to be one.

 ## The course

The first hole at Tralee is really just an excuse to get to the cliffs, and the spectacular view of the Barrow Strand from the second tee eloquently explains what Tralee is all about. One of the best par 5s in the country swings around the cliffs in a kind of Irish tribute to Pebble Beach. If the wind doesn't knock you over, the panorama will. The complexities of the hole, which include a difficult approach to a tiny green backed by an enormous U-shaped trap, seem almost too much to take in so early in the round. If only this could have been the eighteenth.

The third is a short par 3 on a little point with the whole world behind it. There's even a picturesque stone turret in the picture frame, as if the natural wonders weren't enough.

The rest of the front nine cannot live up to the expectations raised by the second and third, and the next few holes offer a rather jarring change of pace which may be inevitable at Tralee. The land is rather prosaic and the holes somewhat ill-defined. The first-time visitor will keep wondering when the course will head back to the cliffs. The eighth hole does so rather gloriously but then you have to wait until well into the back nine for more.

It would be fun to watch the professionals tackle the eleventh and twelfth, but we don't enjoy playing them ourselves. The extremely long eleventh (560 yards from the regular tees) features a steep climb following the drive, and offers precious little charm in compensation.

The twelfth is considered by some to be one of the greatest holes in Ireland (it is certainly among the most difficult). We find it rather irritating. Unless the wind is right at your back, there's no way for an average golfer to get anywhere near the green in two, and you have to lay up almost one hundred yards away at the bottom of a hill.

Fortunately, the thirteenth hole, a lovely par 3 set deep in the dunes, puts everyone back in a good mood. And up ahead is the exciting cliff-side stretch that you've been waiting so patiently for. On a windy day the sixteenth is almost as uncompromising as Ed Seay said it would be, while the fifteenth and seventeenth are exciting short par 4s that are among the most dangerous holes in Ireland when the wind is up, requiring the utmost precision and a rock-steady golf swing. Should you waver, you won't be the first to wreck on the rocks below – countless drowned ships lie at the bottom of the sea.

It may be hard to believe, but this stretch used to be more penal, and even well-struck shots often careened out of civilization entirely. The club brought in Donald Steel to increase the margin for error, though the stirring routing remains very much intact.

The eighteenth seems like the finishing hole on a completely different course. Long and comparatively uninteresting, it faces away from the seaside thrills that make the course so memorable.

If, in the final analysis, Tralee feels more fragmented than a great course should, it is still a worthy achievement and an appropriate legacy for the daring golfers of Tralee, for Ed Seay, and for golf's most exciting player.

Location: Eight miles west of Tralee, through villages of Spa and Churchill on very narrow roads

Restrictions: The club is open to visitors on weekdays (except for Wednesday in the summer months) and Saturdays, from May to October only

Green Fee: €160

Manager: Anthony Byrne

Address: West Barrow, Ardfert, Tralee, Co. Kerry; **tel:** (066) 713-6379; **fax:** (066) 713-6008; **e-mail:** info@traleegolfclub.com; **web:** www.traleegolfclub.com

WATERVILLE

Founded: 1973
Designed by: Eddie Hackett

I have never seen a more consistent succession of really strong and beautiful golf holes than I have seen here.

SIR HENRY COTTON, THREE-TIME BRITISH OPEN CHAMPION

Waterville is a stern and stunning test of championship golf set in the kind of rugged linksland for which Ireland is famous. Beginning on relatively flat land, the course builds steadily to a crescendo of great finishing holes that rumble through the dunes and along the Atlantic shore. Set along the picturesque Ring of Kerry, Waterville is the one place where the Irish architect Eddie Hackett had the money to do exactly as he pleased, and the result is extraordinary.

No golf course in Ireland has had closer ties to America than the Waterville Golf Links, and for a while, at least, those connections were not just

metaphorical. Waterville was the site of one of the first transatlantic cable stations, and you can find a piece of the first cable linking Ireland and America in the clubhouse bar. The employees of the Commercial Cable Company were likely the first to knock a golf ball through the sand dunes here in 1889.

The cable industry didn't last forever, and golf in the area more or less died with it. By the end of the Second World War emigration from the parish of Waterville was endemic. Of those who stayed, few had ever swung a golf club. Noel Cronin, now Secretary-Manager of the club, remembers that the most popular form of entertainment was crossroad dancing.

'You'd have the village of Cahirciveen meeting with the village of Waterville, and vice versa' he says.

Golf began its comeback in Waterville in the 1960s, when Irish-born Jack Mulcahy arrived from America looking for a project to bring him back to Ireland. For locals, Mulcahy must have seemed the incarnation of the American Dream. He had made millions in the chemical industry and was a friend of presidents and movie stars. The contrast with the economic fortunes of the villagers of Waterville couldn't have been more stark.

'He was a real gentleman, a new thing in this area,' remembers Cronin, who used to drive Mulcahy around in his taxi in the early days.

'The course meant so much to the community, and he was responsible, bless his heart, for a lot of employment. This place was pretty depressed when he came. Workmen got wages that they never saw before. The standards of hotels and restaurants really rose.'

Among the British upper classes, Waterville was also known for its fishing. In the catchment area behind the village, the salmon and trout fishing was extraordinary, making it a favourite holiday spot for Charlie Chaplin, among others. In 1968 the estate containing the fishing rights was purchased by Mulcahy, who also bought an enormous manor house for his own use in County Clare.

At first, the golf course received less than Mulcahy's full attention. He still spent much of his time in America (where he was also a notable philanthropist), and when in Ireland he was often busy entertaining the global elite. Among the visitors to the manor in County Clare was the President of the United States (Mulcahy was the second most generous contributor to Richard Nixon's 1972 re-election campaign). He was also distracted by the design and construction of Waterville House, the luxury hotel that would sit on the other side of the village, overlooking Lough Currane.

Eddie Hackett, who had only designed two golf courses in his life at that point, was put in full charge of constructing the links. He reported on progress by phone to Mulcahy in the United States.

'He didn't know what sort of course he was going to get,' Hackett told us in an interview before his death in 1996. 'When the course was finished, he came over and he was mesmerized. It had turned out great you see, with the dunes, as it is now. Except it wasn't green – it was all soil, all black with the rain.

'We walked around, and he was delighted. He couldn't get over what he had. That night in the house over dinner I said "Jack, if you're keen, you have a course out there that has the potential of being as good as any in the world, if you want to".

'And from that day he changed. He came in April and stayed until October. He supervised, he was at the meetings every week. He wanted it manicured. That's when Mulcahy's Peak [the dramatic teeing ground at the seventeenth hole] came into being. He christened it his tee. And why not? It was his money that made it.'

Now that Mulcahy realized he had a great golf course on his hands, he spared no effort to let other people know about it. He planned a grand opening for early 1973, with celebrities such as Sam Snead on hand.

Hackett became alarmed.

'He wanted the course ready in six months,' he said. 'We had to bulldoze an awful lot of dunes, you see, and to stop the sand from blowing I had to put something on it. I couldn't do it the orthodox way because there was no topsoil in winter. So I brought peat dust from a bog around Waterville instead. Eight shillings a load. That was all I paid. I brought in the peat dust, the peat turf, and spread it all around to contain the sand and used it on the greens instead of topsoil. It wasn't good quality, but I got the course made for him.'

Throughout the 1970s Mulcahy promoted Waterville with all his ingenuity. It was a Herculean task. Ireland was still not on the golfing map as far as North Americans were concerned, there were no nearby tournaments to tempt professionals in the area, and the Troubles put a crimp in the tourist trade. So Mulcahy hosted professional tournaments of his own invention and brought in a steady stream of celebrities.

'The moments that I remember the most would be when he brought Bob Hope, Jack Lemmon and Telly Savalas over,' says Cronin. 'As young lads we had watched Kojak on television, and to see him here in reality, it meant so much.'

Gradually, Waterville's fame began to seep into the consciousness of the golf world. Professionals such as Snead, Ken Venturi, Gary Player and Raymond Floyd were persuaded to play what was, after all, the first major new links course anywhere since Turnberry was redesigned just after the Second World War. Floyd would later write that Waterville was one of his five favourite courses, the others being Pebble Beach, Augusta National, Cypress Point and St Andrews. As golf writers made their way to Waterville, the links began to gain the recognition it so richly deserved.

Mulcahy sold the links to a consortium of Irish Americans in 1987, but remained in the village. When he died in 1995, his ashes were buried beside the tee box on his beloved seventeenth hole. After a glowing eulogy by the presiding priest, a flask of Redbreast whiskey – the favoured brand of the deceased – was passed around by the club captain.

The Waterville Golf Links has somehow managed to combine the attraction of a resort golf destination with the charm and personality of a local Irish club. Despite its out-of-the-way location, Waterville attracts thousands of foreign golfers each summer, more than half of them Americans. Visitors are pampered with electric carts, a modern, well-appointed clubhouse and, if they wish, first-class accommodation in Waterville House, where they have access to the fabulous salmon fishing (a bonus that Tiger Woods enjoyed).

Not surprisingly, the village of Waterville (population 500) is given over to the tourist trade in the summer, but by October everything begins to change. The tourists have left and the locals have more time on their hands. Quite suddenly, the accents in the club's lovely bar are more likely to have a Kerry lilt than a Texas drawl.

'Golf has really taken off with the locals,' says Cronin.

'Today every family in town would have at least one golfer, though when I grew up it wasn't like that,' he observes. 'There was a little bit of hoity-toity in golf then. It was a school teacher or a priest or someone up the ladder that was playing. That has changed, and changed for the good.'

The Irish-American businessmen who took over from Mulcahy have managed to keep the goodwill of the locals, while attracting a whole new generation of American celebrities. Mark O'Meara famously won the 1998 British Open the week after honing his game at Waterville with Tiger Woods and Payne Stewart.

'We all fell in love with Payne Stewart,' recalled Mary Huggard of the local Butler Arms Hotel. 'He came in and pulled pints, and played the piano, and everybody loved him. He was absolutely charming.'

Stewart made so many friends so fast that he was named honorary captain of Waterville for the year 2000. But he died in a plane crash in October 1999 before he could take up the post. The club has since erected a bronze statue in his honour near the first tee. In another place, that gesture might not have rung true, but at Waterville it seems an entirely appropriate reminder of the deep Irish-American ties that gave rise to, and continue to nourish, one of the world's outstanding golf experiences.

The course

The American connection at Waterville has continued on the golf course in recent years, with renovations undertaken by Tom Fazio, a celebrated golf architect who rarely works outside of North America. Fazio has added two new holes on the front nine, and lengthened or revised (or both) several others. For all that, Waterville remains true to the vision of Eddie Hackett.

'I walked the place for five days, until I got the feel, and the inspiration as to where to start it, how it would flow,' Hackett told us in 1996. 'It sort of came to me then. I put the first design on an envelope, and it departed very little from that routing.

'It was a lovely site, and it's compact, though there's no cramping. The last twelve holes, they cost us a fortune.'

The opening holes were cheaper because they skirted Waterville's most mountainous terrain, but they are by no means weak. The second was chosen by Christy O'Connor Sr as one of the best eighteen holes in Ireland, even before Fazio added more contours and drama. The third is a dangerous par 4 with a green that leans into the River Inny, and the fourth is a picturesque and unsettling par 3 to a green partly hidden in a circle of shaggy dunes. After an elegant par 5, little touched since Hackett's day, come Fazio's two new holes.

The short sixth is an excellent replacement for the weakest Hackett creation, which involved a clumsy man-made moat, and the seventh is a first class par 4. Both holes make excellent and threatening use of a diverted creek that runs alongside the fairway.

Waterville has few if any flaws now, with one arresting and challenging hole after another. For all its severity, the routing has a lovely rhythm. There are no debilitating walks between holes, no overly theatrical moments. Instead, the course progresses with a persuasive logic, the relatively exposed opening holes gradually giving way to the more muscular and dramatic sections of the course.

There is a kind of aesthetic climax at the eleventh, the aptly named 'Tranquillity', an exquisitely natural par 5 in which the golfer finds himself suddenly secluded from the rest of the course by a row of dunes on a twisting and tumbling fairway. On a lovely day its beauty sends shivers up your spine, a hole you just don't want to end.

The twelfth, The Mass, is a long par 3 over a natural chasm that was used as a place of worship in the days when Irish Catholics had to practise their religion in secret or risk persecution.

'It's one of my favourite par 3s,' said Eddie Hackett, a devout Catholic who attended church daily. 'There's not a bunker on it, either. It doesn't need one and that's the best tribute you can pay a hole.'

Given Hackett's feelings, it's unfortunate that Fazio has inserted a small bunker on the right front of the green, but on the other hand he has also managed to eliminate an unattractive service road that used to mar the hole.

The course ends with six more absorbing holes of great variety. They begin with a reachable par 5 from a spectacular elevated tee, followed by a tough uphill dogleg par 4 called 'The Judge' (at Waterville the names given holes are unusually evocative and precise), and a devilish two-tiered par 4 offering an exciting downhill approach shot. The sixteenth is an intriguing short par 4 shaped like a quarter moon (much altered by Fazio), and the par-3 seventeenth is the famous Mulcahy's Peak with its riveting views and heroic shot over a vast wasteland. The final hole is an appropriately dramatic par 5 that hugs the ocean.

The challenge is multiplied by the fact that no two holes in this stretch are parallel. The ever-present breeze has a different effect on almost every shot.

It is one of the great back nines in the world. And after playing it you will appreciate why Waterville ranks so high among those who have gone before you.

The clubhouse at Waterville is a nice surprise, a low-lying modern building that isn't garish. It's pleasantly low-key inside, the focus on the exceedingly comfortable bar with its turf fire, interesting memorabilia and rather impressive golf art.

'It's where all the lies are told,' jokes Cronin.

It all gives Waterville a sense of tradition out of proportion with its relative youth, but one worthy of a magnificent links that will surely meet the test of time.

Location: At western end of Ring of Kerry; one mile west of town on the coastal road

Restrictions: None

Green Fee: €150

Secretary-Manager: Noel Cronin

Address: Waterville, Co. Kerry; **tel:** (066) 947-4102; **fax:** (066) 947-4482;
e-mail: wvgolf@iol.ie; **web:** www.watervillegolflinks.ie

OTHER COURSES
OF INTEREST

Killarney

Founded: 1893

New course built: 1939

Expanded: 1972 and 2002

Designed by: Lord Castlerosse, Sir Guy Campbell, Dr William O'Sullivan, Fred Hawtree, David Jones and Donald Steel

When anyone sees Killarney, even if he is the basest heretic, he must believe in God.

LORD CASTLEROSSE

Set on the edge of one of the planet's most enchanting lakes, Killarney is the one inland golf experience in Ireland that you won't want to miss. The serene and luscious beauty of its two older courses is a complete departure from the exposed, rugged links that are Ireland's principal legacy to the sport. Each hole is deliberately charming at Killarney. Greens and fairways are thoughtfully framed by woods, lake and the marvellous Macgillycuddy's Reeks, Ireland's highest and most pleasing mountains. On a calm day, this is the mistily tranquil Irish landscape of Hollywood fantasies. Indeed, visiting celebrities such as Bob Hope and Bing Crosby (who crooned

'How Can You Buy Killarney?') helped to make Killarney synonymous with Irish golf in foreign eyes.

◆◆◆

If Ireland has a tourist trap it is Killarney, but then some say that an Irish tourist trap has a charm all its own. Certainly it cannot be denied that each year tens of thousands of people thoroughly enjoy their quaint tours – in horse and carriage or jaunting cars – of the lakes, woodlands and mountains that surround the town. It has all been going on in one fashion or another since Killarney was first discovered by holidaying gentry in the eighteenth century.

It was Lord Castlerosse, the last Earl of Kenmare, who put golf at the centre of Killarney's attractions. Castlerosse was one of the best-known and most outlandish men of his time, the writer of a famous gossip column in a London newspaper, and a notorious glutton and womanizer. Some of his plans for the new golf course at Killarney (laid out over lands on the family estate) were suitably eccentric. He planned to plant acres of flowers and shrubs so that every hole would bloom in a different colour. He wanted to introduce a music system that would play the comforting sounds of Beethoven's Ninth Symphony across the golf course at noon each day. He also hoped to build a radio tower big enough to promote the attractions of Killarney all the way to America.

It didn't all come to pass, but Castlerosse's prediction that the course (which opened in 1939) would become a 'bait' for foreign tourists proved to be accurate. By the 1960s, more than 13,000 visiting golfers paid homage to Killarney's beauty each year, and the course received worldwide attention on *Shell's Wonderful World of Golf*.

'Never in forty-two years of golf have I seen such a beautiful course,' gushed host Gene Sarazen. 'And I've seen them all.'

None of this was lost on Bord Fáilte, the government tourism agency, which proposed to underwrite the construction of a second eighteen holes on land partly purchased from the owners of the old Kenmare estate – if the club would manage it for them.

Once again the driving force was a colourful and domineering figure with a passionate love for Killarney. Dr Billy O'Sullivan, a local golfing hero who won the Irish Amateur in 1949, was determined that the new holes would surpass Castlerosse's efforts. Expanding on the original plans of British architect Fred Hawtree, O'Sullivan insisted that several new holes be laid out along a stretch of wild and swampy shoreline just west of the clubhouse. A generation before, Lord Castlerosse had tramped over his estate in pink plus-fours searching for good golf holes; now 'Dr Billy' could be seen splashing about in his waders doing the same thing.

The two new composite courses – Killeen and Mahony's Point – were unveiled in 1972 to widespread acclaim, and the Northern Ireland professional David Jones made further improvements prior to the Irish Open in 1991.

'They called me up and asked me to toughen it up for the tour pros. And I wrote back and said, "I'm very flattered but I'm not a golf course designer". And they wrote back and said "we don't care, we'd like you to do it anyway". It was brilliant. ... Basically I brought the lake a lot more into play.'

Killeen is much more dramatic thanks to the handiwork of Jones, and it proved to be a formidable test in the Irish Open, which Nick Faldo won in five under par.

Killarney was, by the early 1990s, once again bursting at the seams, and Donald Steel was hired to build a third golf course, the Lackabane, on lands that wind around a rather unattractive factory (environmentalists halted a more ambitious scheme to lease some of the National Park).

Today, more than 40,000 visiting golfers sample Killarney's charms each year, about half of them foreigners. Though the courses are essentially owned by the Irish government, they continue to be very much managed by the club, which with 1,800 members is by far the largest in Ireland. A few dozen don't play golf at all, but instead use the fishing facilities. It all results in a strong and unique local atmosphere in the sprawling clubhouse despite the large number of visitors.

'It's a lovely place to play,' says David Jones. 'And they are great people. One of the great golf clubs in the world.'

We're inclined to agree.

The courses

In common with fine golf courses everywhere, Mahony's Point and Killeen are very much a product of their natural surroundings. There is an aesthetic quality to Killarney, and a self-conscious reverence for nature. Modern architectural gimmicks are noticeably absent. It is perhaps not entirely irrelevant to point out that during the nineteenth century Killarney had a special appeal for the English Romantics who were so fond of lakes and woods. One suspects that Lord Castlerosse, in his own mind at least, had a Romantic sensibility.

It goes without saying that the courses are utterly different from the great Irish links courses. Instead of stark sand dunes, there are gently rolling hills, trees and flowering shrubs. Instead of a roiling ocean there is a glittering lake. Instead of devastating pot bunkers there are sand traps of the more graceful and shallow kind.

The two courses have different personalities. In general, the best of the new holes are on Killeen, and the best of the old are on Mahony's Point.

Killeen is the sterner test. The penal quality of its lakeside holes – built by Hawtree and O'Sullivan, and made scarier by David Jones – is immediately evident. The first hole is a knee-knocking dogleg around a lagoon to a green half-surrounded by water, requiring more confidence and precision than just about anyone has on the first shots of the day. And it doesn't get easier. During the 1991 tournament, some of the best of Europe's professionals complained that the greens on the sixth, seventh, eighth and tenth were unfair – balls were too likely to roll off the green and into a water hazard, even after a good approach.

When it was built, the par-5 seventh also had the dubious distinction of being Ireland's most expensive hole. Constructed entirely over a former bog, the builders had to dig out and remove the peat (eight feet deep) over the entire length and breadth of the hole, replacing it with properly draining soil.

However difficult, Killeen is certainly an exciting course to play, a modern test of golf that is still splendidly natural, still pure Killarney.

Mahony's Point is more old-fashioned, and its memorable holes are the ones fashioned by Castlerosse and Sir Guy Campbell. The latter's contribution consists of what is one of the more exquisite three finishing holes in golf. After a drive over a hill, the par-5 sixteenth descends in gorgeous fashion to a green at the edge of the water, Macgillycuddy's Reeks providing a perfect backdrop. The seventeenth is a terrific par 4 that hugs the outrageously picturesque lake for its entire length, and the famous par-3 eighteenth, over a natural inlet, is a hole so flawlessly beautiful that it seems almost a violation to play it.

Prior to this memorable finish, the best hole is the thirteenth, a singular, rolling par 5 designed by Castlerosse that leads ultimately to a charming, elevated green that is well trapped and frustratingly difficult to breach. Slightly misjudged chip shots will be rejected down the steep hills that surround the green. But the views are ample compensation. Elevated greens – favoured by Castlerosse – remain a feature of Killarney on both courses.

On the whole, less attention seems to have been paid to updating Mahony's Point, and there are more places to relax and enjoy the scenery. The fairways are more generous, and the hazards less onerous. But if it is less consistently challenging than Killeen, it is one heck of a great walk in the park.

Lackabane, the third course at Killarney, is intelligently designed by Donald Steel, well maintained, and no doubt a treat for the members. But because of its location far from the lake, it has little of the charm of the original courses.

Location: Three miles west of town on R562

Restrictions: None

Green Fee: €120 (Killeen); €100 (Mahony's Point); €80 (Lackabane)

Manager: Tom Prendergast

Address: Mahony's Point, Killarney, Co. Kerry; **tel:** (064) 31034; **fax:** (064) 33065; **e-mail:** reservations@killarney-golf.com; **web:** www.killarney-golf.com

---

Cork Golf Club

Founded: 1888

Designed by: Dr Alister Mackenzie

The blaze spread so rapidly from one end of the building to the other that nothing but a few golf balls, four bicycles and some furniture were saved.

CORK EXAMINER, 29 MAY 1945

The story of Cork Golf Club's first half century went up in smoke in 1945, leaving us little idea about the extent of the role that Dr Alister Mackenzie had in the design of its distinctive and memorable golf holes. But it does the designer of Cypress Point and Augusta no discredit to be associated with what is still one of Ireland's finest parkland courses.

✦✦✦

When Cork Golf Club was evicted from its home in Blarney for keeping whiskey in a cow shed, the members took it in their stride. It would be just one of five relocations they would make in nine years before settling on Little Island, the site of a former limestone quarry. Perhaps the fact that British Army and Navy officers were prominent among its founders had something to do with this restless early existence.

The new site was promptly dubbed Rock Farm. Instead of a cow shed, the maturing club erected a comfortable clubhouse more appropriate for its growing role as an exclusive sanctuary of the social elite in Cork City. There was no running water on Rock Farm, however, so it was necessary to pay less fortunate Cork citizens (and there was no shortage of those) a few pennies to haul water up to the clubhouse.

From the beginning, the club was wealthy enough to hire an in-house professional from Edinburgh, and in 1909 the great Harry Vardon was lured to Cork for an exhibition match. The club took up Vardon's suggestion that it snap up some adjacent property (the site of what is now the final five holes) so the course could be properly extended to eighteen holes.

Many of the club's military members did not return from the First World War. But Cork's relative prosperity as an important harbour kept what was left of the city's establishment in the pink, and the club survived the terrible turmoil of the Irish civil war with its finances very much intact.

Otherwise, they certainly wouldn't have been able to hire Dr Alister Mackenzie and his associate Jack Fleming. Thanks to the fire that destroyed all of the golf club's records in 1945, we don't know the details of Mackenzie's involvement. However, it appears he made a single visit, probably on his celebrated 'world tour' in 1926–27 which also took him to Australia, New Zealand and South America, leaving behind a superb if far flung architectural legacy (including Royal Melbourne and the course at the Jockey Club of Buenos Aires).

Mackenzie left much of the follow-up work to his associate Fleming (who would work a year later on Cypress Point in Monterrey Peninsula) and some have speculated that Mackenzie only tinkered with a few greens at Little Island. But it seems unlikely that Mackenzie would have come so far to do so little. There are so many outstanding golf holes that it seems certain that his intervention was pivotal in turning a home-made layout into a truly exceptional one.

Certainly, the transformation was widely and immediately appreciated. Suddenly Cork began to attract a host of major tournaments. There were three Irish Championships (for men, women and juniors) in the late 1920s, and the Irish Open in 1932, in which Henry Cotton finished well back. The challenges to be found on the revised course also thoroughly tested the mettle of a promising junior member, Jimmy Bruen. He turned into a Ryder Cup star, and was arguably Ireland's greatest player before an injury cut short his professional career.

Cork's early glory period was brought well and truly to a close by the deprivations of the Second World War and by the fire that destroyed the clubhouse on 28 May 1945. The system of water porters may have kept the bar going, but it didn't give the fire brigade much to work with.

For a time, the fire seems to have undermined the club's viability, and its common sense. In the immediate post-war years equipment was so scarce that members were reduced to sifting through the ashes of the old clubhouse in search of bits of golf clubs that could be welded together. Yet that didn't stop the club from rashly overextending itself on a new building. The insurance from the fire didn't nearly cover the cost, and there was little money left over for staff. The greenkeepers promptly went on strike.

Things didn't get much better until 1959, when twenty-six members kicked in £100 each to put things on a sounder financial footing. The subsequent introduction of a sprinkler system in 1962 was followed by a rash of professional tournaments. The most memorable performance of all remains the 65 and 63 shot by Christy O'Connor on the final day of a 72-hole championship.

The course

If you're looking for evidence of the inspired hand of Alister Mackenzie you won't see it from the first tee, the start of a simple, straightaway par 4 on gentle farmland. But as you emerge from some greenside trees onto the second tee, you begin to get an inkling of what lies ahead. The second is a visually splendid par 5, descending sharply through columns of trees down towards the wide Lee Estuary. The River Lee will be your constant companion for the next four holes, culminating in the fine par-5 fifth, which combines an intimidating blind tee shot over a chasm and a treacherous approach to a green perched near the water's edge.

Things change suddenly again at the sixth, a very short par 4 played away from the river over engagingly old-fashioned humps and swales. Then, yet another physical feature is introduced. The seventh is a picturesque par 3 over rocky wasteland, and the eighth a spectacularly expansive par 4 played into an enormous depression in the earth. These are the first of the quarry holes, laid out on the remains of the original limestone pit. American visitors who stumble in this very difficult stretch can be consoled in the knowledge that stone from this spot can be found on many historic buildings in the United States, especially in Boston.

If there is a consistent quality to Little Island, it is in its capacity to surprise. In a span of eighteen holes, the landscape shifts any number of times, from farmland, to waterside, to quarry, to rather dense woodlands. And then there is the sixteenth, a short, links-like par 4, that curls in a hook to a delightful green hidden in the swales. By the time you play the flat-out gorgeous seventeenth, a grand par 4 encased in its own little forest, you have long since realized that this is a very special golf experience.

One shudders a little at what a modern designer might have done to this strange and varying landscape, with the possibility of signature bunkers, huge modern greens, split fairways and other efforts to impose a consistent feel on the course. Despite its parkland setting, Little Island, like its principal architect, is closer to the roots of the game, and seems far more Irish than the upscale instant golf courses that have cropped up in the vicinity. Its capacity to surprise comes from the land itself.

Whatever Mackenzie may have contributed to Little Island's lasting charm, it is safe to say that his legacy has been enhanced by the care the members have taken in their efforts to lengthen the course to meet modern requirements. The formidable tee shot on the fifth is their handiwork, as is the eleventh green, which now hangs alarmingly on the edge of the quarry, turning what today's golfers would consider a short par 5 into a delicate challenge.

The eleventh is also where you will find a plaque and a Spanish chestnut tree marking the spot where Seve Ballesteros hit a drive during an exhibition match in 1983. This attempt at glamour by association seems unnecessary on such a wonderful golf course, though it is true that Little Island has been overshadowed in the minds of visiting golfers by the marvellous links courses on the west coast of Ireland, and even by the fancy new developments in the area, such as Old Head and Fota Island. Rest assured, however, that Cork Golf Club is still the best course in Ireland's second city, and one of the very few parkland courses in Ireland we would take a detour to play.

Location: Five miles east of Cork City, on Little Island. Turn south off N25 at Little Island and follow the signs.

Restrictions: None, but call or write in advance

Green Fee: €85–95

Manager: Matt Sands

Address: Little Island, Cork, Co. Cork; **tel:** (021) 435-3451; **fax:** (021) 435-3410; **e-mail:** corkgolfclub@eircom.net; **web:** www.corkgolfclub.ie

---

Old Head

Founded: 1997

Designed by: Ron Kirby

Don't need 'em [the locals]. They don't play Old Head – can't afford it. It wasn't built for them anyway. It's for the international market. We have an annual day for Kinsale's police and fire – keeps 'em sweet. That's about it.

JOHN O'CONNOR, AS QUOTED IN TRAVEL AND LEISURE GOLF

I would appeal to golfers not to avail of the place. By playing there it makes it more difficult for us.

TED TYNAN, FREE THE OLD HEAD OF KINSALE CAMPAIGN

Built on a diamond-shaped piece of land that juts gorgeously into the Atlantic Ocean south of Kinsale, the course at Old Head is the kind of place that gives golf a bad name. Through the courts, the owners have succeeded in barring locals from free access to one of their own national treasures. Golf's international jet set, on the other hand, are able to fly in on their choppers and enjoy some of the planet's most enjoyable scenery. Play a round if you can afford it, but if you see a group of protesters scaling the fences have the decency to let them play through.

90

✦✦✦

First open for play in 1997, the course at Old Head is already world famous and one of the most spectacular courses anywhere. But it is also something of an illusion.

Let's start with the name. The enterprise insists on calling itself Old Head Golf Links, when it isn't on sandy linksland at all; instead more than half a million tonnes of topsoil had to be trucked in to get the grass to grow.

Then there is the design of the course, attributed improbably to a team of six, including three heroes of Irish golf (Joe Carr, Eddie Hackett and Liam Higgins). In fact, most of the important work was done by American Ron Kirby.

The owners also try to attract international members (the joining fee is US$50,000) by promoting the luxury complex as a celebration of things Irish. The reality is that the arrival of a golf course has meant that local people, for the first time in a couple of millennia, are now unable to stroll along Old Head's magnificent cliffs, watch for whales and dolphins, visit the bird sanctuary, or explore the important ruins that are scattered across the property. Unless, of course, they want to pay a small fortune for a round of golf.

Cork poet Diarmaid O Dalaigh obviously doesn't fall into that category. In September 2006 he filed a court action against the owners of Old Head in order to regain public access to the property. He aimed to prove that there was an existing right of way across the course to the cliff paths and historic lighthouse.

It is just the latest chapter in a sorry saga that began in the mid-1980s, when the farmer who owned Old Head offered to sell it to the state as a 'national monument'. One offer came in, but it wasn't good enough, and in 1989 real estate developers John and Patrick O'Connor snapped up the 220-acre site for just £200,000. When the brothers sought planning permission for a golf clubhouse, Cork County Council demanded that public access be allowed during daylight hours.

The O'Connors agreed, and for a few years walkers were allowed to ramble for a small fee, but then the brothers O'Connor asked the courts to relieve them of their obligations.

'When we opened the course we found that people were wandering everywhere,' John O'Connor explained to the media at the time. 'They are a danger to themselves and to each other.'

In 2001, the Supreme Court backed the O'Connors on technical grounds, ruling that public access issues shouldn't have been mixed up with a building application. So the O'Connors were free, legally, to break their promises.

Many locals were amazed.

'The High Court decision that has rewarded the grasping greed of the Old Head golf course owners must not go unchallenged,' roared one Cork councillor. 'The now heavily fortified golf course seeks exclusivity as it markets its access to wealthy golf tourists, tourists who presumably are unaware of the previous unlimited public access that was allowed on the Old Head.'

Local protest groups began a series of annual People's Picnics at the gates of the golf course, often attracting several hundred people, and usually involving an attempt to dodge security guards and scale barbed-wire fences in order to take the traditional walk to the historic lighthouse.

John O'Connor is on record as calling the protesters a 'bunch of tree-huggers,' and certainly Ted Tynan, of the Free the Old Head of Kinsale campaign, is a well-known left-wing organizer in Cork. He told us he simply wanted to do what he had always done.

'I went down to Old Head with my parents, and with my own children,' he said. 'We used to go on picnics on a Sunday, it was like an adventure playground.

'We don't have any problem with the golf course, if only people could walk on the cliffs as they always have. For hundreds of years people have been able to walk on the headlands.'

To some extent, the O'Connors have a point when it comes to safety. In their efforts to amaze the golf world, they have spent millions to ensure that fairways and greens are positioned as close to the 300-foot cliffs as is humanly possible (they even lost a mowing machine to the waves in the process). There are, admittedly, now few places for ramblers to go without being in the line of a golf shot.

That shouldn't be a problem during winter, when the course is closed, but thanks to the court ruling, the proprietors can keep the walkers and whale-watchers out even then.

In a place now dedicated to the pampering of the super rich, it is perhaps worth noting that Old Head has known its share of tragedy. In addition to the notorious sinking of the liner Lusitania (which claimed 1,200 lives in 1915), this was also an area devastated by the Irish famine.

'I went to Old Head, and we met flocks of wretched children,' wrote Asenath Nicholson, an American who travelled through the area in 1851.

'Naught but desolation and death reigned; and the voice of nature, which was always so pleasant on the sea-coast, now, united with the whistling of the wind, seemed only to be howling in sad response to the moans and entreaties of the starving around me.'

The course

Although the official line is that the course at Old Head has been designed by a 'unique team' of six, Ron Kirby set us straight when we bumped into him during our one round here. He was overseeing some work on a green they were trying to teeter even more precariously over the cliffs below.

'A third of the routing is one hundred per cent mine, a third is fifty per cent mine,' said the long-time associate of Jack Nicklaus. 'The original routing was done by [Eddie] Hackett. His routing was counter-clockwise on the front nine, now it's clockwise.

'And one hundred per cent of the strategy is mine. I did all of the greens except a couple. As far as the bunkering, the pin positions, the strategy, I got here in time to do all that.'

Kirby wouldn't say that Old Head was the best course he had helped design, but he said it would be in the top five. He certainly didn't sound like he thought he was building a course for the ages.

'Give them a friendly golf course,' he said about the members at Old Head. 'Give them wide fairways, flat greens, don't get too complicated with the bunkering....There's no trees to direct you, you sort of put bunkers in a cluster. But give them wide fairways, because the wind is the third dimension here.'

The nine holes that hang over the cliffs are certainly breathtaking, and designed well enough. But the golf course at Old Head is essentially a visually stunning, one-trick pony. The inland holes aren't nearly as memorable, and there is as much chance of Old Head being named the number one golf course on earth (John O'Connor's stated objective) as there is for the O'Connors to be named patrons of The Irish Ramblers Club. Old Head is not among the ten best courses in Ireland itself, in our opinion.

And the question remains whether there should be a golf course here at all. While the promotional video for the course speaks, absurdly, of the project helping 'nature fulfil its potential', it is the former owner of the land who no doubt had things right. Surely a place of such natural beauty, and with such ecological, historical and archaeological interest, should have been turned into a public space, and perhaps into a National Park, as Killarney was years before.

Location: About 8 miles southwest of Kinsale. Follow R600 out of Kinsale toward Bandon and Garrettstown and cross bridge at the end of town, following road around to the right, and thereafter following signs to Old Head

Restrictions: None. Note, however, that no trolleys are permitted on the course. A caddie or golf buggy (with forecaddie recommended) must be hired. Children under 12 years of age are not permitted on the grounds or in the clubhouse at any time

Green Fee: €295

Marketing Director: Fiona McDonald

Address: Kinsale, Co. Cork; **tel:** (021) 477-8444; **fax:** (021) 477-8022; **e-mail:** reservations@oldhead.com; **web:** www.oldheadgolflinks.com

Adare Manor Golf Club
Founded: 1900

Designed by: Eddie Hackett

Adare Manor Hotel Golf Course
Built: 1995

Designed by: Robert Trent Jones

These are the odd couple of Irish golf. An unpretentious, century-old club founded by the fourth Earl of Dunraven now sits alongside a showy new course built at much greater expense by an American ex-Marine. It is the American who has the Manor House now, and the Irish Open, but we suspect the soul of Irish golf is more likely to be found next door.

◆◆◆

Tom Kane, who bought Adare Manor in 1987 over the phone, sight unseen, for £2 million, tells a good story about his initial visit to his new purchase. The first buildings he came across were the stables, which he mistook, for a moment, for the main house.

'I said to myself, "What have I done?",' he chortled to me and a cluster of other guests over dinner (I was in Adare as part of a television production on Irish golf).

But then Kane turned round a bend and saw the enormous (there are seventy-five fireplaces) eighteenth-century mansion.

'We call it Holy Shit corner,' he said.

It is the kind of story that goes down well with those fascinated by the rich and powerful (that is, just about all of us). And if Tom Kane isn't powerful, he certainly knows people who are.

Since he turned Adare Manor into one of Ireland's most exclusive hotels, his guests have included movie stars, heads of state and celebrities of every description.

In 2005, a charity golf event organized by J.P. McManus, one of Ireland's richest men, attracted no fewer than thirty-one former Ryder Cup players, including Tiger Woods, a bevy of other celebrities, and forty thousand spectators. Following the success of that event, Adare Manor essentially purchased the Irish Open for the years 2007–2009.

It is not a terrible venue, by any means. The final hole is a theatrical par 5 that ends just across a river, beside the manor, and is the kind of extraordinary finish that any publicity-hungry golf resort owner would appreciate. And while there are plenty of water features, there is also the thirteenth, a wonderfully natural par 4 that seems to start in its own forested world and ends with a stirring downhill approach to a well-guarded green.

The course is among the last attributed to Robert Trent Jones, who was almost ninety when it was completed. He and his team made excellent use of the forests, water hazards and changes of elevation at their disposal.

If the bunkering, and the large man-made lake, seem a little too much like Florida at times, that probably doesn't bother Tom Kane, who used to live there. He has also built a Vietnam War memorial not far from the eighteenth green.

For all the American-style merits of the course, it is what I saw from the manicured fourteenth fairway, while travelling in a motorized golf cart, that intrigued me more. On an adjoining property were some impressive stone ruins. And striding through them were clusters of Irishmen, many with shirts hanging out, pulling trolleys or carrying golf bags over their shoulders. It was the unmistakable, hectic scene of an Irish golf club on competition day. Now *that* looked like fun.

In a break in the filming, I scurried over to the mysterious golfing ground and found myself, confusingly enough, at the Adare Manor Golf Club, though there was no connection to Kane's hotel. The club had a modest clubhouse and its own utterly unique golf course, one that weaved its way around, and right smack through, the ruins of a fourteenth century Franciscan Abbey.

It turned out the club had been around for more than a century, founded by the fourth Earl of Dunraven, who then owned the Manor. Ben Sayers, designer of the fine Castlerock links in Northern Ireland, apparently laid out the original nine-hole course, though the current eighteen-hole routing is based on designs by Eddie Hackett. A year's membership costs rather less than a night's stay in the Adare Manor Hotel's Presidential Suite.

For the club's centenary in 2000, it asked the current Lord Dunraven, who still lived in the area, to be honorary President.

I have no idea how all this went down at Adare Manor itself, where the golf *club* that bears its name seems not to be spoken of at all (certainly not in their promotional literature). But then not all the Dunravens have been that keen on the man who snapped up their former home, either.

Lady Ana Wyndham Quin, daughter of the current Earl, formally objected to Kane's proposal to build 287 housing units on the grounds of Adare Manor. In a submission to the Irish Planning Board, she argued that it would be 'the absolute ruination of Adare village at the hands of unimaginative planners (none of whom live in Adare) and of the five members of Adare Partners, three of whom do not live in Ireland'.

She went on to urge the Board to 'help to uphold the charm, style, fabric and vista of one of the most famously picturesque villages in Ireland'.

We can only guess what Lady Quin thinks about Kane's latest plan to build a 100-bed private hospital on the Manor's grounds. (The Irish government has offered such schemes huge tax breaks to take the pressure off the embattled public health system.)

It isn't the first time the Dunravens have had spats with upstart Americans. In the 1890s, the fourth Earl of Dunraven, the one who built the first golf course at Adare, was expelled from the New York Yacht Club.

It was during one of the first America's Cup races, and the Earl had accused the Americans of cheating.

We want to stress that we have no reason to think that Tom Kane is anything but an honourable fellow. He is a notable philanthropist and a driving force behind Operation Smile, which funds facial reconstruction surgery for thousands of children around the world.

We're just saying that if you happen to attend the Irish Open in the next few years, you may find that the golf is just a little bit more Irish on the course next door.

Adare Manor Golf Club

Location: On N21, southwest of Limerick, follow signs from Adare town

Restrictions: None

Green Fee: €37.50

Hon. Secretary: Pat O'Brien

Address: Adare, Co Limerick; **tel:** (061) 396204; **fax:** (061) 396800; **e-mail:** info@adaremanorgolfclub.com; **web:** www.adaremanorgolfclub.com

Adare Manor Hotel Golf Course

Location: On N21, southwest of Limerick, follow signs from Adare town

Restrictions: None

Green Fee: €145

Manager: Anita Carey

Address: Adare Manor Hotel & Golf Resort, Adare, Co Limerick; **tel:** (061) 605274; **fax:** (061) 396124; **e-mail:** golf@adaremanor.com; **web:** www.adaregolfclub.com

Ring of Kerry

Founded: 1998

Designed by: Eddie Hackett and Ron Kirby

Ring of Kerry is a strange but memorable golf experience that is distinguished by its jaw-dropping scenery. Though built on a steep slope, the course is surprisingly playable, which may be due to the original routing by Eddie Hackett. Nevertheless, this is the one place in Ireland where an electric cart may enhance the enjoyment. Just don't come on a foggy day.

◆◆◆

Some golf courses have nice views. What Ring of Kerry Golf and Country Club offers is a view with a bit of golf attached.

That is no criticism of the golf, which has always been a lot of fun. It is just that the view from almost every vantage point at Ring of Kerry is otherworldly. Officially, the course 'overlooks Kenmare Bay and the Caha Mountains'. But there's something about the perfectly elevated vantage point, and the exquisite framing of blue sea, islands and mountains, set off by the vivid Kerry green of the course in the foreground, which grabs your eyeballs on the first tee and never lets go.

Since the course is built on the side of a hill, and is largely exposed, that view is omnipresent. It doesn't change much either, but no matter. Shank your ball into a pond, and you just need to take a look up and give thanks for being alive.

For all its beauty and prime location on one of Ireland's most popular tourist routes, Ring of Kerry has had a difficult conception. Donal O'Shea, a local man whose family owned the land, died before work on the course really got started, and the original architect, Eddie Hackett, died before the course opened. Their places have been filled, rather haphazardly, by a variety of owners and managers, and by at least three more designers (Roger Brown, Arthur Spring and Ron Kirby).

Construction itself was a formidable challenge, as a quarter of a million tonnes of top soil had to be imported to cover what was essentially a peat bog. The greens were shaped after Hackett died and were, in places, hysterically undulating.

For better or worse, the side-hill terrain gives the course its unique character, and has forced the designers to use their imaginations. We always liked the opening two holes, short par 4s which climbed, quirkily, to the highest part of the property while you still had the energy. Then there were some less memorable holes (not all by Hackett) that were just preparation for a rollicking long hole that sent you thrillingly, and half blindly, over the mountain like a golfing version of Franz Klammer. That hole has been very much redesigned now, as have several others, so it is difficult to know how much of the current course to attribute to Hackett.

With the whimsical greens, occasional blind shot, and repeated changes in elevation, a round at Ring of Kerry took on a sort of giddiness that rather matched the surreal setting.

Things have become rather more sober of late. An outfit calling itself Universal Golf Consulting has been given an eleven-year contract to manage the property, and changes have been made, in the company's words, to 'soften the golf course – including removing rough, re-shaping greens and re-designing holes – to render it much more user-friendly whilst maintaining its championship status'.

We're not quite sure what championships are being referred to, unless it's the Ian Botham Celebrity Charity Pro-Am, won in 2006 by former Ryder Cup player Philip Walton. The truth is, Ring of Kerry is just not on terrain suitable for truly serious golf, and we fear the aspirations of the owners in this regard may never be met. What has been consistent, at least during our visits, has been the excellent conditioning of the course, the first-class clubhouse facilities and the friendliness of the staff.

Ron Kirby, who has spent many a recent summer in this part of Ireland working on Old Head and Skellig Bay, has now reshaped the greens, and is no doubt working on the other changes as well.

Tracing the genealogy of the golf holes at Ring of Kerry is now extremely difficult, but we would like to think the fourteenth is Eddie Hackett's handiwork. It is an uphill beauty in the most heavily forested part of the course, with a green lovingly framed by trees. It is the one place at Ring of Kerry where the beauty and challenge of the golf hole is a match for the views.

The course ends rather oddly on an uphill par 3 played away from the bay (this time not the work of Hackett), and afterwards you have the choice of downing a pint on the clubhouse balcony (that view again) or regaining your sense of reality by visiting one of the excellent pubs in nearby Kenmare. Or, you could turn right on the Ring of Kerry road and head five minutes to Spillane's Bar, known for its decent food and run by a famous Gaelic football star.

We still don't know quite what to make of Ring of Kerry. It will never have the glamour of the 'signature' layouts by great names that have popped up all over Ireland. And it is entirely out of character for us to be fond of a course that is such a strain to walk. But of all the newfangled parkland courses built in Ireland in the last twenty years, this is very close to being our favourite.

Location: On the N70 (the 'Ring of Kerry') at village of Templenoe, about 4 miles west of Kenmare

Restrictions: None

Green Fee: €80-90

Manager: Ed Edwards

Address: Templenoe, Killarney, Co. Kerry; **tel:** (064) 42000; **fax:** (064) 42533; **e-mail:** reservations@ringofkerrygolf.com; **web:** www.ringofkerrygolf.com

---

Bantry Bay

Founded: 1975

Designed by: Eddie Hackett and Christy O'Connor Jr

Ireland's grand old links courses, founded before the bulldozer, feature many invigorating blind tee shots, but Bantry Bay, a much newer parkland course located on the coastline of West Cork, takes things to an illogical extreme. Believe it or not, it is not possible to see the green from the tee on any of Bantry Bay's par 4 or 5 holes. This is such a singular achievement that you may want to pay a visit, perhaps as a convenient stopover between Killarney or Waterville and Cork City. There are other attractions too – fantastic seaside views, a number of very strong golf holes, and some excellent seafood chowder.

Bantry Bay feels like two very different golf courses stuck together, and for good reason. The first five holes are from the original, relatively gentle and traditional nine-hole layout, set amongst many mature trees and almost devoid of bunkers. Designed by Eddie Hackett in 1975, presumably when the club had little money, the holes go up and over the natural ridges in the terrain, with the greens remaining hidden until at least the approach shot.

On the sixth tee there is an almost shocking change of pace. The terrain drops precipitously towards the beach and one embarks on a stretch of nine flamboyant holes, completed in 1998 and designed in a modern vein by Christy O'Connor Jr. Remarkably, O'Connor makes no attempt to balance the number of blind tee shots on the original course, and in fact reinforces this strange and ultimately irritating characteristic of Bantry Bay. There are a few memorable holes on the O'Connor stretch, which is much closer to the sea, but somehow it's not that much fun to play. A handful of ponds aren't used very imaginatively, and it doesn't help that there are two or three punishing climbs.

We wonder if O'Connor Jr – at one time Ireland's most celebrated professional – remembers what it's like to carry a set of clubs, for the steep ascent to the par-3 ninth is just about the most arduous we've come across. It's a pretty little hole to be sure, with breathtaking views, but once you putt out you have to climb *right back down again*. After this bit of silliness, it's fortunate that the par-4 tenth is a beauty – the drive from an elevated tee has to be aimed, thrillingly, right at the ocean to navigate the dogleg properly.

After the grimly steep fourteenth, the course returns rather happily to the Hackett layout, with a stretch of three fine holes. The fifteenth is a sharp dogleg with a severely slanting fairway. The sixteenth doglegs the other way, and begins with a truly dramatic and difficult downhill tee shot (an optical illusion makes right-handers feel they have to draw the ball just to stay in play); and the seventeenth is a dangerous par 3 tucked along the out-of-bounds line. The finishing hole is a comparatively dull ascent to the very friendly clubhouse. But from the tee – surprise, surprise – the green is nowhere in sight.

Location: One mile north of Bantry town on N71

Restrictions: Certain times are reserved for members, but visitors may reserve any day of the week. Sunday play may not be available to visitors during the summer months

Green Fee: €40–45

Manager: John O'Sullivan

Address: Bantry, West Cork, Co. Cork; **tel:** (027) 50579; **fax:** (027) 53790; **e-mail:** info@bantrygolf.com; **web:** www.bantrygolf.com

---

Spanish Point

Founded: 1896

Designed by: Dr Patrick Hillery and others

Spanish Point is a delightful and quirky nine-hole links course eight miles south of Lahinch that has somehow survived for more than a century. The name of the course derives from the 1588 shipwreck of a large portion of the Spanish Armada – the 170 survivors were hanged by the local sheriff and buried on the beach.

Until the 1990s, this was a par-3 course with cows roaming its fairways and fences around the greens, and for years the small group of members used Guinness bungs (the stopper in a beer cask) for tee markers and tobacco canisters to cut the holes. Its most famous member was Dr Patrick Hillery, President of Ireland from 1978 to 1990, who in some quarters gets credit for the modest expansion and redesign that has brought the course, more or less, up to modern standards. The length is still only 4,600 yards, par 64, but there is great fun to be had as you navigate through a handful of very large dunes and try to make sense of the original new layout, which we prefer to think was concocted by the members during an extremely sociable evening in the cosy clubhouse. The first time through can seem like a treasure hunt, but by the 'back nine' you will have been converted by the Spanish Point charm.

Location: At Spanish Point, 2 miles west of Miltown Malbay, off the main coastal road (N67)

Restrictions: Visitors welcome any time except Sunday mornings

Green Fee: €25–30

Secretary/Manager: David K. Fitzgerald

Address: Spanish Point, Miltown Malbay, Co. Clare; **tel:** (065) 708-4198; **fax:** (065) 708-4219; **e-mail:** info@spanish-point.com; **web:** www.spanish-point.com.

DIVERSIONS

THE SOUTHWEST

COUNTY KERRY BOASTS what may be the most beautiful scenery in all of Ireland. It includes the majestic Macgillycuddy's Reeks mountain range and two breathtaking peninsulas, the Iveragh (better known for the name of its principal roadway, the Ring of Kerry) and the Dingle. It is also blessed with the golfing shrines of Ballybunion, Waterville and Killarney, as well as fine links at Tralee, Dooks and Ceann Sibéal. Indeed, an extraordinary golf journey may be had without leaving the confines of County Kerry.

Some may wish to base themselves in Killarney while they play Kerry's golf courses. We think that would be a mistake, but the over-touristed town is nevertheless the beginning point of the Ring of Kerry and full of bed and breakfasts, currency exchanges and other tourist services. Stretching south and west from Killarney is Killarney National Park, which is dominated by beautiful Lough Leane. For those who do not get enough of the Lough when playing golf at Killarney, boat trips and horseback excursions are easily arranged.

Macgillycuddy's Reeks form the spine of the Iveragh peninsula. The tallest peak, Carrantuohill, is also the highest point in Ireland at 3,400 feet. The peninsula is encircled by the 100-mile Ring of Kerry. The scenery, with deep lakes and mountains on the inside of the Ring and cliffs and crashing surf to the outside, is simply spectacular. Most tour buses circumnavigate the peninsula with few, if any, stops in about four hours. You will undoubtedly be stopping, however, at Waterville, which lies almost exactly half way around the Ring from Killarney, and perhaps also at Dooks. Other interesting detours are Staigue Fort, which dates from 1000 B.C., and Skellig Michael, a monastery which was established around 600 A.D. Skellig Michael is located on Great Skellig island and may be reached by boat most days from Ballinskelligs or Portmagee. The trip takes just over an hour and can be thrilling in its own right on a blustery day. Skellig Michael is an eerie and austere site, with its ancient buildings devoid of windows, and populated now by nothing but sea birds.

The otherwise unremarkable town of Killorglin is home to Puck Fair each August, one of Ireland's oldest and largest gatherings. It is also a pagan fertility rite, having at its centre a live male goat which is hoisted onto a fifty-foot high platform for the duration of the celebration. The pubs do not close for the duration of the fair's seventy-two hours, and musicians and dancers seem to be everywhere. It is not for the faint of heart.

Immediately north of the Ring of Kerry, across Dingle Bay, is the Dingle Peninsula. At its end is a fine links course, Ceann Sibéal, and the scenery one passes in getting there is awe-inspiring. Dingle is one of the few authentic Gaeltacht regions where the Irish language is widely spoken. It is covered in ruins, many from early Christian times. One of the best-preserved is the Gallarus Oratory, just east of Ballyferriter, which has been remarkably waterproof for more than a thousand years. The ruins, the barren landscape and the often misty weather combine to create an eerie, mystical atmosphere on Dingle. Its roads can seem impossibly narrow at times, so slow down and take your time. The main centre on the peninsula, Dingle Town (since 2005, known officially as An Daingean), has only about 1,800 permanent residents, but there are well in excess of fifty pubs! This is an excellent place to search out traditional Irish music.

From a tourist's point of view, northern Kerry has little to match Dingle or the famous Ring. This can pose a problem for non-golfers if their companions have settled in at Ballybunion. The limited sightseeing options include Ardfert Cathedral, a Romanesque church about twenty miles to the south (most of the way back to Tralee); and the town of Listowel (ten miles away), which has the ruins of a castle in its main square. If you are driving between Ballybunion and Lahinch take advantage of the car ferry across the River Shannon between Tarbert and Killimer. It will take fifty miles off your journey.

If you decide to take the long way around the River Shannon, or you are using Shannon airport, Limerick will be close at hand. The Republic's third-largest city may be somewhat drab, but interest in it as a tourist destination has soared since the publication of Frank McCourt's *Angela's Ashes* in 1996.

For those whose first order of business upon arriving in Ireland is to get to a pub, the famous (and tourist-packed) Durty Nellie's is just seven miles from Shannon Airport, on the main road to Limerick. Despite the crowds, the pub can be attractive on an evening when the weather is good – walk outside to the bridge and enjoy the fine view of the floodlit Bunratty Castle.

County Clare has two of Ireland's most important natural attractions – the Cliffs of Moher and the Burren. Even in a nation known for some dramatic coastal headlands, the Cliffs of Moher stand out. They stretch north for five miles from Liscannor, which is just a mile or so north of Lahinch. In fact, part of the cliffs are visible from several points on the Lahinch links, but they are much more dramatic when viewed from close range (just how close to the edge you wish to venture is a test of bravery or foolhardiness – the cliff edge is unstable in many places). The cliffs grow progressively higher from south to north, reaching about 700 feet. Perhaps the best vantage point of all to view the cliffs is from O'Brien's tower, at the north end. If the weather is clear you can see the Irish coast from Kerry to Connemara.

The Burren is a vast area of northern County Clare that is often compared to the moon. Burren literally means 'rock', and that is about all you need to know. It is the home of many rare species of flowers, which manage to sprout up between the limestone outcroppings in the spring. It also has literally hundreds of ancient stone forts. All of this is explained nicely at the Burren Display Centre located in Kilfenora. If by chance you are a cave explorer, the area is also for you. But for most, it is an eerie, barren desert.

Two villages in County Clare also merit a mention, if for very different reasons. Doolin, a tiny coastal village about ten miles north of Lahinch, is famous for its traditional Irish music. Try O'Connor's, McGann's or McDermott's pubs (or better yet, try them all – each is renowned throughout the country). If you're travelling to Doolin up the coast road from Lahinch, a stop at Vaughan's Anchor Inn in Liscannor for some of their terrific seafood will also be in order. Meanwhile, Lisdoonvarna is 5 miles to the east of Doolin. It is known as a spa town, but has achieved international fame for its annual matchmaking festival in September. This is not a joke; it is far from unheard of for tourists in attendance (especially young women) to receive serious offers of marriage.

It may be wishful thinking to call the southwestern coast of Ireland the Irish Riviera, but don't be surprised if you find palm trees and other sub-tropical plants in parts of County Cork. This is due to the influence of the Gulf Stream, which keeps the temperature between forty-five and seventy degrees Fahrenheit throughout the year. Indeed, there are many examples of trees and flowers that are otherwise found only in the Mediterranean countries. It is also extremely wet and, it almost goes without saying, very green. 'There isn't much climate,' a local saying goes, 'but there's a lot of weather.'

Cork is the largest city in the southwest by a wide margin and is Ireland's second city. Like any second city, it exhibits a fierce independence mixed with a touch of an inferiority complex. In the pub, for example, this is the only part of the Republic where Guinness does not hold utter superiority. The local Murphy's stout (and occasionally, Beamish) can be found with greater frequency here than elsewhere in Ireland. The city also has large English and French expatriate communities and respected film and jazz festivals.

Cork does not have an abundance of historic sites – much of the city was destroyed in the Civil War. The main attraction may be simply strolling through the compact downtown, sampling from the abundant pubs and cafes. The main shopping area is Patrick Street. The most important tourist attraction is the rather fanciful St Finbarr's Cathedral, built in the 1870s in neo-Gothic style, whose spires are visible from much of the city. Also worthwhile is the Crawford Art Gallery, which has a strong collection of

Irish art, particularly from the nineteenth century.

Some of Ireland's most famous tourist attractions may be easily reached from Cork. The Blarney Stone is located at Blarney, just five miles away. The stone is set high on a hill in Blarney Castle and, as most everyone knows, kissing it is said to confer 'the gift of the gab'. More likely, you will be the victim of the tourist trap, as Blarney is frightfully busy with tour buses and souvenir stands much of the year.

About forty-five miles to the north is Cashel, with the magnificent castle and cathedral on the Rock of Cashel. Much of the current structure dates from the eleventh through fifteenth centuries, though the site was the seat of the King of Munster in the first millennium and is said to have been visited by St Patrick. It is most impressive when viewed from a distance, as it rises up from the flat plains known as the Golden Vale, and is reminiscent of Mont St Michel in France or Assisi in Italy.

Kinsale, just to the west of Cork, is a picturesque village that is widely regarded as one of the country's culinary capitals. It was at one time a true fishing village, but has been considerably gentrified. It is now charming and quaint. The gourmet reputation was built chiefly on the establishment of the 'good food circle,' a group of upscale restaurants which focus primarily on the plentiful seafood available in Kinsale. It makes a very convenient and pleasant night out for golfers playing the Old Head course nearby. The town was also the site of the Battle of Kinsale in 1601, in which the Irish aristocracy and their Spanish allies were defeated by the English. This was a decisive battle in the English occupation of Ireland which would follow for the next 300 years.

The Irish Distillers Ltd complex at Midleton is where the major Irish whiskies, with the exception of Bushmills, are produced. Recently, the Jameson Whiskey Heritage Centre has opened here, with a tour, various audio-visual presentations and tastings all available. Anyone interested in whiskey should take either this tour or the one offered by Bushmills in Northern Ireland.

THE NORTHWEST:
THE GREAT ADVENTURE

ALTHOUGH FAMOUS IN the Victorian age, the fascinating links in this thinly populated region have until recently been largely forgotten. Once a mecca for aristocratic holiday-makers from Britain, the counties in the Northwest were particularly affected by the Troubles, which sharply reduced traffic from Northern Ireland. The lingering sense of isolation in Sligo, Donegal and Mayo make it our favourite part of Ireland. It is here where the sense of golfing adventure is most keen, where you will travel hours on narrow country roads to encounter excellent courses all but unknown outside Ireland. Some of these links are simply astonishing, while others offer an intoxicating mixture of seclusion, great golf, and matchless rural hospitality. Old Tom Morris, Harry Vardon and Harry Colt all left their mark here, but even more notable are the spellbinding contributions from two very Irish architects, Eddie Hackett and Pat Ruddy. And it is a pleasant surprise to learn that in some cases your green fees are supporting community development enterprises. Be it the magnificent light at Rosses Point, the pretzel-like drive to Rosapenna, or the crashing surf at Cruit Island, there is lots to remember in the Northwest.

BALLYLIFFIN (Old)

Founded: 1973

Designed by: Martin Niland and Martin Hopkins

If Nick Faldo is in love with Ballyliffin, why does he want to take it over? The club is our heritage. It is for our kids and their kids and it's not for sale.

KARL O'DOHERTY, HONORARY SECRETARY OF BALLYLIFFIN,

QUOTED IN THE *DERRY JOURNAL*, MARCH 1995

The club members of Ballyliffin rebuffed a lucrative offer from Britain's most famous golfer, and are now the proud custodians of one of the most enjoyable thirty-six holes of links golf on the planet. While the spectacular new Glashedy Links has justifiably won wide praise, the magical Old Links, with its crazy undulating fairways, is every bit as endearing.

◆◆◆

You could understand why the members of Ballyliffin would be starstruck when Nick Faldo's helicopter descended from the skies on a brilliant August morning in 1993. The reigning British Open champion was the number-one ranked golfer in the world, and here he was looking for a game in tiny Ballyliffin.

Perched on the upper reaches of the Inishowen Peninsula, Ballyliffin was both the most northerly, and one of the least known courses in Ireland. Only a few years before, its future had been in grave doubt, and the club council even passed a motion to reduce the course to twelve holes to reduce maintenance costs. Now Nick Faldo, a man who had won the British Open at St Andrews and Muirfield, was calling Ballyliffin 'the most natural links I have ever played'.

Faldo was at the peak of his fame, so his visit to Ballyliffin brought the club new attention. 'Quite why it is not recognized among Ireland's finest courses is something of a mystery,' opined a writer from London's *Financial Times*, who also marvelled at the £8 green fees.

Not a few at the club wondered if Faldo could do for Ballyliffin what Tom Watson did in the 1970s for Ballybunion. The publicity generated by

Watson's regular pilgrimages to the great west coast links had helped make Ballybunion the favourite Irish destination of visiting foreign golfers.

It turned out that Faldo and his management team had a little more in mind than a friendly association. He let it be known that he wanted to *buy* Ballyliffin – or at least rent it for a generation or two. And the numbers being thrown around were pretty spectacular.

You could see how a million pounds could be tempting to a club which had only just got on its feet. This was not Portrush or County Down or Portmarnock, with a century's worth of well-heeled membership. The course had only opened in 1973, after a few members of the old nine-hole course scraped together a few thousand pounds and bought 365 acres of pristine linksland.

The links that Faldo fell in love with was 'built' for just £5,838. The club's finely tuned budget called for an expenditure of £300 a hole, including £33 for each tee, £192 for each green, £50 for resodding and £12 for levelling. Whether or not anyone had an idea of smoothing out the fairways, there was certainly no money to do so.

'Some Scottish guys were brought in at one stage to have a look,' says Martin Niland, a member of the club at the time. 'But they were only a day and a half on site, and we were a bit dissatisfied with the time they spent and what they did. So we ended up doing it ourselves.'

The Scottish visitors were from Frank Pennick's design firm. But when they departed it was left to Niland and fellow member Martin Hopkins to find a suitable routing on the massive property.

'We didn't have proper drawings,' says Niland. 'We just used stakes for the tees and the greens.'

What Niland and Hopkins did have was a good grounding in agricultural science, and among the first thing they did was set up a nursery for the natural fescue grasses they would later lay on the green sites by hand.

Over the years, finishing touches on what is now called the Old Links at Ballyliffin fell to the heroic greenkeeper Dennis Doherty. He did everything on his own with only one piece of automated equipment (a single mower to cut the greens), though in the summer he was sometimes helped by a lad or two from government job-creation schemes.

There were still only a few dozen members, and the club almost went under in 1978, only to be saved by a particularly successful Ladies' Committee bazaar and raffle. Fortunately, golf soon began to take off all over Ireland, and new converts from Derry (the nearest city of any size) and even further afield were looking for clubs that still had room for new members. After a new clubhouse was built in 1987, membership at Ballyliffin *quadrupled*.

Finances were stretched again, however, when the members were persuaded, in 1992, to build a second golf course next to the old one.

By the time Faldo landed his helicopter on that fateful day in August, 1993, the club was well on its way to being almost £500,000 in debt, a sizeable amount for a club with some of the lowest green fees in Ireland.

Faldo's unprecedented offer was both tempting and a little bewildering. A negotiating team was formed, and they were soon whisked away to a fancy hotel in Dublin for secret meetings with the business advisers of the famous professional.

Details of the offer began to emerge. Faldo would take over responsibility for the debt, and sink another £1 million into the club for a new clubhouse and professional's shop. In exchange, Faldo would be granted a lease for a period of thirty-three years, during which time he and his management team would run the entire affairs of the club.

The proposal created an uproar, and media coverage ensured that Ballyliffin's dilemma became a talking point among golfers throughout Ireland. Even members of the negotiating team were split on whether to accept the offer. Details were posted for the members, who attended the decisive annual meeting in record numbers.

After two-and-a-half hours of animated debate, the offer was rejected.

'We simply wish to put any controversy behind us and get on with the day-to-day running of our golf club,' Karl O'Doherty, the club's honorary secretary, told the *Derry Journal*. 'I'm delighted with the outcome and equally delighted that Nick Faldo expressed such an interest in the quality of our club.'

Certainly, the publicity surrounding Faldo's offer did the club no harm. Membership has grown to 1,600, and visitors are now measured in the thousands. The second links opened in 1995 to rave reviews. And in 1999 yet another new clubhouse was built, with luxurious facilities and stunning, panoramic views of some of the most beautiful golf terrain on the planet.

And Nick Faldo remains rather more than just a friend. Now flush with cash, the club hired him to touch up the not-so-very Old Links he loves so well.

The course

In this age of money-is-no-object golf developments, in which a single hole can cost a million dollars, it is cheering to realize that what makes the Old Links at Ballyliffin great is the sheer *absence* of money.

Since the club was all but broke when the course was laid out, they had no access to bulldozers or other machinery. The fairways were routed between the highest dunes, but they retained hundreds of small humps and swales that the wind and the rain had created over thousands of years. As in the days of Old Tom Morris, only the greens were made flat, and it is this bewitching combination of rambunctious fairways and small, straightforward putting surfaces, often on the same level as the surrounding ground, that creates the illusion of stepping back in time. It means awkward lies, bad bounces, and deep hollows that sometimes prevent one from seeing the green. It means that approach shots require consummate skill and a bit of good luck, but once on the green there is a fair crack at making the putt.

The fact that the fairways are not clearly defined, and often just peter out into the rough, only adds to the natural, unadulterated visual quality of the terrain. One feels that this is surely how golf was played in its earliest days. After eighteen holes you begin to wonder if it isn't how it should be played now.

The old-fashioned quality is an illusion, of course. The Old Links at Ballyliffin is less than a decade older than Pete Dye's modernist landmark at Sawgrass. And the good sense displayed in the routing lifts Ballyliffin from an anachronistic curiosity to a full-bodied course of championship calibre.

The most famous hole is probably the least characteristic – a par 3 called the Tank, with a theatrically elevated green set between stocky sandhills.

More satisfying are the many dogleg par 4s, which weave in and out among the dunes at unpredictable and fascinating angles, and which require excellent tee shots and precise seconds.

Despite the arrival of the flashy new Glashedy Links beside it, built with bulldozers and all the technical advantages of the late twentieth century, at least half of the members continue to prefer the Old Links. And all prefer it for inter-club matches, since visiting competitors find the undulations baffling.

Some of the terrain of the Old Links was commandeered in the building of the Glashedy Links, which doesn't pay the same homage to humps in the middle of fairways. But for the most part, the members have left well enough alone as their finances have improved. As a past captain of Ballyliffin told us: 'Some people wanted to create what they call a landing area on some of the holes, but it would take away from the character of the place.'

We have not played the Old Links since it was 'renovated', in 2006, by Nick Faldo, who promised to leave the character of the course alone while 'improving' the quality of the bunkering, and adding a scenically striking hole along the coastal boundary. We're not at all sure such changes were needed, but we're keeping our minds open, and our fingers crossed.

Location: On the Inishowen Peninsula, about a mile northeast of Ballyliffin on R238; about 30 miles from Derry

Restrictions: None

Green Fee: €65–70

General Manager: John Farren

Address: Ballyliffin, Inishowen, Co. Donegal; **tel:** (074) 937-6119; **fax:** (074) 937-6672; **e-mail:** info@ballyliffingolfclub.com; **web:** www.ballyliffingolfclub.com

---

BALLYLIFFIN (Glashedy)

Opened: 1995

Designed by: Pat Ruddy and Tom Craddock

Messrs. Ruddy and Craddock stated that the land was probably the finest piece of links golfing terrain that they had ever seen and the possibilities for developing it as a golf links were mind-boggling.

FROM THE HISTORY OF BALLYLIFFIN GOLF CLUB

Although it shares the same fantastic scenery and magical isolation, the Glashedy Links (named after a striking rock formation offshore) has little else in common with the cosy and quirky Old Links at Ballyliffin. On Glashedy, the earth-moving machines have shaped

relatively wide and smooth fairways that sweep through the high sand hills in majestic curves. The traditions of links golf remain, however. Frighteningly penal pot bunkers determine tactics, and openings to greens reward low, running approach shots. Despite the stunning surroundings, Pat Ruddy has resisted the temptation to build holes that are all theatre, and the Glashedy Links already has the composure and proportion of a classic.

◆◆◆

The Glashedy Links came about by virtue of the kind of good fortune that seems to bless Ballyliffin. In the summer of 1992, Pat Ruddy and his partner Tom Craddock were invited up to the Inishowen Peninsula to make suggestions on how the club might add an additional nine holes.

Ruddy was staggered when he saw the complex of gigantic sand hills – several stories high in places – that loomed over the Old Links, and which were at the club's disposal. What they should consider instead, he said, was using that terrain to construct a completely new eighteen-hole course, of the highest championship standard.

This wasn't just a case of a consultant looking for a bigger contract. Ruddy had recently opened his European Club, a true links south of Dublin, and he was convinced that Ballyliffin now possessed the most fantastic piece of undeveloped linksland left on the planet.

When the members of Ballyliffin used hoes and shovels to construct the Old Links in the late 1960s they had never even considered utilizing the steepest dunes – the very section that Ruddy was now drooling over.

Modern excavation techniques meant that things were different today, Ruddy assured them. The dunes could be tamed and their elevation used to create a series of spectacular links holes. The timing was right too – golf was booming and there was still some tourism development money available for such projects.

The members were eventually seduced by the idea, though it took an eloquent speech by Ruddy at a special meeting to persuade the majority that going heavily into debt would pay off in the long run.

The course

The key to designing Glashedy was getting the golfer to the higher elevations without making the trip a slog, and Ruddy ups the ante by having players make the ascent twice – once on either nine. It is a tribute to his talents that going uphill on the Glashedy is even more fun than going down.

The course starts with a bang. Three difficult and intriguing par 4s that feature deep and strategically placed pot bunkers, high dunes and a threatening out-of-bounds fence, announce that this is a very serious golf course indeed. But while these are super golf holes, it is on the teasingly short par-5 fourth that the true character of the Glashedy reveals itself. The hole winds its way uphill through its own corridor of majestic dunes, and with each step the anticipation mounts. The view is increasingly spectacular, and the fairway seems to funnel right into the sky. The excitement is sharpened by the fact that there is always a chance of a birdie, though a gigantic pot bunker in the middle of the fairway, and sharply rolling terrain in front of the green, make the hole more difficult than it seems. By the time the summit is reached, Glashedy Rock (which does for Ballyliffin what Alisa Craig does for Turnberry) has revealed itself and it is obvious that this is a links like no other. It is an exhilarating moment.

Oddly, the descent from the high ground, at least on the front nine, is something of an anticlimax. It happens all at once on the par-3 seventh, its hugely elevated tee at just about the highest point on the course. The strange pond next to the green doesn't really come into play, and there is nothing to frame the green. The hole itself gets lost in the scenery, which is admittedly magnificent.

It is a momentary lapse. Several solid par 4s follow on lower ground, and then the Glashedy climbs again on the thirteenth, another uphill stunner of a par 5. More or less straightaway, but lined with dunes, the long and difficult hole features such a perfectly framed view of Glashedy Rock at your back that you may wish to do a few neck exercises before making the ascent. Anyone losing their concentration will come a cropper at the green, which features three vicious pot bunkers, complete with steps, that gobble up even slightly errant shots.

As if to reward you for the climb, the views on the fourteenth are equally spectacular. But this is a hole that almost didn't come to be.

'Some of the members objected to what I was suggesting,' recalled

Ruddy in an interview. 'And I knew if you tried to do it at 8 a.m. onwards they would have had their breakfast and come on up and been up your arse.'

'So I said to the workmen, "Lads, we'll do it at three o'clock in the morning". It was dark and lashing rain, but we were up there, with two bulldozers, two diggers and two dump trucks and we had a par-3 hole shaped by breakfast. And not one person said a word.'

The happy result is one of the lovelier short holes in Ireland. Its horizontal green seems like an inviting target from the sharply elevated tee. But craftily placed bunkers – one in front, and one at the back – mean that the ball must be struck high into a stunning ocean view, ride the wind just so, and land softly on the correct section of the sloping putting surface, which kicks loosely played shots into thick rough.

The final holes follow on gentler, more civilized terrain nearer the clubhouse, with the picturesque cottages of Ballyliffin village visible in the distance. But the adrenaline rush of playing the high links holes of the Glashedy lasts well into the nineteenth, where the day's finer moments can be relived in Ballyliffin's comfortable and friendly new clubhouse.

Don't be discouraged if your scores are a little higher than you are used to. When the European PGA Tour stopped here in 2002, no fewer than ninety-five professionals recorded at least one round in the 80s.

Location: On the Inishowen Peninsula, about a mile northeast of Ballyliffin on R238; about 30 miles from Derry

Restrictions: None

Green Fee: €75–85

General Manager: John Farren

Address: Ballyliffin, Inishowen, Co. Donegal; **tel:** (074) 937-6119; **fax:** (074) 937-6672; **e-mail:** info@ballyliffingolfclub.com; **web:** www.ballyliffingolfclub.com

CARNE

Founded: 1995
Designed by: Eddie Hackett

If ever the Lord intended land for a golf course, Carne has it.

EDDIE HACKETT

Carne is a startling links in the most unpromising of places – the remote and thinly populated Belmullet Peninsula. Golf here is a wild ride through Ireland's most rugged linksland, but Eddie Hackett has kept the roller coaster just tame enough to make the trip enjoyable, and to make it a true test of golfing skill. Carne is not only a thrilling golf course, it is a remarkable example of community development in an area of few economic prospects. You will have to go out of your way to get to Carne, through miles and miles of tawny bog, but you will be richly rewarded.

'It all started in this place, right in this room,' said Michael Mangan. He was seated in an easy chair in front of a fireplace in a sitting room of Belmullet's Western Sands Hotel. 'This is where we held our first meeting in 1984.'

It was ten o'clock on a Tuesday night in November, in 1995, and I had just arrived after five exhausting hours on narrow, unlit roads. Despite the late hour, Mangan and Liam McAndrew, the Honorary Secretary of the Carne Golf Course, had donned ties for the occasion. In those very early days, it was an occasion when a golf writer made it all the way to Belmullet Town.

Belmullet is one of those places that looks alarmingly isolated even on a map. The town is stuck out on a talon-shaped peninsula of the same name that looks as if it could break off and float away into the Atlantic Ocean at any moment. The last half of my drive, through empty bogland, was dark and lonely, the light of a passing car something of an event. On the outskirts of the town I passed an experimental power plant, which a sign indicated was built with aid money from the European Community. The plant was powered by windmills, using the unrelenting Atlantic wind. Drained from the drive, and a bit disoriented, my first impression of the dimly lit square of Belmullet Town was that it was as bleak and raw as any I had seen in Ireland – it reminded me both of the market towns I had seen in the Third World, and of the muddy frontier towns you see in old Westerns (I learned later the mud comes from the peat, which stretches in all directions).

But inside the Western Sands Hotel, with a hot whiskey in my hand and a cheese sandwich to cut my long-drive hunger, I listened to Michael Mangan put an entirely different and optimistic spin on what I had seen.

'I've always said that you can market isolation today,' he said with conviction. 'Look what happened to Connemara after they built the golf course. Property values have gone way up.'

Two gulps into my Jameson's and I could already detect an energy and determination in Michael Mangan that would not seem easily contained in this stark place. As the remarkable tale of the development of the Carne golf course unfolded, I was not surprised to find that the first chapter began with Mangan himself.

In the early 1980s, Mangan returned to County Mayo to set up a retail business after spending several years in London. He also bought a small farm near Belmullet that had a one-seventeenth share in a commonage – agriculturally poor land where farmers traditionally share grazing rights. Not being a farmer, the land had no value to Mangan, so he didn't give it another thought.

A couple of years later he heard that the Irish government was using development money from the European Community to persuade farmers to divide up the commonages. The theory was that farmers would be more likely to develop the land if they had control over their own little plot (and didn't need the consent of a dozen or more other families). Each farmer was to get £1,100 towards putting up concrete stakes to mark his property, and five rows of barbed wire to put around the perimeter. Mangan had still not even seen the commonage he had a share in, but he went to a special meeting, picked a number out of a hat, and was awarded a plot.

'The next day I took a walk with my next-door neighbour who showed me where it was,' said Mangan. 'Half of it was what I would call good grazing land, and the other half was just sand dunes. I saw it would be an ideal site for a golf course and that it would be a pity to see it divided up. It was the eleventh hour, but there were no wire fences yet!'

Until this point in the story Liam McAndrew, a much younger man than

Michael Mangan, had kept a respectful silence. But now he burst in.

'We used to have fantastic common areas adjacent to the sea,' McAndrew explained with obvious feeling. 'There were thousands of acres of magnificent land with beautiful beaches. In the summer just about every community would have their sports day and they'd run it on these commonages near the beach, hundreds of people. Imagine what that was like and what it meant to the community.

'Well that's all wired in now. You can't even get on to it, you know. One massive stretch of wire. You can't let kids onto it because they'll get tied up with wire fences. We saw the golf course development as securing one last open area.'

The richness of the tale caught me by surprise and took the edge off my fatigue. Though I had heard through the grapevine that Carne was a special place to visit (its official opening was still a few months away but the course was open for play), I knew nothing of its origins. I ordered a second whiskey and waited for Michael Mangan to take up the story again.

'As I said, five of us met in this very room, and we put five pounds each into a kitty to pay for phone calls. The first thing we did was stall the land commission from proceeding any further.'

The group envisioned developing the commonage as a community project rather than seeing it cut up into economically unviable plots. According to Mangan, the idea quickly gained support in Belmullet, where there was precious little economic activity of any kind. But there were two giant obstacles: all seventeen owners had to agree to sell, and money needed to be found to buy. Even at a modest offer of £500 an acre, a total of £130,000 would be needed, a fantastic sum in Belmullet. Undaunted, Mangan and a few others set up a non-profit company and started lobbying for government support.

But first the farmers had to agree, in principle at least, to sell.

'We conducted seven or eight meetings in this same hotel room,' Mangan said in a tone of voice that I thought still contained a hint of amazement. 'The first night eleven out of seventeen agreed, and every other meeting there was one or two who threw in their hats. Eventually it boiled down to one individual, who had land right in the middle of what would be the tenth fairway. He didn't want to know about money. He wanted to get another seventeen acres somewhere else instead.

'Finally, we went into the dining room there and said, "We can't give you anything that we don't give the others, so the whole deal is off".'

Mangan wasn't sure exactly what happened after he went home, the project seemingly off the rails before it had got started. He did know that a lot of the other farmers were angry at the lone hold-out.

'The following morning he came into the shop and said, "I have to live in this village and I canna be the odd bod out." So he was going to throw in his hat as well.'

Getting the land turned out to be the easy part. The all-volunteer organizing committee didn't realize what it was in for – years of painstaking effort to piece together financing, of navigating through bureaucratic red tape, and then of managing what turned out to be a £2 million project. In order to be eligible for the necessary money, the plans called for the golf course to be only one part of a larger recreational complex.

'It was Trojan work,' said Mangan. 'We kept a fairly tight rein and ran it as efficiently as possible. But quite frankly the size of the work we are doing is too big for a voluntary organization.'

Eighty-four families eventually became shareholders in the project (Belmullet had a population of about 1,500) and hundreds more contributed to local lotteries that raised the money necessary to leverage matching money from government. Eventually, financing was secured through a complicated mix of grants and interest-free loans. But the money didn't always arrive on time, and it is at this point that the saviour of so many golf projects in Ireland – architect Eddie Hackett – makes his inevitable appearance in the story.

'An exceptional gentleman,' said Mangan in a low reverential voice. 'It was never a question of money with Eddie Hackett, it was a question of good results and getting the best out of what we had.

'He was almost eighty years old, but he walked the course for three days, making drawings each night in his B&B. And he was enthusiastic from the very word go. "If ever the Lord intended land for a golf course Carne has it," he told us.

'Eddie wanted to disturb as little as possible the natural territory but there were places we went into where there were just massive sand dunes and we had to create fairways somehow. A few fairways cost twenty or thirty thousand pounds and others cost us nothing.'

At this point I asked Mangan and McAndrew if they could spell out, as best they could remember, the financial details of the project. Even though much of the work had been done years before, the facts and figures jumped off their tongues. They knew the cost of every bulldozer and water sprinkler, the size of every loan, and the amount received each week now that green fees were starting to come in. The only people who made any money out of the development, they said, were the construction workers; under the terms of the government welfare grant they had to be local people who were unemployed. Only now was a paid project manager being hired.

'It was never our intention to take a big bank loan,' said McAndrew, explaining why the course was built in phases. The prudence had paid off. Cash from paying visitors was already ahead of projections, and with a new clubhouse soon to be completed, the future looked rosy. They had just learned that *Golf World* magazine was going to name Carne one of the ten best new courses in Britain and Ireland.

I was surprised to find that it was already last call at the bar. Mangan and McAndrew had become more animated in the telling of their story, their voices containing a mixture of pride in what they had done and excitement about what the future would hold.

Granted, I had not yet played the golf course, had not even left my seat in this unfamiliar hotel in this town I had yet to see in the light of day. But it sure seemed like a textbook example of successful community development to me. I wished that someone from an MBA school somewhere was taking down the details for a case study.

It seemed all the more remarkable when Michael Mangan described the fate of the government scheme to encourage private production.

'The whole thing is reversed now,' he said with a tone of sorrow rather than vindication. 'They're paying farmers fifty pounds an acre *not* to fertilize and to leave it idle for the next five years. And if you wire it in and put *no cattle* in it they'll give another ninety pounds an acre per year. Just let the bushes grow on it. Overproduction you see. The whole thing is reversed.'

The course

The story McAndrew and Mangan told me took on larger dimensions the next day when I finally saw the golf course. The brand new bed-and-breakfast I stayed in, just out of town, had an optimistic air about it, and I was decidedly more upbeat about Belmullet as I headed down towards the beach. It was a windy and cold morning, however, and McAndrew had warned me that there might not be anyone at the two caravans which served as the office and the changing room while the clubhouse was being built. He was right. But the door to the changing room was open, and there was a box in which visiting golfers could deposit their green fee. It was about nine o'clock and there wasn't a soul anywhere.

I was nearing the end of a long trip, and I had seen and revisited some of the greatest links in the world. But playing Carne was still a revelation.

And much of that feeling returns every time we visit. The course hasn't changed much at all, though visiting golfers are well taken care of in a fine clubhouse these days. While Carne is no longer an unknown course, there is still a superb sense of being away from it all

The round begins with a short, careening par 4 with a fairway that disappears from sight between fantastic sand ridges, like some kind of pathway to another world. The magic continues on the second, a secluded par 3 featuring a green set in front of a perfect, pyramid-shaped hill. It is the kind of place you would imagine Druids – Ireland's pagan holy men – performing strange rituals.

On the third tee everything suddenly changes, and you find yourself looking inland from a high tee, soaking up superb views of farms and bog and a body of water called Blacksod Bay.

The third hole descends into more low-lying terrain, and the rest of the front nine is laid out on the bay side of the first hole. The linksland is relatively sedate compared to what lies ahead, but first-time visitors will find it rambunctious enough.

The par 4s are particularly fine, requiring well-positioned drives and precise irons to some of the loveliest green sites in Ireland – each one tucked into a natural theatre of mounds. None of the holes are overpoweringly long. The front nine is an engaging battle of wits rather than brawn, over dramatic golfing terrain.

On the back nine everything is turned up a notch. The tenth hole is played parallel to number one, on similarly undulating terrain, and is an outstanding, rollicking par 5 of exceptional beauty. The eleventh and twelfth, although perhaps just a bit too similar as a golf challenge, are short dogleg par 4s played between steep sandhills of astonishing size. Then the mood changes again, as you emerge from the fantasy of dunes to a long, dangerous par 5 with panoramic views of the Atlantic and endless stretches of deserted cliffs and beaches.

After a pretty, if uneventful, par 3, the course climbs back into the hilliest terrain of all. The fifteenth is an arresting par 4, with a valley between tee and green and a fairway featuring undulations that could be used for freestyle skiing events at the Olympics. The sixteenth is a wonderful steep-drop par 3 to a green encircled by shaggy yellow dunes.

But it is the seventeenth that is Carne's *pièce de résistance*. The tee has grand views of the ocean behind, but the challenge in front is just as stunning. The drive has to find a narrow plateau of a fairway – only twenty-five yards wide in places – set along the edge of a chasm, to be followed by a long approach to a green perched just as precariously. To top it off, the hole is played through a surreal, heaving landscape right out of a science fiction novel. Being surrounded by dunes is nothing unusual on Irish courses, but these are gigantic and raw, with gaping wounds of white sand.

The tee box on the eighteenth tops all that has gone before, so high up you can see the Atlantic behind as well as Blacksod Bay in the distance. And all of the incredible, heaving linksland in between.

Needless to say, the hole itself is spectacular, not to mention provocative. The huge swales in the landing area for the drive make the fifteenth fairway seem like an airport runway, and Hackett left intact an incredibly deep valley just before the green.

'It creates a conundrum, all right,' Hackett once told us. 'But I always say you are entitled to stiffen the exam at the end of the round. Maybe in years to come, people will fill in that valley on eighteen and take away the mounds on the fifteenth, but I won't do it. That goes against the grain for me, because it's all natural.'

And now there are nine more holes to look forward to, perhaps as early as 2007. They are being designed by Jim Engh, the 'hottest' American golf architect of the moment, who has long admired the wild links courses of northwest Ireland.

'The terrain is just jaw-dropping,' he says. 'It's one of my favourite places on earth.'

You won't be the first to be a bit dazed by your initial visit to Carne. It is a little unnerving to find such a wonderful golf course in so unassuming a place. Michael Mangan found the land, and Eddie Hackett gave it form, but the entire community of Belmullet can take pride in making it possible. It is their masterpiece.

Location: On Belmullet Peninsula, one-and-a-half miles west of Belmullet town, follow signs from town square

Restrictions: None

Green Fee: €55–60
Manager: Mary Tallott

Address: Carne, Belmullet, Co. Mayo; **tel:** (097) 82292; **fax:** (097) 81477;
e-mail: carngolf@iol.ie; **web:** www.carnegolflinks.com

CONNEMARA

Founded: 1973
Designed by: Eddie Hackett

Looking back it was a growing and achievement point and self-believing point for the community. They had never done anything like this.

FATHER PETER WALDRON, FOUNDING MEMBER OF CONNEMARA

In a tale fit for Hollywood, Connemara was built by the local community of Clifden, at the urging of their parish priest. The result is a links profoundly unlike any other in Ireland. Winding its way at times through great slabs of rock, Connemara is a raw and exposed place, wide open to the relentless Atlantic winds. It is also uncommonly beautiful, as majestic and uncompromising as the region that gives it its name. Connemara is golf at its most elemental – a striking example of a course dictated by nature, and all the better for it.

◆◆◆

Building a golf course had not exactly been part of Peter Waldron's future plans when he accepted a place in the venerable seminary college at Maynooth, not far from Dublin. The heart of Catholic learning in Ireland, Maynooth sent wave after wave of young priests across Ireland to take up positions of intellectual, educational and moral authority that had been the lot of the priesthood for a millennium.

When Waldron graduated in 1968 and was posted to Clifden, a small town of a thousand souls in remotest Connemara, the biggest threat to his new parish was economic rather than spiritual. Much of the land was agriculturally poor, the fishing industry seemed to have little or no future and tourism was still in its infancy. Young people were leaving in droves for the streets of London and New York.

The young priest wondered whether golf could be part of Connemara's salvation. He had played since the age of ten and he knew the Irish Tourist Board was subsidising the development of a course in Westport, in neighbouring County Mayo. Could a similar project attract more visitors to the parish and keep jobs in the community?

Clifden was different from Westport, however – poorer, smaller and more remote. The only clubs the men and women in Connemara were likely to have swung were hurling or camogie sticks. Life was mostly an effort to put food on the table.

And if golf was to be part of the answer, there was the small matter of where it would be played. On his rounds of the parish, Father Waldron found it hard to look at a vacant piece of land without imagining a flagstick on it, and on more than one occasion he found himself lamenting that the most promising holes always seemed to be on bogs.

Then one morning in June 1969, Father Waldron found himself, quite by accident, on a pretzel-like road past the primary school in the village of Ballyconneely.

After a hundred yards or so, the road suddenly opened up into a wide stretch of grassland. Father Waldron stopped the car in amazement and found himself walking ankle-deep through this unexpected 'prairie'. To his left it extended to the edge of the headland, some fifty feet above the crashing surf. To his right it rose gradually into a wild tumble of Connemara rock. In the distance the Twelve Bens provided a stunning backdrop. But it was the sudden expanse of grass and sea and sky that overwhelmed him.

Although he was very much alone, Father Waldron let out an audible sigh, followed by a self-mocking chuckle. 'Here then, Peter, is your golf course!'

When Peter Waldron gave us his account of the history of Connemara, the club had long since become a successful part of the golf fraternity on the west coast of Ireland. But in 1969, nothing was certain. To move the dream forward, the priest joined forces with Graeme Allen and Paul

Hughes. The latter had just bought the Abbeyglen Castle Hotel, and handled the financial aspects of the golf project. In today's parlance, Father Waldron was the chief social mobilizer. He also led the painstaking negotiations with twenty-two different landowners (one of whom was in America). Everything was done on faith alone, with agreements drawn up in principle without a penny in the bank.

A group of local business people gave their early endorsement to the venture, but the turning point was a public meeting at Clifden House Hotel in February 1972.

Paul Hughes told the packed assembly that golf was the kind of destination activity needed to turn the community around economically. Father Waldron reported that his recent trip to Boston had been successful; he had secured agreement on the sale of the last piece of land.

The response was enthusiastic. Modest contributions were made on the spot, everything from £1 to £500. More importantly, a committee was elected to manage the enterprise as a true community project.

Although a few thousand pounds was raised, the course had to be designed and built on a shoestring. Enter Eddie Hackett, the former professional at Portmarnock who had recently taken to designing golf courses.

'Eddie was a saint,' said Father Waldron. 'He told us, "I'll design the course for you and you can pay me when you can. We'll put pins in the virgin soil. You just have to promise me one thing – even if you can't mow the grass at first, you'll stick to the right design".'

Hackett moved very little soil, and weaved the course through the stark Connemara rock that protruded through the grasses.

Joe Clark, a local builder, agreed to do the first landscaping for £365. Someone had discovered a book on clubhouse development from England, so a structure was put up with more enthusiasm than sense, around a rock that stuck up through the floor of the bar.

'We were learning as we went along,' said Father Waldron. 'And you could sense what it was going to do for around here. The community responded so well…. It was a great time, really a great time, busy, difficult.'

The tribulations were not quite over. At the last moment, some land speculators unveiled a document that indicated they owned a small piece of land where the clubhouse had been built. They had to be bought out with money the project didn't really have.

The debts kept piling up, and there was no money yet from the tourist board. But the community persevered, and on 7 June 1973, Father Peter Waldron and Eddie Hackett were in the first official fourball to play over the Connemara links.

The conditions were still crude and the golfing visitors had not yet materialized. There would be only a handful of paid green fees that first year.

But it was there. The community had made it happen without the help of any big developer or big government grant. What had been done elsewhere for millions of pounds had been done here for a hundred thousand. And when the money did start rolling in, it would go to the local bed-and-breakfast owner, the lad who worked with Joe Clark on the greenkeeping crew, and the waitress in the Abbeyglen.

'It was a destiny,' Father Waldron said. 'And all the other chaps and women who got involved it was their destiny too. It's one of their great stories. And that's the way I'd like to see it remembered. It is their story, it is their place.'

The course

No one appreciated the peculiar appeal of Connemara more than Eddie Hackett. We met him at the golf club in 1995 when, at the age of eighty-five, he was in the process of laying out an additional nine holes closer to the seashore. One got the feeling that Hackett, a deeply religious man, believed it was something of a miracle that a golf course took shape at all in Connemara's distinctive rock-studded landscape.

'You'll notice that the rock doesn't interfere with your play at all,' he said with a mixture of pride and lingering amazement. 'And we didn't move one rock.'

Connemara has few of the high, wild dunes that characterize many of Ireland's links. The terrain, especially on the front side, is relatively flat, and completely exposed to the winds that whip off the sea. Above, ever-moving clouds orchestrate endless shifts in shadow and light. With the imposing Twelve Bens mountain range astride one horizon, the crashing sea stretching across the other, and a tumultuous sky overhead, it is easy to feel very small indeed.

With more money, and a different designer, the land on the front nine might have been torn up and reshaped to provide more 'feature' and contour to the holes. That could well have irreparably harmed the elemental quality of the place. Though straightforward, the front nine has enough subtle variation in bunkering and green sites to keep one's interest. But it is on the glorious back nine that Connemara comes into its own.

The excitement really begins at the twelfth – a terrific, undulating dogleg that pulls you right into the most rugged part of the course. Then, you come to Connemara's show-stopper – the astonishing par-3 thirteenth. After being so exposed to the elements, you suddenly find yourself secluded in a kind of rocky basin. Everywhere you look there is wasteland, except for a green that is miraculously situated among a wild jumble of rocks, vegetation and marshland. The tee shot, obviously, is all carry. The full power and majesty of the hole is best taken in by moving back to the championship tees – take out a driver and an old ball, and go for it!

After the seclusion of the thirteenth you emerge, with adrenaline flowing, to an elevated tee, where there is a full view of the rest of the course and the ocean shore. From here to the clubhouse there is one excellent hole after another, featuring stunning downhill drives and dramatic greens set up in the rocks or on high, natural plateaus.

Topping it off is a fine finishing hole, a dogleg of well over 500 yards. After yet another elevated drive, you must contend with a creek crossing the fairway and an out-of-bounds fence on the right that encroaches ever more menacingly as you approach the green, which is elevated, undulating and well-guarded by pot bunkers.

It is one of the better inward nines in Ireland, and at close to 3,600 yards from the regular tees (200 yards farther from the back sticks), it is a severe test even on a calm day, which is about as common as a kangaroo at Connemara.

The club's success enabled it to purchase additional land closer to the sea, and after years of legal wrangling, an additional nine holes have been built, arguably Eddie Hackett's final creation.

On that very inclement day in 1995 when we joined up with him, Hackett was trying to solve a conundrum forced on him by the local government council, which had ruled that some of the property used in an earlier version of the layout was off limits to golf course development. To compensate, he had to figure out a way of using some land *between* the holes of the championship course, and link it to the new seaside holes. After two hours in the pelting rain, he was triumphant.

'That was a tough morning [but] I feel grand,' he said. 'I feel great because it has gone on our side... And it's not a Mickey Mouse nine holes. Because it has the exhilaration of the ocean over there.'

The new nine is indeed a great deal of fun, with a series of tricky short par 4s darting along the shore and across a winding natural stream. It then finishes with four stern holes very much in keeping with the back nine of the championship course.

'I didn't know what was going to happen, but it has worked out well, you see,' Hackett continued. 'The main thing is I'm satisfied that three holes are out there [by the sea]... You don't see it on the map. You should, but you don't. You would in a house where every nail is counted. But a golf course is different.'

Location: Ballyconneely, 5 miles south of Clifden; follow N59 from Galway to Clifden, then follow signs for Ballyconneely on the coast road

Restrictions: None

Green Fee: €60-65

Manager: Richard Flaherty

Address: Ballyconneely, Clifden, Co. Galway; **tel:** (095) 23502; **fax:** (095) 23662; **e-mail:** links@iol.ie; **web:** www.connemaragolflinks.com

COUNTY SLIGO (Rosses Point)

Founded: 1894

Designed by: H. S. Colt and Captain Willie Campbell

Where the wave of moonlight glosses
The dim grey sands with light
Far off by furthest Rosses
We foot it all the night.

WILLIAM BUTLER YEATS, 'THE STOLEN CHILD'

In a country chock full of spectacular golfing scenery, there is nothing quite like the exhilaration one feels teeing it up on the fifth hole at County Sligo. It is a gorgeous, thrilling drop to a wide and welcoming fairway. There are mountains on three sides – including Benbulben, made famous by W. B. Yeats – and up ahead, beyond Rosses Point, the harbour stretches out into the endless sea. Go ahead, 'grip it and rip it' – even a weak shot here will seem to soar – and savour the sense of anticipation and privilege as you bound down the hill towards one of the greatest stretches of links holes to be found anywhere. While Drumcliff Bay never actually comes into play at Rosses Point, it is a constant and magnificent presence, and seems to infuse the links with a special glow and tranquillity.

◆◆◆

Dust off the college poetry anthology before you arrive in County Sligo, because there is no escaping William Butler Yeats here. Winner of the 1923 Nobel Prize for literature, Yeats was often in dire financial straits when alive. But today his name alone appears to enhance the prospects of just about any enterprise – including shops, pubs, museums, hotels, a summer school and, of course, organized literary pilgrimages.

The commercialization of Yeats's name is tame by American standards, however, and in no way diminishes the attractions of Sligo Town. Although devastated by the famine of the 1840s (at the height of the catastrophe as many as thirteen boats, filled with desperate human cargo, left the harbour each day) Sligo recovered to become an important port and commercial centre. Today it is a bustling and charming little city with old narrow streets and exquisite pubs. The surrounding countryside is full of important archaeological sites and contains the scenery that so moved the great poet.

Rosses Point is about five miles from Sligo. William Yeats and his brother Jack, an accomplished painter, spent some twenty summers there at the home of their uncle, George Pollexfen. The beauty of the surrounding landscape and the rich variety of local legends, which Yeats heard first-hand, are incorporated into some of his best writing. In his later years Yeats spent more time in Dublin, but he asked to be buried within sight of Benbulben mountain. The famous epitaph on his gravestone has not, however, been heeded:

Cast a cold eye
On life, on death.
Horseman, pass by!

Though a Protestant, Yeats believed in Irish independence, and it is difficult to believe he would have shared political beliefs with those who started the County Sligo Golf Club in 1894. A cousin of Yeats was one of the founders, but the club was dominated by Freemasons. In any event, Yeats was no golfer. As described in his autobiography, his personal connection to the club seems to be limited to the fact that he had his first sexual experience on the beach beside the course.

County Sligo Golf Club's first captain was Lieutenant Colonel James Campbell. A leading Freemason in the region, Campbell managed to persuade the local branch of the Masonic Lodge to join the fledgling club *en masse* in 1894 as a show of support. Campbell much preferred polo to golf, but he apparently believed the links was an important enhancement to the community. In any event, he and a couple of like-minded business associates ran the club with commendable efficiency in its first quarter-century, and there is a certain no-nonsense tone to Rosses Point that survives even today.

The first nine holes were laid out by George Combe, the guiding force behind Royal County Down, and nine more holes were added in 1907 by the Colonel's younger step-brother Willie. Only the present day twelfth and thirteenth (both the work of the younger Campbell) remain in anything like their original form.

County Sligo is in most respects the work of H. S. Colt. At the height of his career – with Sunningdale, Wentworth and the Eden Course at St Andrews behind him – Colt remodelled the course during a week in June of 1927 for a fee of £50. In fairness to Colt, it should be pointed out that the club rejected his design for the second hole; instead there is now a dull uphill slog which is everyone's least favourite hole on an otherwise masterful layout.

If you are poking around Sligo's clubhouse you will no doubt come across the name of Cecil Ewing. A world-class amateur player in the 1930s and 1940s, Ewing brought much glory to the then little-known club by winning the key match in the 1938 Walker Cup at St Andrews. A large, heavy-set man, he swung with his feet remarkably close together and relied on his forearms to hit the ball lower and straighter than perhaps any golfer of his era. It was the perfect game for Rosses Point where, in Ewing's words, 'when the winds blow, the only hiding place is to be found back at the clubhouse.'

Not that long ago Sligo was something of a well-kept secret, but visits by that roving ambassador of Irish golf, Tom Watson, and tributes by Bernhard Langer and others have helped to establish its reputation outside Ireland. It remains one of our favourite places to play.

The course

The links of County Sligo runs out and back in the manner of St Andrews. You start on high ground near the clubhouse, descend into a kind of plain that is almost level with the beach, and then rise again onto some turbulent linksland on the extremities of the course. On the back nine you retrace the journey, only closer to the sea.

The five holes on the high land near the clubhouse are comparatively ordinary, with the exception of the fourth and its hump-backed green; Henry Cotton considered it one of the best examples of a bunkerless short hole.

The fifth, called the Jump, is a transition hole, and surely one of the best dead easy par 5s anywhere. It is a glorious tease – the fantastic elevated drive makes you feel you can take on the world.

The course exacts a toll for its early favours, however, building slowly but surely in difficulty and interest. The outgoing holes in the plain are fairly flat, though made more intriguing by the threat of a winding creek, and the front nine ends with a lovely par 3 that features a heavily bunkered green in front of a picturesque stone fence.

The second nine is a much stiffer test, beginning with three tight and rugged holes that loop around the cliffs at the end of the narrow arm of land that is Rosses Point. These holes are wonderfully scenic and seem to be in a world of their own. The tilting fairways and undulating greens demand a new level of precision, especially if the wind is up. But they are only a prelude to a heroic sequence of holes which define County Sligo as a championship golf course. The fourteenth and fifteenth are very different par 4s, but both require length and accuracy off the tee and precise long irons or fairway woods (or hybrids) to difficult greens. At well over 200 yards, there is no respite at the par-3 sixteenth either.

It all culminates in the seventeenth, the Gallery, a favourite of Tom Watson and every other professional who has played County Sligo. One of the most difficult holes in Ireland, it doglegs back up towards the clubhouse, stopping at a green perched half-way up the hill. There is a turbulent sort of no man's land at the corner of the dogleg that must be respected as if it were a hazard, and the second shot requires a courageous, uphill carry to a partly hidden target. At 455 yards, the Gallery is punishing yet fascinating, qualities it shares with another famous seventeenth, the Road Hole at St Andrews.

Like its counterpart at St Andrews, the seventeenth at County Sligo gives way to a rather anticlimactic par 4 that at least allows you one chance to calm your nerves before heading into the attractive, Tudor-style clubhouse with its fine bar. Unless it is raining, however, you won't want to stay inside for long.

Location: Rosses Point, 5 miles west of Sligo Town on R291

Restrictions: Weekdays are unrestricted, though no fourballs are allowed on Tuesdays; weekend play available from 11:00 a.m. to 1:00 p.m. and 3:30 p.m. to 5:30 p.m.

Green Fee: €70–85

Manager: Hugh O'Neill

Address: Rosses Point. Co. Sligo; **tel:** (071) 917-7134; **fax:** (071) 917-7460; **e-mail:** cosligo@iol.ie; **web:** www.countysligogolfclub.ie

---

DONEGAL (Murvagh)

Founded: 1973

Designed by: Eddie Hackett; revisions by Pat Ruddy

You don't have to wear your plus-fours or your bow tie to come in here.

PATTY MCLAUGHLIN, MEMBER OF DONEGAL

A big, bold, beautiful links, Donegal is gradually undergoing a successful renovation under the careful supervision of Pat Ruddy. But Eddie Hackett's original conception remains intact. Most everything is writ large at Donegal – with its expansive fairways and greens, panoramic views of the Atlantic Ocean and the Donegal hills,

and generous hospitality of the members. Still not well known, it may yet emerge as one of the great links courses in Britain and Ireland.

❖❖❖

Donegal's history is a fortunate one, made possible by an aristocratic fire sale and difficult soil. For generations, the linksland on the Murvagh Peninsula in Donegal Bay belonged to the family of Captain Hamilton of Brownhall. He had a country home, Murvagh House, not far from the present-day golf course. In a pattern familiar all over Ireland, death duties played a part in forcing Captain Hamilton's estate to cede much of the land to the state in the 1960s. The Forestry Department planned to reforest much of the area.

Any golfer could have foretold what was going to happen next. The sandy linksland proved to be stubbornly uncooperative, refusing to retain enough water even for the hardy species of trees the department had in mind. This was just the opening that a group of local golf enthusiasts, then playing on a modest nine-hole course, was looking for. With the help of a couple of sympathetic local politicians, the group managed to lease the land from the Forestry Department for a nominal sum.

What was a forester's nightmare became a golf architect's delight. Irish designer Eddie Hackett was engaged for his usual modest fee (about £200 at the time) to design a championship links that could be built without a lot of expensive earth-moving machines.

'We just used one old fellow from the area who had a bucket and one bulldozer,' Hackett told us in 1996. 'Some of the greens were just as we found them. We just rolled back the sod, levelled the ground a bit, and laid the sod back on.'

Pat Ruddy, a native of the west of Ireland, was a golf writer in Dublin when he saw the new course.

'At the time it was done it was truly a miracle, a leap into the future,' he recalls. 'It and Waterville were the first two links during my time that were built towards grandeur and scale.'

The club had only eighty members when the full eighteen holes were unveiled in 1976. Since then membership has grown steadily, and today there is a waiting list (there are also several hundred country members from

Northern Ireland). Despite its remote location, Donegal has often been ranked among the top 100 courses in Great Britain and Ireland.

Despite this success, the members grew a bit uneasy as new links were built along the coast of Ireland, and others, such as Lahinch, Enniscrone, Rosapenna and Portsalon, were updated. They began to wonder if their course could, and should, be strengthened as well. Eddie Hackett had passed away in 1996, so the club turned for advice to Ruddy, now a golf architect of considerable reputation, who had recently built a well-received new links at Ballyliffin in the north of the county.

'I spent two years trying to convince them of the gospel according to Pat,' jokes Ruddy, who has introduced a series of changes aimed particularly at enhancing the strategic complexity of the golf course.

One of the members he had to convince was Derek Whaley, now Donegal's club President who, in the kind of coincidence one grows used to in Ireland, had last engaged Ruddy as a caddy at Lahinch in the 1950s. They had not met since, but quickly found themselves on the same wavelength.

'Pat has given a whole new life to Murvagh,' says Whaley. 'He does what he thinks the game requires, not what anyone else thinks.'

By Irish standards, there are good practice facilities here, and you will want to prepare yourself well for the stern test that Donegal presents. Afterwards, the large clubhouse bar is a neighbourly place, though after a pint or two you may wish to retire to one of the lovely pubs in Donegal Town only nine miles away.

The course

For the tranquil quality of any round at Donegal we can thank the zealous Irish Forestry Department, as the drive into the club from the main road passes through a dense wall of national forest. The club just about has the Murvagh Peninsula to itself.

The sense of being away from it all is reinforced by Eddie Hackett's sensible use of the generous quantities of land he was afforded. One result is length – Donegal was once the longest course in Europe. More importantly, the holes are widely spaced from each other, and even on busy days one is secluded in a way that is unusual on a natural links. While sand ridges define Donegal's holes, they are less vertical than, say, Ballybunion's; they echo instead the gentle Donegal hills that serve as a visual backdrop for many of the greens. The sweeping fairways and large putting surfaces perfectly match the sprawling quality of the linksland.

That is not to say everything at Donegal was built to Eddie Hackett's specifications. Without a building crew of his own, Hackett was at the mercy of others.

'He would lay out the course and leave it to the local farmers to finish the job,' says Pat Ruddy.

Hackett may have worked largely without bulldozers, but he was clearly at the height of his powers as an architect. He composed a steady rhythm of excellent golf holes that inject new energy into a tired cliché: Donegal does indeed test every club in the bag.

After a gently rolling opening stretch, the golfer is confronted with the Valley of Tears, an aptly named par 3 with a fiercely sloping green set in wild-looking dunes. There is no place to bail out, and many find themselves in a voracious bunker near the bottom of a steep hill in front of the green. It may be the hardest sand save in Ireland.

'We didn't have to touch that green, it's just as nature put it there,' Hackett told us.

'A lot of people said you couldn't play that hole, and I said that's one of the best holes and I hope you never change it. Of course, then they got to love it.'

There is an attractive unity to the holes at Donegal. They are all cut from the same cloth, and the changes of pace are logical and welcome. The many sweeping, generous fairways on the front nine, for example, are punctuated by the penal fifth hole and the deliciously tight and curvy par-5 eighth. And the two short doglegs at nine and ten are well-deserved respites after several extremely long par 4s. The back nine is equally forceful and absorbing, if lacking in seaside thrills. It is, in short, a splendidly balanced course, one that effectively uses the double circular routing that Old Tom Morris invented at Muirfield.

It is onto this solid foundation that Pat Ruddy is adding additional layers of strategy.

'Eddie tended to leave it as nature presented it,' says Derek Whaley, who saw both Hackett and Ruddy work on Murvagh.

'Pat sets up the course that, yes, will play comfortably if you do it his way. If the big hitters want to hit hell out of the ball and take their chances, they'll find themselves up to their neck in muck and bullets.

'He's adjusted the line of a hole and so forth and made it into a different challenge.'

Ruddy's first intervention is on the opening hole, which has always been the easiest and least interesting on the course. It now boasts a double plateau green and a provocatively placed central bunker in front.

'It's a simple but in-your-nostrils design,' says Ruddy, with his usual flourish. 'Inexpensive but strategically tormenting.'

Ruddy has also created what he calls an 'early test of a man's nerve' on the second, introducing two menacing fairway bunkers that push longer hitters closer to the out-of-bounds line on the right.

There are new fairway bunkers and greens on the fourth and the ninth, while on the back nine Ruddy has introduced new hazards entirely on the twelfth and fourteenth, par 5s he suspects were not in the end built the way Hackett intended.

'I took little streams and waved them about like Carnoustie, with a horseshoe effect,' he says.

The streams are, indeed, reminiscent of the one that famously vexed Jean Van de Velde at the 1999 Open. They are innocuous looking, unless you are contemplating a make-or-break second shot on either of the par 5s, and present the sort of strategic dilemmas that Ruddy is gradually introducing all around the course.

The most dramatic visual change has been at the eighteenth, where an opening has been bulldozed through a dune leaving the hole's challenges much more obvious from the tee.

'It's now one of our signature holes,' says Whaley. 'Already the whole thing looks like it has been there for 250 years. It shows that it doesn't pay to be totally dictated by nature.'

Though Ruddy is now semi-retired as an architect, there is an understanding that he will oversee further changes at Donegal. When he is through, Murvagh will be the only links in Ireland that combines the genius of Ireland's two greatest golf architects. And that, surely, will be something for golfers to savour for many years to come.

Location: Murvagh, about 3 miles south of Donegal Town on N15 – the turn-off of N15 is not well-marked

Restrictions: Visitors may play any day of the week, though certain weekend morning times are reserved for members

Green Fee: €55–70

Secretary: Sean Diver

Address: Murvagh, Laghey, Co. Donegal; **tel:** (074) 973-4054; **fax:** (074) 973-4377; **e-mail:** info@donegalgolfclub.ie; **web:** www.donegalgolfclub.ie

DUNFANAGHY

Founded: 1906

Designed by: Harry Vardon; refinements by James Brogan

Number 13 is the longest hole on the course, and requires 4 drives to reach the green, a stream being crossed on the way.

NINETEENTH-CENTURY TRAVEL GUIDE TO DONEGAL

When Dunfanaghy celebrated its centenary in 2006, it was, as much as anything, a coming-out party. After decades of suffering every indignity imaginable – from pestilence to flooding to ball-eating cows – this sporty links, not much changed since Harry Vardon's time, is at last able to show off its true charms. Recent Ryder Cups have brought a bit of glamour as well. There are more McGinleys in Dunfanaghy that just about anywhere else on the planet, and favourite son Paul has made a habit of bringing the trophy home for all to see.

Golf on the links at Dunfanaghy – a modest holiday village on the shores of Sheephaven Bay in Northern Donegal – dates back to at least 1886, when the *Derry Journal* reported on the opening match of the season at a course owned by the Stewart Arms Hotel.

An expanded railway line meant well-off residents of Belfast could make it with ease to Letterkenny, and from there steam ships, or a 'two-horse car' were available to take them to the world's first golf resorts in Rosapenna and Portsalon. Dunfanaghy doesn't seem to have been quite so exclusive, but the golf links were obviously an asset for the hotel, which used it to lure visitors for several decades.

DUNFANAGHY

The first course was laid out by the professional at nearby North West golf club. But in the early twentieth century, Harry Vardon, who was visiting Rosapenna, was persuaded to come down to Dunfanaghy and suggest a new routing for the course. Though more research would need to be done, the links at Dunfanaghy may be as close to Vardon's original layout as any in the world.

In part, that's simply because the golfers at Dunfanaghy – who formed themselves into a club in 1906 – have had little time for course improvements. Just keeping the links open has been challenge enough. Though a popular holiday spot for those seeking a rustic and picturesque vacation, the village was still without electricity in the 1950s. Conditions on the golf course were rudimentary too. The clubhouse was a garden shed. There were no man-made bunkers. And because the property was owned by several landowners, boundary fences criss-crossed the fairways. To make matters worse, the creek that crossed the course flooded each year, submerging half the course in the winter months.

And then there was the great plague of 1953. Myxomatosis disease spread from France to Ireland, killing millions of rabbits. This may have been viewed as a something of a blessing by more established golf clubs in Ireland, which considered rabbits a nuisance. But in Dunfanaghy, according to club historian Rev. Denholm Moore, 'the outcome was devastating … grass started to grow where grass never grew before.'

As the club had but a single hand mower, the only way to keep the grass down was to introduce cattle and sheep. Extra fences were erected around greens. Then the cows on the third fairway started to eat the golf balls.

'Players searching for their balls in the fairway were confronted with this beast, with long strings of rubber hanging from its mouth as it chewed away contentedly,' recalls Moore.

With no full time greenkeeper, it was all the club could do to keep the course open for the traditional holiday season, from 12 July – when vacationers from Glasgow came over by ferry – to the middle of August. Few locals played the game at all. In 1967, there were only sixteen members.

As the Irish economy began to expand, along with golf's popularity, that began to change. In the mid 1970s, two ditches were dug that solved the drainage problem and added a new hazard to the golf course. And in 1980, the club appointed their first full-time greenkeeper. His job was made easier when the club smuggled in a proper motorized mower from Northern Ireland (thereby avoiding the substantial excise tax).

This can-do attitude was also used to tackle coastal erosion. Club members filled jute bags with concrete and placed them on the eroded sandbanks, a solution that is still working today.

The biggest breakthrough came in the late 1980s, when the four landowners agreed to stop using the course for grazing. Suddenly, golfers could distinguish the rough from the fairway, greens could be enlarged, and it was possible to play a bump and run without fear of rattling the ball off some metalwork. The true character of Dunfanaghy links began to emerge.

The finishing touches were made by James Brogan, one of Irish golf's more remarkable figures. Now the club president, he caddied at Dunfanaghy in his youth and learned the game playing with only one club – a three wood. Finally, he was given a proper set of clubs by Mick McGinley, father of the Ryder Cup star. Brogan took over greenkeeping duties in 1983, and by the end of his tenure the Vardon-era course had been stretched to almost 6,000 yards, a couple of excellent new tees had been introduced, and Dunfanaghy was ready to join the modern era.

By now the Celtic Tiger was roaring, golf was very much in vogue, and the local membership was growing by leaps and bounds. A proper clubhouse was built and the club started the process, now completed, of buying up the land on which the course is located. It took government grants (from Dublin and the European Community) and a whopping £500,000 loan, but now the thriving club has control over its own destiny.

The course

Par is 68 at Dunfanaghy, but the course offers a full-fledged golfing experience, especially when the wind blows. The links terrain here is not rambunctious, and the first six holes are particularly flat. With the wind behind, as it often is, these are the holes to score on, though out of bounds is ever-threatening on the right side, and ball-gobbling creeks meander just in front of greens.

The golf changes sharply at the seventh, where a new tee offers stunning views of the course, and also presents a formidable challenge – a 230-yard par 3 into the teeth of the prevailing wind. That's followed by an unusual dogleg par 4 that includes two blind shots, and the lovely par-3 ninth, which requires a dramatic shot over the beach from an elevated tee.

The back nine starts off in similarly exciting fashion. The tenth is an excellent short par 4, once more played across the beach, rewarding (or punishing) the brave golfer who tries to cut the corner and challenge the green.

The back nine can play very hard indeed into the wind, and includes a series of tough par 4s that require decent carries off the tee to avoid creeks and rough; the only par 5 on the course (the stern, uphill sixteenth); and a great par 3 next to ocean at the seventeenth.

As befits a holiday course (60 per cent of the members still come from Northern Ireland) Dunfanaghy is beautifully set, with lovely views of the seaside, the surrounding hills and the village itself. And it offers an enjoyable contrast to the high-octane golf found at the new links in Ballyliffin, Rosapenna and Portsalon. After the round, you'll find a welcoming club that very much appreciates what it has.

Location: On N56, half a mile east of Dunfanaghy village

Restrictions: None, though the tee is reserved for members on parts of Saturday and Sunday

Green Fee: €30-40

Secretary: Sandra McGinley

Address: Kill, Dunfanaghy, Co. Donegal; **tel:** (074) 913-6335; **fax:** (074) 913-6684; **e-mail:** info@dunfanaghygolfclub.com; **web:** www.dunfanaghygolfclub.com

ENNISCRONE

Founded: 1922; Redesigned: 1974 and 2002
Designed by: Eddie Hackett and Donald Steel

Enniscrone is ... the sort of course that brings out the best in you by challenging at every turn with a shot you want to make. I was concentrating on golf now, but somehow it felt more like a game than it does at home. I was playing golf and the key word was playing.

STEPHEN GOODWIN IN THE WASHINGTON POST

Another of Eddie Hackett's low-budget miracles, the links close by the village of Enniscrone in County Sligo may offer Ireland's most enjoyable game of golf. Although a championship test from the back

tees, Enniscrone is also pure delight for the middle handicapper, with a series of thrilling elevated tee shots, marvellous par 3s, and some truly sublime linksland. Donald Steel has now added six more holes in terrain that was off limits to Hackett, and returning visitors will find that the new Enniscrone is better than ever.

There may be no group of golfers who have shown more patience, and been more deservedly rewarded for it, than the cluster of determined men and women who decided to expand the golf course at Enniscrone in the late 1960s. Until then, it had been a flat, uninspiring nine holes of golf which hardly made use of the muscular linksland that rose beside the Bay of Killala, just south of the village.

'There were only about twenty or twenty-five members at the time,' remembers Jim O'Regan, a former treasurer of the club. An earnest and obviously sincere man, O'Regan turns deadly serious when discussing the club's frustrating history.

'There was a determination to achieve the goal, to develop a product of high quality against the odds,' he says. 'That was very much in people's minds.'

Although fundraising in the local community was successful enough, the area had only a few hundred families, and the club was understandably short of cash. Just as understandably, it turned to Eddie Hackett, Ireland's national architect. As he had done in so many other cases, Eddie charged a modest fee, and worked with local volunteers and contractors to somehow build a championship course on the cheap (the budget was about £4,000). Hackett revamped several of the holes on the front nine as best he could, and designed an entirely new back nine deep in the dunes. Many of the new holes remain among Hackett's finest creations, and from the beginning the members knew they had a jewel.

The project was plagued by the lack of proper financing, however, and the new holes took five years to build. Even then, the links was too raw and ill-maintained to attract visitors. The club teetered on the brink of financial calamity.

It must have been dispiriting for the members to see their new golf course, truly a diamond in the rough, sit unnoticed. Until the course was in better condition, nobody would visit. But until people started visiting there would be no money for improvements. It was a Catch-22 that lasted almost a decade.

When we first visited Enniscrone in 1988, things had improved somewhat. The course had grown in and was in excellent shape. After a thrilling round of golf, we had a whiskey in the ramshackle clubhouse and were astonished to learn that only a handful of visitors were making their way to what we felt was an extraordinary golf course. Sean Connery had played it (a photograph of the actor had pride of place on the wall) but the members seemed resigned to it being always the 'undiscovered gem.'

'It was frustrating,' says O'Regan. 'But by getting there the hard way you're more aware of the achievement, and you appreciate its value.'

In 1989, the corner was finally turned. Taking what must have been a huge financial risk, the members built a new clubhouse. Irish golfers were travelling within Ireland as never before, but they were looking for clubs with decent facilities.

'At first we didn't put a lot of stock in a clubhouse because we were more determined to have a fine course,' says O'Regan. 'But from the point of view of attracting visitors, the decision to build a new clubhouse has been a major boost to us.'

Indeed, the number of annual visitors to Enniscrone has grown from a few hundred to over 12,000 today. A new eighty-two-room hotel is being built on the doorstep of the links, and property prices have gone up tenfold in the village in a decade.

As the money flowed in, the club felt confident and flush enough to try to incorporate even more of the tumultuous linksland that Eddie Hackett had used for the new back nine. With the addition of six new holes, designed by the accomplished British golf architect Donald Steel, Enniscrone cracked *Golf World* magazine's top 100 courses in the world. It has been a meteoric rise, but success doesn't seem to have gone to anyone's head.

'The quality of life is important here,' says O'Regan. 'No matter who you are, no matter if you are low-waged, or middle income, or a millionaire, once you turn the avenue into the club here every fellow is the same. That's the policy of the club.'

The course

The opening two holes at Enniscrone used to be notoriously bland, given the delights that followed, but with expansion the club has been able to banish them to a new third nine. Now the main course at Enniscrone has one of the hardest opening holes in Ireland. It is the old sixteenth, doglegging sharply uphill around the clubhouse, to a marvellous green set in the dunes.

It is a startling beginning worthy of this remarkable links, and it is a tribute to Donald Steel that the second, third and fourth – all new holes – are up to the mark as well. They take the golfer much closer to the sea than was possible before, and two are par 5s devised in a way that Eddie Hackett would surely have admired. They weave, rise and fall with the natural terrain, and feature no green-side bunkers. It is almost as if Steel is making a statement that, as Hackett himself never tired of saying, 'nature is the best architect.'

'I met Eddie a number of times,' says Steel. 'He was a kindly, affable, whimsical man. And I guess we had the same philosophy, to make sure the golf course blends into the landscape, and is not a blot on the landscape.'

Enniscrone never feels like the work of more than one architect. Steel cleverly introduced a new green on the long par-4 fifth (the old eleventh) to connect his new holes to the original routing. So from the sixth to the thirteenth we are able to play the original Hackett design in the sequence he intended. As before, the progression is entirely satisfying, beginning with a couple of sedate but strategically interesting par 4s, and a demanding par 3, and then taking us to two par 4s that run over surprisingly low land alongside Scurmore beach.

The ninth is gorgeous, a slight dogleg quite close to the water that narrows at the green. The tenth used to be great fun as well, and featured an eccentric, hogsback fairway. It was, alas, flattened by the members in what was surely their only misstep (though subsequent changes have improved the hole somewhat).

All is immediately forgiven as you start to look for the next tee, up high in the sand hills. The eleventh is a wonderful bunkerless par 3 to a green perched perfectly in unruly duneland, and it is followed by our favourite back-to-back par 4s in Ireland. This is not because they are overly difficult, but because they are so beautiful, so natural, and so thoroughly delightful to play.

The drive on the twelfth is hit over a dangerous valley and between huge dunes. When you reach your ball you notice that the second shot is just as dramatic – the target is a lovely yet devilish green on a natural plateau set in the side of a hill. Though the hole measures only 350 yards from the back tees, there is no bunker of any kind.

It only gets better as you climb even higher to the thirteenth tee, where there is a sudden and marvellous view of the ocean. The drive, however, is unnerving – an off-kilter and very downhill affair to what appears to be a small island of fairway in a sea of dunes. It's not quite as difficult as it looks and, as on the twelfth, a straight drive of even modest length will have you clicking your heels with joy. The reward is a very short iron to a picturesque green set perfectly in natural swales.

We now remain in the high linksland, and it is here that five of Hackett's better holes have either been abandoned or moved to the third nine. We miss them, but it must be admitted that Steel's new trio of holes are often dazzling. They consist of two more par 5s and a long par 4 that once again favour natural beauty and movement over man-made obstacle, and which offer striking views of the sea. Although Steel was able to move more earth than Hackett ever did at Enniscrone, he has been faithful to the original landscape.

'The structure of the dunes was there and we tried to interfere as little as possible,' Steel says. 'I'd never seen linksland like that. And you want to do something that is worthy of the task.'

Finally, we are back to the closing holes of the original course. The seventeenth remains a stunning par 3 set in high dunes overlooking the sea (and a few caravans), while the eighteenth has been modified by Steel. We have rarely played a course where it is so much fun for a golfer of average length to drive the ball, and the eighteenth is no exception. At the request of the club, Steel has taken out the blind tee shot (which we rather liked), leaving an admittedly impressive downhill drive to a fairway and green that have been made more distinctive and difficult, if a bit less natural.

For Enniscrone's growing legions of admirers, it a relief to know that Eddie Hackett's posthumous partnership with Donald Steel has been an unmitigated triumph.

Location: Six miles north of Ballina, turn off R297 at sign

Restrictions: Weekdays are best for visitors; some weekend play may also be available

Green Fee: €55–70

Secretary-Manager: Michael Staunton

Address: Enniscrone, Co. Sligo; **tel:** (096) 36297; **fax:** (096) 36657; **e-mail:** enniscronegolf@eircom.net; **web:** www.enniscronegolf.com

NARIN AND PORTNOO

Founded: 1930

Designed by: The Members

A ball may be cleaned and dropped without penalty if manure interferes with stroke or stance.

1991 SCORECARD AT NARIN AND PORTNOO

Formerly known to some as Narin and Port*moo*, this formidable links, cobbled together by the members themselves, no longer has cattle roaming its fairways. Now that you don't have to watch where you are stepping, and with no more electric fences to chip through, there's time to focus on some raw and riveting golf holes. If the club ever gets to play the two new par 5s they have constructed along the sea, and build a new clubhouse, the reputation of Narin and Portnoo will surely rise. For the moment, this is still Irish golf at its most splendidly unpretentious.

◆◆◆

'We had a bit of a celebration, that's for sure,' says Willie Quinn, honorary secretary of Narin and Portnoo Golf Club. 'And we also had a photographic session. We certainly considered it one of the club's great achievements.'

Somewhere else, Quinn might have been talking about a big inter-club victory, or the opening of some new holes or a flashy clubhouse. But at Narin and Portnoo such unbridled joy could only be caused by one thing: the removal, after more than seventy years, of the last cow from the links.

The happy occasion, in 2002, marked the end of an era in Irish links golf. Not so very long ago livestock were as familiar to Irish golfers as a stiff breeze. Typically, courses were on land leased from farmers who retained grazing rights. Even the posh members of Portmarnock had to contend with the cow of Maggie Leonard, who lived behind the first green. The cow allegedly ate some of the stray balls, while the sharp-tongued Maggie kept the rest, secretly passing them on to an enterprising member in exchange for a half-ton of the best coal.

Other clubs actually *encouraged* grazing as an inexpensive way to improve course conditioning in the absence of expensive grass-cutting equipment. Members at Portstewart voted to open up many of their holes to flocks of sheep, while Lahinch offered its lush rough to the village donkeys. Of course, Lahinch has always been way out in front in the use of animals – their famous goats have been used to forecast the weather for years.

After the Second World War, golfers became fussier, and the amiable coexistence with livestock began to fray. The official history of The Island Golf Club notes rather irritably that cattle could still be found on the course in the 1970s, and that they 'trampled greens, used the flagpoles as scratching posts and generally caused nuisance and damage. The dung they left on the course was more often than not in the wrong place and of no immediate benefit for the course.'

It is a problem Willie Quinn can relate to.

'One of the biggest problems was that prior to Captain's Day or other big events, the green staff would have to go around tidying up after them, which meant nothing else got done,' he says. 'And people would get a shock to the system, if you know what I mean, at the electric fences.'

Until the 1990s, Narin and Portnoo hosted about seventy head of cattle; golfers were forced to enter many greens through a gate in a high fence.

Vigilance was important at all times. Club member Tony Boner told us about a day when his playing partner left his golf bag too close to a cow while putting. What happened next will go undescribed, but Boner recalled that 'it was a frosty morning and you could see the steam rising off his bag all the way up the next fairway'.

Those malodorous days are now history, as the club now owns almost all of its land, and has negotiated a new, grazing-free lease on the rest of it.

Narin and Portnoo opened as a nine-hole course in 1930, and has had a variety of unlikely benefactors. It is, for example, undoubtedly the only links that owes its start to a German prisoner of war. Interred during the First World War on the Isle of Man, William Hammersbach settled in Portnoo after the war and leased and operated the local hotel. Though he had never hit a golf ball, Hammersbach knew that the sport had to be good for tourism, and his staff largely built the course under direction from the professional at Bundoran.

Then, after the Second World War devastated the local economy, the club was only kept alive by support from the local dramatic society.

The golf club finally regained its moorings in the mid 1950s, and in 1965 the members managed to extend the course to a full eighteen holes, for the princely sum of £150.

Due to its remote location, Narin and Portnoo does not get many foreign golfers, but it has always been a popular holiday spot for vacationers fleeing the Troubles from Northern Ireland, attracted by the area's tranquillity and its pristine beaches. More recently, many Dubliners who can't get into clubs nearer to home have become country members, and there are now more than a thousand members all told.

The course

Narin and Portnoo is a traditional out and back layout and the first few holes are relatively gentle (there's even a small lake by the second). The whole front nine is a slicer's nightmare, however. The prevailing ocean winds whip across from the left (and slightly from behind) and more often than not there is out-of-bounds on the right. The one occasion when the wind is directly behind you, at the short par-4 ninth, the rock-hard green is backed by the Atlantic Ocean.

By now you are climbing through much wilder territory, and this sequence of holes at the turn is what the course's reputation rests upon.

The tenth, in particular, is excellent, an ocean-side par 4 requiring all the faith at your disposal in tackling the blind, uphill, upwind tee shot. The eleventh is a colossal and endangered par 3 along the water's edge. There used to be one hundred yards between the tee and the cliff. Now there's about ten feet, and the club had planned to retire the hole by building two spectacular new par 5s along the sea.

The new holes were actually in play for a while, but Ireland's national planning authority upheld an appeal by an environmental group, and ordered an environmental assessment.

'We're hoping to have an answer soon, subject to any other objections that may follow,' says Willie Quinn with more than a trace of weariness in his voice. 'I tell people that Narin and Portnoo has finished up as the meat in the sandwich. We fell between the stools.'

Quinn's lapse into metaphor is understandable, as the club was apparently given a green light by the county council before building the two new holes.

'The environmental assessment will show that what the golf club has done has actually been a great addition to the dunes,' insists Quinn, who points out that the club has paid for erosion control, stopped the harvesting of sand by local inhabitants, and been a boon for a rare flower that seems to just love the pond beside the second.

'People who make these decisions should come see what we have done.'

Though there are no guarantees, Narin and Portnoo seems to be taking the appropriate steps to get the new holes back on stream. If they succeed, the course will be over 6,800 yards from the back tees, and will be all anyone can handle.

As it is, when the usual winds are up, the finishing holes wear you down like no others in Ireland, requiring loads of patience and one wind-cheating shot after another. There is a breather on the sixteenth, called High Altar, but it's no bargain. Considered the signature hole by many, it is only 120 yards from the tee to an exposed and elevated green that drops off on all sides. Three-irons into a gale are not uncommon.

There is, most certainly, enough to contend with at Narin and Portnoo without living and breathing obstacles. Though the challenge is immensely enjoyable, you may well end up wondering how such a little-known and modestly long links could do so much damage to your handicap.

Location: Near village of Narin, about 6 miles north of Ardara

Restrictions: None, but it's a good idea to make a reservation in the summer

Green Fee: €35-40

Manager: Sean Murphy

Address: Narin, Co. Donegal; **tel:** (075) 954-5107; **fax:** (075) 954-5994; **e-mail:** narinportnoo@eircom.net; **web:** www.narinportnoogolfclub.ie

NORTH WEST

Founded: 1891

Designed by: W.H. Mann, Tom Gilroy, Harry Vardon and Eddie Hackett

The course provides a variety of hazards sufficient to satisfy the requirements of the most enthusiastic golfer. Sand pits, bunkers, cart ruts, sloughs, rabbit holes, and the risk of getting on the sea beach or the railway constitute the difficulties to be surmounted.

DERRY JOURNAL, 5 AUGUST 1891

One of the nine original members of the Golfing Union of Ireland, this venerable links near the town of Buncrana, just twelve miles northwest of Derry, has shrunk over the years and, as a result, has become progressively *more* old fashioned. In the late nineteenth century, North West was considered a big muscular links, and a writer of the period marvelled that it was 'absolutely without a cross'.

◆◆◆

As the twenty-first century begins, that is no longer true. The loss of four holes to the relentless surf has led to a variety of rearrangements, and today there are three crossing holes (including the seventeenth, which crosses the fourth *and* the eighteenth) and some fairways are quaintly claustrophobic. But sprinkled between a few makeshift holes are several exciting and impressive challenges that would bring honour to any championship golf course. The setting, between the sea and the Mouldy Mountains, is lovely, and it is a joy to strike the ball off the firm links turf, and to run the ball onto the swift greens.

North West's history is more than a little fuzzy. Ireland's first great golfer, Tom Gilroy, is thought to have had a hand in the original layout; Harry Vardon may have contributed a few new holes at a later date, and Eddie Hackett is credited with laying out several holes on the front nine (replacing holes washed into the sea). What is certain is that the course has been continually adapted to Mother Nature's whim. On one particularly grim night in 1922, the combination of a record high tide and gale-force winds destroyed four holes in a single evening, and the resolute members of North West have been building, and rebuilding, ever since.

North West (or Lisfannon, as the links is sometimes known) is one of Ireland's oldest courses, and for many years was considered one of the best. The subtle terrain and the fine quality of the turf even invited comparisons to St Andrews. In 1950, at a time when the course had not yet suffered the worst effects of erosion, an Irish golf writer described the qualities of the links in a way that remains more or less true today:

> There is certainly much in common between St Andrews and Lisfannon, such as concealed runs and bumps approaching greens that look easy enough to run on to. Difficulties, too, as at St Andrews do not always catch the eye on the tee. Moreover, the sandy subsoil with dry turf and short grass, making it necessary to pick up the ball cleanly, are similar. The holes are very well varied, with many sandy knolls and pleasing undulations, but the general tendency is flattish.

There are still enough surprises and clever holes to make an exceptionally fine fourteen-hole golf course. The seventh is a fine par 4, with its crow's nest on the right, and requires a pinpoint drive to a plateau to see the green. The lovely tee shot over wasteland on the eleventh would look great on any links.

For those hooked on the boisterous terrain that characterizes most links courses on the northern coast of Donegal, Derry and Antrim, North West will perhaps be a disappointment. But for those connoisseurs of links golf interested in the sort of courses that defined the game in its formative period, North West is an essential, and thoroughly entertaining, detour.

Location: At Lisfannon on R283, 2 miles south of Buncrana and about 12 miles from Derry

Restrictions: None

Green Fee: €28-33

Secretary: Michael Jordan

Address: Lisfannon, Fahan, Co. Donegal. **tel:** (074) 936-1715; **fax:** (074) 936-3284; **e-mail:** secretary@northwestgolfclub.com; **web:** www.northwestgolfclub.com

PORTSALON

Founded: 1890

Designed by: Pat Ruddy and others

Portsalon golf course [is] one of the best, if not the best course in Ireland.

GOLFING MAGAZINE, AUGUST 1896

Saved from extinction and now modernized, the links at Portsalon is situated in a remote and picturesque setting every bit as stunning as Pebble Beach. This is the best-value golf experience in Ireland, a genuinely championship test that combines modern design with a handful of holes that have survived, more or less, from golf's golden age. The criss-crossing fairways are now gone, but playing at Portsalon is still a journey of discovery, one that combines sweet nostalgia, an exquisite slice of golf history, and some of the most enchanting and challenging links golf anywhere.

Though it was one of the four founding members of the Golfing Union of Ireland, Portsalon is not well known today, even in Ireland. But in the twilight of the Victorian era it and Rosapenna (just a few miles away) were golf destinations of the highest order. They were among the very first golf resorts, the Pinehursts and Gleneagles of their day.

Situated on Lough Swilly, a fjord-like finger of the Atlantic, the Portsalon Hotel and Golf Links was founded by one Colonel B. J. Barton, High Sheriff of Donegal and later aide-de-camp to Edward VII and George V. The resort even ran its own steamer to ferry guests from the train terminus farther south.

The golf hotel at Portsalon survived the Second World War, but then the stream of aristocrats dwindled. The hotel declined rapidly, and the once glamorous links became a ghost of its former self. The few travellers who came upon it paid their green fee in Rita's Bar, a local watering hole. Records show that in 1975 a mere £174 was spent on golf course maintenance.

As the 1980s began, Portsalon teetered on the edge of extinction. One of the rare visitors, American golf architect Tom Doak, wasn't sure what to make of it:

> What passed for the clubhouse was about the size of a snack hut at a typical American club, and there was no one on duty. The first few holes seemed to still be in use, though the fairways consisted mainly of clover, and a white ball would have been impossible to locate and the holes themselves were marked with only the shortest pieces of plastic pipe and a makeshift flag.

From a golfing perspective, things changed for the better when the Portsalon Hotel went up in smoke; in 1984 the adjacent land, including the golf course, was put up for sale. A clutch of local golf enthusiasts discussed buying the course, but their semi-formal 'club' had exactly £67 in the bank. The asking price was sixty-eight *thousand* pounds – a pittance, in retrospect, but a fortune for a handful of rural families in a small village in one of the most depressed areas of a relatively poor country. No bank would loan them the money, so the club members organized a lottery of a thousand tickets at £100 apiece. Much to their own astonishment, the scheme worked. On 28 November 1986 the deed of the land was solemnly transferred in a ceremony in Rita's Bar.

'I remember Portsalon golf club long ago when it was the exclusive domain of a chosen few and locals earned one shilling and six pence a day for caddying if they were lucky,' said club president Neil Blaney in a speech. 'It is appropriate that Portsalon is now owned and run by local people for the benefit of this community.'

The club spent the 1990s reviving the course that had lain almost dormant. Although many holes were superb, there were several criss-crossing fairways, and at 5,900 yards the members became worried that the links might be regarded as something of an anachronism.

This concern was only heightened when news began to seep in about the new and spectacular links courses at nearby Ballyliffin and Rosapenna, both designed by Pat Ruddy.

So when forty acres of land adjacent to the course became available, they snapped it up (for another £295,000) and asked Ruddy to have a go at their place too.

'We got Pat in and said, "there's a green field for you," though obviously there are some very good holes on the old course which he wouldn't want to touch,' says Sean McCormack, a senior club official at the time.

'It was becoming dinky stuff by modern standards,' recalls Ruddy. 'So you had this most historic club now subjugated by Ballyliffin and Rosapenna. Second thing, there were three blind crossover points.'

Ruddy has his own theory on why the fairways at Portsalon were so entangled.

'They did it so the golfers would wear the same place down a number of times, wear it down, keep the grass down. That was OK when there were ten people golfing a day and they were cutting the greens with a scythe.'

The new, much safer course opened in 2003 to rave reviews from anyone who bothered to make the trip. Unfortunately, not many did.

On the suggestion of Ruddy, the club sought to host the 2005 Ladies Irish Amateur Close Championship, the second oldest tournament for women in the world. Portsalon had already hosted the event – exactly one hundred years before! – when it was won by May Hezlet, the best woman golfer of the age. The twenty-first century version of the event was a great success, and Portsalon, after a half century of hibernation, was once again an important part of the Irish golfing fraternity.

'The changes have given us tremendous profile status-wise,' says McCormack. 'We are back in the front row of links courses around the country.'

The course

It is difficult to compete with Portsalon for sheer golfing pleasure. A century after an obscure Portrush pro named Thompson laid out the original course, its seaside setting remains breathtaking. Situated on the curve of a perfectly arched and often deserted beach, with the Knockalla mountains all around, Portsalon offers a series of unsurpassed views from its many elevated tees.

It would be worth a detour just to hit a golf ball in such surroundings. What a delightful surprise it is, then, to discover that the links itself is outstanding, an unpredictable roller-coaster ride that is not quite like anything you have experienced before.

The excitement begins at once. The first hole is an uphill dogleg around a high cliff next to the bay that just dares you to cheat too much. (The tee box for the old par-3 second used to be found *under* the same seawall you just played over, but has been abandoned.) The new second, a longer version of a very old hole, begins with a thrilling downhill drive over the corner of the beach and then requires a demanding approach shot over a small river. Those who lay up are bothered by two ancient rock formations that used to guard the green.

The next two are fine natural holes from the original course, and then Ruddy treats us to eight new holes of real variety and challenge, with bumpy and often narrow fairways, occasional hidden bunkers, and a couple of double greens, all effective reminders of Portsalon's historic past. The glorious beach is a constant visual companion, though you no longer tread as one used to, Robinson Crusoe style, through drifts of sand to get from green to tee. Keep the ball in play because the rough on the new holes can be fierce.

The eighth is a lovely par 3 with dunes all around, and is no doubt meant to be reminiscent of the old fifth. That had a tiny green shaped like an hourglass, and mounds so close to the putting surface that anyone hitting a wayward tee shot had to try a zany bankshot on their second.

As much as we adored Portsalon's former collection of singular, old-fashioned golf holes, it is clear that some had to go, on the grounds of either safety or maintenance (when a green is so small that only one pin position is possible then every golfer walks on the same section of ground). And perhaps there would always be only a limited number of enthusiasts for a par 3 (another hole on the old front nine) that was both blind *and* crossed another fairway!

Ruddy and the club have been judicious in choosing what original holes should remain, and the new holes are first class, even if they have not quite settled into their surroundings yet. If you want to know how much Ruddy cared about the project, just ask him about the thirteenth.

'It was a defining moment,' says Ruddy. 'It was supposed to be an echo of the tenth at Shinnecock Hills [a dogleg par 4 on the famous course in New York state that has hosted four US Opens]. And the next thing the word comes out they were putting the new clubhouse and car park there.

'So I resigned. I said "you can put the clubhouse anywhere, it doesn't matter, but you don't put it down on one of the greatest holes in the world". I went home and thought that was the end of it.'

The club would not confirm or deny this chain of events, but suffice to say Ruddy was back to finish the job six months later. And the new hole is, if not the best in the world, certainly a good one.

The old Portsalon reasserts itself at the very next tee, and it is to Ruddy's eternal credit that he has left the Matterhorn intact. It is a singular double-dogleg through rocks and dunes that looks about 800 yards long from the elevated tee. Once again, the views of the beach are stunning.

The incoming holes are all survivors from the old days. But in the middle of the eighteenth fairway is one of the oddest man-made contraptions you'll ever see on a golf course. In order to meet the needs of the people who use Portsalon's beach (named second best in the world by an American publication according to the locals) Ruddy has built a subterranean channel with a metal grate of a roof.

At one level the pedestrian subway is a great success. The bathers have historic rights of way here and used to hold up play for ages on warm weekend afternoons. On the other hand, the angular roof is just above the level of the fairway and prevents balls from rolling over it. Depending on the wind conditions and the tee you use, it can force a frustrating lay up, and generally spoils the other changes Ruddy has made to what should now be a good finishing hole.

But in the broader scheme of things, it's a hiccup we can all live with if it means that Portsalon can remain a viable proposition. Annual green fees now exceed £100,000, but that is not a vast sum, given the relatively modest membership and the increase in maintenance the bigger course demands.

If nothing thrills you more than coming across an unexpected and out-of-the-way wonder in your travels, then include Portsalon on your itinerary. We used to think that Portsalon was one of the twenty best courses in Ireland. And that was *before* Ireland's leading architect added his jolt of excitement (and more than a thousand yards).

The days when Portsalon was the haunt of the British nobility may be long gone, but the golf has never been better.

Location: At end of R246 on Fanad Peninsula

Restrictions: None

Green Fee: €35–40

Secretary: Cathal Toland

Address: Portsalon, Fanad, Co. Donegal; **tel:** (074) 915-9459; **fax:** (074) 915-9919; **e-mail:** portsalongolfclub@eircom.net

ROSAPENNA

Founded: 1892

Designed by: Old Tom Morris, Harry Vardon, etc.

Sandy Hills Links built: 2003

Designed by: Pat Ruddy

It would be difficult, if not impossible, to find country better suited for golf than that around Rosapenna. There are fine natural hazards, the turf is good and the scenery is delightful ... There is rare cliff scenery, and the air is bracing and exhilarating.

1908 TRAVEL GUIDE TO DONEGAL

The ghosts of Old Tom Morris, James Braid and Harry Vardon still whisper at Rosapenna, but now it is the vivid Irish architect Pat Ruddy who has thrust this historic golfing resort back onto the world stage. There is almost too much to take in at Rosapenna, and we're not talking about the rugged Atlantic views. There is a bewitching, old-fashioned links from golf's Golden Age, a new championship course in vigorous dunes that is astonishing from first tee to last, and another nine holes that are just beginning to mature. Contemplating the golf choices ahead of you over breakfast in the seafront dining room (fresh kippers anyone?), you can't help but wonder if Rosapenna, in its own unassuming way, has once again become the very best golf hotel in the world.

'I was out there this morning on the eleventh hole,' shouted Frank Casey over the phone. 'We've got a bulldozer working there, and I found a golf ball that must be at least one hundred years old. I was pretty happy to find that I can tell you.'

It made us feel good, too, to think that Rosapenna's rich golfing heritage was something you could still touch as well as feel. In a moment of fancy, we imagined someone carrying out an archaeological dig on the site of the old Rosapenna Hotel (destroyed by fire), using toothbrushes to lovingly brush the soil away from mashies, niblicks, gutta-percha golf balls and perhaps a bottle of 1884 Château Latour.

They were all there, once, at Rosapenna.

We imagined the shiver that Frank Casey must have felt when he found that golf ball. It must have been like reaching back through time, like shaking hands with Old Tom Morris. 'At Rosapenna,' the local wags would surely be saying, 'the rough is so thick it takes you one hundred years to find your golf ball!'

We had called the owner and manager of the new Rosapenna Hotel and Golf Links for an update on his expansion plans. As usual, Frank Casey's matter-of-fact voice was full of plans and optimism and hard work. Casey is the kind of honest, straightforward fellow who gives entrepreneurs a good name – he's determined to turn dreams into reality, but he's not going to harm anyone along the way.

'The peace in Northern Ireland is going to make a tremendous difference to Donegal,' he said. 'We've had more English tourists in the last six months than in the last fifteen years. And Donegal is the natural place for people from Northern Ireland who may have been going to Scotland [during the Troubles].'

The recent boom in golf in Ireland has spawned any number of fancy new golf hotels with luxurious appointments and lush American-style courses. But Rosapenna is utterly and gloriously different. It has a story behind it that none can rival. And it begins before the first golf course was even built in America.

The links at Rosapenna Hotel was established in 1890 by the Earl of Leitrim, one of Ireland's biggest landowners, after a design by Old Tom Morris, golf's first great professional. The Earl built a splendid hotel out of Norwegian pine next to the links on picturesque Sheephaven Bay, and promoted it as a wilderness retreat for the English nobility.

Not that the guests were roughing it. The Rosapenna had its own orchestra, a first class wine cellar, and formal evening dress was expected at dinner. Recreation included lawn tennis, croquet, hunting, fishing (on a private lake) and the new art of photography (the hotel boasted its own dark room).

'Nothing is wanting to promote the comfort of visitors or enhance their pleasure or sport while staying at this liberally conducted establishment,' enthused an 1896 guidebook to Ireland.

Photographs and postcards from the era show gentlemen golfers in waistcoats and bow ties (and often with a pipe) and lady golfers in corsets, long dresses and long sleeves. Only the caddies – in bare feet – strike a discordant note, a reminder that the resorts were only for the few. In the late nineteenth century, Donegal was as impoverished as the Third-World countries where many golf resorts are built today. The local Irish peasantry lived in thatched huts, and the terrible famines of the 1840s, when fully a third of the Irish people died or emigrated, were a living memory.

Irish independence did not immediately alter the class structure, and Rosapenna flourished until after the Second World War. But in 1962 a fire broke out in one of the hotel's guest wings. As the smoke seeped into the dining room, it is said that the Duke of St Albans ordered another bowl of soup, explaining to the waiter that he wanted to be 'the last person to eat in the Old Rosapenna'.

And so he was. The building was destroyed, and a newer, less majestic hotel gradually took shape. The golf course deteriorated rapidly under a succession of indifferent owners. By the late 1970s it was difficult to distinguish it from the surrounding grazing land.

But then the story takes one more, happily ironic turn. The golf hotel at Rosapenna, designed as a playground for English aristocrats, was to be rescued by the descendants of their barefoot Irish caddies!

The saviour was Frank Casey. He bought the rundown hotel complex for £500,000 in 1981. It turns out that Casey's father had been the Old Rosapenna's head waiter, and had served the Duke of St Albans his famous bowl of soup.

'When I was a boy, no local would dare think of going into the front door of the Rosapenna Hotel,' remembers Casey, who left Donegal as a young man to seek his fortune. 'It was full of Bentleys and Rolls-Royces.'

Casey is a thoroughly practical man and can't quite see the romance in his own story – the son of the head waiter returning as owner. He insists the decision to purchase and revive the golf course was strictly business.

'Everyone who comes here has a set of clubs in the boot,' he says. 'The golf course puts heads on beds and makes the money.'

Casey spent the 1980s and much of the 1990s gradually bringing the hotel and golf course up to standard. Occasionally, golf architecture aficionados would make a fuss over the green complexes, but for most guests it was just a fun and sporty course to play over. There was a front nine of gently rolling links holes and charmingly natural greens; followed by a wild tramp of a back nine around a scenic hill, with makeshift shots over ramparts and roads.

But Frank Casey knew he had a problem. The shots over the road were becoming a safety issue. On the other hand, he had an opportunity. The property he purchased in 1981 included a whopping 800 acres of land, much of it pristine linksland. Although much too rugged for anyone in Morris's or Vardon's time to work with, Casey asked Eddie Hackett in to see if the land could be used to replace the road-hopping holes of the original layout, should that become necessary.

Then two events intervened to change the course of work at Rosapenna. Hackett passed away (in 1996), and the Glashedy Links at Ballyliffin, designed by Pat Ruddy, was opened to widespread astonishment and acclaim. This is what you could do in the high dunes of Donegal.

Casey quickly hired Ruddy to build an entirely new links at Rosapenna through some of the wildest terrain. As it happens, Ruddy had walked through the dunes years earlier, long before Casey bought the hotel.

'It is just turbulent hill country all the way, stem to stern, no moment of relenting,' says Ruddy. 'The mental juices ferment on it, it's high drama all the way.'

As always with Ruddy, this was to be a hands-on affair. Though he was the operator and designer of one of the top 100 courses in the world (The European Club near Dublin), he uprooted himself, and his wife, and moved onto the site of the new course. The hotel was closed for the winter season, so Ruddy and his wife spent the winter in a fifty-year-old holiday home. This 'shack in the hills', as Ruddy calls it, had a metered electric heater, and would be their home for five months.

'We had to put money in it every time we boiled the kettle – my wife spent more than the fee keeping it heated.' Ruddy jokes.

It would have been a cold lonely winter for some (and long-suffering is an adjective that comes to mind for Mrs Ruddy). But for Pat Ruddy it was a chance to create something special.

'On other sites you have to make things up and introduce drama. Here you had to tone it down.'

Frank Casey is the kind of hotel owner who still fills in at reception and greets his guests every night at dinner, so he obviously admires a similar streak in Ruddy.

'He didn't just give some workers a set of plans,' says Casey. 'He worked out there in the dunes with the shapers and machine men until he got a green, fairway or a bunker just the way he wanted it.'

The result is a revelation, a links every bit as breathtaking as Ruddy's seminal courses at Ballyliffin and the European Club. And possibly even better.

'I believe if you do something good it will work commercially as well,' says Ruddy. 'I've tried to give them the unashamedly best course possible.'

Sandy Hills Links

There is surely time for the new championship course at Rosapenna to be renamed, for 'Sandy Hills' deserves to be called something far more distinctive. From the first tee, it is obvious that what lies ahead is something very remarkable indeed.

Almost 500 yards from the back tees, the opening hole is a mammoth downhill par 4 that carries you swiftly and thrillingly inside the ridges of dunes that Old Tom Morris could only marvel at. Many of the features that characterize Sandy Hills are evident from the start – the elevated tee, the undulating and natural looking corridors of play, the absence of fairway bunkering, and the slightly raised green framed in the sand hills.

Indeed, it would be difficult to find a more thrilling set of downhill tee shots than those at Sandy Hills, though they are often as unsettling as they are beautiful. The challenge of most holes is laid out marvellously before you, but Ruddy makes great use of the hilly terrain to slightly obscure the best landing area, which often looks much less generous than it actually is. It is especially intimidating since the rough at Sandy Hills is, at least for the moment, the most unforgiving in Ireland.

Don't make the mistake of attempting the back tees at Sandy Hills. With the rough so deep, it is a course that plays to major championship difficulty year round. The normal men's tees, at almost 6,400 yards, are test enough, and if you keep your drives in play you will be able to properly appreciate the exciting approach shots that are presented throughout.

In routing the course, one of Ruddy's most difficult tasks was deciding how to navigate down in to, and up out of, the valleys.

'I'm a great believer in a goodly percentage of downhill drives,' says Ruddy. 'But the challenge [at Sandy Hills] was getting the greens elevated, but keeping the floor visible.'

Ruddy's solution was to route and shape the course so that both the principal landing areas and the greens were raised off the valley floor. The golfer, when playing well, never descends too far too quickly, or has too uphill an ascent.

Instead, a good drive will often leave you with the satisfying drama of an approach played from one plateau to another, more or less at eye level. And it means the countless elevation changes that add so much energy to the course never feel like an ordeal.

There are many variations on, and exceptions to this theme of course, and Sandy Hills does not get repetitive or boring. It is also one of the most tranquil courses we have ever played.

'Because of the kind of ground it is, creation of solitude was simple,' says Ruddy. 'On a high percentage of holes, you don't notice anyone else. If you wish you can be alone with your thoughts, and try to make the ball behave!'

It is misleading, really, to single out golf holes on a course that is so consistently exhilarating, but from an aesthetic point of view it would be hard to ignore the sixth, a short par 4 that leads to a gorgeous green location, set in front of beach, sea and hills. A natural chasm narrows the fairway near the green, and a small bunker in front is an understated but very real threat.

'The golf course is only beginning, and we have only one fairway bunker put in,' says Ruddy. 'We can transform it yet. Like a piece of sheet music, a lot of quavers and notes can be added or subtracted.'

It is an immense tribute to Ruddy that we can't think of a hole where a fairway bunker would substantially improve things. The terrain itself asks ample questions; for example, the many small chasms that bite into the fairway are as visible, and threatening, as any bunker.

Around the greens Ruddy has also shown restraint. The putting surfaces are ample enough to be playable in the winds that often sweep off the sea. And the bunkers are modest in size, and often partially obscured, never a scar on the landscape. But they have a purpose – you can run the ball onto the greens at Sandy Hills, but you have to be accurate.

A new golf pavilion has been built by the first tee, to cater to the many golfers who aren't staying at the hotel, and Frank Casey Jr, a two handicap, is intensely involved in the golf operations. Pat Ruddy obviously sees a parallel to the European Club, where his own family helps to manage things.

'It will take another generation to bring it on. A golf place like that, it takes more than a generation.'

Sandy Hills may indeed get better with age. But this vintage links is definitely worth savouring right now.

Old Tom Morris Links

Though few reliable records survive, we do know that the original course at Rosapenna, laid out by Old Tom Morris, was lengthened and revised by Harry Vardon in 1906, with the new and longer rubber-core ball in mind. Vardon promptly declared that 'Rosapenna Links can now take rank with the best championship courses in the United Kingdom'.

It is thought that James Braid assisted Vardon and that H. S. Colt (designer of Royal Portrush) made slight revisions sometime in the 1930s.

If so, the Rosapenna that Frank Casey rescued was an amalgam of the efforts of four of the greatest names in golf history. It was good enough to host several Irish championships between the World Wars.

It is the front nine that the connoisseurs want to play, a true links with greens that melt beautifully into the surrounding terrain (note that Pat Ruddy has added a few longer tees). But many others will find the back nine more exciting, even though most of it is played on hilly meadow grass and is not a links at all.

The change of pace begins in earnest on the uphill eleventh, an adaptation of an Old Tom original, where a decent drive is needed just to clear the busy road that heads into Rosapenna village.

The short par-4 twelfth may also be Old Tom's. The choice is to lay up 220 yards out in front of another road (as Morris surely intended) or let it all hang out and try for the green. There is more than a bit of anticipation for the big hitter as he crosses the road and slips through the cattle gate – will he have an eagle putt, a blast from a pot bunker, or an impossible shot from the fierce rough?

The thirteenth is a lovely sweeping dogleg, apparently laid out by either Braid or Vardon, that sweeps downwards towards Mulroy Bay. After that, the holes on the trek home are various shades of eccentric.

Morris-Ruddy Links

Frank Casey plans to replace the last eight holes of the Old Tom Morris Links (and the first hole) with an entirely new nine designed by Pat Ruddy. Ruddy's holes skirt around the large dunes, and thus follow terrain more in keeping with the front nine of the original course.

'I tried to match the original nine by taking a minimalist approach, not overly embellishing, creating something that might have happened in the days of Morris,' says Ruddy.

We've toured the new holes, and they look wonderful. We expect they will provide an interesting and thought-provoking counterpart to the old front nine, and are certainly very different in conception from Sandy Hills. One thing they have in common, though, is a terrible name: the new composite course is to be called the Morris-Ruddy Links.

Golf archaeologists will be pleased to learn that the old back nine will remain, in truncated form, with the road crossings removed, and will be used as an 'Academy Course' by the hotel's very active golf school.

In our view, Frank Casey has done the world of golf a very big favour. Though Pat Ruddy's magnificent new links will surely be the main attraction in years to come, the magic of the Old Rosapenna will still linger. It will remain possible to feel transported back in time, to an era of waistcoats, steamships, brassies and gutta-percha balls. And it is satisfying to know that this wonderful golf destination is now as Irish as a glass of stout around a peat fire.

Location: Rosapenna, 2 miles north of Carrigart off R245, 25 miles north of Letterkenny

Restrictions: None

Green Fee: €75 (Sandy Hills); €50 (Old Tom Morris); €110 (both courses on same day)

Manager: Frank Casey

Address: Rosapenna, Downings, Co. Donegal; **tel:** (074) 915-5301; **fax:** (074) 915-5128; **e-mail:** mailbox@rosapennagolflinks.ie; **web:** www.rosapennagolflinks.ie

STRANDHILL

Founded: 1931

Designed by: John McAlister, John McGonigle and Martin Niland

We've never moved any earth. It is exactly as it was.

FRANK CARROLL, PRESIDENT, STRANDHILL GOLF CLUB

Overshadowed and at one time perhaps a bit overawed by their famous and fancier neighbours across Sligo Bay at Rosses Point, the members at Strandhill can be justly proud of their unusual, varied and thoroughly entertaining links, much of which they have devised themselves. And there are at least a couple of wild and wonderful holes that you will never forget. It may be that the course's personality merely reflects the quirky streak of the golfers who play over it. After all, where else in Ireland do you find a club so enthusiastic about winter golf that it's harder to get a tee time on a Sunday in January than July?

In common with many clubs in Ireland, Strandhill started with nine holes, laid out crudely over the fields of the local landowner. Frank Carroll, now the club's president, joined in 1964, when 'you needed fourteen or fifteen balls to get around. There was no grading of rough. It was fairway, green and wild wild bents [high grass].'

Golf grew in popularity in Ireland in the 1960s, partly due to the exploits of Irish sporting heroes such as Christy O'Connor. For most people in Sligo, however, membership at the established club in town – Rosses Point – was out of the question. The alternative was Strandhill.

'It was still a very elite sport at the time,' remembers Carroll. 'We came from a different social grouping altogether than Rosses Point, which was set up by military men of the old [British] regime. It was very restrictive. You would have to be interviewed. A lot of people wouldn't qualify for membership and couldn't afford it anyway.

'We also attracted a lot of caddies and other people who worked in Rosses Point but who weren't allowed to play there.'

By 1970, the club was large enough to merit an eighteen-hole course. The original nine holes skirted carefully around the fierce dunes on the property, and the professional at Rosses Point – John McGonigle – was hired to figure out a way to somehow cross over them. Since there were no earth-moving machines available, McGonigle had to be imaginative, and the outlandish thirteenth hole is one of the happy results.

'There was no bringing in a contractor or anything like that,' says Carroll. 'It was all done by voluntary labour. A friend of mine used to cut the bents with a horse and cart.'

Further changes were recommended by club member and agronomist Martin Niland, who had helped to lay out the enchanting links at Ballyliffin Old in the early 1970s. They included three new holes (the formidable finishing stretch) which opened for play during Niland's captaincy in 1985. In true Strandhill tradition, it was a do-it-yourself affair. The first step was to get rid of the waist-high grass that covered the area where the new holes were to be.

'You probably wouldn't get permission these days, but it was very dry at the time and we just set fire to it,' says Niland. 'It took about two hours, and I remember all the lost golf balls exploding, Dunlop 65s and the old Commandos with the rubber cores.'

Strandhill's unique way of doing things extends to its club competitions. The club's bizarre passion for winter golf seems to have developed during the Second World War, when members cycled to the course in what most of us would call the off-season. Since then the obsession has only intensified, and today upwards of 400 members converge on the course most Sundays from November through March, no matter how frigid and frightening the Atlantic winds.

The attraction is Strandhill's famous Winter League, a pairs match-play competition with *eight* divisions that is as idiosyncratic as the course itself.

'You can't get into the car park on a Sunday,' says Carroll. 'And when the men are finished, the ladies go out! The great thing about it is you get to meet everyone. And there's usually a jar or two afterwards in the clubhouse.'

For one season at least, the post-round pints had to be downed in a caravan, following a disastrous clubhouse fire in 2005. But now there's a brand new facility, and talk of expanding the golf course. The future looks rosy indeed.

And while Strandhill is still not quite on a level with Rosses Point in golfing terms, the social and economic changes in Ireland over the last generation have led to a welcome shift in relations between Sligo's two most important clubs.

'It's changed dramatically,' says Carroll. 'In social strata terms, we are very much at par really. We have a tremendous relationship with them.'

For a time the good relations were further cemented by an annual charity competition which entailed teeing off at Rosses Point and playing to the eighteenth green at Strandhill by way of a series of small islands in the bay that separates the two courses. Played at low tide, with boats ferrying the golfers between shots, the hole played to a par of 27. Not your typical fundraiser. But then there's nothing typical about Strandhill.

The course

With so many golf clubs in Ireland making haste to suddenly update links that have stood the test of time, Strandhill is a refreshing throwback to the days when golfers played over the exact terrain they were presented with. And what exciting terrain it is. The opening holes are decent but sedate, and it is only at the plateau green at the fourth that you are given a hint of the pleasures to come.

The fun begins in earnest at the fifth, a terrific par 5 with no fewer than three memorable elements. First, there is a thrilling, elevated tee shot that encourages you to smash the ball into the wide blue yonder, but in reality requires careful calculation as to how much of the dogleg you want to chew off. Then, after a good drive, you find yourself on the most sensationally undulating fairway in Ireland. Finally, there is the approach to an unusual, sunken, saucer-shaped green. It's pure delight from start to finish.

There are two more good holes in this stretch. The sixth is a par 4 leading to one of the two beaches that border the golf course. You then descend to play a truly picturesque, if relatively straightforward par-4 right along the strand itself.

After a few comparatively ordinary holes there's another outstanding sequence in the middle of the back nine. It begins with the incomparable thirteenth, John McGonigle's singular contribution to the world of golf architecture. This right-angled and short par 4 begins with a wildly disorienting blind drop-shot to an unearthly hollow, bordered by gigantic dunes. Those tempted to take a straight line for the green court catastrophe, but then *every* line is nerve-wracking. If you do find the fairway (and the first time through you will have no idea where to aim, or which club to use), the second shot will require a bold short-iron to a green that is itself tucked inside more giant sand hills. It is a strange yet charming hole, and one that rewards good golf shots.

The fourteenth is a short par 3 played to a lovely green set in high dunes, and the fifteenth may be the best hole on the course. It's another sharp dogleg par 4, but uphill this time, requiring a tee shot accurately placed between two dunes, followed by a strong and accurate approach to a sharply elevated green that seems even higher with Knochnarea Mountain looming behind it.

There's nothing wrong with the final three holes either, even if they seem a bit too *normal* after the unexpected surprises that are Strandhill's hallmark. They may be the hardest three holes on the course, and were laid out by Martin Niland, and approved by the club committee after they invited Eddie Hackett in to have a look.

'Eddie spent four or five hours on the course,' says Niland. 'He gave the nod of approval and everyone was happy.'

The club has recently purchased sixty more acres of heaving linksland beyond the fourth green, and has hired Martin Hawtree to design four new holes there, in theory enabling the club to turn a few of the weakest holes into a much-needed practice facility. At the time of writing, these proposals were bogged down in environmental assessments. But even if the plans do go ahead, we trust the members will preserve the best of their endearing links.

Location: Follow R292 for approximately 5 miles from Sligo Town to village of Strandhill, and follow signs

Restrictions: Weekdays are best for visitors, but some weekend times may also be available

Green Fee: €40–50

Secretary: Sandra Corcoran

Address: Strandhill, Sligo, Co. Sligo; **tel:** (071) 916-8188; **fax:** (071) 916-8811; **e-mail:** strandhillgc@eircom.net; **web:** www.strandhillgc.com

OTHER COURSES
OF INTEREST

Cruit Island

Established: 1986

Designed by: Michael Doherty

The finest nine-hole links in Ireland, Cruit Island is set in as magnificent a setting as one could ever hope to find. In a country of wonderful par 3s, the sixth hole is one of the greatest of them all. On the rest of the course, you will find no par 5s, but lots of wind, blind tee shots and rollicking links terrain. This is truly golf at the ends of the earth. Visitors may not be plentiful, but if they make the journey they are sure to be welcomed warmly.

Just finding Cruit (pronounced 'Critch') Island golf club can be a daunting task. It lies at the end of a three-mile, one-lane dirt track in one of northwest Ireland's most remote corners. But do persevere. For at the end of this road lies one of the most spectacular, unspoiled nine-hole golf courses in the world.

We were fortunate enough to play our round with Hugh Gillespie, president of the club from 1998–2001, in what he estimated was a Force 5 to 6 gale.

'We'll play in this, but not much more than this,' he said.

A club competition had been cancelled earlier in the day due to high winds and rain, but conditions had improved just enough to allow us to have the course to ourselves in brilliant sunshine.

The drama starts immediately at Cruit Island. On the first tee you are asked to make a knee-knocking drive over a massive, gaping chasm to a landing area which appears to be set between massive dunes. In fact, once out of sight, the fairway plays eccentrically over the road you just came in on, before doglegging right at a ninety-degree angle.

The second hole is also blind, and probably the weakest on the course, but it does serve to get you where you need to go, out into the thrilling clifftop terrain that contains holes three through seven.

The third hole is relatively short and very downhill, but often plays into the prevailing wind. It gives you the first panoramic vista of the Atlantic coastline, Aranmore and Owey islands, and Mount Errigal. The fourth plays back up the hill, with a tee box that feels like it is perched right on the edge of the sea, and then the fifth is a wacky, blind and downhill dogleg-right par 4 that is reminiscent of the thirteenth at Strandhill, but with a unique, plateaued green which drops off severely at the back and left.

These holes are great fun, particularly if you have found a way to control your ball in the wind, but they are all a prelude to what comes next. If there can be a signature hole on such an unknown links, then it is surely the sixth – a 150-yard par 3 (though it can play to almost any club in the bag, depending on the wind) with nothing between tee and green but two heaving inlets of the crashing Atlantic. The green is a long but narrow sliver with more ocean behind. This is one of the outstanding par 3s in Ireland, and it alone makes all the trouble you took to find Cruit Island worthwhile.

If you're not jaded by this point, you'll find that the vista from the tee box on the seventh is perhaps the most panoramic of all, but don't let it detract from the fact that a well-placed drive is required to have a short approach into a green perched at the far end of the course. The eighth and ninth are pleasant finishers which get the usually wind-buffeted players back to the exceptionally cosy clubhouse.

Gillespie told us that despite the very remote location, Cruit Island is a vibrant club with 300 mostly local members. It was established in 1986 on land originally leased from the Bishop of Raphoe, though the land is now owned by a private landlord. The course was laid out by Michael Doherty, the professional at the City of Derry club. Cruit Island is open for play year round, though the small but very comfortable new clubhouse (built in 2002) is only open on weekends in winter. The club would like to expand to eighteen holes some time in the future, but as yet has been unable to secure the necessary land.

Location: Near Kincasslagh, 5 miles north of Dungloe. Turn off R259 opposite the former Viking House Hotel, where a small sign indicates 'Galfchursa', then proceed 3 miles to the clubhouse, bearing right past the cemetery and crossing a causeway to the island, then following the (eventually, dirt) road until it runs out at the clubhouse

Restrictions: None

Green Fee: €25 (deposit in honour box if clubhouse closed)

Hon. Secretary: Joseph Gillespie

Address: Cruit Island, Kincasslagh, Co. Donegal; **tel:** (074) 954-3296; **e-mail:** cruitisland@eircom.net; **web:** www.cruitislandgolfclub.com

---

St Patrick's

Founded: 1994; Redesigned course: 2008
Designed by: Jack Nicklaus

Long the most tantalizing piece of golf terrain in Ireland, St Patrick's was the eccentric project of a hotelier who didn't play golf, but had more untouched linksland at his disposal than anyone, anywhere. For a decade, St Patrick's thirty-six holes lay almost dormant, and they included the last work by Eddie Hackett and the only links golf ever designed by a woman. Barely maintained, the courses attracted only a trickle of visitors, who were in turn charmed and irritated by the primordial state of the links. Now Jack Nicklaus has arrived, and nothing will ever be the same again.

We met twenty-something Joanne O'Haire at a restaurant after a round at Royal County Down in the late 1990s. We couldn't resist asking for a few free golf tips, and she was game enough to analyse our lamentable swings in the parking lot. Later, over pudding, when the conversation turned to the great golf in Donegal, she mentioned in passing that she had designed a golf course up that way. We were several pints to the good, and we wondered what on earth she was talking about.

A little later, on one of our pilgrimages to Donegal, we found out. Quite visible from the course at Rosapenna were the unmistakable ribbons of fairway on a great mountain of linksland across Sheephaven Bay.

After our round, we jumped in the car to investigate. Trudging through the 'fairways' at St Patrick's was in turns a mystical and mystifying experience. There was a shut-up caravan on a grass lot where we presumed the first hole was, and a sign suggesting we pay our green fees at the Carrigart Hotel. There were pins in the ground, but no clubhouse, no scorecards, no directional signs and almost no bunkers. The fairways were not cut sufficiently to give them much definition. This was golf in the nineteenth – no, make that the eighteenth – century. Golf as orienteering.

It turned out that St Patrick's was the pet project of the owner of the Carrigart Hotel, Dermot Walsh, a non-golfer who knew something about linksland from his days in Dunfanaghy, where he owned some of the property that the golf club plays over. At Carrigart, he owned a whole lot more – a massive 350 acres – and while he initially planned to build a caravan park, he decided to put up a pair of golf courses instead.

The first was laid out to a full 7,000 yards by an elderly Eddie Hackett, with a little help from local lass Joanne O'Haire, a fine amateur golfer at the time. On the second course the roles were reversed, with O'Haire taking the lead.

Even on the Hackett course there was a slightly crude up and down quality to the routing, but many holes were mesmerizing, with fantastic green sites, and crazy, rollicking fairways. It would be Eddie Hackett's last work, and he made his last visit to the course just a few weeks before his death.

And that's almost the end of the story. For more than a decade, St Patrick's hibernated (there was no greens staff until 2001), attracting a trickle of determined Germans who had obviously got wind of it from somewhere. Martin Hawtree was asked to suggest improvements to the site at one point, but the course remained in a charmed state of suspended animation.

Golf had moved on in Donegal, however, driven by a trio of spectacular new links courses designed by Pat Ruddy. With Sandy Hills, Ruddy's new offering at Rosapenna, actually touching the O'Haire course at one point, the commercial potential of St Patrick's was becoming obvious.

Finally, in 2006, Walsh sold out to the Relton Development Group, which promised that the golf would be used to attract guests to a 'luxury hotel, with a spa and complete leisure facilities, to be managed by a world-renowned international hotel operator.' We can hardly wait.

There's no question that Nicklaus has been smitten by St Patrick's. Following the 2006 Open at Hoylake, he spent sixteen hours on the site, which is apparently an eternity for a man who has worked on more than 250 courses worldwide. His verdict was that the Hackett and O'Haire courses are to be entirely discarded. An Ocean Course will fully utilize some land close to the sea that Hackett had no access to, while a second course will be slightly inland.

If nothing else, the Nicklaus 'signature courses' will offer a fascinating point of comparison with Ruddy's work, right next door.

And we expect there will be someone around to take your green fee.

Location: Immediately south of Rosapenna, with access by one-lane dirt road; enquire at Carrigart Hotel for detailed directions

Restrictions: Closed for reconstruction until further notice

Manager: Relton Development Group

Address: Magheramagorman, Carrigart, Co. Donegal; **tel:** (074) 915-5114; **fax:** (074) 915-5250; **e-mail:** info@stpatricksgolflinks.com; **web:** www.stpatricksgolflinks.com

DIVERSIONS

THE NORTHWEST

T HE NORTHWEST OF Ireland is one of the most rugged and remote areas of Western Europe. There is uninhabited land on a scale much more familiar to an Australian or Canadian than a European. It is not uncommon to find the road blocked by livestock. The scenery, particularly along the north Donegal coast, is often stunning.

Galway is a tourist and university centre and a convenient base for exploration. It is a vibrant place, particularly in summer, and has become known as an artistic centre – there is an Arts Festival each July. And it overlooks the famed Galway Bay, notable both for its scenic beauty and its oysters.

Galway is a town of considerable historic interest. It was an Anglo-Norman colony for centuries, dominated by fourteen families who became known as the 'fourteen tribes of Galway.' They stubbornly kept the native

Irish outside of the city and remained intensely loyal to the Crown. Galway grew in importance as it became a significant port for trade with Spain (particularly in wine), and architectural reminders of the period can be found throughout the old town. The best is probably the Spanish Arch, which now houses a small civic museum.

The town also contributed the word 'lynch' to the English language. The Lynch family was pre-eminent among the fourteen tribes and in 1493, James Lynch was Lord Mayor of Galway. His son, Walter, stabbed a visiting Spanish merchant to death and was sentenced to be hanged, but because Walter was so popular (or the townspeople were so afraid of the Lynchs) no one could be found to carry out the sentence. James Lynch, who as Lord Mayor was the judge in the case, executed his son personally, and lived the rest of his life as an unhappy recluse. The incident is commemorated on a plaque in the Church of St Nicholas, formerly the Old Jail.

Western County Galway and County Mayo, though remote, contain some of traditional Ireland's most rewarding sites. The Irish language is spoken along the north shore of Galway Bay, and within that bay are the famous islands of Inishmore, Inishmaan and Inisheer – the Aran Islands that inspired the lyrical plays of J. M. Synge. Inishmore is the largest, and can be reached from Galway by air or ferry. It has lots of limestone, a few interesting pubs and no trees. The main tourist attraction is the impressive fort, Dun Aonghasa. There are also excellent views of both the Cliffs of Moher and the mountains of Connemara from this vantage point. The middle island, Inishmaan (Inis Meain in Irish) is the least visited, and did without electricity until 1978 and telephones until 1987. A large pier has now been built to allow access to Inishmaan, however, and ferries operate from Galway to Inishmaan in the hope that tourism can replace the dying fishing and farming economy.

Just northwest of Galway town is the island-dotted Lough Corrib, with its outstanding salmon fishing, and further west is the Connemara region, dominated by the mountain range called the Twelve Bens. This is a raw and other-worldly landscape. Even at the height of tourist season the dominant experience is likely to be solitude, unless you are fortunate enough to happen upon a herd of wild Connemara ponies. The area has been used in feature films dealing with rural Irish life, including *The Field*, starring Richard Harris, which was shot at Leenane, and the John Wayne classic *The Quiet Man*, filmed in and around the village of Cong. Connemara National

Park, near Letterfrack, has a visitors' centre which describes the region's landscape and natural history. But just about anywhere you go in Connemara will yield fine natural scenery.

In central County Mayo, about twenty miles east of Castlebar, is the village of Knock. The Chapel of Knock has been a place of pilgrimage since an apparition of the Virgin Mary, Saint Joseph and Saint John appeared in 1879. Even though it was raining that day, the area around the figures is said to have remained dry. In modern times, more than half a million people make the journey to Knock annually, and the little village has, understandably, been rather overwhelmed. In 1976, a huge new church was built in the village, and in 1986 an airport (now known as Ireland West Airport Knock) opened at Charlestown, just 10 miles away. Despite predictions of failure, the airport has proved to be a success (over half a million passengers passed through it in 2005), and the influx of visitors – the majority from Britain, and by no means all religious pilgrims – has had a profound effect on County Mayo.

The region around Sligo Bay is known as Yeats Country and promoted as such. The literary tourist will want to visit Yeats's grave at Drumcliff, as well as Lough Gill (made famous in 'The Lake Isle of Innisfree') and Lissadell House. The County Museum, in Sligo, has a section devoted to Yeats. Next door is the County Art Gallery with a good collection of Irish works, including a few by Yeats's brother Jack. Also extremely prominent (and very visible from the golf links at Rosses Point) is the distinctive flat-topped Benbulben mountain, in sight of which Yeats asked to be buried. Even if you are not interested in Yeats, Sligo is a friendly and interesting town, with many vibrant pubs and restaurants. Some of the best are to be found along the River Walk.

County Donegal is a region of thatched cottages, pine forests and superb coastal scenery. Donegal tweed is perhaps its most famous product, and is widely available in Donegal Town. At the centre of town is a large square known as 'the diamond,' and most of the shops, pubs and hotels can be seen from this point. The coastal road from Donegal to Narin and Portnoo yields much worthy scenery, with the fishing village of Killybegs worth a brief look. At Portnoo, there are miles of beautiful sandy beaches, but the weather will seldom cooperate with any plans for an afternoon's swim.

The northern part of Donegal is divided into four spectacular peninsulas – Horn Head, Rosguill, Fanad and Inishowen. The Rosapenna Hotel and

DIVERSIONS

golf courses are on Rosguill, while Portsalon is situated in a commanding spot on Fanad overlooking Lough Swilly, and Ballyliffin sits at the apex of Inishowen. The roads are winding and narrow. You are unlikely to travel more than thirty-five miles an hour no matter what your form of transportation. It would be a shame to go faster in any event, for an imposing cliff or secluded bay may be just around the corner.

THE EAST:

CAPITAL LINKS

Golfing visitors to Ireland have sometimes overlooked the Dublin area in their rush to sample the undeniable charms of Ballybunion and the other famous links on the opposite side of the island. But the eastern seaboard of the Republic now boasts a string of world-class links, and a handful of charming second-tier choices. They have very different characters, ranging from the rollicking duneland of The Island and the European Club, to the subtle stateliness of Royal Dublin and Baltray. And one of the most ancient and convivial cities in Europe is also at your doorstep. A good strategy is to enjoy Dublin at weekends and golf during the week, when starting times are much easier to come by. The capital is now one of the wealthier places on the planet, and it is money that brought the Ryder Cup here, to the less than inspiring K Club. A staggering amount has been invested in similarly luxurious new parkland courses aimed at the millionaire and corporate market. They offer an undeniably high standard of conditioning and creature comforts for those who would rather be in Palm Springs. Sample these if you like, but not at the expense of the great links golf on offer.

COUNTY LOUTH (Baltray)

Founded: 1892

Designed by: Thomas Gilroy, Tom Simpson

This is just about as fine a piece of links land, ordained by nature for golf, as we have ever seen.

TOM SIMPSON, 1937

Although deeply respected in Ireland, the superb links beside the village of Baltray, an hour's drive north of Dublin, is little known elsewhere. Masterfully overhauled by architect Tom Simpson before the Second World War, Baltray (as the course is better known) demands accurate driving and an inspired short game. It is one of the most intelligently bunkered courses in Ireland, and each slick and undulating green presents a unique challenge. There is no breathtaking seaside scenery at Baltray. You will find few of the giant dunes and elevated tees so common on Irish links. But there is one entirely absorbing hole after another. Add one of the country's most commodious and friendly clubhouses (it doubles as a bed-and-breakfast) and you have one of Ireland's most satisfying golf experiences.

Arrive at an Irish golf course by yourself, and there are two things that are gloriously uncertain – the weather and who you may end up playing with. One of the first times I played Baltray I hit the jackpot on both fronts. It was a Monday in temperamental November, but the morning was lovely and calm. I teed off just in advance of a large 'society' of boisterous Dublin journalists, more than content to savour the joys of one of my favourite links in quiet solitude.

No one had hit off the first for some time (I had waited around for a possible playing companion), and the course seemed entirely empty before me, but on the fourth tee I ran into two gentlemen who were using that hole to start their round. They played twelve holes each day, they told me, beginning on the fourth, and cutting across from the eighth green to the twelfth tee. But would I like to join them until that point?

It was a fortuitous meeting, for one of my temporary companions turned out to be none other than Peter Lyons, a member of County Louth Golf Club for more than fifty years and a former President of the Golfing Union of Ireland. Lyons passed away in 2005, but on this day some years before he was an astonishingly youthful eighty-three years of age, and he moved and played in a dignified and graceful manner that could still be admired.

His memory turned out to be as crisp as his play and, to my delight, he vividly described the day, in 1937, that the great British architect Tom Simpson marched up the very same fairway. The fourth today, it was the opening hole of the old course then in use, and Lyons remembered Simpson saying, 'If all the holes are like this, I won't have much to do.' Simpson had been engaged by the club to update the course, and he did, in fact, leave the hole alone. It remains a decidedly old-fashioned and intriguing par 4 with no bunkers, but with a fairway that heaves and gyrates just before the green.

Simpson, however, changed every other hole in the links, which had been originally laid out in 1892 by Thomas Gilroy, the first captain of Royal Dublin. In his written report to the members of Baltray, Simpson was brutally frank:

> It would be idle to pretend that in its present form and condition it is a good golf
> course . . . Unfortunately, those who were responsible for the design of the course
> as now planned, failed to observe and/or take advantage of the glorious
> possibilities that the ground afforded . . . The bunkers on your course, so far as
> they exist, serve no useful purpose whatever in governing the play of the hole. The
> weakest point of all is your one-shot holes, they are featureless and badly sited.

As Peter Lyons, his friend Jim McCullen and I stood on the tee of the par-3 fifth, the efforts of Simpson and his assistant Molly Gourlay were plainly evident. Baltray's par 3s are now considered among the loveliest in Ireland (they may well be the work of Gourlay, as she paid special attention to the short holes). The fifth calls for a precisely struck short iron to a pretty, elevated green that falls off on all sides. As we putted out, Lyons pointed to the pot bunker that lies smack in the middle of the fairway on the long sixth.

'Simpson put that bunker there just to create controversy,' he said. 'He claimed that if you made a perfect course it would be of no interest. He told us that half the people will say that bunker shouldn't be there, and the other half will say it is perfectly placed!'

I avoided the bunker, and found the rough beside the green in two on the par-5 hole. But then I found my chips bouncing back and forth across the small, elevated green.

'The greens can be difficult,' sympathized Lyons, who had hit four shots, all straight and accurate, to within ten feet of the flag. He holed the putt for a par, while I took an eight.

I knew from the club history book that Peter Lyons had left his mark on Baltray in a variety of different ways, over an astonishing number of years. A past captain and past president of the club, he donated the trophy for the inaugural East of Ireland championship in 1941. Played each year at Baltray, it is one of Ireland's most prestigious amateur tournaments. And here he was, more than fifty years later, three strokes better than I over four holes.

The last hole we played together was the eighth, a good, deceiving dogleg around some dunes. Lyons pointed out the spot where an over-zealous club captain (hoping to improve on Simpson's work!) built a new green. The members ignored it, and Simpson's original design remains intact.

Lyons had mentioned that he was also a member at Portmarnock, so as we shook hands I asked him about the difference between the two clubs.

'Well I score better there, for one thing,' he said with a smile. 'And I guess you'd say the social life is busier here. You don't see anyone after dark at Portmarnock.'

With that we parted company, Lyons and his playing partner resuming their specially tailored round at the twelfth.

I played the ninth by myself, but started the back nine with two new companions – a man in his late twenties named Sean, I believe, and his mother. They were delightful companions and filled me in on what it was like to belong to Baltray today.

By now I had found some rhythm and somehow managed to outplay Sean, who seemed to want to impress me with his prodigious length off the tee. Baltray is the kind of course that rewards sober second thought, however, and nowhere is that more true than on the marvellous trio of successive par 4s that starts on the 410-yard twelfth.

The twelfth is the kind of complex dogleg that you find only on links courses. Thanks to dunes of various sizes and some well-placed bunkers, there are any number of possible lines on the drive, and the fairway narrows at the elbow of the dogleg to challenge the ambitious. The approach shot, which looks radically different depending on where you have hit the tee shot, is played rather thrillingly between the largest dunes on the course to a half hidden, saucer-shaped green.

The even longer thirteenth is set picturesquely among the dunes that run along the ocean (the crashing surf is hidden but noisy behind them), while the 322-yard fourteenth is one of the most memorable short par 4s in Ireland.

With the wind in your face, the tee shot on the fourteenth is an intimidating, if short, drive over a wasteland of dunes, setting up a pitch to a severely undulating green that rejects all but the most perfectly placed shots. Elsewhere on Baltray, Simpson has used bunkers to great effect, but on the fourteenth there are none. Instead, he has used the natural slope of the land to create a gem that is tantalizing and frustrating for both long and short hitters alike.

The rest of the back nine is just fine – there are really no weak holes on Baltray – with more doglegs, well-placed and deep pot bunkers, and green sites that always make you think. Baltray represents Simpson at the height of his considerable powers.

Sean and his mother, who played in mixed competitions as a team, confirmed to me that Baltray's reputation as a sociable club was well intact. The family had been members for years, but with the recent golf boom the waiting list was now a mile long. Sean was hoping to be in good enough form to bag a turkey in the pre-Christmas competitions that are a tradition at Baltray and most other clubs in Ireland.

After only eighteen holes, I felt that my various companions had given me a taste of Baltray past and present. I entered the locker room with the immensely contented feeling generated by fascinating golf and warm, good-humoured Irish conversation. In the summer, when there is more light, you will want to play two rounds at Baltray, although it is easy to get side-tracked by the comfortable bar. The clubhouse is a converted hotel, and still has rooms for rent. Some visitors use its bed and breakfast as a base for golfing trips up and down the east coast (the dining room is also very good).

I was soon joined in the clubhouse by the Golfing Society that I had left behind on the first tee. Being journalists and Irish, they were eager interlocutors, and I was soon swallowed up in a grand debate about politics, the latest Dublin plays and, of course, the best courses in Ireland. One of the journalists, it turned out, had even written a successful golf thriller, *Operation Birdie*, about an IRA attack during a British Open at Turnberry.

It was a lovely end to a day that, like the course itself, took many unexpected twists and turns, all of them agreeable. The kind of day that makes travel anywhere, and especially in Ireland, so worthwhile.

Location: Baltray, 3 miles east of Drogheda on R167

Restrictions: Weekdays other than Tuesday are best for visitors; weekend times are possible, subject to availability

Green Fee: €115–135

Manager: Michael Delany

Address: Baltray, Drogheda, Co. Louth; **tel:** (041) 988-1530; **fax:** (041) 988-1531; **e-mail:** reservations@countylouthgolfclub.com; **web:** www.countylouthgolfclub.com

EUROPEAN CLUB

Founded: 1992
Designed by: Pat Ruddy

What I'm trying to do at the European Club is accelerated evolution. To do what St Andrews did in 400 years, what Royal Dublin and Portmarnock did in 100 years, and do it in fifteen.

PAT RUDDY

A fascinating links south of Dublin that was conceived, designed and developed by Irish golf writer and impresario Pat Ruddy, the European Club is a successful labour of love that makes wonderful use of one of Ireland's last stretches of muscular linksland. Already a familiar presence on lists of the world's top golf courses, it is one of Ireland's most challenging and satisfying links, with a host of classic doglegs through tall dunes, grand views from elevated tees, and a trio of exciting holes that hug the ocean. And, for the most part, Ruddy has kept well within the boundaries of the Irish golf tradition. This is a modern course, but an intensely Irish one.

◆◆◆

'This last winter a substantial offer came in, and I learned a little bit about myself,' said Pat Ruddy over the phone just before this book was published. The offer was for the piece of land that changed him from a little known sports writer into an important figure in world golf. Ruddy had turned the property into an asset worth tens of millions of pounds, but not in the popular manner of building expensive houses on the property. At the European Club, only the golf has ever counted.

'I had to consider it, you know, I'm not home alone,' Ruddy says in reference to his family's future. You can tell by his voice that he's rather proud of the offer he received, but it's not long before the serious tone has been replaced, in classic Ruddy fashion, by an outrageous comic metaphor.

'I've been pondering the Cookie Monster in Sesame Street,' he says. 'There's a quiz [show] and he has the choice between a million dollars and a jar of cookies. He went for the cookies. Well I'm a Golf Monster. I reckoned I'd stay where I was.'

The story of how he got there is a remarkable one. Ruddy was a middle-aged golf writer who had only dabbled a bit in course design when an advertisement in a Dublin paper caught his eye in 1987. A stretch of seaside land fifty miles south of Dublin was for sale at a place called Brittas Bay, and the advertisement suggested it might be suitable for a caravan park or a golf course.

Ruddy was curious enough to take a helicopter ride to see how it looked from the air. He was stunned. It was a fantastic, heaving piece of linksland, with huge dunes reminiscent of Ballybunion. It was also the only undeveloped linksland on the entire east coast.

He couldn't really afford it, but he managed to come up with the finances to buy the land.

'It was only after I had been there a while that the enormity of the ground grew on me,' Ruddy remembers. 'I went in there for days on end with grass over my head.'

Ruddy knew he had found his life's project. But he also knew how little he had in the bank. He would have to work slowly, doing most of the work himself with the help of his children.

'We built this ourselves, ninety per cent, [and] I can drive every machine,' he says with obvious pride. 'The money was being gobbled up, every penny. I re-mortgaged my home, sold my insurance policy, drove an old car, did everything to do this. You can't define that in money terms, the feeling you have for the place afterwards. The bond is so tight.'

Just when he needed it most, Ruddy was struck with a bolt of good fortune. For the first time in twenty years, the Irish Tourist Board started giving out tourism grants to golf course development projects. The European Club received its share, which made it possible to speed up construction. Still, it was five long years before the course opened on St Stephen's Day in 1992. Guests had to change in temporary trailers.

'I'm very lucky that I'm in it for the sheer love of it,' says Ruddy, who used to water the greens at night by the light of his car headlights. One night a pump beside the seventeenth green began to leak and Ruddy found himself up to his waist in water.

'I had to decide whether I was going to dive down after the valve or not. I looked up at the sky, and it was a very lonely moment for a "rich" developer. And I knew whether I did or not the next day fellows are going to say "your greens are lousy"!'

The European Club was an instant hit. The club attracted twenty thousand visitors in 1994, and critical acclaim followed.

As the club has climbed high into the global rankings there has been the usual backlash, as critics try to find fault with the upstart that has moved into such elite company. No doubt some critics are a little off put off by Ruddy's relentless and occasionally clumsy efforts at promotion.

'If you're too modest they think you know nothing and have nothing, and if you say you think you have it, they think you're pompous and a jackass,' says Ruddy, whose ready wit can become a tad caustic when he is riled.

We think a man who has created a masterpiece with little at his disposal but the love of the game should be given the benefit of the doubt.

'[How it will rank] on a world scale is very intricate, and the dividing factor at the end of the day will be the intangibles,' says Ruddy, warming to the subject. 'You're talking about soul, about feel for the game.

'There are two types of golf courses. One is the drop-from-heaven type – you get $15 million, stir it around in a bowl, throw it on a field and you have instant golf. It may not be great golf but it's very impressive. Like a lady painted to the nines in a miniskirt, it looks good. But in most cases it's not as good as it looks. It's commercially driven, not dream driven. A trading post in golf, not a golf place.'

And a golf place is what the European Club most definitely is.

The course

Pat Ruddy states his intentions from the opening tee shot. Intimidating fairway bunkers faced with railway ties give exactly the right message. The European Club is a serious test of golf.

But it is a beautiful place too. The aesthetic and strategic qualities of the course emerge forcefully on the third, a lovely par 5 that meanders ever so naturally through high dunes down towards Arklow Bay. The bunkering is restrained, rather than showy, and the effect is pure Irish links. The green is nestled in a natural amphitheatre and partially protected by the sand hills. And while there is a choice of attack, with enough room to bounce the ball onto the green, a nasty hidden bunker collects approaches from the unwary.

The majority of the holes at the European Club take their cue from the third. While Ruddy has taken pains to provide a new twist to every hole, there is a satisfying consistency of style. Typically there is a drive from an elevated tee and an intriguing channel to be followed through the dunes. The channel usually narrows as you approach the target, and well-conceived slopes and bunkers make the greens more tightly guarded than they appear from the fairway. Although we are fond of the many blind shots that distinguish Ireland's most venerable links, it must be admitted that few courses look as good from the tee as the European Club.

While Ruddy makes allowances for the average golfer with forward tees, he never panders to them.

'When Johnny Miller was here he said it was the first course he'd played with eight par 5s,' he says with genuine glee. What Miller meant, of course, is that it often *feels* as if the European Club has eight par 5s, especially from the back tees of almost 7,500 yards. In reality there are only two.

'You have guys going in with a three or four iron,' says Ruddy. 'And if you ask him to do it ten times in a round he has got to know how to play.'

Part way into the back nine there is an exhilarating change of pace. The twelfth, thirteenth and fifteenth skirt the ocean, with the beach very much in play. The contrast between the holes carved through high dunes and the relatively flat, exposed seaside holes is invigorating. The walk to the extremely elevated twelfth tee, when the ocean suddenly comes into full view, is one of the most exciting moments on a very exciting golf course.

For all his earnest efforts at the European Club, Ruddy can't resist an opportunity to have some fun (this is a man who placed a box on the scorecard so golfers could record 'What My Score Should Have Been'). He has built a couple of additional, and rather superb par 3s as holes 8A and 12A, and constructed what he claims is the longest green in the world at the twelfth.

'It's 126 yards long,' he says. 'I went over to St Andrews and played the widest double green and made this eight yards longer than it was wide. It reintroduces the great art of putting, the good three putt, as opposed to the "shit-I-missed-it" three-putt!'

While it was obviously a thrill to have Tiger Woods visit in 2002 ('It was great to see the machine being driven by the best,' Ruddy says), you get the feeling he was most pleased that the greatest golfer of the age seemed to share his notion of a golfing good time. According to Ruddy, Woods immediately wanted to try his luck at the longest putt in golf.

'I don't know if Nicklaus would have done that,' he says.

'But despite all the fun, I think we have a serious golf course, with scenery added, and fun added, but a serious golf course. I don't know of others where the designer is there working for years trying to achieve the ultimate. It may be serious golf in the wrong direction, but it's serious golf nonetheless.'

At the thirteenth we see how good Ruddy is at revising his own creation. Previously a fairly straight hole along the sea, the tee box has been moved a hundred yards or so to the left, creating a dramatic dogleg with a drive that seems to send you right into the ocean.

'If you go at the hole you go over bad land,' explains Ruddy. 'But playing it safe, for every degree off line you get five yards closer to the beach.'

The fifteenth also plays to the water's edge, and the sixteenth is a much improved par 4 that skirts some farm land. The seventeenth is an exquisite return to some of the best dunes land on the property. It is a pretty and unaffected par 4 in its own little valley, lined with gorse and a variety of bushes and grasses.

We are happy to report that Ruddy has at last done away with the only true blemish on the course, a pond on the eighteenth that he has turned into a twisting stream. It's now a fine, if brutally hard finish, and in its revised form is perhaps the last piece of Ruddy's glorious puzzle. His dream of building an outstanding modern course in true links style has come true.

In recent years, Ruddy has vastly improved the conditioning at the European Club, taken out a dozen or more bunkers (then put a few back in), altered greens, and added gorse and flowering bushes to enhance the visual experience. What he hasn't focused on are the post-golf amenities. The European Club has the most modest clubhouse of any of the world's great courses, and until recently at least, was the only one where you couldn't get a glass of beer.

But something as inconsequential as where you change your shoes isn't what drives Pat Ruddy. He's more interested in posterity.

'I don't think even in the modern age that it is possible to plop a classic down,' he says. 'It needs polishing afterwards, polishing and refining. Old ones like Pine Valley, and Oakmont, they took years. Even if you are a bit stupid, years of effort gives you a chance.'

Location: Brittas Bay, about 35 miles south of Dublin on N11, and 5 miles south of Wicklow town

Restrictions: None

Green Fee: €150

Manager: Sidon Ruddy

Address: Brittas Bay, Co. Wicklow; **tel:** (040) 447415; **fax:** (040) 447449; **e-mail:** info@theeuropeanclub.com; **web:** www.theeuropeanclub.com

THE ISLAND

Founded: 1888

Designed by: Fred Hawtree and others

The Syndicate were very careful in whoever they invited to become annual ticketholders. The invited members were from the 'best circles' and nobody who worked with their hands or whose religion differed was invited.

WILLIAM MURPHY, *A CENTURY OF GOLF ON THE ISLAND*

For close to one hundred years the only way to get to The Island was by rowing boat. And for the first half-century you needed an invitation. Originally the private preserve of a clutch of well-to-do Dublin bachelors, The Island almost went bankrupt in the 1950s, and has only recently reasserted itself as one of Ireland's premier courses. But if you think The Island's history is topsy-turvy, wait until you play the links. It's an up-and-down journey over some of the world's most rambunctious linksland. Raw and stirring, The Island

would not be out of place on Ireland's wild west coast, and there are a number of singular golf holes that burn into the memory.

✦✦✦

In 1887, four of Dublin's more eligible young men, frustrated at the prohibition on Sunday golf at the Royal Dublin Golf Club, rowed across a channel between the village of Malahide and a peninsula of all-but-deserted linksland known locally, if erroneously, as the 'island.' According to local lore, Jonathan Swift had used it for romantic outings in the seventeenth century, but for the most part the land was suitable only for grazing.

Sure that the lumpy terrain would make for terrific golf, the four headed back to Dublin, and persuaded six other men to join them in forming a syndicate to secure the land and build a course.

The group consisted of five bankers, three lawyers, a soap-making industrialist and a brewer. All were bachelors. The attraction between man and linksland can rarely have been so strong, for six of the ten never did marry – satisfied, one presumes, with the pleasures of running their own little golf paradise.

Coming from the upper crust of Dublin society, it was no great strain for the bachelors to come up with the £10 necessary to rent the property, and for the next half-century The Island prospered as the preserve of the Syndicate – as they were known by all – and their well-off Protestant friends. Only the Syndicate had any say over the development of the club, though they invited a select few to become annual ticketholders. It was not just a question of keeping out Catholics and tradesmen, a common practice at other early clubs. The Syndicate's sense of caste was more refined than that. Distinctions were made, for example, between retailers, who were deemed to be not of sufficient social standing to play the links, and wholesalers, who presumably exerted themselves less and earned considerably more.

In the Syndicate's attempts to preserve the sanctity of the club, caddies presented a special problem.

'With a view to keeping the Links as private as possible, the club desires to discourage the use of caddies,' stated regulations published in 1897. 'They are strictly prohibited on Sundays and may not be brought up on the links on that day by Club boats or otherwise, and on week days shall only be brought over when all other passengers are accommodated.'

The sense of splendid isolation that the founders craved was enhanced by the fact that there was no road to the club. All visitors arrived in a large rowing boat – it could hold twenty people – that crossed the channel at regular intervals (an arrangement that lasted until 1971). Although women were not represented in the Syndicate, they made up almost half of the ticketholders, and The Island was known as much for its social scene as for its golf course.

'I think one of the great charms of the Island is the picnicking which precedes or follows the golf,' a leading journalist of the time wrote. 'There are no distracting elements such as liquor bars, but this does not mean that a guest will be thirsty. There is no professional but the club enjoys the services of excellent boatmen, who also act as greenkeepers.'

Irish independence altered the power structure that had made The Island possible. At first the Syndicate was unmoved and continued to run the club according to the old rules. But by the 1930s, as the original Syndicate members began to lose interest or die off, and as Ireland suffered economically, the condition of the course began to deteriorate. Ticketholders from other religions and professions were let in, but few resources were allocated for the upkeep of the course, which began to resemble, quite literally, a cow pasture, as cattle damaged greens and left their droppings everywhere.

Finally, after the Second World War, the Syndicate's heirs handed the club over to the annual ticketholders – the people who actually played the course. In the next two decades the new, democratically constituted club, which had far fewer resources than the original founders, desperately tried to keep The Island afloat. A proposal to reduce the course to nine holes in 1963 was only narrowly defeated, and in 1971 the membership gave serious consideration to selling the club to an American millionaire.

But the members persevered, and their fortunes truly changed with a brave decision to take out a sizeable loan to build a new clubhouse in 1975, and to make enhancements to the course. Although the redesign was undertaken painfully slowly, over fifteen years, it was also famously successful. Today The Island is like some long-neglected but lovingly renovated old building. It has quite suddenly blossomed into one of Ireland's golfing treasures.

The course

The Island has almost nothing in common with the classic Dublin-area links of Portmarnock, Baltray and Royal Dublin. Instead, its camel-hump dunes seem imported from Ballybunion. Whereas its Dublin neighbours are graceful, spacious and only moderately undulating, The Island is twisty, hilly, cranky and unpredictable. Although the redesign removed its zaniest and most anachronistic features, the comments of an Irish writer in 1908 hold just as true today:

> No one can walk around The Island and declare the course uninteresting. It is full of weird and wonderful interest which might assume the nature of nightmares to a golfer whose unlucky star is in the ascendant . . . The hazards throughout are natural and fearful.

It is unclear who designed the original course in 1887, or who made the first set of amendments shortly before the First World War, although one can imagine the Syndicate members stalking their terrain in waistcoats, flasks in hand. Several holes remain, at least in part, from that time, including the fifth through the ninth, and the eleventh and twelfth.

The recent enhancements are a rare example of a historic course that has been made substantially better. The British architect Fred Hawtree mapped out the changes in 1973. These were slowly implemented with the assistance of Eddie Hackett. The revised layout respects the often crazy, natural terrain and thus retains some of the quirky and charming character of the original course. It also remains true that no two holes at The Island are much alike.

Notable among the new additions are the rather grand first hole, an uphill par 4 cut through an enormous sand bank, and a strong finishing stretch. But some of the most memorable holes are leftovers from the previous course. The best may be the thirteenth, a cliff-side carry of 200 yards across an inlet. And next up is the notoriously skinny fourteenth – a short par 4 that slithers like an eel along the water's edge (recently the hole has been lengthened and its green slightly enlarged).

The two nines are quite different in character. The short front side, with eight tight par 4s and one par 3, is at once claustrophobic and charming. The fifth and the eighth, with their blind tee shots and zany, undulating fairways, have a strong nineteenth-century flavour.

The back nine is tougher and bigger, starting with Hawtree's long par-5 tenth; it's a hundred yards longer than any hole on the front, and tempts long hitters to flirt dangerously with an out-of-bounds fence. The contrasting quality of the nines is compelling, and every round is made more memorable by terrific views of Ireland's Eye, and of sailboats in the harbour.

Martin Hawtree, son of the designer whose work has served The Island so well, has drawn up a master plan for the club that would alter some of the idiosyncrasies of the routing, and break up the unusual opening sequence of eight par 4s.

'It's so unclassical in its format, with the first short hole coming at the ninth, and with what some would call ridiculously narrow fairways at the eighth and fourteenth' Hawtree says. 'Of course, you can also argue that they are unique features of the place, and quite intriguing.'

Although Hawtree has already implemented some modifications to three greens, the club seems in no hurry to launch into a more radical overhaul. Hawtree says his master plan has been 'diluted in committees' and that at a recent club meeting, a decision on the next phase of his work was put off due to a lack of a quorum.

If, after a generation of uncertainty, the members at The Island seem pretty content with what they have, who can blame them? Word about the quality of their revitalized links has spread quickly, and visitors are now charged some rather stiff green fees. However, the air of elitism that characterized the club's early years has disappeared for good. After almost 120 years, you could say that The Island has finally come of age.

Location: Four miles from Dublin Airport; take R126 east off the M1 and follow to end. You are sure to get lost at least once

Restrictions: Visitors are welcome at designated times on weekdays (no times available Wednesday afternoons), and on weekends after 3:30 p.m.

Green Fee: €125

Secretary-Manager: Peter McDunphy

Address: Corballis, Donabate, Co. Dublin; **tel:** (01) 843-6205; **fax:** (01) 843-6860; **e-mail:** info@theislandgolfclub.com; **web:** www.theislandgolfclub.com

LAYTOWN AND BETTYSTOWN

Founded: 1908

Designed by: The Members

Other players [on tour] would see a difficult pitch, but I was so used to seeing tight sandy lies at Bettystown that whenever I saw a little grass under the ball it looked easy.

DES SMYTH

Located just across the River Boyne from Baltray, the rollicking links at Laytown and Bettystown is definitely worth a visit on its own merits. You will find golf holes and shots of every shape and description here, and it is no wonder that it produced Des Smyth, one of Ireland's gentlest but most enduring golf stars.

Can there be a more idyllic place to grow up than the holiday village of Bettystown in the Ireland of the 1960s? Not according to Des Smyth.

'I started hitting it up and down the beach when I was five years old, no different from anyone else,' he tells us over the phone from Texas, where he is competing in the latest PGA Champions Tour event.

'Money didn't mean anything because nobody had any,' says Smyth, whose father was a butcher. 'It was perfect. We knew everyone in every house and you could walk in any front door and get a glass of milk and a biscuit.'

In the summer, life in Bettystown revolved around the golf club, with its links course and tennis courts. It was situated about a mile down the coastal road from the village.

'We'd join up [for the year] for about five dollars in American terms,' he says. 'We'd often play thirty-six holes in a day, except when there was a junior tennis tournament, and then we'd play eighteen. During the week, the senior members only played after work, so we'd have the course to ourselves most of the time.

'And in the evenings the tennis club would organize hops, with bands playing in the hall in the golf club. There was never any fighting or any problems. At the end of the summer you went back to school and lived your normal life.'

Smyth's rosy recollections may seem too good to be true, a kind of Irish version of *Happy Days*. But there can be no denying that conditions at Bettystown must have been conducive to learning the game of golf. The club produced more fine golfers in the mid-1960s than any other in Ireland. They included Smyth's brother Val – who old-timers will tell you struck the ball better than Des – and Declan Branigan; both represented Ireland internationally.

'One year I started to practise through the winter,' remembers Smyth. 'A summer later I was as good as most of the guys. And then the next summer no one could beat me.'

'Looking back, the club produced so many quality players. Certainly it was the small elevated greens that developed iron play and the short game. In those days golf was all about arms and hands.'

Smyth's golfing education was made possible by the foresight of a couple of local farming families who laid out the first course before the First World War. The Laytown and Bettystown club was formed in 1909, and it began to thrive as the area became popular as a small holiday resort in the 1930s. Visitors would join the club for a month or two during the summer and then head back to Drogheda or Dublin.

The course itself has always been a work in progress. Though the club has from time to time brought in professional golf architects to have a look, it has ultimately always decided to do things its own way. Though individual holes may change, the marvellous golfing terrain has not.

And neither has the camaraderie in the clubhouse. For Des Smyth, it was a much-loved anchor in a life that was, by its very nature, going to be itinerant.

'I turned professional when I was twenty, and was basically on the road after that,' he says. 'All my socializing was done at the club.'

Incredibly, for a two-time Ryder Cup team member, Smyth only played one tournament in the United States before his fiftieth birthday, the Bay Hill Classic in 1989. And you have to wonder if his love of his home area is at least partly responsible. Smyth eventually married a woman from 'the other side of the river [Boyne]' (he makes it sound like another country), and now spends a lot of time at Baltray and at nearby Seapoint, which he helped design. It is all of ten miles from where he grew up and his ties with Laytown and Bettystown remain strong.

A massive portrait of Smyth now dominates a staircase in the clubhouse and on the walls you will find details of his exploits, which are remarkable. They include eight victories on the European tour (spread over four decades), and appearances in five World Cups for Ireland. He also played on five Dunhill Cup teams, and his 1988 victory at St Andrews with Ronan Rafferty and Eamonn Darcy caused something of a sensation in Ireland.

When Smyth finally went to America in 2004 to play the Senior Tour, he achieved instant success, earning more than $3 million and winning two tournaments in his first three years. Smyth was also vice-captain of the winning European Ryder Cup team in 2006, a tremendous honour with the event taking place in his home country for the first time.

There's another honour, just on the horizon, that you feel will be as satisfying to Des Smyth as any other he has received. In 2009, the centenary of Laytown and Bettystown, he will be Captain of the club that has meant so much to him.

The course

Bettystown (as the links is usually called) is one of those courses with a charm and variety that only comes from *not* having a single designer associated with it.

The 300-yard par-4 first is one of those holes – too short to please most golf architects, but tight and fun (and more than a bit scary in a wind) for a mid-handicapper.

The second used to be a long, partially blind par 3, the site of many a practical joke by Des Smyth and his pals.

'We'd hide in the banks and if we saw an old farty four ball, and one of them slipped it over the hill we'd put the ball in the hole and then watch their reaction,' he says, before adding just a bit apologetically – 'just a bit of fun, you know'.

You might be thankful for such assistance on what is the second hole today; a heavily undulating par 4 that requires a strong second to clear a hollow in front of a sharply elevated green. It's the start of a great stretch of tumbling golf holes that takes you uphill in the exciting manner of Ballybunion, with approaches to dune-protected green locations made even trickier by off-kilter and slick links terrain. Indifferent chip shots can see the ball roll right off the green again.

It all leads to three new holes laid out by the members only a few years ago. The sixth is a lovely par 3 with a plateau green, and views of the sea and the Mountains of Mourne in the distance. Then there's an exciting downhill par 4 over a lone tree that, while surely out of place on a links course, adds a peculiar dimension to a hole that narrows dramatically near the green to tease the long hitters.

After one more decent, uphill par 4 we are now high in dune country again, to contemplate the ninth, a fantastic par 3 with a green partly hidden in sand dunes that wouldn't look out of place at Carne.

It is a peculiar, almost quirky front side, and as much fun as any in Ireland.

After the excellent and stern par-4 tenth, the terrain on the inward half is noticeably flatter. And while some extra length gives the holes backbone, and demands some serious golf, they are not quite as enjoyable.

It is only right, however, that Bettystown's engaging personality reasserts itself on the closing holes.

The seventeenth is a cute, short par 4 around a dune, and (now that Dooks has been redesigned) the eighteenth is the most singular finishing hole in Irish links golf.

It's an old-fashioned classic, a looping dogleg par 5 requiring at least a couple of leaps of faith. The fairway is mostly hidden on the tee shot, which is hit through rough dunes, and for those who want to go for the green in two (the hole is only about 475 yards) there's another wall of dunes about fifty yards before the green. It may sound strange, but somehow these blind shots seem fair and challenging rather than bizarre.

It will certainly give you a talking point as you tally up your score (and it will be higher than you think it should be) in Des Smyth's favourite bar.

Location: On R150, just north of the village of Bettystown and just south of the River Boyne

Restrictions: None, though access will be easier on weekdays

Green Fee: €60–75

Secretary: Helen Finnegan

Address: Bettystown, Co. Meath; **tel:** (041) 982-7170; **fax:** (041) 982-8506; **e-mail:** links@landb.ie; **web:** www.landb.ie

PORTMARNOCK

Founded: 1894

Designed by: W. C. Pickeman and others

The charm of Portmarnock is difficult to describe. There is little sign of artificiality, and it is one of the most natural links in the world.

HAROLD HILTON, 1902

Only ten miles north of Dublin, Portmarnock is a world classic. Understated and enchanting, ever changing in the most natural of ways, yet full of energy, intelligence and beauty, Portmarnock is like a great piece of classical music – its genius seems to come from within. There is no reason to expect that such a course should evolve here – there are more interesting stretches of linksland, and there has been no famous architect to guide things. Yet the value of Portmarnock, like St Andrews, seems only to grow over time.

As Royal Portrush is to the North, Portmarnock is to the Republic – an undeniably great golf course that has been at the centre of things since golf was established in Ireland. Even the land Portmarnock sits on has a famous pedigree, as it was owned by the Jamesons, the great distilling family, and for years a Jameson was president of the club. The club's flagpole came from the family yacht. To be at the centre of Dublin society in the nineteenth century meant being Protestant, of course, so that's what Portmarnock was. The club's first professional was admonished for 'compromising matters by taking an Irish wife'.

It didn't take long for Portmarnock to acquire a reputation, both for the quality of its golf course and for being one of Ireland's most desirable clubs. By the turn of the twentieth century the great amateur Harold Hilton had called it the 'most natural links in the world', and by 1905 there were 350 members and a waiting list to get in. In the same year the fine clubhouse, still in use, was built.

Women were not allowed to join, however. The first mixed foursome competition at the club was met with shock by many members, who argued that 'the club had fallen from its high estate in sanctioning such a competition'. In fairness, however, there has always been a gallant side to the club's chauvinism. Until 1905 no green fee was charged to women, who were allowed to play during the week, and Portmarnock has held the Irish Ladies Championship three times. Portmarnock was also the site of the British Ladies Amateur in 1931.

Although women are still not able to join, Portmarnock changed with the times in other respects. The honorary secretary in 1921, for example, was both Irish and a Catholic. But the club has remained, until this day, a refuge for Ireland's elite.

When Eddie Hackett became the professional at Portmarnock in 1939 he was told to remove his car from the parking lot and to eat his lunch in the kitchen.

'That's just the way it was in those days,' he told us in an interview. 'The professionals saluted the members. I didn't mind, I loved the game so much.'

If no one seems to hold a grudge against Portmarnock, despite its occasional airs, it is perhaps because the members have always known that the most important thing about the place is the miraculous golf course itself. The club has hosted countless Irish and international tournaments and visiting golfers have always been given a cordial welcome.

'The club is exceptionally hospitable to strangers,' wrote Englishman Edward Markwick in the *Golfer's Magazine* of August 1900. 'When properly introduced, you are accorded a week's free play; and your bodily comforts will be excellently looked after by a very obliging steward. If you are alone you will presently be accosted by some member and offered a game, and a drink, with the genial hospitality so peculiarly Irish.'

There is an appealing air of mystery about the origins of the great links, though it is established that William Chalmers Pickeman, a Scottish insurance executive, rowed over to evaluate the golfing potential of the peninsula on Christmas Eve in 1893. Pickeman designed a number of the very early Irish courses, and since Portmarnock was his pride and joy (he was honorary secretary until 1917) it is probable that he is responsible for getting the links on the right track. He certainly had a hand in early designs, and he may have been assisted by Mungo Park, who served as professional for one year.

On the whole, however, Portmarnock seems to have mostly evolved.

PORTMARNOCK

The first greens were placed on the most natural sites available, and tees, fairways and hazards were more or less put where they had to be, given the impossibility of moving earth. Not that things remained static. As the decades passed the members added bunkers, extended tees, moved the odd green, and even added a hole or two (the last addition being the dramatic par-3 fifteenth, in the 1930s). But the course never underwent an extensive remodelling. The integrity of the original links, dictated by nature, seems to be intact.

Today, Portmarnock is over 7,000 yards from the championship tees, and has withstood challenges from the greatest players in the game. It is interesting that no fewer than seven Masters champions have won tournaments at Portmarnock (Sam Snead, Arnold Palmer, Ben Crenshaw, Bernhard Langer, José-María Olazábal, Seve Ballesteros and Ian Woosnam) for the course shares certain features with Augusta National – both have surprisingly generous but undulating fairways, and each demands approach shots of uncommon skill to carefully guarded and difficult-to-hold greens.

In recent years, many of the world's great players have been introduced to Portmarnock at the Irish Open, played here on twelve occasions between 1976 and 1990, and again in 2003. But while Portmarnock will undoubtedly remain the finest links course never to host a British Open, it has a surprisingly rich history of hosting other major competitions. In 1949, for example, one of golf's major championships, the British Amateur, was played at Portmarnock, a situation made possible due to southern Ireland's ambiguous status as a Free State within the British Commonwealth. Before the tournament the Irish Prime Minister declared Ireland a Republic, but the tournament went ahead as scheduled, and was won by Max McCready.

In 1991, the Walker Cup was held at Portmarnock. The American team, led by Phil Mickelson, won by 14 to 10. Mickelson created a bit of a sensation in the practice round by hitting two balls onto the fifteenth green – one left-handed and one right-handed.

But the most important tournament ever played at Portmarnock was the 1960 Canada Cup (later renamed the World Cup). In the 1958 Canada Cup, played in Mexico, Portmarnock's club professional Harry Bradshaw had teamed with Christy O'Connor to win the Cup for Ireland. The victory caused great excitement in Ireland, where golf had been in the doldrums for many years, and the 1960 event at Portmarnock was played in glorious weather in front of colossal galleries. It didn't hurt, either, that Arnold

Palmer was on hand to lead the United States to victory, in partnership with Sam Snead. Even today, that tournament is cited as a turning point in the popularity of golf in Ireland. Once again, Portmarnock was at the centre of things.

Which begs the question why Portmarnock was not on the world's television screens during the 2006 Ryder Cup, held instead on the lush parkland fairways of the K Club.

'A course like Portmarnock would have been a magnificent choice,' lamented television commentator Peter Alliss, a former Ryder Cup player. 'I care passionately about this event, so I find this rather sad, losing the Irishness of links golf. It's all because of money, money, money.'

Former European Tour executive director Ken Schofield, who was closely involved in the selection of the Ryder Cup venue, admitted the obvious: 'Portmarnock bowed out – they couldn't afford the bidding war.'

The course

Portmarnock starts in a serene and welcoming way, with a short, easy par 4 along an estuary separating the peninsula from the mainland (the green has recently been moved a little closer to the water). It's the last time salt water comes into play on the course until the fifteenth, and for the most part Portmarnock's attractions are something you feel in your bones rather than see. Since the links is sealed off on three sides by the sea, the impression is one of seclusion, and there are few elevated points to remind you of what is out there, beyond the linksland. Everything seems designed to help the golfer focus on the task at hand.

The next couple of holes are also short par 4s, but far more confusing and challenging. The fairways are less well-defined and the greens are bunkered in a quirky and dangerous manner. These are classic examples of holes that you just know you will birdie *next time*.

Now Portmarnock flexes its muscles, with three very long and splendidly natural holes through graceful dunes. The fourth and fifth have only one bunker between them. After the short seventh, there are four more classic par 4s.

By this time it will be clear that you will be playing low to the ground at Portmarnock, in the fashion of the older Scottish links, and that the view from the tee will tell you very little. Even when the drives aren't out-and-out blind, it is still difficult to see exactly where to play. The holes curl in one direction, then another, and the landing area is often partially concealed by fescue-covered hills. The greens are just as unsettling. The quirky swales, formed by the elements, don't adhere to expected patterns, and the size, or even existence, of the pot bunkers is not always obvious.

Although all of the holes are good, the fourteenth and fifteenth have probably generated more praise than any others. Henry Cotton, so it is said, thought the fourteenth to be the greatest hole in golf, and while that is surely an exaggeration there are few holes where birdie looks so plausible and bogey is so much more likely. It is only about 380 yards from the men's tees, and the beautifully natural plateau green looks enticing from any position on the fairway. It is only when you get to the putting surface that you realize how tightly guarded it is, with slopes that reject all but the best shots into severe pot bunkers.

The greatness of the fifteenth, a long but lovely par 3 along the shoreline, is apparent from the tee. The sudden view of the Irish Sea, after so many holes played in the middle of the linksland, is rather startling, and complicated by the knowledge that the ball could land on the beach. The rough to the left of the convex green is no treat either, and the wind is always stronger here than at any other place on the course.

If your nerves are still steady and you can avoid the panoply of fairway bunkers, then the short par-5 sixteenth offers a birdie opportunity. Don't expect similar chances on the final two holes, both par 4s, which are long and uncompromising.

Portmarnock may not have trademark features – such as the giant dunes of Ballybunion, the flowering whins of County Down, or the dramatically shaped fairways of Royal Portrush. In common with the Old Course at St Andrews, Portmarnock invites metaphors, not photographs. It is a mood as much as a place, its charm an accumulated effect of the variety, intelligence and grace of the layout. There is a wonderful sense of proportion at Portmarnock, a feeling that every piece is in the perfect place. If Mozart had been a golf architect, this would have been his masterpiece.

Location: Ten miles north of Dublin; just south of Malahide on R106

Restrictions: There are tee times available for visitors on weekdays (except Wednesdays), as well as limited availability on Saturday afternoons and Sundays.

Green Fee: €165–190

Manager: John J. Quigley

Address: Portmarnock, Co. Dublin; **tel:** (01) 846-2968; **fax:** (01) 846-2601;
e-mail: secretary@portmarnockgolfclub.ie **web:** www.portmarnockgolfclub.ie

PORTMARNOCK HOTEL

Course Built: 1995
Designed by: Bernhard Langer and Stan Eby

As well as golf, a selection of outdoor activities such as archery, clay pigeon shooting or even quad-bikes can be arranged to provide escape from a hectic conference schedule.

LINKS AT PORTMARNOCK BROCHURE

It has always been difficult to find much that is inspiring about the golf hotel developed by the late sports agent Mark McCormack, with its soulless corporate focus, and its attempt to benefit, by name association, from its famous neighbour. Yet, for all that, the links itself has a surprising amount of character.

Given the lacklustre history of the infuriatingly named 'Links at Portmarnock', the news in the *Sunday Times* in 2005 was at least novel.

The 140-bed hotel and golf course property had been purchased for €60 million. The price was hardly a surprise given Dublin's super-heated property market. What was unusual, according to the *Sunday Times*, was that the new owners wanted to *swap it for another course entirely*.

The idea was to trade the course, lock, stock and barrel, to an existing Dublin golf club, which would in turn vacate its own golf course so that a housing development could be built on it. The members would make a killing, and so, presumably, would the property developers.

But then the Links at Portmarnock has always been a business enterprise first and foremost.

Developed in 1995 by the International Management Group (IMG) of the late Mark McCormack, the agent for Arnold Palmer, Tiger Woods and a host of other superstars, the course and hotel should never be confused with the 'real' Portmarnock further along the Velvet Strand. There are no full golf members here, though the hotel does a good business in weddings and corporate meetings.

Promotional literature brazenly refers to the hotel course being 'founded in 1891', an allusion, one supposes, to the fact that the Jameson family (of whiskey fame) played some golf here on a long since abandoned nine-hole track.

Today's course was built in the early 1990s, and the project represented an opportunity to develop one of the last true links courses on the planet. What IMG apparently saw, however, was an opportunity to raise the stock of one of their clients – Bernhard Langer. Though the German professional had little design experience at the time, he was installed as the head architect; in-house designer Stan Eby would do most of the work. The idea of a celebrity architect, backed up by a sort of 'ghost designer', was a marketing gimmick that McCormack helped invent with his first client, Arnold Palmer. And while the result is rarely a world-class golf course, it has tended to make money for everyone concerned.

The course

Eby says Langer made several visits to the site, and he is careful to emphasize the German professional's contribution. However much involvement Langer actually had in the design, the personality of the Portmarnock Hotel course is uncannily like that of Langer the golfer – intelligent but overly deliberate.

The routing is decent enough, with good use of doglegs and fine green locations, and the bunkering is nothing if not thorough. There are about one hundred bunkers in all, and while they add to the strategic challenge of the round, they are overly uniform in shape, and rather too obviously positioned. As a result, the holes sometimes feel like something laid out on a draughting table.

'Bernhard wanted to make sure there was nothing funny about the holes,' says Eby. While the comment is no doubt intended as a compliment, it alludes to the major flaw in the course – the lack of whimsy or unexpected pleasures, and a reluctance to let the land speak for itself.

After a fairly bland stretch of opening holes (enlivened immensely by a cemetery on the first, as at Ballybunion!), the interest begins to build in earnest on the seventh, which requires an unsettling drive over whins. The eighth is a lively dogleg left with an elevated green set in dunes, and number nine is very natural short par 3 to another raised green.

The back nine is played almost entirely in energetic duneland, and begins well with a challenging driving hole that features a six-pack of circular bunkers on the left side for the overly bold. A series of good holes leads to the fifteenth, an excellent par 4 that plays over a couple of oddly shaped (at last!) bunkers at the neck of the dogleg, and then to a green guarded on the left by two more pot bunkers.

The sixteenth is perhaps the best drive on the course, a hugely elevated tee shot where you have to decide on the lesser of two evils, bunkers on the right or gorse and heavy rough on the left. The seventeenth is a strong par 3 and there is a more than respectable finish through an alley of dunes to a raised green.

If, in the end, the care taken in designing the course is rather too obvious, it is still an invigorating round of golf.

Afterwards, you could try to find an authentic Irish pub, but the well-appointed drinking facilities in the Hotel will probably be too much of a temptation. And here, at least, there is some real history worth noting. The bar area was once part of the former mansion of the Jameson family, renowned for their excellent Irish whiskey.

Location: Just south of Malahide on R106

Restrictions: None

Green Fee: €125 (discounts for hotel residents)

Golf Director: Moira Cassidy

Address: Portmarnock, Co. Dublin; **tel:** (01) 846-0611; **fax:** (01) 846-2442; **e-mail:** golfers@portmarnock.com; **web:** www.portmarnock.com

ROSSLARE

Founded: 1905

Designed by: Fred Hawtree, the Members

Rosslare is indeed a fine course in the making, and now that the club owns the links and the ground adjoining, there are great possibilities about the place as a golfing holiday resort.

THE IRISH FIELD, 3 APRIL 1926

It is hard not to warm to the village of Rosslare, with its loveable and affordable links golf, and very Irish holiday atmosphere. The combination of a microclimate just a bit sunnier than the rest of Ireland, wide sandy beaches and pure linksland has proved irresistible to generations of families from both Ireland and the United Kingdom (the ferry from Fishguard, Wales, lands only seven miles away). There's no getting around the fact that Rosslare is a bit out of the way to fit into the itinerary of the nomadic golfing tourist, but a visit will be amply rewarded.

◆◆◆

'We call it the hangover classic,' says Austin Skerritt, with a twinkle in his eye. The long time and much-loved professional at Rosslare is speaking about a year-end golf tournament for the staff of the nearby Kelly's Hotel.

'The staff dinner is on Sunday night. And we have the classic on the Monday morning. One year I asked the local sergeant to come down in uniform and ask the golfers to blow into the (breathalyzer) bag. The one who scored the highest got a bottle of whiskey!'

We were delighted to catch up with Skerritt, one of the great gentlemen of Irish golf, just before his retirement as head professional at Rosslare. For more than a quarter century he personified the down-to-earth, laid back hospitality for which the club is renowned.

Skerritt is the son of a Lahinch butcher, and one of seven golfing brothers who had 'a handicap of 4 or 5 combined.' Three became professionals, including Paddy, who led the 1967 British Open at Carnoustie after 45 holes.

'We caddied for our school books,' Austin Skerritt remembers. 'And in Lahinch, in the shops, nothing was spoken expect golf.'

Today, Rosslare has some of the same relaxed feel that Lahinch used to have. And while you won't read much about Rosslare in the golf guides, this terrific course on the (relatively) sunny south-east coast of Ireland is very much part of Ireland's golfing fabric.

Rosslare was one place where family holidays and golf came together, and in this regard the club's history is inevitably intertwined with that of Kelly's Hotel, a Rosslare institution that predates the golf course's founding in 1905. The current proprietor's great grandfather, one William Kelly, was instrumental in keeping the club afloat when the original developer went bankrupt in 1908.

That was good business, of course, and the hotel and the club benefited from the relationship. The first members of the club were generally the elite of nearby Wexford, especially bankers, and club competitions were timed to co-ordinate with the arrival of trains from the town. According to Tom Williams, the club's historian, 'those engaged in trade, salesmen and factory workers were …rejected out of hand' for membership.

Wexford had been a centre of rebellion since at least the time of Oliver Cromwell (who killed thousands in reprisal), and it is perhaps not surprising that the golfing ambitions of the local establishment met with hearty resistance. When the club expanded the course to eighteen holes in the late 1920s, local farmers physically stopped the work for a time, and the greenkeeper was repeatedly threatened. Reports of vandalism of greens and fairways by donkeys, goats, sheep and cows continued for several decades.

Tough times after the Second World War meant that the club couldn't be so choosy about its membership, and by the 1960s the era of social elitism was a distant memory. Rosslare hit its stride again after Austin Skerritt arrived in 1968. He organized a pro-am tournament that attracted the leading Irish professionals and garnered nation-wide attention. And when Kelly's Hotel reopened after a complete renovation, Skerritt began a golf school there that only gained momentum as the years went by.

Over the years thousands took instruction, and more than half were usually beginners, so it's safe to say that few individuals in Ireland can have introduced more people to golf than Austin Skerritt.

Though Kelly's Hotel has played a big part in bringing in paying visitors, Rosslare remains a members' club, and it is the members who have had to battle with the Irish sea. The treacherous waters around the course have sunk no fewer than 124 ships, and have also claimed several original golf holes, and a clubhouse, through relentless erosion. Scientists suggest the expansion of the nearby harbour has played its part too. The club has spent the better part of a century, and a great deal of money, coming up with schemes to protect the shoreline, and rearranging holes when that hasn't worked. Only in recent years has the battle begun to go the members' way.

The course

The original nine-hole course at Rosslare was extended to eighteen holes in 1928 with the help of British designer Fred Hawtree, and the newest holes (roughly holes four through thirteen) are on the more rambunctious links terrain. Given that continual alterations have been necessary to counteract the damage inflicted by Mother Nature, it is a tribute to the club that the present layout retains so much charm.

The opening two holes actually play through and around some trees, but then the links character of the course asserts itself with authority. There are a series of increasingly wild holes, some with heavily undulating fairways, culminating in the exhilarating par-5 seventh that winds its way through muscular dunes right along the ocean. If you've been stumbling to this point, you can forget a low round, because the eighth is where the course turns around, and in classic links fashion you fight the prevailing breeze for most of the back nine. The eleventh is the best hole on the course, a gigantic and original par 4. The fairway is cut into two by a wild ridge, which forces a blind approach to a wonderfully sunken green (it used to be a par 5, and probably should still be).

Few of the tees are elevated at Rosslare, and finding the fairway with a drive is often intimidating and unsettling. This is certainly the case on holes twelve and thirteen. Then comes the fourteenth, a fiendishly difficult 160-yard par 3 directly towards the sea that calls for a low punch shot that can somehow both carry the front bunker *and* stop on the green.

Into the prevailing wind the fifteenth and seventeenth are macho par fours that can break all but the sturdiest of games, and it is almost disorienting to finish with a gentle par 5, downwind at last, with a green nestled between a stone fence and a few trees.

In recent years, Rosslare has added an additional twelve-hole course, called the Burrow, designed by Christy O'Connor Jr, which helps to soak up many of the high handicappers taking advantage of the many 'golf getaway' packages offered by Kelly's. Some of the holes are on excellent terrain, and offer the club an insurance policy if erosion gobbles up any more holes on the championship course.

Even if you aren't staying at Kelly's, you should check out its astonishing collection of modern Irish art, which make a gorgeous, if somewhat incongruous, backdrop for its decidedly middle-brow clientele.

In a country chock-a-block with links courses, Rosslare is surprisingly isolated. Heading west, the next links course is Waterville, a distance of more than 200 miles. On the other hand, it's not far from the famous Waterford Crystal factory, and that's how Deane Beman, long-time head of the American PGA Tour, discovered Rosslare. He used to visit Waterford regularly to check on the trophies being made for PGA tournaments.

Location: Immediately north of the village of Rosslare on the coastal road; 5 miles north of Rosslare Harbour and 10 miles south of Wexford

Restrictions: None

Green Fee: €40–60

Manager: John Hanrick

Address: Rosslare, Co. Wexford; **tel:** (053) 913-2203; **fax:** (053) 913-2263; **e-mail:** office@rosslaregolf.com; **web:** www.rosslaregolf.com

ROYAL DUBLIN

Founded: 1885

Designed by: H. S. Colt; revisions by Martin Hawtree

Made Possible by: Captain Bligh

By any standards, this is as good a traditional links as you will get.

CHRISTY O'CONNOR SR

One of the oldest and most historic clubs in Ireland, and indeed the world, Royal Dublin is a subtle and intelligent links on an island that appeared magically in Dublin Harbour in the nineteenth century. The island is also a bird sanctuary, and there is an unlikely sense of seclusion on this traditional and relatively flat golfing ground that today lies in the shadow of factory chimneys, only fifteen minutes from the heart of the capital. This used to be the most exclusive club in Ireland, but the staff and members at Royal Dublin are genuinely happy to see you.

◆◆◆

Not many clubs can claim to have helped change the course of golf history, but Royal Dublin is one of them.

The club's initial eighteen-hole course (the first in Ireland) was laid out on Easter Monday in 1885 by a Scottish banker named Lumsden, who tramped around Dublin's Phoenix Park with eighteen jam jars and the same number of red flags. Golfers all around the world should be glad he did, because the next year the newly formed Dublin Golf Club was patronized by the most famous and influential golfer in the world at the time.

Arthur Balfour wasn't a great golfer (he had an eleven handicap) but he was one of the most dashing politicians of his day. Ireland was still part of the United Kingdom, and Balfour had recently taken up the extremely sensitive position of Irish Secretary. A predecessor in the position had been assassinated in Phoenix Park by Irish separatists only two years earlier, and Lord Balfour's determination to play his weekly round of golf at the Dublin Golf Club, no matter what the risk, became the talk of Britain. He took a modest bodyguard of two detectives with him, one to carry his clubs and the other to act as forecaddie. This demonstration of golfing courage contributed to the Balfour legend and helped to ignite the golf frenzy that soon overtook the upper classes in England, Ireland and America. (Between 1885 and the turn of the century, the number of golf courses outside Scotland grew from a handful to over one thousand.)

Dubliners who used Phoenix Park for other purposes were baffled by the game. As was the fashion of the time, members of the Dublin Golf Club wore a red coat and knickerbockers as a kind of warning signal to passers-by, and members of the club were soon dubbed the 'Red Loonies.'

Though famous throughout the golfing world, Phoenix Park became soggy in the winter months, and the indefatigable Lumsden persuaded the club to move to an island in Dublin harbour that owed its existence to, of all people, William Bligh. In the early 1800s, before the Bounty set out on its infamous voyage, Bligh helped to chart Dublin Bay for the British Admiralty. One of his recommendations was that a wall be built in Dublin harbour to prevent silting in the shipping lanes. Bligh's suggestion worked, and the soil that was displaced created an island on top of a submerged sandbank on the other side of the wall.

By 1890 North Bull Island had grown to 600 acres, with a sandy soil that was perfect for links golf. The course was laid out by Thomas Gilroy, Royal Dublin's first captain and unquestionably the best player in Ireland in the nineteenth century. Gilroy was so good that Ireland's first handicapping system used his scores as the definition of 'scratch'!

Given the island's youthful age, the terrain for the new links was rather flat, but its beautiful turf (at a time when course maintenance was primitive) and proximity to downtown Dublin (only a fifteen minute ride by horse and carriage) made it the club of choice for Dublin's elite. Membership fees dwarfed those at most other clubs, and the members had the means to build Ireland's largest clubhouse, complete with staff quarters, clubmaking shop (the young Eddie Hackett, later to become Ireland's greatest architect, worked there in the 1920s) and a residence for the club professional.

More than a quarter of Royal Dublin's membership were lawyers, and the legal fraternity's fascination with the game was the subject of many jokes, including one printed in the *Irish Golfer* in 1899:

Judge (to small boy whose head only tops the front of witness box):

'Do you know the nature of an oath lad?'
Boy: 'Yes, Sir, I used to be your caddie.'

It was a golden age for Royal Dublin. Also known as Dollymount, after an adjacent neighbourhood on the mainland, the club was patronized by a series of Royal Viceroys to Ireland, who underwrote tournaments that attracted the greatest players of the age. In 1910, the London-based writer Bernard Darwin called Dollymount one of his favourite courses, and Royal Dublin's young club professional, Michael Moran, was fast becoming one of the sport's dominant players. Moran won five straight Irish professional championships in 1909–1913, and at the age of twenty-five came third in the British Open of 1913, despite a third round of 89. His nickname of 'Dyke' was apparently used widely in Ireland to indicate a birdie.

Like so much in the world of the Anglo-Irish, Royal Dublin's golden age came to a crashing halt in 1914. The course was taken over by the British military as a training facility, and the grand clubhouse became an officer's mess. Michael Moran, just reaching the prime years of golfing life, died at the front.

By the time the members of Royal Dublin got their links back, the southern part of Ireland was independent and the country had endured a mean and bloody civil war. Royal Dublin quickly began the process of rebuilding. Before departing, the British military had paid the club £10,000 (an enormous sum at the time) to repair damage to the clubhouse, and the club's largely Protestant membership, though hardly thrilled at the prospect of Irish independence, were not as vulnerable to the winds of change as the landed aristocracy who had spearheaded the formation of golf courses in other parts of the country. There seems never to have been a thought to take the 'Royal' out of the club's name, despite Ireland's new status.

There were enough resources to engage H. S. Colt, one of the premier architects of the age, to redesign the links. His work met with immediate acclaim, though some of his plateau greens wouldn't take, due to the extremely porous nature of the sandy soil on North Bull Island.

Disaster struck again during the Second World War, this time in the form of a fire that destroyed the fine old clubhouse. By some accounts, this may have been a blessing in disguise. The trials and deprivations of the war, combined with the intimacy of a temporary clubhouse, seem to have broken down social barriers. Though still an exclusive club, Royal Dublin was perhaps more Irish than it had ever been before.

As the explosion in interest in professional golf took hold in the 1960s, Royal Dublin played host to several championships, including the Irish Open in 1984 and 1985. The course produced two memorable winners – Seve Ballesteros and Bernhard Langer. In fine weather, Langer finished twenty-one under par to win by four shots, and he fired a course record 64 as well.

The latest chapter in Royal Dublin's evolution began in 2006, with the completion of a significant overhaul by Martin Hawtree.

In reviewing the course, Hawtree says he didn't feel the front nine had retained much of Colt's genius, perhaps because of military use of the ground during the Second World War.

'But I saw more evidence of Colt in the shaping on the back nine. And the sixteenth seemed to me a classic Colt short par 4.'

Though Hawtree has rerouted the sixth through eighth holes, his major contribution has been to reintroduce raised greens, a feature of Colt's original design.

'We raised low-lying greens with imported filling material,' says Hawtree. 'This allowed me to get more hollows and deeper bunkers, and more links features.'

All eighteen greens have been redeveloped, a project that Hawtree says had the full blessing of the membership.

'If it were in England a lot of the older members would not want bulldozers around. But at Royal Dublin the older members were saying "This is not for me, its for my grandchildren".'

Or grandsons, at least. Women are allowed to play Royal Dublin as guests, but cannot join as members. It is surely ironic that one of the most famous clubs in the country, which did so much to foster golf in Ireland (and elsewhere), should be, in this respect at least, so absurdly behind the times.

The course

On our first visit to Royal Dublin, in the days before the Euro, we were joined on the first tee by Pierce, a member of the club for twenty-five years who was, he explained, recovering from a triple bypass operation.

'We'll play a pound, pound, pound, then,' he informed us, pulling a sweater over his rain jacket. The tone in his voice was not one that invited objections. Then he asked us for our handicaps, calculated how many strokes we would give him, and pulled out a driver that looked at least sixty years old. After watching us butcher our first shots, he stroked a low screamer right down the middle that seemed to roll forever.

The match was already doomed, of course, but we didn't mind. For Pierce was both a charming companion and an invaluable guide through Royal Dublin's hidden obstacles.

Writing in 1910, Bernard Darwin noted that at first Royal Dublin 'looks a little flat, and bare, and even dull; we do not see where the holes are and whence and whither the players are going and what they are trying to do.'

Almost a century later, we were still not entirely sure what lay ahead. With so few spots of real elevation, the course's strategic strengths seemed only to fully emerge in retrospect, after we had played each hole. The bunkers, for example, were often hidden, a feature that reminded Darwin of the world's oldest course.

'Save possibly at St Andrews, I feel as if I have been in more bunkers at Dollymount than on any other course,' he wrote. 'This seems to be *the* feature at Dollymount, the amount of low cunning, if I may so term it, with which the bunkers are placed.'

Though not as visually impressive as the more undulating Irish courses, we found many strong holes at Royal Dublin, beginning with the third. This 400-yard par 4 featured an intimidating tee shot that had to be struck boldly to the right side of a misleadingly narrow opening between sandhills. The green was well guarded with bunkers, though as on most other holes, there was room to run the ball onto the green.

'The turf is light under your feet, isn't it?' Pierce exclaimed proudly as we reached the eighth green. 'You have to pick them off the fairway clean.'

The turf was, indeed, a delight, and we couldn't help but admire Pierce's ability to clip the ball off the grass without taking a divot.

Royal Dublin has an old-fashioned out-and-back layout, and as we made the turn it was hard not to feel privileged to be playing golf in such a secluded and tranquil spot in the midst of an urban industrial centre. Although factories loom next to the course on the mainland, the island itself is a bird sanctuary and biosphere reserve.

'They're manuring all the time,' Pierce told us as we picked our way through some goose droppings. Long-legged hares were also out in force on the fairways, and we learned later that birds gather by the tens of thousands in marshes to the north of the course during the winter. There is an interpretive centre beside the ninth green, and the beach on the south side of the island is a hugely popular public playground.

We lost our first pound on the ninth, of course, and fared little better as we started the back nine. The eleventh hole, though, we thought the best on the course. The tee was actually *out of bounds* and the challenge was to hit the drive back into play over a creek that runs parallel to the right edge of the fairway, while keeping the ball close enough to the creek to leave a manageable shot to the green.

The next two holes were brutishly long, but were followed by a very short par 5 and the quirky and tantalizing sixteenth. A par 4 of a mere 270 yards, it was much-complicated by the scattering of a dozen pot bunkers and an extremely undulating green.

The round ended splendidly, with a right-angled dogleg around a piece of land called 'The Garden' that is emphatically out-of-bounds. Though short for a par 5, it required a brave shot over a huge chunk of The Garden to reach the green in two. It is here that Christy O'Connor completed a now legendary eagle, birdie, eagle finish to win an important professional tournament in 1965.

We also finished in triumph, securing a birdie and a par between us, but this was not nearly enough to dent the lead that Pierce had amassed. Perhaps feeling that this good-natured humiliation was sufficient, Pierce dismissed our determined efforts to make good on our debt. Instead, he showed us the way into the commodious Royal Dublin clubhouse, with its four comfortable bars, decent food, first-class snooker tables and lively hospitality. We stayed for dinner and then succumbed to the attraction of the pubs of downtown Dublin, which after all were only a few minutes away.

Location: On North Bull Island in Dublin harbour, about 4 miles north of the city centre

Restrictions: Weekdays (except Wednesdays) are best for visitors; there are also limited times available on Saturday afternoons and Sunday mornings

Green Fee: €150–170

Chief Executive: Paul Muldowney

Address: North Bull Island Nature Reserve, Dollymount, Dublin 3; **tel:** (01) 833-6346; **fax:** (01) 833-6504; **e-mail:** info@theroyaldublingolfclub.com; **web:** www.theroyaldublingolfclub.com

ST ANNE'S

Founded: 1921

Designed by: The Members, extended by Eddie Hackett and Paddy Skerritt

We've golf and cards and a song or two,
and we're oft times stuck in the sand,
but you have to travel a long long way,
for a better club than St Anne's.

POPULAR ST ANNE'S CLUB SONG (WRITTEN BY PADDY LAVERY)

Royal Dublin isn't the only golf course on Bull Island, that miraculous bit of natural golfing terrain created by accident in Dublin Harbour in the nineteenth century. St Anne's Golf Club may not have the airs and connections of Royal Dublin, but the links golf is almost as good, the setting unique, and the indomitable spirit of its membership is worth celebrating.

From the beginning, St Anne's has been a labour of love, and something of a healthy contrast to its privileged neighbour that shares the three-kilometre strip of duneland called Bull Island. Whereas Royal Dublin was founded by the very upper crust of the Anglo aristocracy, St Anne's was cobbled together by a dry goods salesman and a couple of employees of streetcar companies. Lore has it they were sneaking a few holes on Royal Dublin when they were shooed away by army officers who had taken over the famous course for artillery practice during World War I. They were told to hit their golf balls further down the island, out of range of the guns, and it is here where they set up the first rudimentary holes of what would become St Anne's.

For more than fifty years, St Anne's was widely known as the best nine-hole course in Ireland, and the quality of its greens was famous throughout the land. Like everything else at St Anne's, they had to be made on the cheap. Michael Collins, the club's legendary greenkeeper (he served the club for *sixty-one* years) came up with an ingenious fertilizing mixture of oxblood and soot – ingredients he could get for free in the Dublin of the time.

As late as the 1950s, annual fees were only £4, and in stark contrast with

Royal Dublin, St Anne's had a raucous women's section. No one let the shabby clubhouse ruin a good time, and on weekends the adjacent beaches made a perfect playpen for children. The camaraderie was reinforced by the difficulty of the journey in just getting to St Anne's. For decades, members would gather in the morning at the south edge of Bull Island, where the train station was, and then walk or cycle along the beach (past Royal Dublin) to the club. Even when cars became more popular, there was always a risk of getting stuck in the sand dunes or getting caught at high tide (Volkswagens, with their heavy engine in the rear, were considered the best at getting through the soft sand). The club printed a schedule of tides in its fixture book. It was a do-it-yourself kind of club. Members hauled in the first electrical cable themselves in 1974 (the city wouldn't make the connection), and the course didn't have a reliable source of fresh water until a Diviner was employed in 1992.

Along the way, St Anne's has also had to fight tooth and nail just to survive. Their first landlord was the formidable Lady Ardilaun, of the Guinness family, who allowed the club to lease the land as long as she couldn't see the clubhouse from her window. Later, the city ran a causeway through the middle of the course, ruining several holes, and for a while the Irish Tourist Board threatened to turn the entire island into an amusement park. At first, being next to the well-connected Royal Dublin probably helped keep the ferris wheels at bay. More recently, a growing environmental awareness of the site as a bird sanctuary made golf seem like a relatively benign usage. Today the island is a UNESCO designated biosphere, and the golf course has a long-term lease and looks set to stay.

In Ireland, St Anne's was also famous as the home club of Paddy Skerritt, who startled the golfing world by leading the 1967 British Open at Carnoustie after 45 holes. At the age of 42, he won the 1970 Alcan International at Portmarnock (beating the likes of Lee Trevino in his prime) igniting what a Dublin paper called an 'an orgy of joy' among the throngs of spectators.

The course

While the original course was member-designed, the links was professionally extended by Eddie Hackett (with help from Paddy Skerritt) in the late 1980s. There were numerous teething pains as the new holes grew in, however, and the new layout (some greens and teeing sites were further revised by architect Eddie Connaughton in 2003) is only now reaching maturity. Like Royal Dublin, St Anne's navigates its way through rather sedate dunes, and holes ten through thirteen are not really links holes at all.

But the rest of the course features classic, if relatively flat, links fairways leading to distinctive plateau greens, and there are some fine holes in the mix, such as the testing opener that plays along the beach, and the seventh, a dogleg par 4 with a hidden burn in the driving area and a narrow plateau green set amongst low dunes. The front nine lies at the north end of Bull Island, and it is very exposed to the wind, with fine views of Dublin Harbour and the Howth Peninsula. After the parkland stretch which opens the back nine, the drama picks up again at the sixteenth, a short par 4 with an elevated tee and a panoramic view of the course and its setting.

The course finishes with an intriguing dogleg left par 4 with a long finger of duneland running almost the entire length of the fairway, or at least so it appears from the tee. It's really more of an optical illusion than a difficult hazard, but the drive must be threaded down the right side, from which a narrow green protected by a mound on the left and a devilish pot bunker on the right may be safely reached. From there, it's back to the clubhouse and the company of the members, who truly are some of the friendliest and most spirited in the east of Ireland.

Location: On North Bull Island, in Dublin Harbour (enter off Causeway Road, not Bull Road as for Royal Dublin)

Restrictions: None; but visitors should book in advance

Green Fee: €80–95

Manager: Robbie Gaine

Address: Bull Island Nature Reserve, Dollymount, Dublin 5; **tel:** (01) 833-6471; **fax:** (01) 833-4618; **e-mail:** info@stanneslinksgolf.com; **web:** www.stanneslinksgolf.com

OTHER COURSES OF INTEREST

The K Club

Founded: 1990

Designed by: Arnold Palmer and Ed Seay

The K Club Palmer Course is a relentlessly mundane track that has no business representing Irish golf. It's like having Keira Knightley invite you to her bedroom – to move furniture. It's like going to Rome for dinner and ordering fish and chips.

BRUCE SELCRAIG, WRITING IN THE *IRISH TIMES*

The saga of how the Ryder Cup came to the K Club is well documented, and is fairly straightforward. Michael Smurfit, the paper-packing millionaire, bought the event by pumping money into the European Tour for more than a decade. Now this very pleasant parkland layout outside of Dublin has become world famous. But if you have shelled out in excess of €300 in the expectation of playing a course worthy of one of the great events in sport, you will be crushingly disappointed.

♦♦♦

After years of build-up, the first Ryder Cup in Ireland seemed to go by in a flash. With the Europeans cruising to a smashing victory, the principal drama was the emotional presence of Darren Clarke, who had lost his wife to cancer earlier in the year. The good-hearted enthusiasm of the Irish galleries was universally admired, and their unreserved claiming of Clarke, who comes from Ulster, as one of their own sent a strong message to the world that there is only one Ireland.

The course used for the Ryder Cup was cleverly rerouted, with the seventh and eighth holes, perhaps the best two on the course, becoming the sixteenth and seventeenth. This created some do-or-die excitement as the greatest players in the world flirted with the water. But the choice of the K Club also made the matches a celebration of target golf. The varied kinds of approach and recovery shots that make Irish golf so fascinating were conspicuous by their absence.

From the beginning, the Irish public has been ambivalent about the K Club's selection as the first Irish venue for the Ryder Cup. Everyone knew it was hardly the test of golf that Portmarnock or Waterville or the European Club would have been. But everyone also knew that without Smurfit's money, the event might not have come to Ireland at all.

'The Ryder Cup is a cash cow for the Tour, so yes, money was at the top of the pile of reasons the K Club won out,' said Ken Schofield, former Executive Director of the European Tour, on the eve of the 2006 competition.

At least the K Club is better than The Belfry (the English course which has hosted the Ryder Cup on four occasions), with a nice mixture of water hazards and forested areas, and occasional moments of intimate charm that recall Killarney. Ostentatious mounding is kept to a minimum, and the drainage problems that made the club something of a laughing stock in Irish golf circles in the early years have been solved.

It is hardly news, however, to point out that the K Club represents almost the inverse of the qualities and values that make golf in Ireland so attractive to the visitor. Whereas the great links of Ireland have been laid out to fit in with the natural terrain, promotional literature from the K Club brags about reinventing the landscape by moving 'a million tonnes of soil' and creating a cluster of man-made water hazards. Most golf clubs in Ireland take pains to be accessible to everyone, but the K Club shamelessly caters to the hugely wealthy and has begun to restrict public access in the summer months.

The hotel is architecturally splendid, with a main 'house', built in 1832 that is crammed with paintings, including a room devoted to the work of Jack Yeats, the poet's brother. For sheer irony, however, you might want to search out the corridor that has an exhibit on Irish revolutionary heroes. If it is still there, it is rather interesting, albeit terribly out-of-place in this celebration of the aristocracy.

Money attracts money, and Dublin business journalists have written that the Ryder Cup, while costing Smurfit a fortune, may well make him two more. Bill Clinton and Michael Douglas are among those rumoured to be looking at purchasing property on the wider estate (which also entitles you to a golf membership). The members include a clutch of Ireland's richest men, and two of those on the top of the world's wealth table – Bill Gates and the Sultan of Brunei – have also been spotted here.

Anyone can apparently join, if they can stump up €80,000 in initiation and another €7,000 each year after that (the annual fees have recently been hiked, much to the dismay of those locals who joined at more modest pre-Ryder Cup levels). And the published perks aren't all that generous, unless you count the 'individually assigned member's locker' – a benefit we would have thought wouldn't need to be spelled out at all.

The K Club is all about fame by association. Make your way past the Bentleys and Maseratis in the parking lot and you will find a couple of unexceptional golf courses, at least by the high standards of Ireland. The second course, named the Smurfit after one of its co-owners, has been opened to underwhelming reviews, and in some ways seems the Irish equivalent of the garish golf resorts that Donald Trump has begun opening in the United States. Despite being described as 'an inland links' course, the Smurfit is as much about target golf as the original Palmer course. And if you are worried about the future of the sport, you won't want to read the K Club's own description of the seventh hole on the Smurfit:

> This hole will probably be regarded as the most dramatic in Europe. It has a series of water cascades and water features which are just some of the factors of this development. In its construction, the fairway was dropped some sixty feet below its original height. A large man-made quarry/rockface has been developed along the entire length of the golf hole. This was done using technologies developed by a company called Rock & Waterscape who are based in California....Their main

core business is working with the likes of the Disney organisation, Seaworld, and Universal Studios.

Quite unnecessarily, we are told that these excesses have 'never been attempted before in Europe'. Like so much about the K Club, it would be nice to think they will never be tried again.

Location: Straffan, 17 miles southwest of Dublin off N7

Restrictions: The Palmer Course is open to visitors (non-hotel residents) Sunday to Wednesday only from 1 April to 30 September

Green Fee: €370 (Palmer Course); €225 (Smurfit Course)

Director of Golf: John McHenry

Address: Straffan, Co. Kildare; **tel:** (01) 601-7200; **fax:** (01) 601-7299; **e-mail:** golf@kclub.com; **web:** www.kclub.com

---

Druids Glen

Founded: 1995; Druids Heath Course: 2004
Designed by: Pat Ruddy

Perhaps the most successful, in golfing terms, of the posh parkland complexes that have sprung up around Dublin, Druids Glen boasts thirty-six challenging holes by Pat Ruddy, who has shown his versatility by designing two ambitious and satisfying parkland courses not all that far from his seminal achievement on links terrain at the European Club. But no matter how they dress up the resort with Irish trappings, the inspiration here is mostly American, from the island green to the self-proclaimed title of the Irish Augusta. It's no Augusta, and Druids Glen has little in common with the links courses that have made Ireland famous in the golf world. But you can certainly have a couple of exciting, if overpriced, rounds of golf here.

◆◆◆

For the capital of a country with such a rich golf tradition, it is remarkable just how unremarkable Dublin's parkland courses used to be. Woodbrook, for example, which held the most lucrative professional tournaments in Ireland in the 1960s and 70s, would never have been considered worthy to host big events in other golfing countries. And other Dublin clubs, apart from the handful with links courses, weren't any better.

'They have a nice social atmosphere, but not great golf and it never will be,' says golf architect Pat Ruddy, who played a big part in shaking up the golf scene in Dublin in the early 1990s.

'I said it was time we did a new wave, and put up a nice middle-of-the-road clubhouse and did a very nice job and you do pay as you play and maybe have a small membership, and it should do awful well.'

Ruddy had the ear of an Irish businessman, who invited him to design what would become St Margaret's Golf and Country Club, just off the ring road north of Dublin, and convenient to the airport. Built over a rather featureless and flat piece of ground, St Margaret's was never going to be a world beater. But with its excellent conditioning, large quick greens, flashy bunkers, artificial mounding, and man-made water hazards, St Margaret's was among the first courses that tried to look like the ones Irish golfers were seeing on TV from America. It was aimed firmly at the corporate market, and seems to have always done rather nicely.

It also established Pat Ruddy, then in partnership with top amateur golfer Tom Craddock, as something more than a sportswriter with a home-made course.

Then, Irish businessman Hugo Flinn provided Ruddy the resources, and the piece of land, to do something more ambitious.

'He said "Pat, you've built Ireland's best seaside golf course, now build its best inland course",' says Ruddy. 'I told him the south of Dublin is the place to be, it's where the rich population of the city is and not enough golf courses. Eventually we found Woodstock [the name of an old estate]. And in the middle there's a glen and an ancient Druids altar, and I said we'd call it Druids Glen.

'We've moved mountains of rock in some cases and fitted into a very nice site that's a bit like Augusta in that it's turbulent ground with plenty of timber and water.'

The developers of Druids Glen have always made clever use of the pieces of Irish history at their disposal. The clubhouse is a converted eighteenth-century manor, which contains a few well-presented displays of historical interest. And the ancient Druid theme is played out in the corporate logos and on the golf course, where there are floral arrangements with Celtic symbols, and even a Druid statue. These attempts at charm might have been endearing in the hands of a real Irish golf club. But at Druids Glen, the historical references have been processed too many times by a public relations machine aimed squarely at the corporate market.

Shortly after its opening, Druids Glen hosted the Irish Open from 1996 to 1999, and the owners very much had the Ryder Cup in their sights. While they were outbid by the K Club, Druids Glen will always be notable as the scene of the first professional triumph of a nineteen-year-old Sergio García, who scorched the course in 64 in his final round at the Irish Open in 1999.

To American visitors, the courses at Druids Glen will seem familiar. Basketball star Michael Jordan, after a whirlwind tour of Irish courses, most of them links, said that at Druids Glen he felt he was in the American midwest. It might be a bit more accurate to say that golf here fits the global mould of a high-end corporate golf experience. And now there's an international luxury hotel on the property to underline the point.

Nevertheless, it is remarkable how well Pat Ruddy, so immersed in links golf, matches and even surpasses the work of better-known American design teams at their own game. Ruddy has designed another eighteen holes, called Druids Heath, on a less wooded piece of farmland next door, and claims to be trying to capture something of the feel of the famous English heathland courses.

There are good holes and originality aplenty on each course (though Druids Glen is marred a little by a clumsy island green) and both reach a climax just after the turn. The twelfth at Druids Glen is a picturesque, heavily flowered par 3 that uses elevation, natural water features, and the resort's famous landscaping skills to great effect. The thirteenth is just as compelling visually, but is also one of the most demanding and memorable inland holes in Ireland. The same twisting river is cleverly crossed twice, and there is a dramatic, sheer rock face on the right of a dangerously tilting fairway that gives everything a claustrophobic feel. The approach, to a narrow but very long green, with water mostly all around, is equally unsettling.

But the best sequence on either course may begin on the Heath at the twelfth, a monumental par 4 played up to a ridge and then down, thrillingly, to a green guarded by a pond. The thirteenth is a much shorter and quirkier dogleg, with a single intimidating tree bothering the line of both the drive and the approach shot, which is also played over water. And the short fourteenth is one of those marvellously natural looking holes – in this case carved out of a quarry, rimmed with gorse and exposed rock, and punctuated by small pot bunkers – that looks perfect the first second you look at it.

Location: About mid-way between Bray and Wicklow town; exit N11 at Newtownmountkennedy and follow signs

Restrictions: None

Green Fee: €175 (Druids Glen), €125 (Druids Heath)

Golf Director: Barry Dowling

Address: Newtownmountkennedy, Co. Wicklow; **tel:** (01) 287-3600; **fax:** (01) 287-3699; **e-mail:** info@druidsglen.ie; **web:** www.druidsglen.ie

---

Mount Juliet

Founded: 1991

Designed by: Jack Nicklaus

It doesn't seem like a European course. It seems like an American course. A lot of guys that play our tour feel right at home.

CHRIS DIMARCO, PLAYING AT THE WORLD GOLF CHAMPIONSHIPS EVENT

AT MOUNT JULIET

Three hours' drive south of Dublin, the golf course at Mount Juliet is an immaculately groomed playground for the rich and chauffeur-driven. Twice home to one of the tournaments in the World Golf Championships, the course has played host to probably the strongest field ever to play in a golf tournament in Ireland (and it is the one place on the island where Tiger Woods has won a tournament). None of this makes the golf here anything special, however.

'Do you smell it?' asked Sean, our playing partner, as we walked down one of Mount Juliet's immaculately groomed fairways. 'There's a dog kennel over there. You can smell the dead meat they give to the dogs.'

MOUNT JULIET/POWERSCOURT

We tried not to inhale and asked Sean how he had come to be a member at Mount Juliet, one of Ireland's most expensive courses. He seemed out of place with his tattered golf bag (which he carried like a suitcase) and running shoes. He grew up in the area, as it turned out, and could remember the parties at the old manor house (now turned into a luxury hotel), to which locals of his family's class were definitely not invited. Sean had joined the club as part of a corporate membership package – really just ten people banding together and sharing the fees. He was actually self-employed and lived in a fairly distant town. But he had the flexibility to drive down to Mount Juliet on a fairly regular basis, and could stay with his parents, who still lived nearby.

Mount Juliet was principally a resort, and somewhat out-of-the-way for the regular player. Membership was a bit thin.

'We don't have much of a club atmosphere,' Sean said. 'But it's our own fault really.'

On the fourth hole, a terrific dogleg to a green that juts out into a pond, we passed a man sitting beside the green with a walkie-talkie.

'He's making sure that no one fishes balls out of the water,' Sean explained. Apparently the chemicals in the pond could damage the green, and a professional tournament would start in a week's time.

Sean pointed out some other interesting sights. On the seventh hole, for example, we passed a controversial new house, apparently purchased by a rich Canadian. The neighbours (we couldn't see any) had for some reason complained about an enormous skylight the owner was proposing.

Soon afterwards we saw a helicopter fly across the course.

'I think it's the Prime Minister of New Zealand,' Sean said.

Since we met Sean, Mount Juliet has played host to three Irish Opens and two World Golf Championships events, restricted to the top fifty golfers in the world. Even the pampered professionals were amazed by the quality of the greens. They also ate the course alive. In 2002, Tiger Woods shot twenty-five under par, and there were a pair of course-record 62s, by Sergio García and Retief Goosen. Ernie Els won in 2004.

For the average golfer, the conditioning of the course is always a treat, and when Mount Juliet opened it was an opportunity for Irish golfers to sample the kind of lush parkland golf that is commonplace in North America. Now that several other similar courses have opened much closer to Dublin, Mount Juliet is no longer special. And Jack Nicklaus's course, though decent enough, isn't the sort of wonder you would drive for two hours, and then pay a very high green fee, to play. As at the K Club, the best holes involve water, and there isn't as much of it here.

There is, however, one intriguing addition to the golf attractions at Mount Juliet – a par 53, eighteen-hole putting course, complete with water hazards and sand traps.

Less exciting are the excesses of the hotel, now managed by Hilton's Conrad chain, which boasts one of the more vacuous corporate slogans: 'the luxury of being yourself'. The organized hunts seem to have been discontinued, but there's still horseback riding, trapshooting, archery and fishing (some kind of world trout championship was held here) and the obligatory spa. Monster houses are popping up in supposedly 'discreet locations' around the property; every time you spot one through the trees it's a reminder that the comforts of Mount Juliet, like the aristocratic world it so earnestly celebrates, are aimed at a depressingly small slice of humanity.

Location: Near Thomastown, about three hours southwest of Dublin; follow signs from Thomastown

Restrictions: None

Green Fee: €130–160

Manager: Colin Donovan

Address: Thomastown, Co. Kilkenny; **tel:** (056) 777-3064; **fax:** (056) 777-3019; **e-mail:** info@mountjuliet.ie; **web:** www.mountjuliet.ie

Powerscourt

Founded: 1995

Designed by: Peter McEvoy (East course) and David McLay Kidd (West course)

The two golf courses at Powerscourt estate south of Dublin are no better or worse than other upscale golf course developments in the Dublin area. But they *have* contributed to the restoration of an important historic landmark. The elegant Powerscourt House, which overlooked one of the world's great gardens, was gutted by fire in 1974. It has taken a generation, but the building has been stitched together again by a regretful Slazenger family, and is now a proud

POWERSCOURT

part of one of Ireland's great tourist sites. It is one place where, as Walter Hagen used to say, you should stop and smell the flowers.

◆◆◆

There was a fortified castle at Powerscourt in Norman times, erected to protect the area south of Dublin situated 'beyond the pale'. Richard Wingfield, later the first Viscount Powerscourt, was granted land here in 1603 by King James I, and a descendent built the imposing classical mansion in the eighteenth century. But it was with the development of its magnificent formal gardens in Victorian times that Powerscourt's fame grew beyond Ireland. The Duchess of York, a descendent of the Wingfields on her mother's side, likes the place so much she has said she wants her remains sprinkled over the grounds.

In an independent Ireland, the upkeep of the massive property (14,000 acres) was too much even for Viscounts, and the property declined, eventually ending up in the hands of Ralph Slazenger, whose father had started the sporting goods empire. The Slazengers, related by marriage to the Wingfields, spent a decade painstakingly restoring the house.

Then, in 1974, just as the work was coming to an end, a chimney fire swept through the historic building in a blaze that caused widespread dismay in Ireland.

'In those days there was only a volunteer fire brigade so they were ringing around to get everyone going,' says Ralph Slazenger's granddaughter Sarah, who was a young girl at the time. 'And so it was hopeless really by the time they arrived; there was nothing left of it.'

Contents that were salvaged were later sold off in a rather controversial manner and the house was boarded up until, in 1990, the next generation took control of the property.

'I hadn't been in since the fire,' recalls Sarah. 'It had trees growing up on the inside of it. The external walls were completely intact and in pretty good condition. But all the floors were gone, all the staircases. You'd stand in there and look up and just see the daylight. There was nothing there at all.

'The driving force behind us wanting to restore the house is that there is some guilt associated with the fact that the fire happened on our watch if you like.'

Sarah's father (Ralph's son) took a year off from his medical practice to see what could be done with the estate. And in order to pay for the repairs, the family decided to build a golf course.

Englishman Peter McEvoy, the former British Amateur champion, was hired, ably assisted by estate manager Tom Clark, who knew the property inside out.

'And we were just amazed at how popular it was,' says Sarah, who became marketing manager for the property. 'We seemed to be hitting the time just when golf was taking off in Ireland, and people were desperate to get into new courses because all of the traditional members' clubs were completely full.

'The golf was such a tremendous success that it was a catalyst really for getting the house back. We opened the golf in July and started work on the house in September.'

The inside of Powerscourt House is by no means in the same shape as it was when Sarah Slazenger ran though its glamorous halls and passageways. Though the ballroom and a few other rooms have been magnificently restored, other parts of the structure have been converted into eating places and a boutique department store. But there's a pleasing sense of style and restraint to the entire complex, and a real effort to explain its historical context.

The House's crucial role, however, is to act as a worthy backdrop to the famous gardens, the creation of the sixth Viscount Powerscourt and, especially, his son, who travelled across Europe looking for statues and ornaments. Anything he couldn't buy, he copied.

The gardens are a great delight to visit, a formal but exuberant combination of ponds, terraces, cascades, wooded walks, magnificent sculpture and, rather endearingly, a pet cemetery.

The combination of architecture, art, gardens and shopping has made Powerscourt into a popular outing for Dubliners, as well as an international tourist destination. A second course has also boosted Powerscourt's lucrative share of the corporate golf market around Dublin.

Slazenger makes no apology for the more commercial aspects of the enterprise.

'Yes it has to make money because otherwise the estate is not going to survive long term, and the pressures will come as they do on other estates to sell off bits of it. And our whole philosophy is that we wanted to keep it together, to keep it intact. I suppose we would like to pass it on better than we found it if you like. So we're working hard to achieve that.'

The financial pressure is surely off now, what with the recent granting of a contract to build a massive and luxurious Ritz-Carlton hotel on the grounds. We don't know if it is a step in the right direction. But it will pay more than a few bills.

In a place as rich in history and creativity as Powerscourt, the golf courses inevitably play second fiddle, but they are decent layouts that make excellent use of the outstanding views of the Wicklow hills. McEvoy's East course starts and ends in exciting fashion, and has large, highly undulating greens which we rather liked, but which were reportedly toned down after complaints.

'Our design brief was that we want you to fit a golf course into Powerscourt, rather than fit Powerscourt into a golf course,' says Sarah Slazenger.

The newer West course is the work of David McLay Kidd, a still-young Scottish architect who made his name with the much-heralded Bandon Dunes course in Oregon. His Powerscourt contribution is slightly more flamboyant that McEvoy's, taking advantage of a number of natural water features.

If all you do is golf at Powerscourt, there's a rather fine clubhouse quite separate from the restored House. But it would be a shame to come all this way and not have a peek at the gardens. And you might keep your eye out for a novel by Sarah Ferguson. Rumour has it she's working on a story based on a heroine who lives in a mansion that golfers, however unwittingly, have helped to breathe new life into.

Location: Near village of Enniskerry, just off M11. In the village square, take the road to the left of the clock tower and continue up the hill for a third of a mile

Restrictions: None

Green Fee: €130

Manager: Bernard Gibbons

Address: Powerscourt Estate, Enniskerry, Co. Wicklow; **tel:** (01) 204-6033; **fax:** (01) 204-6031; **web:** www.powerscourt.ie/golfclub

Seapoint

Founded: 1996

Designed by: Des Smyth

With the membership at adjacent County Louth Golf Club bursting at the seams, Seapoint no doubt provides a much-needed outlet for local golfers wanting to join a quality golf course.

The front nine is played over sedate terrain that often appears to be parkland in nature (though the club seems to insist that the entire course has links qualities). But the back nine takes a trip through some indisputably authentic linksland next to the sea (you can get a glimpse of these holes from the fourteenth tee at Baltray).

Designer Des Smyth, a former Ryder Cup player, does a decent job, but there are few magic moments, and one is rarely left admiring the course's tactical subtleties. The decision to build to an exciting climax on the closing holes (the par-3 seventeenth is the best on the course) has some logic, but it leaves the first part of the round devoid of much drama.

Almost from the start, work has been carried out on the course to enhance the conditioning and the finer points of the design, and this has been largely overseen by Declan Branigan, a fine amateur golfer who played with Smyth at nearby Bettystown in his youth. So Seapoint is very much rooted in the local area despite an equity-style membership structure. If the number of homes being built nearby is any indication, the club is seen to be a desirable one.

Seapoint gives you a tantalizing taste of links golf, but a round here is no substitute for a game on the sublime County Louth links next door. It could, however, be used as a perfectly respectable warm up.

Location: At Termonfeckin, about a mile north of Baltray along the coastal road

Restrictions: Weekdays are best for visitors

Green Fee: €60–100

Secretary/Manager: Kevin Carrie

Address: Termonfeckin, Drogheda, Co. Louth; **tel:** (041) 982-2333; **fax:** (041) 982-2331; **e-mail:** info@seapointgolflinks.com; **web:** www.seapointgolflinks.com

THE EAST

DUBLIN IS ONE of the most accessible of the great European cities. Much of it is easy to walk around, and its people are famously easy and fascinating to engage in conversation. Founded by the Vikings in the tenth century, Dublin is a city of satisfyingly monumental buildings, interesting museums, artistic activity and cosy pubs – and home to about a fifth of the island's people. Working-class tenements and grand living have long existed side by side in Dublin, which has been the home, at various points in their lives, of the writers Swift, Wilde, Yeats, Joyce and O'Casey. Dublin's energy and contradictions still foster the development of world-renowned artists, although in keeping with the times they are as likely to be rock musicians as serious writers.

In some ways, Dublin was at its grandest in the eighteenth century, when the ruling aristocracy had its own Parliament and a degree of autonomy from London. Much of the most impressive public architecture dates from that period.

But in terms of wealth, there has been no time like today. The recent economic boom in Ireland has made Dublin one of the world's wealthiest cities. It was ranked sixteenth in a worldwide cost-of-living survey in 2006, when average house prices were flirting with €500,000.

The tourist attractions of Dublin are, by and large, contained in a one-square-mile block on the south side of the River Liffey. The famous O'Connell Street Bridge is the main downtown artery for north–south travel. If you are on foot, a more appealing option is the quaint Ha'penny Bridge, open to pedestrians only. Depending on the amount of time you wish to take away from golf, Trinity College, the National Museum, Temple Bar, the Guinness Brewery museum, the National Gallery, St Patrick's Cathedral, the Grafton Street shopping mall, Christ Church Cathedral and Dublin Castle are all worth a visit. On the north side of the river, take a quick walk down the grand boulevard of O'Connell Street past the General Post Office, an important site in the 1916 uprising. Note the statues of Irish patriots and the ill-conceived Spirit of the River Liffey statue (referred to by some Dubliners, with typical Irish wit, as 'the floozy in the Jacuzzi').

The latest monument to attract controversy is the Spire of Dublin, a 393-foot needle that pierces the sky over O'Connell Street. It is built on the site of a statue of Nelson that was blown up by the IRA in 1966. Although Dubliners are coming around to it, the structure has inspired nicknames ranging from 'the stiletto in the ghetto' (a reference to low-income areas in the vicinity) to 'the erection on the intersection'.

The famous Book of Kells in the Trinity College Library is an illustrated version of the four Gospels of the New Testament created by the monks of the monastery at Kells. The pages glow with the most intricate of illustrations, done in luminous 'paint' which was somehow fashioned from insects in the eighth century. The book is exceptionally fragile – only one page is on display per month. The college itself was an Anglican bastion from 1591 to 1873, when it was opened to Roman Catholics (though it remained largely Protestant until the 1960s). Guided tours are available in the summer months when classes are not in session.

The National Museum is worth a visit for its exhibits on the founding of Dublin by the Vikings, its material on the 1916 uprising and the War of Independence, and its collection of ancient gold objects, most notably the

DIVERSIONS

Tara Brooch. In the same complex of buildings, which is immediately southeast of Trinity College, are the National Gallery, the National Library and the Museum of Natural History. The National Gallery contains a decent collection of European painting from the Renaissance to the nineteenth century (the collection of Gainsboroughs is particularly strong), but is probably more interesting for its portraits of Irish literary giants Swift, Joyce, Shaw and Yeats.

A museum of an entirely different kind is the Guinness Brewery Visitors' Centre and museum at the Guinness Brewery, St James Gate, just west of the downtown area. Although the brewery itself is not open for tours, the entire brewing process for Guinness stout is explained in detail, after which samples are provided. A visit here might start to explain the remarkable hold that this unique product has had over Ireland for two centuries. At the very least, you will find no larger collection of Guinness souvenirs anywhere in the world.

Dublin's two cathedrals are Christ Church and St Patrick's. Christ Church is the older of the two, in the early Gothic style of the twelfth century. St Patrick's was founded at roughly the same time but was almost completely rebuilt after a fire in the fourteenth century. It was built just outside the city walls in an attempt to evade municipal jurisdiction. It was the home of Jonathan Swift for thirty-two years, and he is buried here. It is a legacy of British rule in Ireland that both Christ Church and St Patrick's are Protestant cathedrals; St Patrick's is the national cathedral of the Church of Ireland, while Christ Church is the Church of Ireland cathedral for the diocese of Dublin.

Modern Dublin is perhaps best seen on foot in the Grafton Street shopping area. Between Trinity College and St Stephen's Green the street is closed to vehicles. It has a collection of shops with the greatest variety of merchandise in Ireland – whether you wish to purchase Aran sweaters, Donegal tweed, Waterford crystal or heraldic items, they are all available here. And you're never far from a pub. Dublin is also one of the great cities of the English-speaking world for bookshops. Try in particular Fred Hanna, on Nassau Street opposite Trinity College, or any of Waterstone & Co., Hodges Figgis, Eason & Son Ltd or the Trinity College Library Shop.

The district just south of the river and roughly between Trinity College and Christ Church is known as Temple Bar. It was a prime focus of Dublin's redevelopment in the 1990s, and is now the centre of Dublin's considerable nightlife, and an international attraction in its own right. It sports various galleries, boutiques, cafés, pubs and late-night dance clubs, as well as the Irish Film Centre.

Dublin Castle was constructed by the Normans in 1204 and remained as the symbol, and usually the seat, of the English rule of Ireland until 1922. Much of the present complex dates from the eighteenth century, however. The State Apartments are the portion of the castle that is open to the public for tours when not being used for state occasions, such as the inauguration of the President of Ireland.

The Irish are passionate about sports, both the international sports of soccer and rugby and the Irish games, hurling and Gaelic football. An All-Ireland final in either of the latter provides an excellent insight into Irish sporting culture. Both are held at Croke Park, on Dublin's north side, in September, but you may have to use your ingenuity to obtain a ticket. No less passionate are the supporters of the national football (soccer) and rugby teams, especially given the remarkable success of the football team throughout the 1990s. Football and rugby internationals are normally held at Lansdowne Road stadium, south of the river in Ballsbridge. The main rugby union season (the Six Nations Cup) is from January to March. The national football team will have home matches throughout the year, either friendlies or qualifying matches for the World Cup or European Championship. Any home match for either team is a national event. A game against England is likely to bring Dublin to a near standstill. (Lansdowne Road is closed until 2009 while it undergoes redevelopment; in the meantime, the constitution of the Gaelic Athletic Association has been changed to allow 'foreign games' at Croke Park.)

Dublin also has an extensive theatre scene, highlighted by the historic Abbey Theatre. The current Abbey Theatre was built in 1966, after the 1904 original burned down. W. B. Yeats was its first director. The Dublin Theatre Festival, held annually in September, is also excellent.

St Patrick's Day (March 17) is, of course, a national holiday, but even in Dublin don't expect the raucous celebrations of Boston or New York. Bloomsday (June 16) is not an official national holiday, but it is a lively event just the same. It commemorates the travels around Dublin of the protagonist of James Joyce's *Ulysses*. Tourists and Dubliners alike turn out in striped blazers and straw hats to retrace Leopold Bloom's walk around the city, while readings and other events occur at various venues. Any day of the year may be made a personal Bloomsday by obtaining the *Ulysses* map of Dublin from Tourism Ireland. It sets out an extensive walk with twenty-two stops in all. True Joyce fans will also visit the James Joyce museum in the Martello Tower at Sandycove (also described in *Ulysses*).

To the south of Dublin stretches a coastline of some of the better beaches in Ireland, with the lovely Wicklow mountain range rising in the background. The southeast region claims to be the sunniest part of the country, but it is doubtful that Bermuda feels particularly threatened. The valley of Glendalough, nestled between the Upper and Lower lakes, contains the ruins of one of Ireland's most important monasteries. It is worth a visit but can be heavily touristed in the summer months. Further southwest is the town of Kilkenny, perhaps Ireland's best-preserved medieval town. Kilkenny's castle, the Black Abbey and St Canice's Cathedral are the main medieval architectural attractions.

NORTHERN IRELAND:

HIDDEN TREASURES

In golfing terms, the north and south of Ireland have never been separated. The Golfing Union of Ireland, founded in 1891, administers golf over the entire island, and is the oldest union of its kind in the world. That it decided to remain united after independence was no doubt partly due to the strong cultural ties among the Protestant elite which completely dominated golf at the time. In any event, the Golfing Union has had a salutary effect on the development of the sport in Ireland, and there is a genuine attempt to keep sectarian issues out of the game. If and when the Troubles recede into memory, the great golfing treasures in the 'six counties' will no doubt become even better known. Northern Ireland boasts two of the world's greatest courses – Royal County Down and Royal Portrush – and a number of other links of real substance. And it is one place where we would not discourage you from considering a tree-lined diversion. The area in and around Belfast boasts parkland courses of impeccable pedigree that are well worth playing, and several newcomers that at least give you good value for your money.

BALLYCASTLE

Founded: 1890

Designed by: Various

Ballycastle lies at the foot of a very pretty glen in County Antrim, about fifteen miles to the east of the Giant's Causeway, and lately its already not inconsiderable attractions have been completed by that necessary adjunct to all well-regulated neighbourhoods – golf links.

GOLF MAGAZINE, 1897

At times, Ballycastle just seems kind of slapped together – part parkland, part links, with fairways that run too close together, a couple of holes that appear too quirky by half, and a clubhouse that almost touches the eighteenth green. It shouldn't really work as a golf course, yet there is an undeniable exhilaration to be had in playing golf on the high linksland they call the Warren, which overlooks so much beauty, and so much Irish history. Amidst the views and legends you will also find many testing and intriguing golf holes.

If you were a teacher taking students on a field trip to discuss Ulster's history and lore you could do worse than to ask them to play a round at the Ballycastle Golf Club. The history lesson begins on the first three holes, which encircle the atmospheric ruins of the Bonamargy. It is in this sixteenth-century friary that the heroic figure of Sorley Boy MacDonnell is buried (hook the ball on the par-3 third and you may well end up in the graveyard). MacDonnell and his clan ruled this part of Ulster from his impressive Dunluce Castle along the coast at Portrush. After losing the castle in a siege to the English in 1589, MacDonnell somehow managed to reclaim it by raising his men in baskets up the cliffs.

The next history stop is the twelfth tee, high up on a cliff overlooking the ocean, where a fine view can be had of the island of Rathlin. For such a rocky and barren place, Rathlin has been awfully busy over the centuries. This is where the Vikings first attacked Irish soil in 795, where Saint Columba performed a miracle in the sixth century, and where Robert the

Bruce took refuge in 1306 before returning to Scotland to defeat the English at Bannockburn. According to legend, a diligent spider in one of Rathlin's caves inspired Bruce to coin the phrase, 'If at first you don't succeed, try and try again.'

The island was also the site of a massacre in 1595 when an English fleet trapped the clan of the MacDonnells (who had been put on the island for safekeeping). On a more peaceful note, Marconi made his first successful commercial transmission of the wireless between Rathlin and Ballycastle in 1898.

By then the golf course had been in use for almost ten years, on land provided free of charge by Miss Kathleen Boyd, a descendant of Colonel Hugh Boyd, one of Ulster's first industrialists. He developed the town of Ballycastle into something of an industrial centre in the eighteenth century.

The Boyd family's legacy is clear to see from the bench at the hugely elevated seventeenth tee. There is a spectacular view of the golf course, the still-bustling town and Ballycastle's sweeping beach. In the distance are the massive promontory of Fair Head (with its 600-foot cliffs) and the famous Mull of Kintyre in Scotland.

There are any number of legends associated with the evocative landscape and the narrow channel that divides Ireland and Scotland. But while legend and history have been passed down with some precision, the origins of the Ballycastle Golf Club are something of a mystery. The club was all set to celebrate its centenary in 1991 when plans were set a flutter by a putter discovered in East Sussex. It had been presented to Naval Commander Alfred Malcolm Causton for his 'indefatigable exertions in founding the club in 1890'.

The centenary committee let out a collective 'Oops!' and moved up their plans by a year.

If Commander Causton was the driving force in establishing the club, Kathleen Boyd must come a close second. Not only did she provide much of the land for the course free of charge, she was the club's Lady Captain for *forty-seven years* and often held women's committee meetings in her manor house. It was no doubt partly due to Boyd's example that Ballycastle had more lady members than men as late as 1953. The club's strong programme for junior girls produced two national champions in the 1960s.

Boyd's long reign as captain is typical of the extraordinary continuity that marks Ballycastle's history and which is part of the charm of the course itself. Between 1894 and 1972, for example, the position of greenkeeper was held by only two men, which may explain in part why much of the original nine-hole course used at the turn of the century was preserved for so long. Despite recent alterations to relieve congestion, holes six to nine survive in much the same form as they were in 1906, while most of the rest of the course dates from 1926, when two distinguished members of Royal Portrush, Major C. O. Hezlet and Sir Anthony Babington, were asked to suggest an extension.

The course

Ballycastle consists of two entirely different sections. The first five holes are parkland in style and rather flat and sedate, although the opening hole does flirt with the River Margy. The most interesting hazard, of course, is the ruined Bonamargy, which comes into play on the third.

To freshen things up a bit, the head greenkeeper asked his son to have a look at the bunkering. That might seem odd, except the greenkeeper was Godfrey Clarke and his son was Darren, the best player from Northern Ireland since Fred Daly.

'We drove around in a buggy,' says Brian Dillon, who was captain at the time. 'Those new bunkers on the first five holes were Darren's idea. We got free advice, but we entertained him afterwards with the black stuff!'

The club actually went a step further, making Clarke an honorary member of Ballycastle in 2000 after he defeated Tiger Woods in the finals of the World Golf Championships match-play event.

'He's a great guy, and still has his feet on the ground,' says Dillon.

(Since their initial collaboration at Ballycastle, father and son have joined forces on the design front, and Godfrey is overseeing the development of Darren Clarke-designed courses as far away as South Africa.)

The Clarke family's new bunkers have helped strengthen Ballycastle's opening stretch, but to cross the Cushendall Road back towards the clubhouse to the sixth tee is to enter a different, and much more satisfying, golfing world. This is the Warren (you will still see a lot of rabbits), the linksland on which the course's original nine holes were first laid out.

It is an unusual piece of golfing ground. Unlike most Irish linksland, the Warren has few high dunes; instead, it is creased with deep crevices that suck stray balls off the fairways and greens, which are typically on the highest ground and very exposed to the wind. Here, Ballycastle has the delightful feel of a 'found course' that was up and running before golf architecture became a growth industry. One hundred years later the holes still seem fresh and unpretentious.

The Warren also used be a claustrophobic place, with shared fairways and constant shouts of 'fore!' But with the addition of new land, and two new holes at the farthest end of the course, the most problematic areas are congested no longer. Sadly, that meant the demise of the old par-4 seventh, a terrific dogleg that dipped into a valley and then required a heroic uphill approach reminiscent of the second at Ballybunion. The only problem was that it shared its fairway with two other holes!

Fortunately, one of our favourite fairways in Ireland – the Hog's Back on the sixth – is still intact, and if there is a way to keep the drive from sliding into the rough we haven't discovered it. The seventh rolls along the beach and features an anxious and very beautiful downhill approach, while the eighth is a short and quaint par 4 up a hill to a knob of a green.

Holes nine through seventeen are played on a higher piece of linksland across another road, and it is here that the views are bound to stop you in your tracks. The ninth is the most theatrical hole on the course, requiring a semi-blind approach to a severely sloping green set high in the dunes, while the tenth may be the windiest hole in golf. Only 115 yards in length, it features a tee set out on the edge of a cliff. It is a breathtaking spot, and it doesn't really matter that the green is far too elevated for such a short par 3. Just remember to pack your hat away and batten down the hatches on your golf bag.

The next six holes are played up and down the side of a steep slope, and in the summer a principal challenge is inventing ways to keep downhill approach shots from bounding over the hard and well-guarded greens. Number thirteen and fourteen are the two new holes added to this stretch (designed by the members), and are very much in character with the holes around them.

Ballycastle ends with a flourish. The seventeenth has perhaps the most elevated tee of any par 3 in Ireland (this is where you take out the camera) while the eighteenth is an excellent par 5 over rollicking terrain that now features a well bunkered green that is not quite so close as it once was to the club's parking lot. Of course, when the hole was first laid out the motor car had only just been invented, and it is part of the attraction of Ballycastle that its oldest holes are also its most exciting.

Location: One-half mile east of town on A2, about 20 miles east of Portrush

Restrictions: None, except for competition days

Green Fee: £20–30

Secretary-Manager: Brian Dillon

Address: Cushendall Road, Ballycastle, Co Antrim, BT54 6QP, Northern Ireland; **tel:** (028) 2076-2536; **fax:** (028) 2076-9909; **e-mail:** info@ballycastlegolfclub.com; **web:** www.ballycastlegolfclub.com

CASTLEROCK

Founded: 1901

Designed by: Ben Sayers

Hills and valleys alternate in the course... and the natural hazards provided in the rough ground, furze, bent, sand and drains render the links exceptionally attractive to golfers who appreciate sporting chances. Some of the holes, both out and home, Mr. Sayers described as 'the best he had ever seen'.

BRITISH GOLF MAGAZINE, 1908

A true Irish-style links on the Causeway Coast, Castlerock may be Northern Ireland's most rugged golf course, with a host of long, demanding holes through impressive and intimidating sandhills. When the wind is up, as it often is, Castlerock can be a tiger – everything seems to be played uphill or upwind, and approach shots bound off the hard and fast greens. This is an underrated course and hugely enjoyable to play.

Although little-remembered today, Ben Sayers was one of the most colourful characters in golf at the turn of the twentieth century. The club professional at North Berwick in Scotland, Sayers was known to cartwheel around the green after making an important putt. He competed in every British Open between 1880 and 1923, and was perhaps the best player of the era never to win the championship. He was also a famous club and ball maker. But his most enduring contribution to the game may be the exciting links in the coastal village of Castlerock. Despite a partial rerouting made necessary after the Second World War, the links still takes its inspiration from the layout Sayers recommended in 1908. It is one of only three remaining courses designed by the flamboyant Scot.

Any history of Castlerock, however, is incomplete without reference to the august figure of Frederick Hervey, fourth Earl of Bristol and Anglican Bishop of Derry, who built an enormous castle just west of the present town in 1750. The only remnant of the estate is the Mussenden Temple, which the Bishop used as a library. In an unusual gesture of religious tolerance, he allowed Catholics to celebrate Mass in the temple, as there was no church nearby.

The Bishop had very fixed ideas about how the village that inevitably grew up around his estate should develop, and stipulated that no houses should be lower than three stories. The stone buildings in the town centre are evidence of that edict.

Not surprisingly, the original golf course was built on lands owned by the Bishop's descendants, in 1901. The links was the main attraction of a recreation club established by a group of Anglican and Presbyterian ministers and local business and professional men. By 1908 the club was ready to invite Ben Sayers to completely revise the home-made nine-hole layout and expand it to a full eighteen holes. Enhancements were apparently suggested by H. S. Colt in the 1920s, and many of the present-day bunkers and contours were the work of David Lyttle, the club professional and head greenkeeper.

Five of the holes disappeared in the late 1940s, when the landlords took back land for a housing development. In compensation, the club received ownership of the golfing ground that remained, and some additional land. Unfortunately, there wasn't much money in post-war Northern Ireland, and the cost of developing new holes put immense financial strain on the club. The club soon started to sell sand from its most gigantic dunes in order to make ends meet (the contractors eventually hit the water table, and there has been a slight drainage problem on the first hole ever since). But the club persevered and the newly built holes (the first, second, eighth, ninth and tenth) were more or less in their present form by 1960.

In recent years, David Jones has been called in to freshen up the course a little (he also converted the first hole into a dogleg), but this has not changed Castlerock's essential character.

If you have time, you may also want to check out the eccentric, nine-hole Bann course, with its giant dunes, blind shots, and bunkerless fairways and greens. It features a par 5 by the ocean that many feel is world class, and may be the only links course designed by brothers (while members of the club).

The course

Despite the changes that have been necessary, there is no doubt that Ben Sayers deserves credit for moving the club in the right direction. Castlerock often has the feel of a championship layout, and its greens are known locally for their quickness. While driving is not nearly as strategic an exercise as it is at nearby Royal Portrush, the approach shots call for accuracy and courage. The prevailing wind at Castlerock is almost never helpful. The longest holes are usually upwind, requiring long and demanding irons to greens that are tucked between high dunes and fierce rough. Downwind approach shots are much shorter, but the green is often tightly trapped, perched on a devilish plateau, adjacent to a burn or out-of-bounds fence, or all of the above. On a truly windy day in summer, when the greens are hard and fast, even a wedge shot can be treacherous.

Castlerock's best known hole is the fourth, called Leg of Mutton. It combines a threatening creek on the left, a railway track on the right, and a raised green that is extremely difficult to hold. After a straightforward par 5, the front nine ends with four fine holes, usually into a stiff breeze. The sixth is a dogleg over a burn just in front of the green, while the seventh and eighth may be the best holes on the course – strong par 4s that feature greens set naturally and challengingly in the dunes. No bunkers are required. After the ninth, an extraordinarily difficult par 3 over 200 yards of gorse and rock, you will be ready to recuperate in the rustic halfway house.

The back nine offers more of the same, a mix of expansive and quirky downhill holes and formidable uphill ones. Against the wind, the par-5 fifteenth is perhaps the best, with its semi-blind tee shot and a narrow, twisting fairway that leads to an elevated green set in the dunes.

Castlerock finishes on an idiosyncratic note, a dogleg around an enormous mound to a sharply elevated green. It is the only green left from the original 1901 course, and if the eighteenth is unlikely to be copied by any modern architect, it is an engaging reminder of the club's turn-of-the-century origins. Castlerock has long had a reputation for being an informal and welcoming club, and the clubhouse, if not an architectural gem, boasts one of the friendliest bars in Northern Ireland.

Location: In town of Castlerock, 6 miles northwest of Coleraine

Restrictions: Weekdays are best for visitors; weekend play after 3:00 p.m. is also available

Green Fee: £60–75

Manager: Mark Steen

Address: 65 Circular Road, Castlerock, Co. Londonderry, BT51 4TJ, Northern Ireland; **tel:** (028) 7084-8314; **fax:** (028) 7084-9440; **e-mail:** info@castlerockgc.co.uk; **web:** www.castlerockgc.co.uk

PORTSTEWART

Founded: 1894

Designed by: A. G. Gow, Des Giffin, Willie Park Jr

Men pretend that they go [to Portstewart] for golf, and better golfing they will not find anywhere, but in the depths of their hearts they go to the wind-blown spaces in search of beauty and to hear the old music that has been played there for a million years – the lark's song, the sound of the waves, the curlew's call, the plover's flute – and inhale an air that is at once redolent of the mountains and the sea, the fragrance of flowers and the faint piquant incense of a thousand turf fires in the mountain homes across the Bann.

THE NORTHERN CONSTITUTION NEWSPAPER, 1933

With the addition of seven splendid holes, the venerable links at Portstewart well and truly emerged from the shadow of its magnificent neighbour, Royal Portrush, in the early 1990s. There are actually fifty-four links holes here, but it is only the championship course, the Strand, that you will need to play. The front nine is among the best anywhere, and the first hole is in a class by itself. Wonderfully situated between a gorgeous stretch of Atlantic beach and the River Bann, Portstewart offers links golf at its thrilling and scenic best. Enjoy.

PORTSTEWART

◆◆◆

Almost from its founding in 1792, the seaside resort of Portstewart has competed for holiday-makers with neighbouring Portrush, only a few miles down the road. Two hundred years later, the fact that Portstewart usually came out second best has its rewards, for today it seems a more graceful and restful place than its relatively brash rival. (It also has the highest house prices in Northern Ireland.)

For its first century, Portstewart was more or less ruled by the Cromie family, who owned most of the town's land and leased it out to residents. By all accounts, the Cromies were a rather moralistic and domineering lot who tended to put principle ahead of good sense. In 1855, John Cromie made the fateful decision to keep the railway from coming into Portstewart because it ran on Sundays. Portrush had no such qualms and immediately began to prosper at Portstewart's expense.

The introduction of golf in 1895 was just one in a long line of attempts to lure vacationers back to Portstewart. The civic chest-beating even made its way into the club's original constitution.

'Portstewart has been regarded as an old-fashioned Derry village, nestling quietly and quaintly by the seashore, beyond the sound of the rushing railway train,' the document states. 'Portstewart, like every other watering place of any pretensions, has [now] provided its visitors with a golf links. After all this, who can truthfully say that Portstewart lags behind?'

The early members at Portstewart were all well-to-do, but the first among equals was, naturally, the heir to the Cromie estate. Robert Acheson Cromie Montagu, the first captain and president, was also something of a sandbagger, winning more than his share of the handicap competitions.

Britain's social structure gradually evolved and the club's membership broadened. The town's moralistic bent remained, however and it almost bankrupted the golf course in the cash-scarce years following the First World War. Each year at the annual meeting, a determined group of evangelical members would block motions to allow a bar in the clubhouse and golf on Sunday – reforms long since adopted in Portrush and the rest of Ireland, north and south. The motions finally passed in 1950, but not before opponents had cited everything from the Communist Menace to Creeping Materialism in their crusade to keep Portstewart dry and

Sabbath-observing. In the records of the fierce debates one can get a taste of the kind of impassioned rhetoric that would fuel the Troubles two decades later.

The Portstewart links, like many in Ireland, has undergone constant evolution. The current course has its origins in a layout designed in 1910 by A. G. Gow, the greenkeeper at Portrush and formerly at North Berwick in Scotland. This routing appears to have stayed more or less intact until the 1960s. Bill Rodgers, a local historian, believes that Willie Park Jr, who is often given credit for the design, made only a few changes during his visit in 1913. The members themselves have been less reticent, and have fiddled with the course from the start, most notoriously in 1931, when dozens of new bunkers were dug in preparation for a tournament. The members spent the next decade gradually filling them in again.

To their everlasting credit, however, the members had a collective stroke of genius in 1951, when Portstewart was selected to be a site for qualifying for the British Open held at Royal Portrush. They decided to move the first tee high up on a perch overlooking the course, and to push the first green deep into the dunes. The result was one of the most satisfying first holes in all of golf.

By the 1950s Portstewart had gained a reputation as a first-rate – if not outstanding – links, and members took pride in the fact that the British Open competitors actually found Royal Portrush easier than Portstewart. But next to the jewel that was (and is) the Dunluce course at Royal Portrush, Portstewart found it hard to sparkle. The club kept trying, but revisions to the back nine in the 1970s were not widely acclaimed. The only thing left to do was to extend the course into the wild terrain of Thistly Hollow.

Thistly Hollow was a particularly treacherous stretch of giant sand hills, covered by a thick layer of sea buckthorn, that had tantalized members for many decades. It had long been considered too expensive to develop the land, but modern earth-moving equipment had changed things. In typically Portstewart fashion, the task of designing the new holes was given to a local who had spent his childhood playing in the wild wasteland – the Greens Convenor and school teacher, Des Giffin.

The work was completed in 1992. Although it is still possible to find a particularly crotchety member in the bar who grumbles that the course was better in the old days, the new holes are splendid.

The course

If first impressions are important, it's no wonder that Portstewart has many friends. The first tee perches above the course, and there is a terrific panorama of ocean, sand hills, the River Bann and even the hills of Donegal in the distance. Jogging down the steep incline you feel swallowed up by the linksland. Exposed to the wind, which is usually in the golfer's face, it takes a brave first shot to be long and straight enough to attack the green, which is guarded by dunes and is really but a rumour at the end of a marvellous vista.

The second hole is almost as breathtaking and every bit as nerve-wracking – another steep drop from the tee to a narrow strip of fairway that rises up to a sloping green set in the sand hills. When the wind is howling there doesn't seem to be anything one can do to keep the ball in play (an illusion, actually). A professional could perhaps overpower the hole, but it's a stirring challenge for an average player.

The rest of the front nine is high-octane excitement, as you twist through Thistly Hollow via elevated tees and tricky, undulating greens. The fairways are narrow and hard and the rough unforgiving. The sixth is the best of a series of fine par 3s, a 'Five Penny Piece' set up alone in the elements, and dropping off sharply on all sides. On a blustery day it can take a long iron to traverse its 127 yards, and it is always a thrill to see your tee shot land softly on the green. Many members hate the new eighth, a severe and downhill dogleg that seems to lean in all the wrong directions – like those funhouses at the fair where the floor moves. The lies are usually downhill *and* side hill, the green slopes wickedly as well, and a couple of vicious pot bunkers swallow up the shots of anyone who bails out. We rather like it.

The back nine begins with two uphill, upwind slogs and another difficult par 3. But just when the fun is threatening to turn into an ordeal, everything changes in exhilarating fashion on the hugely elevated thirteenth tee. The towering dunes of Thistly Hollow are now behind you, replaced by the idyllic Bann, and you are likely to see fishermen casting picturesquely from the shore. The prevailing wind is, at last, right at your back and in front of you are two shortish par 5s that, relative to the tight terrors of Thistly Hollow, seem to be wide open. On a truly windy day you get almost light-headed, so drastic is the transformation – from hitting three good shots to reach an upwind par 4, to needing a good drive and an eight iron to reach a par 5 in two. You return to earth with the fourteenth – a dandy par 3 into the wind, and three stiff par 4s that have been around for more than a century.

It's all terrific fun and certainly Portstewart need no longer feel it is 'lagging behind'.

Location: Just west of town centre on the Strand

Restrictions: Visitors welcome anytime except Wednesdays and Saturdays before 3:00 p.m.

Green Fee: £70–90

Manager: Michael Moss

Address: 117 Strand Rd., Portstewart, Co. Londonderry, BT55 7PG, Northern Ireland; **tel:** (028) 7083-2015; **fax:** (028) 7083-4097; **e-mail:** michael@portstewartgc.co.uk; **web:** www.portstewartgc.co.uk

ROYAL COUNTY DOWN

Founded: 1889

Designed by: Old Tom Morris, George Combe, H. S. Colt

Many people know Newcastle and it is perhaps superfluous to say that it is a course of big and glorious carries, nestling greens, entertainingly blind shots, local knowledge, and beautiful turf . . . the kind of golf that people play in their most ecstatic dreams.

BERNARD DARWIN

Set dramatically in the foothills of the Mountains of Mourne, Royal County Down is recognized by all who have played it as one of the finest and most beautiful golf courses in the world. Much of the course's unique beauty comes from its fiercest hazard – the flowering gorse and heather that line its fairways. Then there is Slieve Donard, the graceful peak that rises up behind the town of Newcastle, creating a perfect backdrop for a course that seems to have been created with a postcard in mind. As striking as they are,

253

photographs don't do Royal County Down justice. On a sunny day, when the gorse is in full bloom and the scent of peat fires is on the breeze, the combination of scenic splendour, world-class links golf and the marvellous sense of isolation can be transporting. These are the links of heaven. You won't want the day to end.

◆◆◆

It was two o'clock on a sunny Saturday afternoon in April, my turn to play off the first tee, and I was finding it damned difficult to figure out which of the golf balls I was seeing was mine.

It was all very embarrassing. After all, it's not every day you are invited to Captain's Day on possibly the finest links course in the world.

Things had started well enough. As is the case every other Saturday at County Down, the members were playing a series of fourball matches. My name had been put into the hat, my partner and opponents set by the 'Hat Man'. The stakes were a pound and '50 pence on the bye'.

So far so good. If only someone had advised me on how to navigate the pre-round lunch, which at County Down is eaten with the members of your group.

Not that the food wasn't lovely – a shank of lamb in the wood-panelled dining room, washed down by some very acceptable claret. Along with most everyone else present, I had consumed a couple of gin and tonics (or was it three?) in the members bar upon arrival, but I felt things were well under control. I could still walk and talk in a straight line, the company was intelligent and often hilarious, and there was still a round to play on just about everybody's favourite golf course.

But then came the *coup de grace*. One of my dining companions, a High Court Judge from Belfast, asked me rather matter-of-factly:

'Some Kummel?'

'Uh, why not?' I said, assuming he was referring to some kind of pudding. Instead, kummel turned out to be a caraway-scented spirit consumed in significant quantities (I later learned) by many of the posher clubs in the United Kingdom.

I had one, and then the judge offered me another. The slightest of smiles on his face made me feel my manhood was somehow being questioned.

'Absolutely!' I replied, downing another shot. And the match was over before it even started.

You won't be surprised to learn that the kummel-pouring judge was not my partner, but one of my opponents. Nine of the world's most gorgeous golf holes flashed before my eyes before I had sobered up enough to hit a single ball cleanly.

The caraway in Kummel is supposed to be a relaxant (and no doubt so is the 39 per cent alcohol) but in my own experience it doesn't appreciably help one's putting, chipping or driving. Or walking.

But then I'm not a member of Royal County Down.

'How do they hit the ball after all that....drinking?' I slurred to the nearest caddie after my fourth consecutive shank.

'Oh, they say many couldn't hit the ball without it,' was the reply.

It wasn't until the fourteenth hole that I realized our group had one too many in it. A rather agile man was rambling beside us through County Down's famous rough. A very attentive gallery of one.

'The judge's bodyguard,' I was told.

That bit of information, a reminder of the Troubles that can still not be left entirely behind in Northern Ireland, at least for those who live there, had a sobering effect, though it was far too late to salvage the match.

There were rather more coffees after the match than before, and by dinner time the club was just about empty.

It had been a magical, if tipsy day, and it had all come about because that year's captain had been given an earlier edition of this book for his birthday. He wrote us a letter to point out what he thought were inaccuracies.

Was he going to sue us? Complain to the publisher? No, he thought he'd invite us to be his guests on the most important date of his captaincy. A classy gesture we're not soon to forget.

Needless to say, you don't have to be 'properly introduced' to have a magical time at Royal County Down, a blessedly tranquil place where golf, on a warm summer day, can turn into a kind of dream.

In common with all Irish clubs established before the turn of the century, the miracle began with a cluster of well-off Protestants – this time from Belfast – who wanted to spread the game of golf into Ireland as an upper-class pastime.

They hired Old Tom Morris of St Andrews to design the original eighteen holes in 1889, but by 1902 only six of his holes were left. George Combe, an early captain, and one of the leading figures in Irish golf, made a series of alterations. Combe was something of a golf pioneer, introducing metal cup-liners to Ireland, inventing a wooden teeing box to protect the turf in wet weather, and devising a new handicapping system, parts of which were adopted worldwide.

Combe also brought over luminaries such as Harry Vardon from England to play the links and to comment on the design. As head of the greens committee until 1913, Combe has to be given much of the credit for nurturing County Down into a great links. Finishing touches were made on the advice of H. S. Colt in the 1920s, and today Royal County Down is generally recognized as one of the top ten courses in the world.

One of the course's champions was the great golf writer, Bernard Darwin. Reporting in 1957 for *The Times* on a tournament held at Royal County Down, Darwin was full of praise:

> I am ashamed to say that I had not recognised Royal County Down as one of the world's greatest seaside courses. I now say that I have seen nothing finer, either as a test of the game or from the point of scenic splendour.

Although it has never hosted the Open Championship, Royal County Down is the site of the 2007 Walker Cup. It has also hosted the British Amateur, the Curtis Cup, a handful of British Senior Opens and no fewer than seven British Ladies' Amateur Championships.

While Royal County Down is a prestigious club it is in no way sectarian, though that didn't prevent it from being the target of a car-bomb attack on a Sunday morning in 1977. In a show of bravado of which the club is still proud, the debris was cleared up and the day's tournament went off as scheduled.

Although the bombing was by far the most serious and potentially tragic attack, the club's centenary book rather tantalizingly reports that a band of suffragettes vandalized the club back in the 1920s without providing any more details. If the members' chauvinism was at the root of the incident, things have changed for the better. Though they have their own clubhouse, women have equal rights on the main links, and can of course still play on the improved second course (initially built for the ladies). It has been over-hauled by David Steel.

The course

In addition to a beautiful setting, County Down has its own unique architecture, characterized by blind tee shots, some of the fiercest rough in Ireland, and deep pot bunkers that are set back a bit from the greens. Although the course has changed since the days of Old Tom Morris, the strategy for surviving at Royal County Down has not – don't miss the fairway. The knee-high fescue and ball-swallowing gorse make 'U.S. Open rough' seem tame by comparison.

Royal County Down is the world's greatest advertisement for the return of the blind shot from the tee. In the nineteenth century, when there were no bulldozers to level the undulating duneland where golf was first played, it was common for the drive to be played over a sand hill onto a fairway unseen from the tee. The following description of a long-since rearranged hole at County Down was published in the *Irish Golf Annual* of 1895:

> The tee of the 'Alps' (233 yards) is in the centre of an arena surrounded on all sides by towering sandhills. Right in front, and at a distance of 100 yards from the tee, stretches a terrible bunker. There is no playing round it; you must take your trusty club in hand and go for it; and who shall describe the feelings of that player who gets away a 'bonnie lick' as he stands and watches his ball rise straight over the guide-post and fall out of sight beyond. Crossing the 'Alps' by the steps the ball is seen lying on beautiful turf at the foot of the sandhills.

After the first round at County Down, the blind shots seem more like a challenge than a trick. They often provide lovely moments of surprise – the natural beauty of the course unfolds in a series of revelations as you climb over each rise. Besides, as Tommy Armour once said, 'a blind hole is only blind once to a golfer with a memory.' And since the changes made by Harry Colt, there have been no blind approach shots, at least not if you hit your drive in the correct portion of the fairway. The play to the green is usually clear and dazzling – and when surrounded by flowering gorse and heather, the greens are exceptionally beautiful.

Like any great golf course, Royal County Down is more than the sum of its parts, and much of its charm is intangible. The course has a pace of its own – each hole seems to tilt and bend in a different way, with the fairways narrowing and widening at unexpected and strategically interesting moments. The level of difficulty also ranges widely – from a par 5 that can be easily reached in two downwind, to the terrifying par-3 fourth, which requires a picture-perfect carry of 217 yards over a stunning expanse of whins and bunkers.

There is only one water hazard at County Down, a rather irrelevant little pond on the seventeenth that somehow cost Bernard Darwin a berth in the quarter-finals of the Irish Amateur in 1931. But the fierce rough makes every hole feel as if it is lined with danger. In the summer, the firm fairways will send the ball great distances, and there is almost always one line that enables you to avoid bunkers and run the ball onto the green. Keep the ball in play and you will be able to savour everything that County Down has to offer. If you have a wayward driver, leave it in the car.

Royal County Down's only shortcomings used to be found on its final three holes, and Donald Steel has gone some way to addressing these. The quirky, short par-4 sixteenth was just getting too short, even for good amateur players, so Steel has created an entirely new curving hole, still of tantalizing distance, full of the kind of options, risks and rewards that make County Down so special. He has also helped to tighten the final two holes.

The course still ends a little anticlimactically, and its wonderful seclusion is somewhat marred by some holes from the second course that come a little too close. But to dwell on such details is a little like parsing a haunting lyric for its grammar. As with a beautiful poem or song, Royal County Down is best appreciated in its glorious entirety.

Location: Golf Links Road, Newcastle (behind the Slieve Donard hotel)

Restrictions: Visitors are permitted Monday, Tuesday, Thursday and Friday, and on Sunday afternoons

Secretary: James Laidler

Green Fee: £120–150

Address: 36 Golf Links Rd., Newcastle BT33 0AN, Northern Ireland; **tel:** (028) 4372-3314; **fax:** (028) 4372-6281; **e-mail:** golf@royalcountydown.org; **web:** www.royalcountydown.org

ROYAL PORTRUSH

Founded: 1888; Redesigned: 1933

Designed by: H. S. Colt

[Portrush] is truly magnificent and Mr H. S. Colt, who designed it in its present form, has thereby built himself a monument more enduring than brass.

BERNARD DARWIN, 1951

Site of the only British Open played in Ireland, the Dunluce links at Royal Portrush Golf Club is one of the masterpieces of golf architecture. Compared to some Irish links, the terrain is rather sedate, and the natural setting, while nice enough, is not in a league with County Down or even nearby Portstewart. It is the intelligence, precision and balance of the design that captivates at Portrush. Each hole presents a new and elegant challenge, yet each seems cut from the same cloth. Then there is Calamity, one of the world's most famous par 3s, and the glorious exclamation point that every great course seems to have.

◆◆◆

Now that solutions to the unrest in Northern Ireland seem conceivable, and the possibility at least exists that the British Open could return to the magnificent links in the busy seaside resort of Portrush, the number of visitors are swelling. And although everyone is friendly and helpful enough, there is an air of we-are-doing-you-a-favour-just-letting-you-play-here that one doesn't normally find in Ireland. It is, of course, the kind of thing that descends on just about any place where demand exceeds supply.

It is hardly a new phenomenon for Portrush, which was one of the world's most popular golf courses *more than a hundred years ago*. In the roaring '80s and '90s – nineteenth-century variety – Portrush was a fashionable and hopping holiday destination. There were regular ferries from Glasgow, fast trains from Belfast, and a tramway that whisked visitors to the nearby Giant's Causeway ('Worth seeing? Yes; but not worth going to see,' Dr Johnson said of the famous attraction). Portrush was a 'progressive' Victorian resort, meaning you could have a good time there, and the year-round population of 1,600 swelled several-fold during the summer months. Golf was exploding in popularity all over the British Isles, so when a couple of Scottish-born golf enthusiasts persuaded the Earl of Antrim to lease them ground for a links, it was an instant hit.

Golfers from Scotland, England and other parts of Ireland poured into Portrush. In 1900, a major British magazine described Portrush as the 'St Andrews of Ireland', and promised that the visitor would be treated with 'plenteous kindness and whisky'. By the turn of the century there were already seven hundred members (almost three hundred of them women), making it the largest golf club in Ireland, and one of the largest in the world. Most members were from out of town, including one hundred from Lancashire! In 1908, no fewer than seven thousand paying visitors played the course – a colossal number for the time – and just as today there were moves to restrict play.

It was also a glorious time for women's golf at Portrush. There were more female members than today, and two of them – May Hezlet and Rhona Adair – were probably the best women golfers in the world as the century ended. Between them they won the British Ladies Amateur Championship, then the world title for women, four times in five years. Years later Rhona Adair made a celebrated trip to America and beat Margaret Curtis (who later donated the Curtis Cup) on the twentieth hole of an exhibition match at Merion.

The links used in the 1890s was nothing like today's, but by all accounts it was outstanding for its time. Its most notorious feature was the world's largest man-made bunker – 150 yards across. In early photographs it resembles a meteor crater.

Despite the success of the club, members decided in the early 1930s to move the course to undeveloped linksland nearer the ocean. H. S. Colt was paid £212 for his design (a considerable sum for the day) and construction cost another £6,000. It was money well spent. Only eighteen years later the course hosted the British Open.

Bernard Darwin, reporting on the 1951 Open for *The Times*, had never before seen the Dunluce course. He was, to say the least, impressed.

'The first Open Championship ever held in Ireland was begun at Portrush yesterday,' he wrote, 'and I must to my shame confess that I have never before seen this grand course. Let me at once pay it my respectful compliments.'

The tournament was won by Max Faulkner, who never broke 70; he was to be the last British-born champion until Tony Jacklin in 1969. American stars were not present (this was before the Palmer revival) so the drama centred mostly on whether Bobby Locke would win his third straight Open. Locke failed, but did manage to lend his name to a famous corner of the golf world at the fourteenth.

A second of golf's major championships – the British Amateur – was played at Portrush in 1960, with the Irish star Joe Carr triumphant, and in recent years the British Senior Open has visited Portrush on a number of occasions.

As with so many links, Portrush is in a constant battle with the elements. In the early 1980s, erosion threatened the fifth green and sixth tee, perhaps the most charming corner of the course and certainly the one with the best views. A £200,000 relief scheme was launched, and by the mid-1980s Portrush was peddling life memberships at $500 a pop to any American willing to help out.

That would have been quite a bargain, as Portrush now charges about half that for a day's golf. The erosion problem seems well under control now, the sport is booming again in Ireland, and Portrush, with its British Open pedigree, was the first in Northern Ireland to feel the benefits.

The course

Portrush's charms are not easily defined, and one is extremely hesitant to go where Bernard Darwin has gone before. In his report on the 1951 British Open, the dean of golf writers described the Dunluce course this way:

The course does not disdain the spectacular, such as the one-shot hole called 'Calamity Corner' with its terrifying sandy cliffs and its Gadarene descent into unknown depths to the right of the green; for the most part, the course does not depend on any such dramatic quality, but rather on the combined soundness and subtlety of the architecture. There is a constant demand for accuracy of driving, the more so at present as the rough is really worthy of its name and the approaches are full of varied interest. In particular there are one or two holes of the despised length called 'drive and pitch' which are entirely fascinating, such as the fifth, with its green almost on the brink of the sea, and the fifteenth. The greens are full of interesting undulations and altogether I find it hard to imagine a more admirable test of golf.

Nothing has happened since to date Darwin's assessment. Colt's fairways remain elegant, clearly defined, well proportioned and full of purpose. Every tee-shot presents a different challenge – the bunkers are never in the same place, the doglegs never turn at the same angle, and the elevation never seems quite the same. There is a dance-like quality to playing Portrush; it sweeps you along and swings you in a most rhythmic way, but never off your feet.

A pair of holes midway through the outward half offer a good example. The fourth is a long, fairly straight par 4 made special by exquisite fairway bunkering, the roll of the fairway, and the marvellous, if strenuous, approach shot to a green half hidden in a little dell. The hole that follows is, by contrast, a short dogleg par 4 that offers all range of hitters increasingly risky ways to cut the corner, and a tricky and exposed seaside green guarded by the most subtle of knolls. The way the fairway snakes through the sand hills – never very wide, with few steep descents or inclines, but never flat – is pure Portrush, and in this case there are no bunkers at all.

Of course none of these nuances apply to Calamity, the mere sight of which can suck the air out of your lungs. Unless, of course, you hit a one iron like Jack Nicklaus. Colt set this 205-yard par 3 along the ridge of a deep chasm, leaving only a modest space to bail out on the left of the green, which has since become known as 'Bobby Locke's Hollow'. In the 1951 Open, Locke played to the spot each round, preferring to chip his second shot rather than risk disaster from the tee. Unfortunately, for most of us Bobby Locke's Hollow is not much easier to hit than the green itself. Calamity is a hole in the heroic mould, a great crashing of cymbals that only calls attention to the subtle charms that are more characteristic of Portrush.

Since Colt liked to test more than a golfer's length, the average player does not feel overwhelmed by Portrush and can fully appreciate its allure and challenge. There are six par 4s under 400 yards, and the four par 5s are all about 500 yards or less.

If there's a breather, it comes at the pretty, short eleventh hole. But you are unlikely to do better than Graham Marsh. He scored an ace here twice during the 2004 Senior British Open, the only time that's happened in a top-flight tournament.

In all, six Senior British Opens have been played at Portrush in recent years, and several have been decided at the par-5 seventeenth, which features one of the largest bunkers in Ireland (about 220 yards from the tee, it is terrifying for the slice-prone but, alas, not much in play any more for the professionals). In 1995 Brian Barnes, son-in-law of Portrush's Open champion Max Faulkner, made a spectacular eagle here in a playoff to outduel American Bob Murphy.

And in 1997, sixty-one-year-old Gary Player calmly got up and down from a difficult lie in a greenside bunker, enabling him to become the oldest champion ever. Player was visibly emotional afterwards, aware that this was likely the last time he would win such a big event. But he thought the course was ready to stage an even bigger one.

'This is one of the greatest Open courses,' he said. 'And I would love to see (another) British Open round here one day,' he said.

Amen.

The **Valley Links** at Portrush is by no means a weak test of golf, and has gained in our estimation. There are some lovely natural holes, often with minimal bunkering, and since the vegetation and terrain in the valley is quite different (the rough has more heather and the fairways, with the exception of an occasional steep descent or climb, are generally flatter) it has a very different feel from the famous Dunluce. Though it has obviously received less attention and care than its famous sister course, the Valley Links is still used for some fairly important regional competitions. One of its biggest fans is Tom Doak, the celebrated American golf architect and writer, who particularly admires the four finishing holes, and calls the Valley 'an exceptional, overlooked layout, perhaps the third best in Northern Ireland'. We wouldn't go that far, but you may want to go judge for yourself.

Location: Just east of town on Bushmills Road (the A2 highway)

Restrictions: Best days for visitors are weekdays, except for Monday mornings and afternoons on Wednesday and Friday. Weekend play is possible after 3:00 p.m. on Saturdays and during the late morning and after 2:00 p.m. on Sundays

Green Fee: £105–120 (Dunluce); £35–40 (Valley)

Secretary: Wilma Erskine

Address: Dunluce Rd., Portrush, Co. Antrim, BT56 8JQ, Northern Ireland; **tel:** (028) 7082-2311; **fax:** (028) 7082-3139; **e-mail:** info@royalportrushgolfclub.com; **web:** www.royalportrushgolfclub.com

OTHER COURSES OF INTEREST

Ardglass

Founded: 1896

Designed by: The Members

[The course] stretches over the extensive verdant plateau known as the Downs, surrounded on three sides by the sea: On the North by Ardglass Bay, on the East by the Irish Channel, and on the south by Killough Bay. Precipitous, riven headlands border the sea and the prospect is altogether singularly beautiful.

DOWN RECORDER, 1898

Venturing forth into the wind to subdue the first four holes at Ardglass is one of golf's most formidable adventures. Scrambling up the ridge of a rocky cliff, with the crashing surf of the Irish Sea filling the ears, it seems fitting that your progress should be covered by a battery of cannons, poised in front of Ardglass Castle, and pointed directly at the first green. For this is golf's version of a military siege, with shots rejected by all manner of rock formations, earth embankments and stone walls. So what if the rest of the course can't keep up to the spectacular drama of the opening quartet? If it did, you might never reach the nineteenth hole, with its promise of a pint in one of the most intriguing clubhouses anywhere.

◆◆◆

If *Candid Camera* wants to do a golf segment, may we humbly suggest that they stick a hidden microphone in the back tee of the first hole at Ardglass, and wait for a group to turn up that hasn't played the course before. If our own experience is any indication, a variety of comical double takes will be followed by some combination of the following queries (expletives have been deleted):

-Is this some kind of a joke?
-You want us to play over *that cliff?*
-Is the bar open yet?

OK, the opening hole is not quite as hard as it looks, but then how could it be? A relatively short, but steep 327 yards, it requires a hefty uphill drive over a seam in the high cliffs that provide Ardglass with its stunning sea views. After that there are strange rocky mounds and fierce swales to navigate, and one the world's cruellest bunkers is placed right in front of the elevated, and mostly hidden green. If the wind is howling in your face, as it was on our first visit, then it seems less like a golf hole than a training exercise for a crack team from the Special Forces.

Then the course really gets tough. We hit driver into the breeze on the 162-yard second, which is played across Howd's Hole, a steep crevice in the side of the cliff that makes your stomach churn should you be foolish enough to peer into it. This being Ireland, it's all in play, of course, and the nauseating descent hasn't stopped the occasional rock climbing enthusiast from going after his errant golf ball. A prominent local surgeon once ventured a little too far into Howd's Hole, and had to be rescued *by ship* from the rocky shore below.

The third and fourth holes, both par 4s, also follow the cliff edge, and are equally exhilarating, if not quite as life-threatening, and by now you are beginning to think that, compared to this, Pebble Beach is nothing special.

Ardglass Golf Club was founded during the British golf boom of the 1890s by a group of local Protestant luminaries who leased land around the Ardglass Estate. The impressive manor on the site had been built in the 1790s on the site of a fortified medieval trading station, and considerable portions of the fourteenth-century structure were retained as an attachment to the new residence. The most important and fascinating resident was William Ogilvie, a former tutor who married his employer, the Duchess of Leinster, after her husband died. A good thing for Ardglass, for when he moved to the town in 1806 at the age of sixty-six he set about transforming the sleepy backwater, building hot sea baths and hotels to attract visitors, digging out the town harbour, and donating land and money to both Protestant and Catholic churches. (Ask for the excellent club history by George Rice if you wish to learn more.)

The estate had fallen on hard times by the time Ogilvie's great-grandson, Aubrey De Vere Beauclerk (himself a descendant of Charles II's mistress Nell Gwynn) agreed to lease the property to the fledgling golf club. The members laid out the first seven holes in April 1896, bought the property and manor outright in 1927, and finally extended the course to eighteen holes in 1970.

After the fantastic opening stretch of holes, the rest of the course, much of it built on relatively flat farmland, used to be something of a let down, and there was a sense that Ardglass could benefit from the touch of a professional designer. The members obviously agreed, hiring the services of former Northern Ireland touring professional David Jones, who is also responsible for the successful changes to the Killeen course at Killarney. In 2003, he added three holes to Ardglass on newly purchased land at the far end of the course, next to the sea, and these additions (the ninth, tenth and eleventh) add considerable excitement where there was little before. That said, the best hole remains the short twelfth, which drops dramatically towards the sea, and which has fortunately been left untouched.

There have been real losses as well, however. Two charming, if old-fashioned holes were sacrificed in the new routing. 'The Wall' was a singular par 5 that required a second shot over an ancient six-foot stone fence, while 'The Downs' was a quirky par 3 perched up high in the winds that had been around for a century.

If the first hole at Ardglass is the most terrifying, the last is the easiest – a downhill par 4 that slaloms its way towards an eighteenth-century sundial and the impressive clubhouse. You half expect someone from British Heritage to charge you admittance, but instead you are welcomed into a convivial club bar, where you can take a deep breath and make sure everyone from your expedition to Ardglass is accounted for.

Location: At the seaside in the town of Ardglass, near the town centre

Restrictions: None, though weekdays are best

Green Fee: £35–50

Manager: Deborah Polly

Address: Castle Place, Ardglass, Co. Down BT30 7TP, Northern Ireland; **tel:** (028) 4484-1219; **fax:** (028) 4484-1841; **e-mail:** info@ardglassgolfclub.com; **web:** www.ardglassgolfclub.com

Royal Belfast

Founded: 1881
Designed by: H. S. Colt

My greatest memory at the club? Getting in.

Member of Royal Belfast Golf Club

The members of Northern Ireland's oldest club are a little paranoid about their status as, well, members of Royal Belfast, but that shouldn't stop you from playing one of the finest parkland courses in Ireland.

Designed by H.S. Colt in 1927, Royal Belfast is beautifully situated rather high up on the shore of the Belfast Lough, and the views of the harbour are a constant treat. Apart from some minor tweaking, the original layout remains intact, and for this, at least, the members need to be heartily congratulated.

Of the three jewels Harry Colt built in Northern Ireland (Belvoir Park and Royal Portrush being the others) Royal Belfast is perhaps built on the least promising landscape. There is much open and seemingly featureless ground and, except for the views, water plays a minor part. Instead, Colt used changes in elevation to outstanding effect, with strategy influenced by finely placed bunkers, subtle doglegs and the natural undulations of the fairways and greens. Although in places there are plenty of mature trees, they serve mostly as backdrops and only occasionally influence shot-making. The result is a parkland course that often has the spaciousness and feel of a links, and the exposure to the sea only adds to the impression.

The 174-yard eleventh is one of the best uphill par 3s we have played. The hole begins on the edge of the cliff, where the views of the harbour are at their most sublime. In the sharpest of contrasts, the tee shot must be hit up a steep slope into what appears to be a chaotic jungle of bushes and trees and gorse. The surface of the green is nowhere in sight. This could so easily have been a deadly slog of a hole, but Colt somehow knew that if he made the pin half visible through a V-shaped opening in the riot of foliage, it would provide a delightfully tantalizing, if intimidating target. As it turns out, the hole is a kind of visual joke, for the green has a surprising amount of safe area around it. But it is hard to convince yourself of that on the tee, and there is more than enough trouble to swallow up the shot of anyone whose nerves truly get the best of them.

This gem is book-ended by two terrific and entirely different par-4 holes. The uphill, 307-yard tenth features a classic risk-reward tee shot over a gorse-filled gully (how much of the dogleg do you cut off?) with a narrow, tricky green that challenges even a short approach shot. The 430-yard twelfth, on the other hand, rollicks back down the same hill, with a broad fairway that seems to invite a freewheeling drive. This is an illusion of a different kind, however, as the natural contours of the fairway (and the green) will kick wayward balls into very difficult spots.

The rest of the course is only marginally less interesting and it is peculiar that Royal Belfast has hosted relatively few competitions. It could be that the club finds it just a bit difficult to mix with outsiders, for its notion of hospitality seems to have changed little from the era of its founding, a time when social class really counted for something. The early history of the club is chock full of Lords, and it is no surprise that the club was able to secure the 'Royal' designation only four years after its inception, even though the course at the time was little more than a peat bog.

The club moved twice before finding its current home. The writer of a club history positively sighs with satisfaction when he arrives at the point when the club was able to purchase the Craigavad House (now the clubhouse) and Demesne in 1925: 'It was felt that here at last an opportunity presented itself of acquire a really dignified home for the Club.'

Built in 1852 by Thomas Turner, the same architect responsible for Belfast's famous Stormont Castle, the clubhouse is certainly handsome. The commodious main lounge has panoramic views of Belfast Lough, so bring a jacket and tie if you can, as the casual bar isn't anything to write home about. There is a full-fledged dining room as well.

They've removed the Keep Out sign in the driveway that used to be the only indication that you had arrived at Royal Belfast, but they still don't like it much if you just show up. Not that the course is crowded, even on weekends. Still, if you write and phone ahead the club will gladly accept your green fees.

A word of warning. Although the members sometimes let it drop that they receive visits from their 'friends from Augusta', the conditioning of Royal Belfast is not in that sort of league, especially early in the season. During one visit (about Masters time, in fact) the greens of a public course down the road were in rather better shape.

Location: On Station Road, just off the A2 (the primary road from Belfast to Bangor), turn left on to Station Road if travelling from Belfast

Restrictions: Any day except Wednesday and Saturday; always make reservations in advance

Green Fee: £46–56

Manager: Mrs S.H. Morrison

Address: Station Road, Craigavad, Holywood, Co. Down, BT19 0BP, Northern Ireland; **tel:** (028) 9042-8165; **fax:** (028) 9042-1404; **e-mail:** manager@royalbelfast.com; **web:** www.royalbelfast.com

---

Belvoir Park

Founded: 1927

Designed by: H. S. Colt

The 1920s were a tough time in Belfast, so it took a group of luminaries to pull off the feat of building a world-class golf course in the midst of an economic depression, with memories of the Irish Civil War still fresh.

Nothing would have happened had the land not been donated by one Lord Duramore, on a lease of a mere 10,000 years; and the first captain was the Lord Mayor of Belfast. But the key figure was Anthony Babington. A long-time Attorney General of Northern Ireland, and also an active member of Royal Portrush (where the sixteenth hole bears his name), it was Babington who convinced the club to hire Harry Colt for the job of designing its new course.

The result is a quiet triumph, with the same kind of natural flow and strategic excellence that makes Portrush such a joy to play. It is to the members' credit that they have made few changes to the original design, though over the years they have had the foresight to plant more than 40,000 trees. The legacy is a beautifully forested course that is a shockingly peaceful oasis in an area of Belfast overrun by noisy urban sprawl.

A hole that the members *have* changed, and arguably not for the better, is the third. Among the hardest holes you will play in Ireland, it is an uphill, sharply doglegged par 4 of 435 yards which was always difficult, but which now is all but unmanageable. Not only has the new green been set farther back, and higher up, it is also now guarded in front by two bunkers and a steep embankment. In a final masochistic flourish, the members have also made the green *humpbacked*, ensuring the rejection of even the most heroic two iron or three wood by a mid-handicapper. The end result is out of kilter with Colt's usual careful balance between risk and reward.

Things get back into stride on the fourth, a lovely, steep downhill par 3 with five vivid sand traps guarding the green. The next three holes make their way gently and prettily through the flattest terrain on the course, a place where good scores are essential. The eighth is a devilish and pretty hole of only 130 yards, and the ninth is a short par 5 with a gyrating fairway and a severely sloping green that has been turning an easy birdie into a frustrating bogey for seventy-five years.

The back nine is more muscular, difficult and consistently exciting, played over severe dips and valleys and made even better by the mature trees that have grown up since Colt first laid out the course. There are two terrific dogleg par 4s at twelve and thirteen, and the sixteenth is a superb par 3 of understated elegance, requiring a perfect long iron to a green placed on slightly elevated land behind two deep bunkers, The trees around the hole are set well back, and it's a hole that wouldn't look out of place at Portrush. Certainly, the simplicity and natural beauty of the hole is a reminder of golf's links heritage.

The seventeenth is another fine par 4 through dense forest that requires a long, heroic second over a deep crevice to an elevated green, but this time with the kind of opening (dangerously narrow, but fair) missing on the third.

As at Portrush, the eighteenth is a bit of an anticlimax, but there is plenty of exceptional golf at Belvoir Park to make the post-round drinks satisfying. Given its upper class pedigree, Belvoir Park is a surprisingly informal club, and you shouldn't have much trouble joining the members in their boisterous bar. And once there you are as likely to put down a pint with a policeman as a judge.

Location: Newtownbreda, about 4 miles southeast of central Belfast. Take Ormeau Road toward Saintfield and Newcastle if travelling from the city centre

Restrictions: Any day but Saturday

Green Fee: £45–55

Secretary/Manager: Ann Vaughan

Address: 73 Church Road, Newtownbreda, Belfast BT8 7AN, Northern Ireland; **tel:** (028) 9049-1693; **fax:** (028) 9064-6113; **e-mail:** info@belvoirparkgolfclub.com; **web:** www.belvoirparkgolfclub.com

Malone

Established: 1895
Designed by: John Harris and Fred Hawtree

Another golf club ... has just been organised in the beautiful suburban district of Malone, within easy distance from our city, either by train or by tramcar, and judging from the zeal and energy displayed by its promoters the new club augurs well to be one of the most successful ventures of the kind which has so far been undertaken in the province of Ulster.

BELFAST NEWS, 29 APRIL 1895

Malone Golf Club is one of the most colourful and famous in Ireland, and it is surely the only club in the world to ask Alister Mackenzie for its money back!

In 1919, the future designer of Lahinch, Augusta National and Cypress Point was paid £300, a considerable sum at the time, to lay out a new golf course on what was already Malone's third home in Belfast. No sooner had the work finished than the club's members were grumbling and demanding a refund.

In response, Mackenzie's firm insisted that 'the plan of the course and the design of the greens are what may be termed quite good' and 'that if a fault does really exist in the quality of the work done, it is due to a lack of understanding of Dr Mackenzie's instructions by workmen who carried out the job.' Malone prevailed in the dispute, and Mackenzie refunded two-thirds of his fee.

It is entirely possible that Mackenzie was more than a little hard done by, as his handiwork was good enough to establish Malone as one of the premier courses in Ireland. By 1931, it had attracted 850 members, and was reported to be the among the largest twelve golf clubs in the world. And it was with real remorse that, forty years later, the members decided they had to abandon the Mackenzie course because of encroaching housing developments.

The designer of the next course, John Harris, fared as poorly as Mackenzie. A new generation of members proved as grumpy as their predecessors, and started complaining even before the first ball was hit in the summer of 1962. Among the criticisms was that the picturesque twenty-seven-acre lake on the new property didn't come into play once! (Harris later maintained that he had been told to route the holes away from the water.) Another architect, Fred Hawtree, was brought in to redesign most of what is now the back nine, and several holes on the front side were rejigged by the members themselves.

Malone's large and motivated membership (there has always been an active Ladies section) have made significant volunteer contributions to the administration of the sport in Ireland, and for many years Malone teams were feared throughout the land in Ireland's much loved inter-club competitions. As agitation for Catholic rights in Northern Ireland began in earnest in the late 1960s, however, Malone's prominence attracted less welcome attention. Catholic nationalists considered golf clubs to be bastions of the Ulster establishment, and the club's official history recalls the morning when civil rights protesters 'delivered a number of children to the Club with the sole purpose of disrupting golf by sitting in the bunkers.' In February, 1972, things turned far more grave, when a bomb blew up much of the clubhouse.

There have not been any serious incidents since, and Malone has evolved into a comfortable twenty-seven-hole complex – built on a former estate – with members also enjoying trout fishing, squash and lawn bowling. If the club has had turbulent relations with its architects, it has done better with greenkeepers. Malone has long been renowned for the quality of its greens and the dry condition of the fairways, even in winter. An ambitious tree and flower planting programme on the current property has even led to some hyperbolic comparisons with Augusta.

Killarney would be a more reasonable comparison, for Malone has a similarly intangible charm, its many picturesque holes enhanced by the presence of the lake, the careful landscaping, and views of the impressive nineteenth-century clubhouse. (And like Killarney, there's a fishing club!) Nevertheless, the course itself simply does not have the strategic quality offered by Belfast's other major clubs – Belvoir Park and Royal Belfast – which have left their classic H.S. Colt designs more or less intact. Perhaps Malone's members have had too much say in the layout, and tee shots in particular are often devoid of strategy or difficulty.

It also remains baffling why the lake, though serving as a pretty backdrop, still only affects the golfer on the fifteenth and eighteenth holes, which are, not coincidentally, among Malone's best. It is hard not to conclude that Malone would benefit from the kind of adjustments that David Jones made so successfully to bring water into play on the Killeen course at Killarney. For if some enhancements could be made to what is already a fine golfing experience, then Malone's second century might well turn out to be as illustrious as its first.

Location: Opposite Lady Dixon Park on Upper Malone Road in Dunmurry, 5 miles from the city centre

Restrictions: None

Green Fee: £55–60

Manager: Nick Agate

Address: 240 Upper Malone Road, Dunmurry, Belfast, BT17 9LB, Northern Ireland; **tel:** (028) 9061-8363; **fax:** (028) 9043-1394; **e-mail:** manager@malonegolfclub.co.uk; **web:** www.malonegolfclub.co.uk

Clandeboye

Founded: 1930

Designed by: William Robinson and Baron Von Limburger

In 1927, Belfast linen merchant William Robinson defied all local opinion by clearing one hundred acres of bracken, gorse and stone from land about twenty miles east of town that only he could see had the makings of a top-flight golf course. The land was leased from the estate of Lord Dufferin (former Viceroy of India and Governor-General of Canada) with the proviso that it be turned into a proper members' club within six years.

Robinson had little machinery at his disposal except a Model T Ford to cart away stones, and work had to be stopped at least once when he ran out of funds. But the new course, which he laid out himself, was a smash hit, and the Clandeboye Golf Club has thrived ever since. Although Robinson died in 1947, his layout eventually attracted top-flight golf tournaments, including the 1963 Hennessey tournament, then the richest in Ireland, which Christy O'Connor won by a phenomenal seventeen strokes.

In the minds of some, the club committed a sacrilege in 1970 when it destroyed nine holes of Robinson's work to create a new eighteen-hole championship course designed by one Baron Von Limburger (then an associate of Peter Alliss). Alas, Limburger's Dufferin course is competent, but bland, requiring little accuracy off the tee and featuring hazards that seem designed for high handicappers. The controversy hasn't completely died out even today, partly because you can see what might have been on Clandeboye's second course, the Ava. The front nine is left over from Robinson's original course, and here you will find holes bursting with personality, even if the distances are more in tune with golfers of the 1920s than those of today. The second hole on Ava is the best hole on either course, a heavily undulating par 5 through dense woods that requires two brave shots to get through a narrow opening to the green.

Although there is plenty of good-value golf here, and a highly picturesque setting, neither of Clandeboye's courses can now be ranked among Ireland's best. But there's a friendly unpretentious atmosphere (perhaps a legacy of the founder's mercantile roots) that goes down well with visitors. A choice of convivial bars awaits in the spacious clubhouse, and on Sunday afternoons there is an unusually strong following for Formula One racing on the gigantic television screens. Former ace driver Eddie Irvine, who hails from the local village of Conlig, is a member of the club.

Location: Near village of Conlig, south of Bangor and north of Newtownards. Take A21 south from Bangor, exiting at Bangor Road/Main Street, follow until reach Tower Road

Restrictions: None

Green Fee: £27.50–33 (Dufferin); £22–27.50 (Ava)

Manager: John Thomson

Address: Tower Rd., Conlig, Newtownards, Co. Down, BT23 7PN, Northern Ireland; **tel:** (028) 9127-1767; **fax:** (028) 9147-3711; **e-mail:** office@cgc-ni.com; **web:** www.cgc-ni.com

Templepatrick

Founded: 1999

Designed by: David Jones

If it weren't for David Jones, at one time Northern Ireland's best professional golfer, the Hilton Templepatrick Hotel & Country Club would be just another anonymous, corporate development. But Jones has spent the better part of a decade dreaming about how to turn the property into a piece of golfing magic. It hasn't been easy.

'The very first morning we started to strip topsoil we found a three thousand year old Bronze Age settlement in the middle of the third fairway!' recalls Jones.

The Templepatrick property is reputedly on the site of a church started by St Patrick himself, but the archaeological finds were from an earlier millennium. Eventually, the government sent in a team of archaeologists to excavate.

'They were all over it,' says Jones. 'They found arrowheads, axe-heads, drainage systems. The eighteenth green is on a funeral cremation site.'

Archaeological frustrations were only one of many on the project, which began in 1992 when Jones was still in a fledgling golf course design partnership with David Feherty. By the time work began in earnest, Feherty had long since taken the leap to television golf commentary, and Jones was on his own. Templepatrick is the first championship course he has created from scratch.

At the time of our visit, Templepatrick was too new to make judgments about, but from a design standpoint it may be the most ambitious inland course to be built in Northern Ireland since the great Harry Colt courses of the 1920s at Royal Belfast and Belvoir Park. The five lakes on the estate, the stream that feeds them and the river that serves as the northern boundary are all used to great strategic advantage, and you only have to listen to Jones to realize that everything has been agonized over.

'I had my drawings, but I came here and supervised every element of the construction myself on a daily basis,' says Jones, whose home is only a thirty minute drive away. 'I knew it like my own back garden.'

It is the kind of personal passion and connection that is usually missing from a corporate golf retreat. And it doesn't hurt that Jones's work was implemented by Frank Ainsworth, the once legendary greenkeeper at Malone Golf Club who has also designed several decent courses himself. The Royal and Ancient recently lauded the course for its successful efforts to retain indigenous fescue grasses on the greens.

None of this makes Templepatrick a real golf *club*. The main objective is putting bodies in the bedrooms of the hotel, which inevitably has a numbing corporate quality to it. But if it takes a few thousand golf-hungry business travellers (Templepatrick is only five minutes from the Belfast International Airport) to help make Jones's dream a reality, perhaps that will be a fair trade off.

Location: Just north and west of crossing of M2 and A57, 5 miles from Belfast International Airport

Restrictions: None

Green Fee: £45

Manager: Patrick Stapleton

Address: Castle Upton Estate, Templepatrick, Co Antrim, BT39 0DD, Northern Ireland; **tel:** (028) 9443-5500; **fax:** (028) 9443-5511; **e-mail:** reservations.templepatrick@hilton.com; **web:** www.hilton.co.uk/templepatrick

Galgorm Castle

Founded: 1997

Designed by: Simon Gidman

The grandson of Lord Brookeborough, who served as Northern Ireland's Prime Minster from 1943 to 1963, is the driving force behind Galgorm Castle, a new golf development situated about twenty miles northwest of Belfast. When Christopher Brooke returned from Dubai in the early 1990s to inherit the exquisite seventeenth-century plantation house, where he now lives, he quickly determined that only by building a popular golf course could he afford to keep the surrounding estate. The fact that he had never picked up a golf club didn't deter him, and has arguably left him with a refreshingly open mind.

He made Irish history, for example, by hiring a woman as his first head golf professional. And in the rather funky clubhouse, Brooke's taste for fine food is reflected in imaginative offerings that certainly bear no resemblance to a golfer's fry.

The terrain on the estate is perhaps too exposed (the ongoing tree-planting programme will help) and flat to have the makings of a superior golf course, but architect Simon Gidman has done a satisfactory job with what he had to work with, and there is a lovely stretch from the tenth to the fourteenth – where the trees are denser and the River Main threatens – that shows what he can do. The condition and drainage of the course is already good, and the fact that the energetic Brooke is very much a hands-on owner probably means that the complex will move from strength to strength.

Indeed, Brooke is such an engaging fellow that it is hard not to reflect on how some things, at least, have changed in this still troubled part of the world. Brooke's grandfather once notoriously encouraged farmers to hire only Protestant agricultural workers, and he remains a polarizing historical figure. To spend a pleasant day at thoroughly ecumenical Galgorm Castle is to see a more optimistic picture of Northern Ireland. If you are so inclined, there is a variety of first-class accommodation on the estate that could, conceivably, be used as a base for golf in other parts of Ulster.

Location: Just southwest of Ballymena town centre on A42

Restrictions: None

Green Fee: £28–35

Secretary: Barbara McGeown

Address: Galgorm, Ballymena, Co Antrim, BT42 1HL, Northern Ireland; **tel:** (028) 2564-6161; **fax:** (028) 2565-1151; **e-mail:** golf@galgormcastle.com; **web:** www.galgormcastle.com

---

City of Derry

Founded: 1911
Designed by: Unknown

City of Derry is not a great golf course, but it is the best in Northern Ireland's second largest community, and over the years the members have done more than might be expected with their fairly uninspired strip of sloping, partly treed land that runs along the main road.

Of particular note are a trio of surprisingly memorable par 3s. The eighth has a 'postage stamp' feel, with an exposed, slightly elevated green that is difficult to hold; the twelfth is guarded by brutal bunkers and set in a pretty cluster of trees; and the fifteenth sends you down a severe drop over gorse bushes. At the higher elevations there are fine views of the River Foyle and the Donegal mountains, particularly on the genuinely gorgeous par-4 fourteenth. There are some dull holes, but for the most part City of Derry will keep you occupied with a variety of engaging little surprises, such as the ancient, earth-covered stone wall you need to cross on the fourteenth, aptly named Aintree after the steeplechase venue.

Today Derry, or Londonderry, has forged a reputation as a kind of edgy cultural centre, but it is impossible to escape politics in a city where people can't even agree on its name. In all likelihood, it won't be until 2008 when the final report is published of the public inquiry into Bloody Sunday, the day in 1970 when British troops shot dead fourteen unarmed funeral goers.

It would be surprising if the City of Derry Golf Club, only a short drive from the town centre, had escaped the Troubles, and it has not. A bomb damaged the clubhouse in the early 1980s, and a few years later a policeman was shot dead in the parking lot. But to dwell on the past is to do the people of (London)Derry a disfavour, and you will meet a great number of friendly folk at the City of Derry Golf Club who just want to get on with their lives.

Location: On A5 (Victoria Road), just south of the city centre

Restrictions: Monday through Friday are the best days for visitors

Green fee: £25–30

Secretary: Noreen Allen

Address: 49 Victoria Road, Prehen, Londonderry, Co Londonderry, BT47 2PU, Northern Ireland; **tel:** (028) 7134-6369; **fax:** (028) 7131-0008; **e-mail:** info@cityofderrygolfclub.com; **web:** www.cityofderrygolfclub.com

Roe Park

Founded: 1993

Designed by: Frank Ainsworth

It is no doubt a backhanded compliment to say that the best aspect of the Radisson Roe Park Hotel and Golf Resort is its practice facility, but it is true nonetheless. Engagingly contained inside the stone walls of the old estate's vegetable and fruit garden, the driving range has a charm that the mostly forgettable, if reasonably priced, parkland course lacks.

The most notable hole by a very wide margin is the sixth, an extraordinarily steep and difficult par 3 next to the clubhouse that provides sadistic entertainment to those watching play through the large windows of the swanky bar. The green, so elevated that the pin is barely visible from the tee, lies at the base of an ancient stone turret, and it wouldn't be surprising if the local members pack a catapult as their fourteenth club. Despite being only 132 yards from the back tees, it is fantastically intimidating, with other difficulties including a flurry of gorse, a vicious bunker and a putting surface almost impossible to hold. A singular hole, though one might wish that some of this excess drama would have been spread over the rest of the front nine, which is on the dull side. Better bunkering would improve things considerably.

Those with a vivid imagination can perhaps raise the excitement level by conjuring up St Columba, the semi-legendary figure responsible for converting the Irish to Christianity in the sixth century. It is thought he made a great address to a gathering of Irish nobility (dubbed by historians the Convention of Crumceatt) somewhere on what is now better known as Roe Park's outward half. The staff at the hotel report that other legends –

ROE PARK

Gary Player and Arnold Palmer among them – have visited Roe Park more recently. The back nine, to get us back on topic, is rather better, and includes a couple of water features.

Sixteen miles to the east of Londonderry, and not all that far from the Causeway Coast, Roe Park was developed in the early 1990s on an old estate by three enterprising locals who thought there was money to be made in a parkland golf course appealing to corporate clients. It is now part of the Radisson hotel chain. The course architect is Frank Ainsworth, the long-time greenkeeper at Malone Golf Club in Belfast and the designer of a similar course at Slieve Russell. But the club has recently hired Martin Hawtree to make some improvements.

Location: One mile from Limavady on A2

Restrictions: None

Green Fee: £25–30

Manager: Don Brockerton

Address: Radisson Roe Park Resort, Roe Park, Limavady, Co Londonderry, BT49 9LB, Northern Ireland; **tel:** (028) 7772-2222; **fax:** (028) 7772-2313; **e-mail:** sales@radissonroepark.com; **web:** www.roepark.com

DIVERSIONS

NORTHERN IRELAND

For more than thirty years, tourism to Northern Ireland, particularly from America, has been disproportionately affected by the Troubles and their aftermath. In fact, tourist-related crime was always extremely rare. Encouragingly, more and more people are coming to recognize this fact, and the North now receives more than two million visitors per year, almost double the levels of a decade ago. What they are finding, besides the not-to-be-missed links of Royal Portrush, Portstewart and Royal County Down, are superb coastal and mountain scenery, the only UNESCO world heritage site in Ireland, and natives who are eager to encourage tourism.

Belfast is a city of history and substance. Its greatest glories were in the nineteenth century, built chiefly on textiles, shipbuilding and its excellent harbour. There are many examples of fine Victorian architecture in Belfast, including the City Hall, Belfast Cathedral, St Mark's Church and the Grand Opera House. Perhaps best of all, though, is the wonderfully preserved

Crown Liquor Saloon, located at the outset of the 'Golden Mile' of Great Victoria Street. Its gas lights, snugs and snob screens, intricate woodwork and ornate granite bar, preserved as a National Trust monument, transport drinkers one hundred years into the past.

Travelling south, Great Victoria Street becomes University Road at Queen's University. The university area, also home to the beautiful Botanic Gardens, is an excellent one for restaurants, pubs and bed and breakfast accommodation. The north and west ends of the city (especially the infamous Shankhill and Falls Roads), along with the dock area, are to be avoided after dark.

There are many interesting towns near Belfast. Carrickfergus will be familiar to anyone with even a passing interest in Irish music, and boasts the oldest castle in Ireland, built by the Normans in 1180. Hillsborough, located ten miles to the southwest of Belfast, is one of Ulster's prettiest and most enjoyable villages, with many fine examples of Georgian architecture and some delightful pubs.

The Ulster Folk and Transport Museum makes an excellent day out for those travelling with children. It is located about five miles east of Belfast, at Cultra. It is an open-air museum, which documents the traditional way of life of Northern Ireland. Actual buildings, such as a thatched cottage, a schoolhouse and a shoe shop have been dismantled and reassembled on the grounds to form a village. The attendants are informative and interesting.

After the folk museum it may be convenient to continue to Bangor, a picturesque resort east of Belfast along the prosperous south shore of Belfast Lough. Directly south from Bangor is the Ards Peninsula, separated from the rest of the Province by Strangford Lough. Strangford Lough is a renowned migratory bird sanctuary. The peninsula also contains several charming fishing villages. From the southern end, a short ferry ride from Portaferry and a twenty-mile drive along the coast will bring the visitor to Newcastle and Royal County Down.

Halfway to Newcastle, however, a stop at Downpatrick may be in order. The town is the capital of County Down, and the main attraction is Down Cathedral, the burial place of St Patrick, patron saint of Ireland. Interestingly, this is not a Roman Catholic cathedral, but one of the Church of Ireland.

Newcastle has little to recommend it except its famous golf club. But it does enjoy the lovely backdrop of the Mountains of Mourne. Slieve Donard is the tallest peak, and hiking trails to its summit are well laid out. The beach is also excellent, but the weather doesn't always cooperate.

Proceeding north from Belfast along the coastal A2 road brings you to the beautiful Glens of Antrim, nine enchanting valleys which extend from the Antrim Mountains down to the sea. The town of Cushendall, at the foot of Glenballyemon, is perhaps the most convenient base for exploration of the nine glens.

The Causeway Coast is stunning. It is a string of villages nestled under imposing cliffs, each more dramatic than the last. It culminates in the Giant's Causeway, the only UNESCO World Heritage site in Ireland. The Giant's Causeway is made up of a series of black columns which protrude step-like from the sea. They are said to have been created as a walkway across the Sea of Moyle to Scotland by the mythic giant Finn MacCool. In fact, the Causeway was formed by volcanic eruption of basalt lava, which cooled slowly (probably by sea water) to form the columns. It is likely the most famous attraction in Northern Ireland, and really shouldn't be missed. Despite its popularity, it is admirably preserved in a natural state and only accessible on foot.

Many elevated points along the Causeway Coast offer dramatic vistas. Even for non-golfers, the park bench by the seventeenth tee at Ballycastle Golf Club must provide one of the most glorious views on a sunny day. The entire Causeway Coast, Rathlin Island and even the coast of Scotland are in sight. Further west, from Portstewart for example, the Donegal coastline is plainly in view.

Just to the west of Ballycastle is the Carrick-a-rede rope bridge, a precarious walkway from the mainland to Carrick-a-rede island. Only the brave will attempt to cross it when the wind is blowing. Do not look down in any event. There is boat service to the island for the sensible. The island provides a unique perspective back on the Causeway Coast, as well as housing a fish hatchery and copious sea birds. The rope bridge is open only in the summer.

Londonderry (a.k.a. Derry) is often avoided by golfers, thanks to the Foyle bridge and the new Lough Foyle ferry crossing at Magilligan Strand, which makes Ballyliffin much more accessible to those travelling on a circuit from Portstewart and Castlerock. For the adventurous, though, a historic but at times troubled city awaits. Highlights are the city walls, the last constructed in Europe (in the seventeenth century), and St Columb's Cathedral, the first built in the British Isles after the Reformation. Both figured in the unsuccessful siege of the city led by James II in 1689.

For anyone with energy to spare after golf, the Ulster Way is a hiker's dream. It is five hundred miles long, encircles the entire Province, and passes through the Glens of Antrim, Mountains of Mourne and Giant's Causeway, to name but a few highlights. It is accessible at a myriad of locations and thoroughly documented; details are available from Tourism Ireland and many other sources.

CONTEXTS

EQUAL PARTNERS?

WOMEN'S GOLF IN IRELAND

When we played with men we had to have a chaperon. We had either ninepenny or shilling chaperons. The ninepenny ones were small boys and the shilling ones were slightly older.

MAY HEZLET, BRITISH LADIES CHAMPION, 1899, 1902 AND 1907

ANYONE WHO THINKS that sport's first Battle of the Sexes had something to do with Bobby Riggs and Billie Jean King doesn't know enough about the history of women's golf in Ireland. More than seventy years before the wacky tennis match at the Houston Astrodome, a far more interesting cross-gender tussle occurred in a far more dignified location.

'[I will] no' be licked by a lassie,' Old Tom Morris reportedly vowed before his challenge match at St Andrews with the Irish phenomenon Rhona Adair. It was July 1899. Morris was seventy-seven years young at the time, but apparently thought nothing of the prospect of a one-day, thirty-six-hole match.

His opponent was only seventeen. But Rhona Adair was already known to be able to hit the ball farther than any woman ever had, and she would win the British Ladies Amateur title the very next year.

'She stands up to the ball in a manner quite worthy of the sterner sex,' wrote the great English amateur Harold Hilton. 'There is a determination and firmness in her address which is most fascinating to watch. Lady players, as a rule, appear to persuade the ball on its way; Miss Adair, on the contrary, avoids such constrictions on her methods by hitting very hard indeed.'

It must have been quite a sight – the white-bearded golfing icon and the teenager in her long dress and stiff white collar. It was certainly quite a match. After the first round, Morris led by one hole. He extended his lead to three after twenty-seven holes, and fended off a late challenge to win on the last green.

It is a tribute to the strength of women's golf in Ireland at the turn of the century that Adair, despite her celebrity, was probably not even the best woman player *in her own club*. For Royal Portrush was also home to the great May Hezlet. Between them, Adair and Hezlet appeared in the finals of five straight British Ladies Championships (then the undisputed world title) from 1899 to 1903, winning four of them, and Hezlet won another for good measure in 1907. Hezlet and Adair were also avid badminton, tennis and field hockey players, and they introduced a new athleticism to women's golf. Although the steady Hezlet had slightly the better record, Adair seems to have caused the greatest sensation due to her startling power.

After winning her second British title in 1903, Adair made a historic visit to North America, playing in a long series of challenge matches in the United States and Canada, and losing only once. Her tour was followed with intense interest. The *Illustrated Sporting News* trumpeted the fact that Adair would compose a copyrighted column for the paper during her visit, 'the only one she will write for any American publication, [in which] she gives her impression of America's leading women players and best courses, and tells of the advantages of the game as an important aid to good health.'

Adair's feat of clearing a water hazard of 170 yards (a considerable shot with the equipment of the time) was greeted with astonishment, and she brought home no fewer than sixteen gleaming trophies. The trip also made an enormous impact on the young American player Margaret Curtis, who would later launch the Curtis Cup, the most important international trophy in women's golf.

Adair and Hezlet were by no means the only women playing golf in Ireland. Only a decade after the game took root in Ireland, there were an astonishing 290 lady members of the Portrush Golf Club. Several clubs had as many lady members as men, and Royal County Down found it necessary to establish a separate ladies' course in 1909.

'Golf undoubtedly owes much of its popularity to the enthusiasm with which it has been taken up by what men are pleased to term the weaker sex,' wrote the editor of the *Irish Golfer* in 1899. 'Many conscientious fathers of families can now take their families to the seaside and enjoy their rounds of golf, because their womenfolk also pursue the game, instead of boring themselves to death in seaside lodgings talking scandal or reading trashy novels.'

Needless to say, women put a slightly different spin on the same phenomenon. In the first issue of *Ladies' Golf*, a writer pointed out that before golf 'the comings and goings of. . . more or less attached husbands, who golfed, fished and shot, were veiled in mystery'.

In the early days, golfers of both sexes came from the Protestant upper classes. Typical attire for women consisted of elaborate hats, stiff collars, petticoats, ankle-length skirts and corsets. That so many Victorian women and girls were taking up the sport despite these obstacles was considered by some a trend of the first importance.

'The whole hearted adoption by women of the Royal and Ancient Game marks an epoch in the history of the sex,' reported *Ladies' Golf*. 'Without unduly straining a point, it may be said that golf has been a factor of no small importance in the mental, as well as the physical, development of the modern girl.'

In those days golf was an outdoor adventure with limited clubhouse amenities, and women and girls were given equal access to Irish courses. If the enormous galleries depicted in photographs from the era are any indication, interest in women's competitions in Ireland, especially in Ulster, was substantial. The exploits of Adair and Hezlet undoubtedly added to the credibility of women's golf in Ireland. It is perhaps no coincidence that the British Amateur Ladies Championship has been played in Ireland no fewer than fourteen times, including once at Portmarnock, one of the few clubs which admits no women members.

There has been a steady flow of outstanding Irish women golfers over the years, the best being Philomena Garvey, a seven-time Curtis Cup player from County Louth. But one of the most celebrated never won a major championship. Bridget Gleeson was born in 1963 and raised in the lodge beside the fifteenth green at Killarney's Mahony's Point course. She started hitting balls at the age of two-and-a-half, and by five she was a BBC television celebrity and played in exhibition matches as far away as Canada. She won the club championship at ten. An injury interrupted her career, though she returned to competitive golf and even competed internationally.

Although there have been individual highlights, it seems that the proportion of women players in Ireland (compared to men) began to decline along with the aristocratic lifestyle that allowed some women considerable leisure time. Men began to exert increasing control over the sport as it became institutionalized (and more elaborate clubhouses were built). In an arrangement encouraged by the (all male) Golfing Union of Ireland, women were re-designated as 'associate' members at significantly reduced membership fees. As associates, women were denied voting rights at annual meetings and faced some restrictions on playing time. It is not exactly clear how resentful women were of these changes, although it may not be completely coincidental that Killarney and Royal County Down were both targets of suffragette attacks before the First World War.

This is not to say that women golfers were treated less fairly in Ireland than their counterparts in England and America. Indeed, the degree of participation of women in golf clubs in the Republic is somewhat surprising, given the traditional role espoused for women by the Catholic church and the early nationalist governments. The 1937 Irish constitution stated that 'by her life within the home, woman gives to the State a support without which the common good cannot be achieved.' It was not until 1977 that it became illegal to require women to resign from civil service jobs upon getting married. Divorce was only legalized in 1996 and in most cases women who wish to have an abortion must still leave the country.

By the late 1980s, women's rights had become a central issue in the Republic, and were given further impetus by the election of Mary Robinson as President (a largely ceremonial, yet influential, post) in 1991. The winds of change began sweeping through golf clubs as well, with clubs such as Killarney and Ballybunion offering full membership privileges to women. It will take longer elsewhere, but the trend seems irreversible. The new courses for executives – such as St Margaret's – make no distinction between men and women, though few women as yet are using golf as a business tool. It doesn't help, of course, that two of the most important clubs for networking – Royal Dublin and Portmarnock – don't allow women to join as members.

Portmarnock, in particular, has become something of a lightning rod for women's rights campaigners. When the club hosted the Irish Open in 2003, the National Women's Council of Ireland urged a boycott, saying its men-only membership rules were an 'insult' to women.

Then, a District Court judge ruled that the club should be banned from selling alcohol for a week as punishment for discriminating against women. It was a decision welcomed by the government's own Equality Authority.

'What we are seeing here is something which is of clear importance to women golfers,' said the agency's Niall Crowley. 'It also has wider importance, in that women who have access to clubs like Portmarnock don't just access its recreational facilities. They also get economic and social benefits from the status and networking opportunities which come with membership.'

The venerable club wasn't about to remove its head from the sand just yet, however. Portmarnock won an appeal to the High Court, which ruled that, as a private club, it could do pretty much what it wanted. The European Union has recently entered the fray, but no one is sure what its apparent ban on men-only golf clubs really means.

Today, about sixty thousand women golf in Ireland, triple the figure of twenty years ago. And, happily, there are few additional obstacles to be faced by women travellers wishing to golf while they are in Ireland. Restrictions on visitors almost always apply to men and women equally, and indignities such as male-only lounges in clubhouses are largely a thing of the past. While it should be assumed that most handicapped golf tournaments (such as the Causeway Coast Open) are aimed at men, the Open Weeks held by the clubs usually have mixed and ladies competitions that are open to all comers.

Given that men represent the overwhelming majority of golfing visitors to Ireland, those women who do make the trip can expect an especially warm welcome.

The Nineteenth Hole:

A GUIDE TO DRINKING AND EATING IN IRELAND

When things go wrong and will not come right,
Though you do the best you can,
When life looks black as the hour of night–
A pint of plain is your only man.

FLANN O'BRIEN, 1939

MUCH OF THE charm of drinking in Ireland derives from the characters encountered in the typical pub. With the same four or five beers and half-dozen whiskies available in virtually every pub in the country, an Irishman is said to choose his pub on the quality of the *craic*, or conversation and banter. The Irish are nothing if not lovers of a well-told joke and masters of the ruthless witticism. As well, due to the immense number of expatriate Irish around the world, someone is invariably interested in, or familiar with, your home town or its environs, no matter how obscure. But proceed with caution. The Irish, especially in rural areas, can be conservative and quite proprietary about their local. Ease yourself into the conversation with tact; you will be rewarded many times over.

Although times are changing rapidly in many parts of Ireland, the pub remains at the heart of the community in most rural areas. It is also the typical focus of the local music scene, be it 'traditional' Irish music or modern folk, jazz or rock. Impromptu sessions where local musicians bring their instruments and perform are still quite common. Ask the bartender or a local member before you leave the golf club – they will point you in the right direction.

Like many things Irish, the opening hours of pubs are not exactly set in stone. Officially, they are 10:30 a.m. to 11:30 p.m. (Monday through Wednesday), 10:30 a.m. to 12:30 a.m. (Thursday through Saturday) and

12:30 p.m. to 11:00 p.m. (Sunday) in the Republic, and 11:00 a.m. to 11:00 p.m. (Monday through Saturday) and 12:30 p.m. to 10:00 p.m. (Sunday) in the North. Some rural pubs will close for an hour or two in the middle of the afternoon (euphemistically known as the 'holy hour'), though they are no longer required to do so. In the Republic, closing time can be extended for a myriad of local festivals and race meetings, so one can never be sure when last call will be. As well, it is far from unknown for a rural publican to draw the blinds and lock the front door at closing time and continue to serve for an hour or more. Indeed, a pub can encounter difficulty in enforcing the letter of the law when it comes to closing, and it is not uncommon for staff to spend thirty minutes herding the drinkers towards and ultimately out the front door. If all else fails, certain other types of licensed establishments, such as clubs and discotheques, serve alcoholic beverages – often for a stiff cover charge – after the pubs close, and hotels with bars are obliged to continue to serve residents. Just ask a likely-looking local.

Drinking and driving is taken seriously in Ireland. In order to reduce the rate of road fatalities, which at one time was among the highest in Europe, legislation was introduced in 1994 that reduced the legal blood alcohol limit for drivers to 80 mg and included mandatory licence suspensions. Random police checkpoints are used frequently. In March 2004, smoking was banned in pubs in the Republic of Ireland, and similar legislation is due to come into effect in Northern Ireland in 2007.

Beer

A great many people think Guinness is the best beer in the world. Certainly it is the most recognizable, its name synonymous with *dry stout* on every inhabited continent. It is Ireland's most famous export. No one seems to mind that the national symbol, the harp, is also a Guinness trademark. Like many things Irish, its history is bound up with that of England.

In the eighteenth century, the principal styles of beer in England were brown ale, old ale and pale ale (the Irish were primarily drinkers of a distinctive reddish-brown ale). In London, the practice of a drinker blending the three types of ale in his glass became popular. Over time, this blend became known colloquially as porter, thought to be so named because it was favoured by the porters in London's markets. Enterprising breweries began to do the blending themselves, and porter was born as a distinct product. Porter quickly became London's most popular beer, and as a product of the industrial revolution it was exported far and wide, including to Ireland. It seems it was warmly embraced by the Irish, first in Dublin, and later in the countryside. In 1759 the Arthur Guinness brewery was established in Dublin; by 1799 it was strictly a brewer of porter. In the nineteenth century, Guinness produced two porters of varying strengths (plus an even stronger version for export). The stronger of the domestic porters became known as 'extra stout porter' and was eventually known universally as 'stout.' The weaker porter was simply called plain.

Domestic porter reached its zenith in England in the nineteenth century and was all but extinct by 1935. The Irish, however, had other ideas. Some put it down to their natural conservatism; others say they sensibly realized they were drinking the greatest libation man could devise. In any event, plain porter survived in Ireland until 1974 (and has recently made a comeback), while stout took firm hold as the national drink. It also became a huge success as an export product to much of the world including, ironically, England, the place of its birth.

The period from 1925 to 1955 saw Guinness establish itself as one of the world's great trade names. In the late 1920s a British advertising agency was commissioned to determine what Guinness drinkers liked about the product. The response appears to have been that it was 'good for you'. Thus was born one of the most successful advertising campaigns in history. 'Guinness is Good for You' passed into everyday language. The campaign continued through the 1930s with such slogans as 'Guinness Gives You Strength' and 'My Goodness, My Guinness'. Various animals were introduced, including a seal, an ostrich and a toucan. By 1953 the animals appeared in uncaptioned advertisements, with no further explanation or corporate logo necessary.

There is much hand-wringing among beer enthusiasts with respect to the perceived decline in the quality of Guinness over the last decade.

'Guinness has changed,' wrote Dublin food and drinks writer Tom Doorley. 'It is widely thought to have become lighter bodied. There are dark mutterings that the St James's Gate boffins have stopped adding flaked barley.'

Many similar opinions have been expressed. There is no doubt that, as the younger generation in Ireland has flocked to Budweiser and other light-bodied lagers, Guinness has reacted by, at the very least, insisting that publicans serve it at increasingly colder temperatures ('if it gets any colder, it will be Guinness-on-a-stick', noted one wag). The fuller bodied, bottle-conditioned Foreign Extra Stout was withdrawn from the Irish market in the 1990s and replaced with the mediocre 'draught Guinness in a can'. More recently, the 'Extra Cold' Guinness campaign was perhaps the nadir of Guinness marketing, and mercifully did not seem to catch on with drinkers, though it continues to limp along in some pubs. Guinness sales in Ireland, for whatever reason, are down by almost 25 per cent in the past eight years.

Despite all that, for our money a good pint of Guinness, drunk in Ireland, is still a world-class treat. It is intensely bitter, with strong grapefruit flavours, but with aspects of burnt toast and roasted nuts. At times it is slightly smoky. Much of the flavour will only become evident as the pint warms, as modern serving temperatures are at least ten degrees colder than the ideal and up to twenty degrees colder than the serving temperature of the 1950s and 60s.

Although very bitter, Guinness is also quite smooth, even creamy, with little carbonation evident. This is due to the use of nitrogen in its dispense, which was pioneered by Guinness in the 1960s. Despite the strong taste, Guinness in Ireland is not a particularly alcoholic drink. It contains approximately 4.2 per cent alcohol by volume. So have another; the Guinness served in Ireland, because it is only lightly pasteurized, is a much richer and fuller tasting drink than the beers of the same name exported to other parts of the world.

Guinness is available everywhere in the Republic and Northern Ireland. Because it is filtered and kept chilled, quality rarely varies. Nevertheless, the Irish are inordinately concerned with 'pulling a good pint'. This harkens back to the days, which ended in the early 1960s, when a pint of Guinness was in fact a blend of two different cask-conditioned beers, and considerable skill was required from the barman to get it just right.

Guinness today is kept under nitrogen gas pressure and dispensed through a tight sparkler. No actual pulling is required. Rather, the glass is quickly filled to about the two-thirds mark and left to sit. A dense, creamy head will 'mushroom up' through the beer. When the beer has settled fully, the glass is filled to the brim and again set aside, allowing the mushroom effect to occur anew. A classic tourist *faux pas* is to drink from a fresh pint before it has fully settled; nothing will bring more scorn from the barman or any of the pub's regulars.

Two other stouts, Beamish and Murphy's, are available in parts of Ireland. Both are produced in Cork and are principally available in and around that city. They can be difficult to find in other parts of the country. Beamish tastes much more of roasted coffee beans and cocoa and is less bitter than Guinness. Its head is noticeably whiter. Murphy's is similar to Beamish in character, with more of a roasted, toasty flavour. Neither Beamish nor Murphy's is as intensely dry as Guinness.

It may not seem so at first blush, but dry stout matches extremely well with seafood. Although many novice drinkers will describe stout as 'heavy', it is actually an appetite enhancer (in moderation) because it is so dry. It is particularly good with oysters, and both Guinness and Murphy's sponsor oyster festivals in County Galway in September. Some famous places to try the oyster and stout combination are The Oyster Tavern in Cork and Moran's of the Weir, near Kilcolgan, Co. Galway, which faces directly onto some of Ireland's best oyster beds. Oyster season runs from September to December.

Traditional Irish ales, including micro-brewed stouts and porters, have made something of a comeback in the last decade. There are now a few specialties to be had in the Republic, but one must be willing to search them out, which is not always possible after a long day of golf. We recommend The Porter House, an outstanding Dublin brewpub which brews such previously all-but-extinct treats as plain porter and oyster stout, and the Carlow Brewing Company, particularly their O'Hara's Celtic Stout.

Northern Ireland enjoys a greater selection of pale ales and bitters than the Republic. The cask-conditioned real ales of the Hilden and Whitewater breweries are especially worth seeking out. Hilden, located in Lisburn, has tenaciously clung to life for some twenty-five years, while Whitewater was formed in Kilkeel in 1996. The White Horse, Saintfield, the Hillside, Hillsborough and the Botanic Inn in Belfast, among a very few others, are real-ale stalwarts in Northern Ireland. And in 2006, Belfast's first brewpub appeared, when Molly's Yard was opened by two of the children of the founders of the Hilden brewery.

Whiskey

After dinner, another pint of 'the black stuff' may not appeal. Guinness is sometimes just too voluminous to fit in a satiated stomach. Fortunately, the Irish have invented the perfect solution, in the form of the other national drink, Irish whiskey.

Irish whiskey pre-dates Scotch, at least as a commercial product. No one knows for sure which nation had the first backyard still, but they were prevalent in both countries. It is thought that the process of distillation was introduced to Ireland by missionary monks as early as the sixth century. Bushmills, licensed in 1608, is the oldest commercial distillery in the world, and markets itself as such. It is known that there has been a distillery in the village of Bushmills since at least 1276.

Thus the Irish regard Scotch as something of a latecomer, despite the fact that it supersedes the native drink in worldwide popularity. Most Irish are happy to assume that the modern world is misinformed in the matter – in previous centuries it was the Irish style which predominated. In his 1750 dictionary of the English language, Dr Johnson defined whiskey as 'a compounded, distilled spirit . . . the Irish sort is particularly distinguished for its pleasant and mild flavour. In Scotland it is somewhat hotter.' In the nineteenth century Irish whiskey dominated the spirits trade: there were more than 400 brands, produced by 160 distilleries, for sale worldwide. Now, however, there are two major distilleries, producing the five principal brands: Bushmills, Jameson, Power, Paddy and Tullamore Dew. Happily, a third has arisen in recent times – the Cooley distillery, producer of Locke's, Kilbeggan, Millar's, The Tyrconnell and Connemara peated malt, among others. Prohibition in America, coinciding with the War of Independence and a trade war with England which followed, are thought to be the principal causes of the dramatic contraction.

The difference in taste between Irish and Scotch is readily apparent, even to the beginner. Irish whiskey has none of the smoky, peaty flavour of Scotch and is slightly sweeter. The Irish, at least, would regard it as more delicate, refined and sophisticated. It is distilled in a uniquely shaped 'pot still', and is usually triple distilled, as opposed to just twice for Scotch, which undoubtedly contributes to the smooth body. Irish whiskey is variously described as 'perfumy', 'fruity', 'malty', and 'rounded'. The best Irish whiskies will show the most dry and complex character, because they are blended with only a small amount (or ideally no) grain whiskey, which tends to be sweeter and blander.

Differences between the main brands are subtle but can be detected. Jameson is the most popular Irish whiskey worldwide, and is light and smooth. Paddy has a huge following in the south and west of Ireland. It was named after Paddy O'Flaherty, who worked with such success as a salesman for Cork Distilleries in the 1920s that the practice of simply asking for 'Paddy's whiskey' became widespread. The name was eventually adopted on the label. Paddy is dry and crisp, but perhaps not the most elegant of whiskies. Tullamore Dew is the lightest tasting of the principal Irish whiskies.

John Power & Sons (Power) is our favourite of the commonly available brands. It is drier than Jameson or Black Bush, with malty complexity, lots of 'pot still' character, and a long, spicy finish. It is known colloquially as 'three swallows' and, inevitably, there is an elaborate story behind it. Power was the first Irish whiskey to be sold in miniature 'airplane' bottles, which the Irish apparently felt contained about three swallows of whiskey. The bottles became so popular, and the three swallows reference so prevalent, that three small birds, swallows, found their way on to the label at the neck of the bottle where they remain to this day, a classic Irish pun.

Northern Ireland's Bushmills distillery produces Old Bushmills and its premium brands Black Bush and Bushmills Single Malt ('Bush Malt'). The distillery is located on the banks of the river Bush in County Antrim and is recognized by its pagoda-style malting towers. Guided tours are available year round. Old Bushmills is a standard Irish whiskey, tending towards the sharp side. Black Bush, which is aged in sherry casks, is a distinctive whiskey with little of the dryness that characterizes a Power, for example. Black Bush is rich, smooth and mellow, with evident sherry complexity. It makes an excellent change of pace.

Though hard to find, the best Irish whiskies are the single malt (made from 100 per cent malted barley, and at one distillery only) and pure pot still (made from both malted and unmalted barley only) varieties. Examples of the latter are the exquisite Redbreast, as well as the hard to find Green Spot and Jameson 15 Year Old. The single malts include the firm and smooth Bush Malt, the elegant Tyrconnell, and the delicate pear-drop flavoured Knappogue Castle. All are very much worth seeking out. Finally, one of Ireland's most unique (and pleasing, at least to Scotch-lovers) whiskies is Connemara peated malt, which combines Irish whiskey smoothness with the flavours acquired from malting the grains over a turf fire.

Irish whiskey is meant to be consumed straight up or with a small amount of water. Ice is often available (but rarely needed by the travelling golfer). Far more likely will be the need for a restorative 'hot whiskey' to combat the effects of eighteen holes of wind and rain. A hot whiskey is made by adding boiling water, lemon, clove and sugar to a generous measure of Irish whiskey. At the right time in the right place it is a superb drink.

Food

Until very recently, the term fine Irish cuisine was almost an oxymoron. Guidebooks used to limit themselves to a few euphemisms such as 'the cooking can be variable,' 'the Irish still eat quite a lot of potatoes,' and 'the baking of bread is almost always reliable'.

There are very good historical reasons for the plainness of Irish cuisine. The Lords and Ladies of the Anglo Ascendancy could afford to experiment with exotic tastes. But for millions of Irish peasants, the main challenge was survival. It is estimated that, in 1845, fully one-third of Irish families relied *entirely* on potatoes (mixed with buttermilk) for their food. This reliance on one staple had devastating consequences during the potato blight of the following year and led directly to the Great Famine.

Even in the twentieth century, Irish cuisine resembled British provincial cooking of a particularly low standard, and with a lot more potatoes thrown in.

That has most definitely begun to change. The quality of the restaurants in Ireland has improved considerably in the last ten years. At the high end, it is now possible to find Michelin-starred restaurants in Dublin (Thornton's, L'Ecrivain and the two-star Patrick Gilbaud) and there are a few country-house culinary resorts which specialize in the use of Ireland's abundant fresh fish, meats and produce. But it is not just at high end establishments that standards have risen. People eat out more, there's more competition for the food faddies, and international culinary influences have made serious inroads.

What has been taken in its stride by much of the world has been given a name in Ireland: 'New Irish Cuisine'. This primarily means using fresh local ingredients, fusing in a bit of Asian spice here and there, and trying not to overcook everything. It also means celebrating the few tasty examples of Irish peasant food, usually involving potatoes, such as champ (potatoes and green onions), boxty (a potato pancake) and potato bread.

At the 2006 Ryder Cup in Dublin, all that was newly pretentious in Irish cooking was on display. Bord Bia, the government agency responsible for promoting Irish food, took pains to ensure the event was a showcase for 'Gaelic cuisine'. The main course at the players' dinner was *beef tuath*, the 'Ryder Cup signature dish', consisting of 'two mignons of Irish beef, shallot and wild mushroom crown, organic carrot with garlic and potato foam [and] mead sauce'. (It remains on the menu at the K Club, priced at a mere €65.)

Bord Bia Chairwoman Angela Kennedy could hardly contain herself.

'Linking ancient past to dynamic present, a sense of place and a sense of people, *beef tuath* celebrates the richness of Ireland's heritage, the quality of its ingredients and the genius of its new generation of chefs,' she declared.

It is not clear that all this impressed the American Ryder Cup players, who brought with them a half ton of corn chips and salsa, and downed mountains of un-Irish fare, including waffles, pancakes, maple syrup, bagels and American-style bacon. They even imported beer for those, such as Tiger Woods, who wouldn't touch a pint of Guinness with an extra-long driver.

The term New Irish Cuisine can, of course, mean just about anything to anybody. In a fancy restaurant it might mean seaweed mixed with locally made cream cheese; in a West coast pub it may simply mean re-branding staple fare, as in 'fish hand dipped in our fresh beer batter, served with *Irish* chips' (italics ours).

It must be said that fresh produce is better cooked (i.e. less cooked) just about everywhere in Ireland than it was fifteen years ago. Unless you are in Dublin or Kinsale (the town near Cork that fancies itself the culinary capital of the country), the best bet is often the simplest, freshest, least handled food on the menu. Salmon and lamb can be excellent.

There are no prizes to be won for guessing what will normally accompany the main course. In Ireland the question is often not whether there will be potatoes with your meal, but what combination of potatoes you are going to get. The first time this happens, North Americans will be apt to think some kind of mistake has been made, as in 'I already have three sizeble boiled potatoes on the plate, what is the waitress doing with those French fries?'

Those with a lot of money can avoid misadventure. In the major centres, at least, it is possible to seek out one of the frighteningly expensive restaurants that feature a respectable standard of international cuisine. For the travelling golfer on a budget, however, the principal challenge in smaller towns and villages will be just finding a place to have the evening meal, especially if it is left past eight o'clock. Sometimes hotels and the golf club itself are the only options.

Here are a few tips to help you make the most of Irish cooking.

Where to eat

Breakfast: Veteran golf travellers will know that breakfast is the most important meal, and a well cooked Irish breakfast (or Ulster fry in Northern Ireland) is a perfect preparation for a windswept day on the links. Theoretically, it can consist of bacon and eggs (supposedly an Irish innovation), sausages, baked beans, black and white pudding, and soda bread (or fried bread), but the quality of food preparation in B&Bs is entirely variable. One of our favoured establishments in Dublin used to fry *one* mushroom and *one half* of a cherry tomato with each egg. After a few days of super-cholesterol you may wish to switch to the poached eggs on unbuttered toast. One option is to ask for the porridge when available. In upscale accommodation you may see smoked salmon. Whatever it is, dig in.

Lunch: Eat at the golf club. It is convenient, you will have an appetite, and the prices are usually modest (since you will be paying what the members pay). Toasted sandwiches with soup is as reliable a meal as you can order in Ireland. The carvery in the dining room at Royal Portrush is particularly noteworthy for its quality and reasonable prices. A pint of Guinness adds further nourishment.

Dinner: The final meal of the day is problematic for the golfer in Ireland, due to the discordant mix of long summer days and early-closing kitchens. You will quickly realize that the food served so laboriously in hotel dining rooms is the same stuff they slap in front of you in the bars, only there's too much of it in the dining room version and it costs an arm and a leg. The most economical place to eat is a pub or hotel bar, but the pubs usually stop serving food at an early hour, often eight o'clock. After that you are stuck with full-fledged restaurants, and many of these close early as well. On a Sunday night in a small town, a hotel dining room or a Chinese takeaway can be your only options.

Fast food and ethnic cuisine: Heart stopping fried food (including battered sausages and hamburgers) is still easy to find in Ireland, which has one of the highest rates of heart disease in the world. (For a hilarious account of the evolution of a Dublin chip wagon, read Roddy Doyle's *The Van*.) In the less interesting culinary areas of Scotland and England, a visitor can always take refuge in Indian restaurants, but they are fewer in number in Ireland. Even in small towns there is the inevitable Chinese takeaway, though the food will rarely resemble anything you might find in China. Pizzas have improved markedly.

Vegetarians: If the golf courses were all in downtown Dublin, vegetarians could survive quite nicely in Ireland. As it is, it's a struggle unless you have an unlimited tolerance for vegetarian lasagne. There is plenty of vegetable broth soup, which goes well with the excellent soda bread, but the salads are unimaginative. Cooked vegetables have at least firmed up a little. Once again there is, unfortunately, no escaping the need for chips.

Even when the food is indifferent, an Irish meal is rarely a negative experience. The stout is always superb, and waiters and waitresses in Ireland are terrifically friendly, if not particularly well organized. In Ireland a restaurant is not a place to sample innovative dishes. It's a place to talk with your friends and perhaps a few strangers. And the talk, needless to say, is usually excellent.

A GOLFER'S HISTORY OF IRELAND

IT IS HARD to escape history in Ireland – there are few places where the echoes of the past resound so loudly and meaningfully. What follows is in no way meant to substitute for more complete and authoritative accounts, although it will give you a thumbnail sketch of Irish history, at least, if you are already descending into Dublin, Shannon or Belfast.

Golf is a social game, so it is no surprise that its progress in Ireland has been shaped by the political and economic currents that have so buffeted Irish society in the last century. In fact, golf may have been introduced to Ireland as early as 1606 by a Scottish 'laird' named Hugh Montgomery. A good friend of James I, Montgomery secured much of the Ards Peninsula to start a plantation after the latest of what was already a long line of Irish rebellions against English rule. Montgomery built a school not far from present-day Belfast which included 'a green for recreation at goff, football and archery'. The success of the Montgomery estates encouraged many more English and Scottish Protestants to settle in Ulster, with consequences that reverberate to the present day.

Until that point, Ireland had managed to survive or assimilate its invaders. A bewildering array of autonomous Celtic 'kings' jockeyed for power and territory with each other and with foreign intruders. The Celts themselves had arrived in Ireland at least a thousand years before, and established a civilization full of magic and myth in which a learned caste of poets, historians and druids were revered and powerful. They built the impressive hill-forts that still dot the Irish landscape, and you will find that golf clubs are particularly proud of archaeological discoveries on their golfing grounds.

St Patrick and the Irish church

Given that St Patrick has become almost a mascot of Ireland in the eyes of many foreigners, it is worth pointing out that he was a real human being. An English-born missionary who travelled widely in Ireland in the fifth century, St Patrick was a pivotal figure in the introduction of Christianity to Ireland, and became even more important in legend.

The three centuries following St Patrick's death were in many ways the golden age of Irish influence abroad. The remote and fortified monasteries of Ireland – beyond the reach of the marauding tribes which overran most of Europe and England – became renowned outposts of learning. The Book of Kells, an astonishing illustrated manuscript on display at Trinity College in Dublin, dates from the early part of this period. Irish missionaries and scholars reintroduced Christianity to much of Europe, established monasteries in Germany, France, Switzerland, Italy and Austria, and became the wise men of European courts.

'Almost all of Ireland, disregarding the sea, is flocking to our shores with a flock of philosophers,' complained a European writer in the year 870.

Although Ireland was later invaded by the Vikings and the Normans in turn, Irish kings remained powerful and influential, continually forging alliances with foreign forces (Brian Boru became the first and only Irish king to assert control over all of Ireland when he defeated the Vikings in 1014; but he died in the final battle). Indeed, it was an Irish chief's request for assistance in a local squabble in 1166 that brought an English king (Henry II) onto the Irish political stage for the first time. During the next four hundred years English monarchs gradually increased their control over Ireland, distributing land and power to the English nobility.

Henry VIII's break with Rome in 1533 added an ominous religious dimension to the power struggle between Irish chiefs and the English intruders, and eventually led to Oliver Cromwell's invasion of Ireland in 1649. Battle-hardened, religiously zealous and eager to avenge a particularly bloody Irish uprising in Ulster, Cromwell's army overwhelmed all resistance and killed many thousands, often indiscriminately. Afterwards, Cromwell ordered all Irish landowners to migrate to inhospitable lands west of the River Shannon or face death or slavery in the West Indies. It was the beginning of two hundred years of repressive English rule – the percentage of land owned by Irish Catholics plummeted to just 22 per cent by 1685 and to 5 per cent by 1800.

There was a brief reversal when a Catholic monarch ascended to the restored English throne in 1685, but five years later James II was forced to flee after his defeat by William of Orange at the Battle of the Boyne. Ulster's Loyalists reserve their most enthusiastic marches to commemorate that day.

The Penal Laws

It is difficult to exaggerate the degree of discrimination that Irish Catholics endured for the next century at the hands of the Anglican Ascendancy, the all-powerful ruling class that owed its good fortune to the seizure of millions of acres of Irish land. In an attempt to make this power permanent, it passed a series of draconian measures through the Irish Parliament (which was loyal to the English sovereign). Known as the Penal Laws, they deprived Catholics of the right to vote, to receive a formal education, to hold any kind of public office or to buy land, or even a horse. To a far milder extent, Protestant settlers in Ulster also faced discrimination – those who were Presbyterian rather than Anglican could not hold government office or run for Parliament.

One consequence of this oppression was the first wave of emigration. Remnants of the old Irish nobility fled in huge numbers to France and other parts of Europe, where many enjoyed highly successful military careers. Thousands of Irishmen fought in 'Irish Brigades' in Europe and beyond in the eighteenth century. Fourteen generals in the Austrian army were Irish, as was the founder of the American navy (John Barry) and the liberator and first president of Chile (Bernardo O'Higgins). In addition, no fewer than ten American presidents are descendants of the thousands of Ulster Presbyterians who emigrated to the United States.

The success of Irishmen abroad contradicted Ascendancy propaganda, which justified the Penal Laws by depicting the Irish as uncivilized. Jonathan Swift, an Anglican Dean and author of *Gulliver's Travels*, said it 'ought to make the English ashamed of the reproaches they cast on the ignorance, the dullness and the want of courage of the Irish natives; those defects, wherever they happen, arising only from the poverty and slavery they suffer from their inhuman neighbours'.

The arrogance of the Ascendancy eventually gave rise to an opposition that crossed religious and class lines. The Great Rebellion of 1798, inspired partly by the example of revolutions in America and France, attracted a mix of Ulster settlers, Catholic peasants and Anglican revolutionaries, with support from the French government. Though the rebellion was ruthlessly suppressed, its leader Wolfe Tone became an enduring symbol around which future nationalists could rally.

The Irish Parliament's decision to agree to a complete union with Britain in 1801 and the elimination of legal discrimination against Catholics in 1829 did little to address underlying grievances. The next century saw the birth of popular movements in support of land reform, the formation of underground groups (such as the Fenians) which favoured armed revolt, and endless intrigues around the 'Irish Question' in the British parliament in London.

The Famine

The most profound and devastating event, however, was the Great Potato Famine of the 1840s. In the early nineteenth century potatoes had become the sole food of a third of the population and the livelihood of millions more, and the Irish peasantry was helpless when a potato blight destroyed crops on a huge scale in 1846 and several succeeding years. At least one million people died of starvation and related diseases, and about the same number emigrated to the Untied States and other countries (seventeen thousand died aboard transatlantic ships). Although the British authorities under Prime Minister Robert Peel reacted swiftly in the early stages to set up relief operations, Peel was defeated later in 1846 and replaced by a government grimly committed to a *laissez-faire* ideology.

'The matter is awfully serious, but we are in the hands of Providence, without a possibility of averting the catastrophe if it is to happen,' declared the civil servant in charge of famine relief.

The consequences of the depopulation of Ireland were profound, changing the agricultural economy, creating a culture of emigration (and huge and influential Irish communities abroad) and delivering a death blow to the Irish language. Today the population of Ireland remains 20 per cent lower than it was in 1845.

Though large landowners felt the pinch of land reforms which followed the Famine, the upper classes were largely insulated from the catastrophe. What did sweep through high society was the new fad of golf. No fewer than 110 clubs were founded in Ireland between 1885 and 1900, a rate of growth not equalled since. Golf was for the privileged – wealthy Protestant merchants, aristocrats and Scottish officers sent to Ireland to enforce British rule. In 1901 the *Irish Times* reported that the relative paucity of golf enthusiasts in the southeast of Ireland was due to 'the great amount of time devoted to hunting and the numerous packs of hounds that there are to follow'.

Political change was on the horizon, however. For the first time large numbers of Irish Catholics could vote and be represented in Westminster, and, by voting as a block, Irish nationalist MPs soon found they could influence British politics. Greater autonomy for Ireland in the form of 'Home Rule' was first proposed in 1886 by Prime Minister William Gladstone (who needed the support of Irish MPs to stay in power), but the legislation faced an endless series of setbacks, not the least of which was the public disgrace faced by Charles Parnell – the parliamentary leader of the nationalists – who admitted to an adulterous affair. The machinations in London also raised emotions in Ulster, where most Protestants feared the prospect of rule from Dublin.

Independence and civil war

Still, self-government of some kind seemed inevitable as the First World War started, and it was with some shock that Dubliners woke up on Easter Sunday in 1916 to find their city the site of an armed revolt. Led by Patrick Pearse, the hopelessly undermanned uprising resulted in the deaths of about one hundred people and caused extensive damage to central Dublin. The initial reaction of the populace was indignation – at the rebels. However, the heavy-handed response of the British government (fifteen rebel leaders were executed and thousands were arrested who had nothing to do with the rebellion) turned public opinion around completely, and the rebels soon became martyrs to a rejuvenated nationalist cause.

When the British government did not act swiftly to meet nationalist demands after the First World War, a guerrilla-style War of Independence developed and enjoyed widespread popular support. Once again, the British government was its own worst enemy. Ill-disciplined troops from the war against Germany were deployed, and these 'Black and Tans' became notorious for indiscriminate revenge killings and destruction.

International opinion turned against the British, and hastened negotiations. In 1922, a treaty was signed that created an Irish Free State within the British Commonwealth. However, the six counties in Ulster largely inhabited by Protestant settlers were to remain part of Britain. Not all revolutionary leaders accepted the deal, and the next two years saw Irish shooting Irish in a brief, but mean, civil war between nationalist factions. Ultimately, pro-treaty forces prevailed. Several hundred people were also killed in riots in Northern Ireland, as Loyalists formed their own Parliament and police forces.

What many assumed would be a temporary partition of Ireland quickly became solidified. Unsure of their positions, politicians on both sides played the 'religion card' to shore up support. In Northern Ireland, the minister of agriculture (and future prime minister) went so far as to dismiss 125 Catholics working on his estate 'to set an example to others'.

Economic doldrums

After the heady patriotic fervour of the early 1920s, the rest of the period between the world wars was comparatively dull. Voters in the Free State were overwhelmingly rural and Catholic, and heartily sick of violence and turmoil. A series of conservative governments stressed symbolic measures, such as reviving Irish-language teaching in schools, introducing high tariffs on imported goods from England, and welcoming the influence of the Catholic church over all aspects of Irish life.

Schools were controlled by the church, abortion and divorce were banned, and the state censorship board prohibited thousands of books from being distributed in Ireland, including many by internationally respected Irish writers. As one historian has remarked, the list of banned books made up 'a respectable list of modern classics.'

On the other hand, it was also a time of idealism. There was a surge in interest in Irish music, folklore and culture, and Irish missionaries once again roamed the world – this time ministering to impoverished populations in the emerging nations of South America, Africa and Asia. The mixture of conservatism and idealism was reflected in a radio speech to the nation by the dominant politician of the era, Prime Minister Eamon de Valera:

> The Ireland which we dreamed of would be the home of a people who valued material wealth only as a basis of right living, of a people who were satisfied with frugal comfort and devoted their leisure to the things of the spirit; a land whose countryside would be bright with cosy homesteads, whose fields and villages would be joyous with sounds of industry, the romping of sturdy children, the contests of athletic youths, the laughter of comely maidens; whose firesides would be the forums of the wisdom of serene old age.

Economically, however, the picture was bleak. In Northern Ireland, unemployment rose to 25 per cent, and as late as 1938 more than 85 per cent of rural homes in Ulster had no running water. Things were just as bad in the Free State.

The gap between rich and poor was nowhere more obvious than at golf clubs, many of which continued to thrive despite the prevailing hardships. Many of the best-known clubs (including Royal Portrush, County Louth, Lahinch, Killarney, Royal Dublin and County Sligo) had enough money to pay the foremost architects of the age to redesign their courses. Some also built elaborate clubhouses. Though members of the middle class (Protestant and Catholic) began to penetrate what had been an upper-class domain, golf retained its aristocratic air between the wars.

The sport's elitism did have one salutary effect, however. Since most golfers shared the same religion, class and point of view, there was no incentive to break up the Golfing Union of Ireland. The sport continues to be administered on an island-wide basis today, and Ireland sends united teams to international events.

The divisions between Northern Ireland and the Free State deepened during the Second World War, when the Irish government declared itself neutral (though it cooperated quietly with the Allies). The war years revitalized Ulster's shipping industry, but Belfast suffered from German bombing raids. Throughout Ireland horse-drawn carts made a return to country roads, and golf clubs all but closed down, as there was no petrol to transport golfers to the course. Golf balls were rationed, and golfers used paint (until it ran out) and glue to keep them together.

Post-war Ireland

Things did not get much better after the war, and social pressures were only eased by emigration. Each year during the 1950s some forty thousand people sought better lives in the United States, Canada, England and Australia. The influence of the church in what was now the Republic (declared in 1949) declined very slowly, and the Catholic hierarchy was able to stop a government plan for socialized medicine, arguing that a welfare state was against Church doctrine. Women's rights fell short of those enjoyed in other Western democracies. The constitution declared that the State had to ensure 'that mothers shall not be obliged by economic necessity to engage in labour to the neglect of their duties in the home'.

The 1950s were the Dark Ages for many golf clubs. The aristocrats were now all but gone, but the elitist image of the sport remained. For the young, golf couldn't compete with the attractions of hurling, Gaelic football or (in the North) soccer. And the average person could not afford even the few pounds necessary for a golf membership. Not a single golf course of distinction was built in Ireland between 1940 and 1965.

Ireland finally began to modernize in the early 1960s. A new Prime Minister, Sean Lemass, oversaw policies of economic liberalization and cultural pragmatism, and the notorious censorship board was emasculated. For the first time, the Republic embarked on a prolonged period of steady economic growth. Those looking for work headed to Dublin instead of overseas. A growing middle class began to discover golf, aided by the introduction of television and the heroics of Irish golfers.

Within golfing circles the achievements of Jimmy Bruen, Fred Daly (who became the first and thus far only Irishman to win the British Open, in 1947) and Joe Carr reached mythical proportions, but their performances were less important to the general public. In 1958, however, news reached Ireland that Christy O'Connor and Harry Bradshaw had won the Canada Cup (the forerunner to the World Cup). When the tournament was held in Ireland two years later, tens of thousands of spectators flocked to Portmarnock (it didn't hurt that Arnold Palmer and Sam Snead represented the United States). Suddenly it was okay to be a golfer in Ireland.

Slowly, golf clubs began to grow again. The Irish Tourist Board helped matters by supporting golf course construction in places such as Westport and Killarney. Community-run clubs in Ballybunion, Tralee, Enniscrone, Dingle and Connemara followed suit and built new links of their own, sometimes with glamorous architects such as Arnold Palmer and Robert Trent Jones.

The Troubles

These efforts to attract tourism were undermined by the Troubles. The violence that began in the late 1960s in Northern Ireland followed the first real thaw in relations between Protestant and Catholic groups. A new Prime Minister of Northern Ireland, Terence O'Neill, began to dismantle discrimination against Catholics in employment and housing, but the reforms came too slowly for young Catholics inspired by civil rights movements in America and elsewhere. Street demonstrations turned into violent confrontation with Protestant militants. This led to O'Neill's resignation and a bloody crackdown by his successors. This in turn energized militant factions of the Irish Republican Army (which had more or less given up armed struggle). The new 'Provisional' IRA rushed to defend Catholic neighbourhoods. Some Protestants, who feared the IRA was behind the civil-rights movement, became even more militant in response. What began as a struggle for civil rights became a rigidly sectarian cycle of violence.

The escalation of terrorism in Northern Ireland led, in 1972, to the disbanding of the Northern Ireland parliament by the British government and the implementation of direct rule, an arrangement that has been in place ever since.

More than three thousand people died in the Troubles, which became regular fodder for television newscasts around the world. Given the many aborted attempts at starting a peace process, the announcement of a unilateral ceasefire by the IRA in late 1994 (followed by similar commitments from the Protestant paramilitary groups) caught many of the most knowledgeable observers by complete surprise. One result was that tourism to Ireland, north and south, began to soar, jumping by more than 25 per cent in 1995 alone.

This was followed in 1998 by the Good Friday Agreement, endorsed in a referendum by voters in Northern Ireland and in the Republic. While the political process has remained agonisingly slow, and is by no means resolved, violence has remained at a low ebb.

Boom times

The remarkable resurgence of golf in Ireland, although assisted by tourism, is largely a result of the enthusiasm and increased spending power of the Irish themselves. In the 1970s and 1980s the standard of living increased markedly in Ireland (though there were growing disparities). For the Republic, membership in the European Community helped to diversify trade and proved to be both a psychological and economic boost – Ireland could move out of the shadow of Britain.

Due partly to this new prosperity, Ireland caught the wave of the international golf boom of the 1980s like few other countries. Television helped to fuel the growth, and a new generation of heroes – Christy O'Connor Jr, Eamonn Darcy, Ronan Rafferty, David Feherty, Des Smyth and others – reinforced the sport's popularity in the Republic and in

Northern Ireland. In 1988 and 1990 there were new international triumphs for Ireland, at the heavily televised Dunhill Cup at St Andrews.

In the mid-1990s, the steady economic progress Ireland was making gave way to a volcano of growth (a phenomenon dubbed the Celtic Tiger) that was unmatched anywhere in the world, with the possible exception of China. Fuelled by low corporate taxes, aid from the European Union, an underutilized but educated workforce, and a reduction in bad news from the North, Ireland became a key computer hardware and software exporter. Though there have been hiccups, the wild ride hasn't really stopped, and Ireland moved from being the 'poor man of Europe' to the continent's richest country. (Not everyone has benefited, however; one recent study showed Ireland to have more inequality than any country in the Western world after the United States.)

If there is a man who personifies the link between this new money and the evolution of Irish golf in the first years of the twenty-first century, it is Michael Smurfit. As CEO of Jefferson-Smurfit from 1977 to 2002, he turned a cardboard box manufacturer into what has been called Ireland's first multinational company. Smurfit was also in the vanguard of bringing to Ireland exceedingly high-priced golf, aimed squarely at those most benefiting from the economic boom. When his many millions helped land the Ryder Cup for Ireland in 2006 it was less a tribute to Irish golf than a sign that Ireland had joined the big time in economic terms.

As always, interest in golf has been assisted by a new generation of home-grown heroes. Although the likes of Darren Clarke, Padraig Harrington and Paul McGinley haven't yet won a major championship, they are all successful Ryder Cup players, and all played their part in the victorious 2006 team that demolished the Americans at Smurfit's K Club.

Demand for golf continues to exceed supply, and Ireland is experiencing a boom in golf course construction unseen since the 1890s. The number of member clubs in the Golfing Union of Ireland has swelled from 248 to well over 400 in the last twenty years.

'Golf used to be a middle-aged person's sport,' says Pat Ruddy, who has written about golf in Ireland for more than forty years. 'Now thousands of young people are coming out of big office blocks, all going to play golf by the busloads. In the public houses you used to talk women, horseracing and football, but now they're talking golf as well.'

A LINKS FROM HEAVEN:

IRELAND'S FINEST 18 HOLES

WE HAVE LIMITED ourselves to one hole per course in constructing our dream links. It would not be too long, at 6,677 yards, but its par of 71 would be very difficult to match. We hope it will start as many arguments as it resolves.

1. Portstewart #1 (Tubber Patrick), par 4, 425 yards: Perhaps the best opening hole in links golf, with a dramatic descent from a gloriously elevated tee into an amphitheatre of dunes.

2. Tralee #2, par 5, 590 yards: In their original form, at least, some holes on this links were just too quirky, but #2 is not one of them. Here Palmer and Seay have used Tralee Bay to great effect – creating a sweeping dogleg right with the beach as a constant hazard for the slice-prone. The Dingle peninsula sits brooding on the horizon and there are panoramic views of the entire course from the tee.

3. Portsalon #2 (Strand), par 4, 430 yards: Altered and lengthened, but still a cracker. An elevated tee shot across the beach must skirt ancient-looking rock formations, leaving a heroic approach over a river. The views over the Lough are as stunning as any at Pebble Beach or Turnberry.

4. Royal County Down #4, par 3, 217 yards: This oft-photographed hole is at its most glorious when the gorse is in bloom in early June. It is a beast at any time of the year, however, as the tee-shot is all carry over the gorse until the cluster of eight bunkers in front of the hard, narrow green. The view from the back tee is the most gorgeous of all the vistas on the course.

5. Lahinch #5 (Dell), par 3, 156 yards: This Old Tom Morris original is completely blind from the tee. The green is bordered by high dunes on all sides, a unique green placement which would never be copied today. On your first visit, there is nothing to do but aim for the white stone marker on top of the dune and hope. Also makes some people's Worst 18 list.

6. Rosapenna Sandy Hills #6, par 4, 390 yards: A good drive to the crest of a hill unveils a picturesque approach towards a backdrop of beach, sea and hills, with a natural chasm narrowing the fairway dangerously near the green.

7. Ballybunion (Old) #11, par 4, 453 yards: 'Don't be right, all of Ireland is to your left,' was the advice we received when we first played this hole. How true. Downhill and bunkerless, the landing area for the drive progressively narrows between the dunes on the left and the sea. The second shot is played to a small green on a shelf with trouble on all sides.

8. Ballybunion (Cashen) #15, par 5, 487 yards: One of the eeriest holes in golf, this par five is played over a crest of a hill into a bowl surrounded by the steepest sandhills you can imagine. The third shot is played to a green built high on a plateau. The

unearthly solitude and strange terrain would make it a good location for the first *Star Trek* golf movie.

9. Cruit Island #6, par 3, 160 yards: There are many wonderful par 3s in Ireland, but this one makes worthwhile the considerable effort it takes just to find Cruit Island golf club. The shot is all carry over a deep and craggy Atlantic inlet to a long, narrow green perched at the edge of a cliff, with pounding white surf below. The ever-present wind is usually into the player and from the right, necessitating a medium to long iron despite the hole's modest length.

10. Enniscrone #13 (The Burrows), par 4, 338 yards: A great links hole, a short downhill par 4 that scares and entices, charms and frustrates, all at the same time. Exquisite scenery off the tee, but the narrow, tilting landing area is intimidating and either the wind or the humps and hollows of the fairway conspire to throw many shots off-line and into the fearsome rough. A well-placed tee shot leaves just a wedge to a lovely, but tightly guarded green.

11. Waterville #11 (Tranquillity), par 5, 496 yards: Almost bunkerless, this aptly named hole sends you tumbling through a long, undulating chute lined with stately dunes. You feel cut off from the rest of the world amid the delightfully natural terrain.

12. The European Club #17 (Tom Watson), par 4, 392 yards: One of several holes at Pat Ruddy's masterpiece that provide a fairly generous landing area (this time in a pretty valley), but demand an accurate second to a well-positioned, slightly elevated green protected by natural swales and a pot bunker.

13. The Island #13 (Broadmeadow), par 3, 215 yards: A wake-up call after meandering through the dunes of the first twelve holes at The Island. It is all carry over a half-moon-shaped estuary. There is bail-out room to the left, but to reach the putting surface the water must be negotiated with a long iron or wood. Beyond the green the village of Malahide provides a lovely backdrop.

14. Portmarnock #14 (Ireland's Eye), par 4, 395 yards: The most elegant of Portmarnock's fine collection of par 4s, the line for the tee shot on this dogleg left is said to be 'Ireland's Eye', an island poised on the horizon. The second shot is played over large bunkers to a plateau green that accepts only the most precisely played shot. English great Henry Cotton's favourite hole.

15. Royal Portrush #14 (Calamity), par 3, 213 yards: A treacherous and historic hole with a huge chasm of rough waiting to swallow any shot short or right of the green. Usually played into the wind. Bobby Locke got up and down from the depression to the front-left of the green in all four rounds of the 1951 British Open. This area thus became known as 'Bobby Locke's hollow', and you are advised to keep it in mind, as it is the only conceivable bail-out area. The hole is said to be a source of inspiration for Pete Dye.

16. Carne #17 (An Muirineach), par 4, 390 yards: A treacherous, exhilarating adventure played on a narrow plateau high up in some of the planet's most sublime duneland.

17. Co. Sligo #17 (Gallery), par 4, 455 yards: One of the toughest holes to par in all of Ireland, this severe dogleg sweeps uphill and to the left on the second shot. The green is large but slopes severely from the back.

18. Laytown and Bettystown #18, par 5, 475 yards: Not the best finishing hole in Ireland, but the most fun, with two blind shots, including the approach to a green hiding in the dunes.

GOLFER'S
READING LIST

THE IRISH HAVE always held writers and poets in high esteem. From the bards of the early Celtic kings, to the learned Irish monks that educated Europe, to the poets and playwrights of the independence movement, to 1995 Nobel Prize-winner Seamus Heaney – Irish wordsmiths have been a potent force. Some argue that the introduction of the notorious censorship law in 1929 reflected how well the authorities (and the Catholic church) understood the power of the written word. Today many Irish works that were once banned are considered national treasures, and a law passed in 1979 gave writers tax-free status. Here is but a brief sampling of (mostly) twentieth-century Irish writing.

Accessible fiction

Maeve Binchy's charming stories set in small-town Ireland are on international best-seller lists around the world. Roddy Doyle's affectionate and hilarious accounts of life in working-class Dublin have also made terrific movies; his books include the *Barrytown Trilogy* (*The Commitments*, *The Snapper* and *The Van*) and the Booker-Prize-winning *Paddy Clark Ha Ha Ha*. Michael Collins, a Limerick native now living in Seattle, has a unique take on Ireland and Irish immigration to America in the collection of stories *The Feminists Go Swimming* and the novel *Emerald Underground*. The popular Victorian classic, *Some Recollections of an Irish RM*, by E. O. Somerville and Violet Ross contains much lively and perceptive detail about rural life at the turn of the century. David Hanly's *In Guilt and in Glory* captures the spirit and contradictions of modern Ireland, while Dermot Healy creates an edgy psychological thriller set partly in Sligo in *Sudden Times*. The creator of *Dracula* is Irish, and some say the confrontation between peasants and debauched aristocrat in Bram Stoker's most famous story is full of revolutionary symbolism.

More challenging fare

A master of the short story, William Trevor writes exquisite and often heart-breaking stories that are usually set in his native Ireland. John Banville's unsettling and sometimes bleak psychological novels rank among the best works of literature being produced in English today. Brian Moore's early novels, including *The Lonely Passion of Judith Hearne*, evoke the Belfast of his youth. The poems and essays of Seamus Heaney, winner of the 1995 Nobel Prize for Literature, have been deeply influenced by the Troubles in his native Northern Ireland; they often explore the relationship between art and society. Frank McCourt won the 1997 Pulitzer Prize for *Angela's Ashes*, his memoir of growing up in difficult times in Limerick. Feel free to jump into James Joyce's *Ulysses*, but you might want to cut your teeth first on *Dubliners*, his famous and perfectly crafted group of short stories. William Butler Yeats – winner of the Nobel Prize in 1923 – is one of the century's greatest poets and an important nationalist figure.

Drama

Take away Irish-born playwrights and you would leave a gaping hole in this century's English-language theatre. The Irish influence starts with George Bernard Shaw and Oscar Wilde, and continues with the lyrical tales of J. M. Synge, the wrenching civil war plays of Sean O'Casey, the absurdist masterpieces of Samuel Beckett, and the more accessible, though equally penetrating, dramas of Frank McGuinness, Ireland's best contemporary playwright. (Don't be put off by the titles of McGuinness's plays; *Observe the Sons of Ulster Marching Towards the Somme* and *Carthaginians* are exciting pieces of theatre that illuminate Ireland's inner conflicts.) Reading plays is not everyone's cup of tea, of course, so keep an eye out for local productions of Irish plays, and definitely check out the lively theatre scene in Dublin. Prices are reasonable and the quality is high.

History

Readable general histories of Ireland include John Ranclagh's *A Short History of Ireland* (Cambridge) and *The Oxford Illustrated History of Ireland* (Oxford), edited by R. F. Foster. *Ireland: A Concise History* (Thames and Hudson) by Máire and Conor Cruise O'Brien is well written and illustrated, but assumes prior knowledge of Irish affairs. Terence Brown's *Ireland: A Social and Cultural History 1922–1985* (Fontana) is much more interesting than it sounds. *A Traveller's History of Ireland* (Interlink) by Peter Neville is very accessible.

David Cannadine's *Decline and Fall of the British Aristocracy* (Yale) is a fascinating and exhaustive account of the demise of the landed gentry in Britain and Ireland. *The Great Hunger* (Hamish Hamilton) by Cecil Woodham Smith is a similarly definitive history of the Famine of the 1840s. *How the Irish Saved Civilization* (Bantam) by Thomas Cahill is an illustrated account of the golden age of Irish influence in Europe.

Early Irish Golf (Oakleaf) by William Gibson can be found in better bookstores in Ireland. It is a careful documentation of the development of golf in Ireland and should be of interest to those with a serious golf library. Robert Browning's 1954 classic, *A History of Golf: The Royal and Ancient Game* (A & C Black) contains some material on Ireland. Fans of Bernard Darwin could also peruse *The Golf Courses of the British Isles*. Herbert Warren Wind's famous article on Ballybunion, written in 1967, is reprinted in a collection of writings entitled *Following Through* (Ticknor & Fields).

Centenary books

If you fall in love with a specific course, and it's old enough, you might inquire whether the club has commissioned a special book to celebrate its one-hundredth anniversary. While the quality varies, most centenary books are well researched and make attractive and unique mementos. Many are labours of love, which we think gives them additional charm. There are centenary books on Ballybunion (written by John Redmond), Ballycastle (John Andrews, Michael Page and Tim Sheehan), County Louth (Charlie Mulqueen), County Sligo (Dermot Gilleece), Dooks (several authors), Dunfanaghy (Denholm and Olivia Moore), Killarney (Donal Hickey), Lahinch (Enda Glynn), Portsalon (several authors), Portmarnock (T.M. Healy), Portstewart (Bill Rodgers), Rosslare (Tom Williams), Royal County Down (Harry McCaw and Brum Henderson), Royal Dublin (Liam Browne and Frank Chambers), Royal Portrush (Ian Bamford) and The Island (William Murphy).

Guides

There are many excellent general guides to Ireland, and it would be pointless to list them all here. Browse in your local bookstore to find the one that suits you best. Most are terribly ill-informed about golf, however. The tourist board has some attractive golf brochures that will help get your adrenaline going. Those who want a pictorial record of Irish golf should look for *Great Golf Courses of Ireland* (Gill & Macmillan Ltd) by John Redmond, or *Emerald Gems*, a physically massive coffee-table book on the links courses of Ireland containing the wonderful photography of Larry Lambrecht.

McCarthy's Bar, by the late Pete McCarthy, is a funny and insightful travelogue of a man who stops at every pub he encounters called 'McCarthy's'. *Ireland's Pubs* (Penguin) by Sybil Taylor is an excellent exploration of pub culture, with detailed information on the most historic and worthwhile of Ireland's ten thousand pubs, while the acclaimed spirits writer Jim Murray has produced the very useful *Classic Irish Whiskey*.

Georgina Campbell's Ireland is a comprehensive guide to both accommodation and eating and drinking throughout Ireland. The Irish Hotels Federation's *Be Our Guest* guide is a useful guide to Irish hotels and guesthouses, while The Town and Country Homes Association's *Bed & Breakfast Guest Accommodation* guide is an excellent way to review B&B accommodation. There are also a myriad of general interest publications available from Tourism Ireland.

Film and screen

The Wind that Shakes the Barley, directed by Ken Loach, is a harrowing but brilliant film about the Irish civil war period, and won the Palme d'Or at the Cannes film festival in 2006. One of the more interesting contemporary Irish film directors is Jim Sheridan, who made *My Left Foot*, *The Field* and *In the Name of the Father*. The latter film deals with the Troubles, as does Neil Jordan's *The Crying Game*.

The Commitments and *The Snapper* are wonderful adaptations of Roddy Doyle's comic novels, while *Waking Ned* is an entertaining look at a west of Ireland village turned upside-down by a lottery win. There have also been outstanding film treatments of *The Dead* (the final story in Dubliners), *The Lonely Passion of Judith Hearne* and Maeve Binchy's *A Circle of Friends*.

Film buffs will enjoy *The Quiet Man*, starring John Wayne and Maureen O'Hara, and for a taste of the kind of scenery you will encounter on golf courses in the west of Ireland there's always *Ryan's Daughter*.

Internet

Almost all the clubs in Ireland have websites now and you can certainly get a visual sense of the courses you are interested in playing, though you may prefer to explore a course for the first time with your own eyes, rather than being saturated with photographs ahead of time. There are numerous sites that purport to be virtual guides to golf in Ireland, but they tend to be short on independent information and long on the shameless promotion of the wealthier golf destinations. Bord Failte's website (www.ireland.ie) is an excellent source of accommodation and travel information, as is Tourism Ireland's (www.tourismireland.com).

PLANNING YOUR JOURNEY

Golfing in Ireland is rather different than spending a week on the Costa del Sol or at an American golf resort. With a few exceptions, you will not be patronizing a golf resort at all. Instead, you are accepting the hospitality of fellow golfers. Generally, you will be travelling the narrow, unfamiliar roads of rural Ireland, and staying in cosy bed and breakfasts that often double as people's homes. Here is the practical information you need to successfully plan your golf journey to Ireland.

PLANNING YOUR JOURNEY

IF YOU ARE on a tight schedule or consider the words 'vacation' and 'surprise' to be incompatible, the many tour companies (both within Ireland and in Great Britain) which arrange all-inclusive golf holidays to Ireland are worth investigating. Many specialize in self-drive holidays – they arrange for accommodation, starting times and a rental car, and the rest is up to you. Some also offer guided tours, in which a group of eight or more golfers travels in a chauffeured minibus with a number of other golfers. Differences in price between various packages have much more to do with the type of accommodation chosen than any other factor (with the exception of the increasingly common helicopter tours aimed at the very rich). The most expensive tours use large hotels, while the cheapest will likely use bed-and-breakfasts. It is always a good idea to talk to someone who has used the company before – not merely to check on the company's reliability but to help you decide which kind of tour is best for you.

The advantages of trips arranged in advance with a tour company are obvious. The most important may be the rapidly increasing popularity of golf travel to Ireland (it is estimated that approximately one-quarter of a million people visit on golf trips annually) and thus the need to book the most popular courses months in advance. Also, using a tour operator means that less advance planning is necessary on your part, there are few surprises, and you may travel with a bunch of like-minded people who could become friends (a guided tour holds particular attractions for those who may be travelling on their own).

The disadvantages are just as obvious. You are somewhat insulated from your Irish hosts, there's little flexibility should you want to stay in one place for an extra day (or if poor weather spoils your round), you won't experience the thrill of finding the perfect pub or bed-and-breakfast on your own, and you may find yourself cooped up with that one obnoxious character you can't stand. Self-drive tours offer more flexibility and privacy than guided tours, though they still stick to a pre-planned schedule, which very likely includes pre-paid and non-refundable green fees if you are playing the country's top courses.

So, for a real cultural experience, there is nothing like the excitement and pleasure of planning, and taking, your own journey. This section will help you do just that.

When to go

There is no reason to think of Ireland as a summer destination only. One of our most enjoyable trips was taken in early November. The weather, such as it is, does not change all that much throughout the year (especially in the southern part of the country). It is rare for the temperature to fall below forty degrees Fahrenheit or climb above seventy-five degrees Fahrenheit. The links courses are generally open to visitors year-round (with a few notable exceptions, such as Tralee), and spring and fall are the driest times of the year. In November and March the courses are not in as fine condition as they are in the summer, but as compensation you will often have them to yourself. And the compulsory use of artificial grass mats on the fairways during the winter, so common in Scotland, has not generally caught on in Ireland (though it's worth asking in advance). One important difficulty with off-season golf travel is the amount of light available. In June in Portrush it is light until 10:30 p.m., but dusk begins to fall at 4:00 p.m. in the winter months. For first-time visitors, the best times to travel are probably from the beginning of May to mid-October.

Getting there

We have set out below several itineraries for golf journeys in Ireland which vary according to the number of days available and the arrival and departure points used. Each begins and ends at a course which is convenient to one of Ireland's three international airports or the ferry ports at Larne, Dun Laoghaire or Rosslare. Many of the itineraries rely on booking a flight which arrives at one airport and departs from another – a relatively straightforward procedure. There are multiple daily flights to Dublin from Heathrow, Gatwick, Stansted and Luton, as well as many other British airports, and the options range from Aer Lingus, British Airways and BMI (British Midland), to discount airlines like No Frills, Ryanair and Aer Arann. For those who prefer to drive their own vehicle, there are ferries from Holyhead to Dublin/Dun Laoghaire, Fishguard to Rosslare, Cairnryan (Stranraer) to Larne, and Liverpool to Belfast and Dublin, among others. From the United States and Canada, Aer Lingus has flights to Dublin and Shannon from New York (JFK), Boston, Chicago and Los Angeles. Delta (JFK) and Continental (Newark) also have non-stop flights from New York. Several airlines (including British Airways) offer flights to Dublin and Belfast, via London, from several North American cities. Air Canada offers direct flights to

Dublin, then on to Shannon, from Toronto in the summer months only. In the summer months, there are also charters to Dublin, Shannon and Belfast from various North American cities.

Getting around

If you have not driven your own vehicle, it is a good idea to book a rental car from home, rather than doing so in Ireland. This will almost always be the most cost-effective option, and it is not unheard of for all available cars to be rented out at Shannon Airport, say, in the busy summer months.

A detailed map is a necessity in Ireland, especially if you are intent on finding some of the more remote links we have described. The Michelin road map of Ireland is excellent, as is the Ireland Driving Map produced by Ordnance Survey Ireland. Even with a map, however, you will get lost from time to time. When you are reviewing the map and estimating the amount of time it will take to drive from point A to B, count on progress of thirty to forty miles per hour. Of course, it is possible to make better time on the (still relatively rare) motorways, but narrow and twisting country roads lead to many of the great Irish links, particularly in the west and northwest. Most roads pass through a string of towns which will slow your progress. In some rural areas, livestock on the road remains a real possibility. Also, note that road signs in the Republic can give distances in either miles or kilometres. The old white signs express distances in miles, while newer, green signs give distances in kilometres. Note, though, that there are also new white signs which give distances in kilometres – these will have a small 'km' above the number. To add to the confusion, the locals often do not refer to a road by its 'official' name, especially in rural areas. Asking for directions can be a gamble, but is almost always entertaining.

Advance starting times

Tee times at most of the courses featured in this book must now be arranged well in advance, sometimes several months in advance. Most of the famous links of the southwest, for example, began allotting their 2007 tee times in the autumn of 2006. This is particularly true if you are planning to travel between June and September, when demand is at its greatest. Be sure to inquire whether green fees are for a round or the day, and to specify if you wish to play more than once. If you do, be sure to leave yourself enough time for lunch – Irish clubs will often estimate a pace of play that is quite fast. If you plan to hire a caddie, this should also be specified to the club in advance. Many Irish clubs say they require a letter of introduction (from your home club) and/or a handicap certificate in their official literature, but we have never been asked to produce either of these items. Nevertheless, it would be wise to carry one along if you have one, just to be on the safe side. In recent years, many Irish clubs have added an on-line booking component to their websites, making a homemade Irish tour that much easier to arrange, in our view. At a few of the more traditional clubs, better results may still be achieved by politely contacting the club secretary directly, however.

Motorized buggies (electric carts) are now disturbingly commonplace in Ireland. Nevertheless, trolleys (pull carts) remain the most sensible, and widely accepted, form of club transport in the country (we know of only one course in all of Ireland, Old Head, on which trolleys are banned). Caddies are also available at most of the larger clubs, but visitors are only 'strongly encouraged' to employ them at Doonbeg and Old Head, in our experience. A caddie can add considerable expense for those on a budget, but a round played under the care and guidance of an experienced Irish caddie can be a rare treat, and well worth the cost. We recommend you try a caddie at least once.

What to take

As the departure day approaches, try to pack as lightly as possible. Rental cars in Ireland are not big (even the station wagons) and four golfers sharing one car will have problems if they have brought more than one soft-sided suitcase and a relatively compact golf bag each. Having said that, there are certain essentials. The first is a reliably waterproof rain suit and either one pair of comfortable, fully waterproof golf shoes or a second pair to wear when the first becomes waterlogged. On links courses, umbrellas are more often than not a nuisance in the ocean wind. Two or three all-weather golf gloves will be useful, and some golfers swear by the 'rain gloves' that are now designed specifically for play in wet weather. Bring one wool and one cotton sweater, a wind shirt, and one cotton turtleneck shirt, even in July. A sports jacket and tie is required apparel in certain parts of a few clubhouses, so check in advance with the clubs you will be visiting. Finally, bring enough golf balls to see you through your trip, and lots of tees and pencils. These will not always be available in abundance.

Where to stay

There are few worries when it comes to accommodation in Ireland. The options range from invariably excellent bed-and-breakfasts to luxury hotels, manor homes and castles. A good starting point is the Irish Hotels Federation's *Be Our Guest* guide (for hotels and guesthouses) or the Town and Country Homes Association's annual comprehensive listing of bed-and-breakfast accommodation. Also, the Irish Tourist Board has some very informative publications.

Both 'guest houses' and 'town and country homes and farmhouses' are, generally, what we would call bed-and-breakfasts (B&Bs). The difference is that a guest house must have at least five bedrooms for rent. A large guest house is pretty much indistinguishable from a small hotel. A town and country home or farmhouse may have fewer than five bedrooms and can be more intimate – you will often have breakfast in the proprietor's own dining room, and they will invariably take a personal interest in your journey.

Hotels have certain advantages, though. They may have more amenities, like a bar which is required to stay open as late as you wish, a television in your room and an en-suite bathroom, and there is a certain element of coming and going as one pleases which may not be present in a small B&B.

A third option is to rent an entire house or cottage. There are some wonderful properties available at very reasonable prices, but the obvious disadvantage is being restricted to the area in which your cottage is located. The Irish Tourist Board produces a comprehensive publication called Ireland Self-Catering Guide which lists all of the houses available and gives details on how to book. Bookings are generally made by the week.

We've listed some of our favourite hotels and B&Bs in each region at the end of this chapter.

What it costs

Budgeting is a very personal matter. While prices in Ireland should not be overly surprising to most residents of Great Britain, North American visitors will raise their eyebrows more than once. The sustained economic boom in Ireland has led to extraordinary inflation in some aspects of golf travel, most notably green fees, which have roughly tripled in the last decade at many of the championship links courses. As you can see from the summary at the end of each of the principal chapters, high-season green fees now range from €40 to €200, and in a few cases beyond. Apart from green fees, travellers planning to stay at bed-and-breakfasts should budget a minimum of €40 per day for accommodation (higher in the major cities), and a similar amount for food and drink. There are, of course, high-end hotels (sometimes in grand castles) and restaurants in Ireland where it is possible to spend five times this amount. Competitive and up-to-date prices for air fares and rental cars are easily obtained on the Internet or from any reputable travel agent.

The currency of Northern Ireland is the pound sterling, while that of the Republic is the euro. At press time, the rate of exchange between the euro and the pound was approximately 1.5 to 1. It may be useful to obtain a small supply of euros before leaving home, but automatic teller machines are plentiful in Ireland. Credit cards are widely accepted too, but note that many smaller B&B operators will accept cash only.

Communications

Throughout the book we have given telephone and fax numbers for the various golf clubs. The system of telephone numbers in Ireland continues to be upgraded, as some numbers are currently five digits in length, while others have been updated to six or seven digits. As the number of new telephones continues to increase, the five-digit numbers will be lengthened by one or two digits. Note also that all of the area or city codes which precede the actual telephone number begin with '0'. When in Ireland, the '0' must be dialled, but if you are calling from Great Britain or North America, the '0' is ignored. When dialling from overseas, the country code for the Irish Republic is 353, and for Northern Ireland it is 44 (the country code for all of the United Kingdom). There is also a special prefix required to make a call from the Republic of Ireland to Northern Ireland. In this case, begin with 048, rather than 028.

Ireland has a high rate of mobile phone usage, with the total number of cellular subscriptions exceeding the total population of the country. Cellular coverage, both for telephones and communication devices such as Blackberries, is excellent across the entire island, even in remote outposts such as Carne. Be cautious when using your home mobile phone in Ireland, however, as roaming charges can mount very quickly. If you plan to make a number of calls, renting a local mobile phone may be the best option. In order to make calls from a public telephone, it will be necessary to purchase a Callcard (known as a Phonecard in the North).

SOME SUGGESTED JOURNEYS

HERE ARE SOME itineraries for golf journeys in Ireland. These itineraries are quite golf-intensive – they can, of course, be modified to intersperse some non-golf days or to provide for longer stays in fewer places. What we have set out here is what, from our experience, is *possible* for travellers who want to play as many of the great courses of Ireland as they can in the time available. There will be little opportunity for sightseeing for anyone following these itineraries. It is always a good idea to be flexible when following an itinerary – you might make some new friends and be invited to participate in some unforeseen adventures.

The grand tour - Shannon to Dublin

Two weeks; arrive Shannon, depart Dublin

Saturday	arrive Shannon, drive to Killarney (option: afternoon round at Killarney)
Sunday	Waterville
Monday	Tralee (option: Dooks)
Tuesday	Ballybunion Old (morning); Cashen (afternoon)
Wednesday	Doonbeg
Thursday	Lahinch
Friday	drive to Sligo Town; afternoon round on Co Sligo
Saturday	Enniscrone
Sunday	Rosapenna Sandy Hills
Monday	Portstewart
Tuesday	Royal Portrush (Dunluce)
Wednesday	Royal County Down
Thursday	County Louth
Friday	Portmarnock
Saturday	European Club
Sunday	depart Dublin

A morning flight from Great Britain, or a transatlantic flight (which will invariably arrive in the morning, Ireland time) allows for an afternoon 'warm up' round on the day of arrival. Waterville and Tralee are within driving distance of Killarney, for those who do not wish to be constantly changing accommodation. There is much to be said for moving each night, however, as there is an excellent post-round atmosphere in the bar at Waterville and at the excellent Butler Arms Hotel, both of which may only be properly enjoyed without the prospect of a two-hour drive at its conclusion. Tralee is well worth playing, both for the spectacular scenery and an insight into how a modern American player and designer (Arnold Palmer, with Ed Seay) sees links golf. But for an off-beat treat, the extremely friendly Dooks club is also recommended.

Even though the object of this tour is to play as many of the great Irish courses as possible, Ballybunion may merit a stay of two days (if so, consider leaving Doonbeg to another trip). There are, after all, two exceptional courses at Ballybunion. Again, take the opportunity to compare the modern vision of Robert Trent Jones with the classic Old Course. Decent accommodation can be scarce in Ballybunion – this may be one night's stay that should be booked in advance.

Lahinch is an easy ninety-minute drive to the north, which can be undertaken on the morning before the round. Be sure to check the scheduled times for the short but vital ferry link between Tarbert (Co. Kerry) and Killimer (Co. Clare). A longer drive is in store between Lahinch and Co. Sligo. Get it out of the way as early as possible and consider setting up a base for the next two days. If you have an appetite for more golf, a round at the underrated Strandhill, also in Sligo, might be a possibility. Carne is very much worth a visit as well, but it is a long and lonely drive from Sligo. Otherwise, it would certainly be included in this itinerary.

It is to be hoped that your swing is grooved and your energy remains high, for the heart of the trip is just ahead. Make the three-hour drive north to Rosapenna to visit the outstanding new Sandy Hills links. Even those on a limited budget for accommodation should consider splurging for a stay at the wonderfully hospitable Rosapenna Hotel. Then, it is on to the Portrush/Portstewart area and a base for the next couple of nights. Royal Portrush and Portstewart are only about fifteen minutes apart – and could both be played in one day – but each is worthy of a day to itself.

Next is the beautiful and imposing Royal County Down. While any of the courses on this tour are worth playing twice, this is the one place you should definitely play thirty-six if you have the energy. Besides, there's little else to do in Newcastle, beyond hiking in the majestic Mountains of Mourne. Head out of town after your rounds and travel south to Drogheda, and a round the next day at County Louth (Baltray).

We end the tour by finding a base in the Dublin area for the concluding weekend. The majestic Portmarnock is within thirty minutes of central Dublin, and Pat Ruddy's masterwork at The European Club is to the south (and open to visitors every day of the week, including Saturdays). There are a few other worthy choices in the greater Dublin area as well, of course, including The Island, Royal Dublin and St Anne's, as well as the considerable non-golf attractions of the capital.

The tour can also, of course, be done in reverse order, if a flight into Dublin and departing from Shannon is more convenient. Generally, this will be most important to travellers from North America, where the same plane may fly from the originating city to Dublin, then on Shannon and home (or vice versa in some cases). In order to avoid the annoying wait on the tarmac and commuter flight across the country, begin the tour in Dublin and end the tour in Shannon (or the reverse, depending on your particular flight). Be sure to check with your airline when planning your tour.

JOURNEY 2

The great southwest
One week; arrive and depart Shannon

Saturday	arrive Shannon, drive to Killarney, play Mahony's Point or Killeen
Sunday	Dooks
Monday	Tralee
Tuesday	Waterville
Wednesday	Ballybunion Old
Thursday	Ballybunion Cashen
Friday	Doonbeg
Saturday	Lahinch
Sunday	depart Shannon

For those who have only one week, and who do not wish to change accommodation nightly, a week in the southwest of Ireland is very appealing. All of these courses, with the exception of Doonbeg and Lahinch, are within driving distance of a centrally located base in the Killarney or Tralee areas. If, for some reason, you do not fancy the trip to Co. Clare, either or both of County Cork (Little Island) or Old Head could be substituted.

JOURNEY 3

Undiscovered gems of the northwest

Ten days; arrive Shannon (or, if possible, Knock); depart Belfast or Derry

Saturday	arrive Shannon or Knock, drive to Connemara
Sunday	Connemara
Monday	Carne
Tuesday	Enniscrone
Wednesday	County Sligo
Thursday	Donegal
Friday	Narin and Portnoo (morning); Cruit Island (nine holes, afternoon)
Saturday	Rosapenna Sandy Hills (option: afternoon round on Old links)
Sunday	Portsalon
Monday	Ballylffin Old and Glashedy
Tuesday	depart Belfast or Derry

Here is a tour for those who like their golf peaceful and undisturbed.
Undertaken at any time other than the height of summer, this tour will
likely yield eleven rounds played in splendid solitude. There are two
lengthy drives involved – about three hours from Shannon airport to
Connemara, and about the same distance from Ballyliffin to Belfast.
Commuter flights to Knock or from Derry would shorten travel time
considerably.

Dubliners

One week; arrive and depart Dublin, or Dun Laoghaire or Rosslare ferry ports

Saturday	The European Club
Sunday	sightsee in Dublin (option: St Anne's)
Monday	Royal Dublin
Tuesday	The Island
Wednesday	Baltray
Thursday	Portmarnock
Friday	Royal County Down
Saturday	Druids Glen (option: substitute The K Club)
Sunday	depart Dublin

There has been an explosion of parkland golf courses in and around Dublin. Nevertheless, the classic links courses should not be missed. A week of outstanding golf can be had in the vicinity of the capital. Choose a hotel or B&B to the north of the city, if possible, as all of the courses are in that direction with the exception of The European Club and Druids Glen. The only trip of a substantial distance is the two-and-a-half hour drive to Royal County Down – a must if you have never been before. Fans of modern parkland golf could substitute with The K Club, Powerscourt or Carton House.

The Dublin area is one part of the country where visiting golfers may be restricted to certain days of the week. Baltray, for example, prefers visitors on weekdays other than Tuesday, while Portmarnock, The Island and Royal Dublin welcome guests every weekday other than Wednesday. The European Club will take visitors every day of the week, leaving some scheduling flexibility. Realistically, with a little perseverance and enough advance warning, an early morning or late afternoon tee time should be possible at any of these clubs most weekdays, and even on some weekends. The trip ends with a round on one of Dublin's fine new parkland layouts. Those who can afford it may wish to visit The K Club, site of the 2006 Ryder Cup matches, though note the Palmer Course (where the matches were held) is open only to hotel residents on some summer days. Links purists will substitute Laytown and Bettystown, or St Anne's.

JOURNEY 5

The Causeway Coast Open

One week; arrive and depart Belfast, or Larne ferry port

Saturday	arrive Belfast, drive to Portstewart, afternoon round at Portstewart
Sunday	Royal Portrush (Dunluce) (option: play Valley course in afternoon)
Monday to Friday	play in tournament: Ballycastle, Castlerock, Portrush Valley and Portstewart; off-day: Royal County Down
Saturday	depart Belfast

if additional days can be added:

Saturday	Ballyliffin
Sunday	Portsalon
Monday	Rosapenna
Tuesday	depart Belfast

The Bushmills Causeway Coast Open is one of the great experiences in Irish golf. The tournament is played in four rounds over five days in June (Monday to Friday, with one of the days being an 'off' day) at Portstewart, Castlerock, Ballycastle and the Valley course at Royal Portrush. While free practice rounds are available during the week on each of these courses in the late-afternoons, we recommend that you forgo these. They will impede your ability to socialize with the (mostly Irish) tournament participants, which is at least half the point of going in the first place. Better to arrive the Saturday before and take a look at Portstewart and Royal Portrush before the tournament begins. Take your time, as it stays light past ten o'clock in Northern Ireland in June. Much of the membership of Royal Portrush hails from Belfast, and by noon on Sunday, the course is often all but deserted.

For your off-day (tournament organizers will let you know which day this is), be sure to have made a booking at Royal County Down. It's only a two-hour drive away. If you have only one week available, bid your new friends adieu on Friday night and head home from Belfast on Saturday. If you are able to squeeze a few more days into your vacation, we recommend a visit to neighbouring Co. Donegal. The drives between courses are relatively short, and the modern classics at Ballyliffin Glashedy and Rosapenna Sandy Hills make for a fascinating contrast to the historic links you will have played during tournament week.

It is hard to overestimate the value, exceptional links golf, and camaraderie that is experienced by the typical Causeway Coast Open participant. For this reason, the tournament is vastly oversubscribed every year. To apply for a spot in the tournament, contact the organizer, Jackie Graham, at (028) 7035-1668.

ACCOMMODATION

HERE ARE SOME recommended B&Bs and hotels situated in or near the principal golfing areas. Many hotels have various rates depending on the season. We have based our price descriptions on the high-season rate.

Inexpensive: under €50 per person per night
Moderate: €50–100 per person per night
Expensive: €100–€200 per person per night
Very expensive: over €200 per night

Double occupancy in all cases

The Southwest

A centrally located base in Killarney or Tralee can allow you to comfortably reach most of the famous links of the southwest. On the other hand, changing your accommodation as you move from course to course means less driving and more time enjoying the *craic* in the wonderful pubs and clubhouse bars.

International Hotel, Killarney
(064) 31816
www.killarney-inter.com
There are many hotels in central Killarney, but this is one of the best, with a warm welcome for golfers and a fine restaurant and bar; *moderate to expensive.*

Glenmill House, Aghadoe, Killarney
(064) 34391
www.glenmillhouse.com
Modern B&B with friendly proprietor and spectacular view of the lake, just five minutes from the golf courses; *inexpensive.*

Butler Arms Hotel, Waterville
(066) 947-4520
www.butlerarms.com
Central gathering point for golfers visiting Waterville with exceptionally warm atmosphere was made famous by Payne Stewart's visits in the late 1990s; *moderate to expensive.*

Abbey Gate Hotel, Tralee
(066) 712-9821
www.abbeygate-hotel.com
Modern hotel in central Tralee which opened in 1994; *expensive.*

Marine Links Hotel, Ballybunion
(068) 27139
www.easygolfballybunion.com
Ballybunion Golf Club has pre-sold a
number of tee times to area hotels
and guesthouses, including the
Marine Links Hotel, a town-centre
institution with an outstanding
golfer's bar. The hotel is small (only
ten rooms in total) so must be booked
well in advance; *moderate*.

Teach de Broc, Ballybunion
(068) 27581
www.ballybuniongolf.com
The Irish Golf Tour Operators'
guesthouse of the year in 2005 is as
close as you can get to the famous
links; *moderate*.

The Tides Guesthouse, Ballybunion
(068) 27980
www.linksgolfballybunion.com
Friendly and accommodating B&B
run by a Ballybunion member can
also provide pre-booked tee times;
moderate.

Trident Hotel, Kinsale
(021) 477-9300
www.tridenthotel.com
Fine, water's-edge base for those
ponying up to play Old Head – be
sure to request a harbour view;
moderate to expensive.

Greenbrier Inn, Lahinch
(065) 708-1242
www.greenbrierinn.com
Fine, family-run guesthouse within
walking distance of the links;
moderate.

The Northwest

The considerable distances
between courses make
moving around from night to
night necessary, for the most part, in
the northwest. The one exception
may be the Rosapenna, which makes
a convenient base for its own two
courses, Portsalon, St Patrick's,
Dunfanaghy and perhaps even
Ballyliffin.

Rosapenna Hotel, Downings
(074) 915-5301
www.rosapenna.ie
The standard against which to
measure all other Irish golf hotels.
Lovely rooms, excellent food and
unrivalled hospitality, not to mention
a superb new links on-site. Closed
from November to March; *moderate*.

Sandhouse Hotel, Rossnowlagh
(071) 985-1777
www.sandhouse.ie
Wonderfully situated seaside hotel on
Donegal Bay is very convenient for
Donegal and Bundoran; *expensive*.

Haywoods B&B, Donegal
(074) 972-1236
www.littleireland.ie/haywoods
Cosy B&B run by avid golfers;
inexpensive.

Lisadorn House B&B, Sligo
(071) 914-3417
Very modern and comfortable B&B
just outside town to the north, with
pitch & putt course right across the
road; *inexpensive*.

Drom Caoin B&B, Belmullet
(097) 81195
www.dromcaoin.ie
Excellent B&B just a couple of
minutes from Belmullet village and
the Carne links; has second, self-
contained suite apart from the main
building which will help house larger
groups; *inexpensive*.

Stella Maris Country House Hotel,
Ballycastle (Co Mayo)
(096) 43322
www.stellamarisireland.com
Not terribly convenient for golf, as it
is situated midway between
Enniscrone and Carne, but an
outstanding country hotel known for
the quality of its accommodation and
food. Ireland's small hotel of the year
in 2006; *expensive*.

Teach Iorrais Hotel, Geesala,
Co. Mayo
(097) 86888
www.teachiorrais.com
Luxury thirty-one-room hotel about
15 minutes from Carne, very good
value; *moderate*.

Abbeyglen Castle Hotel, Clifden
(095) 22832
www.abbeyglen.ie
Wonderfully atmospheric castle hotel
built in 1832, it has beautiful gardens,
a traditionally Irish formal dining
room, and exuberant after-dinner
sing-a-longs. The owners were
instrumental in the founding of the
nearby Connemara links; *expensive*.

 The East
To be sure, cosmopolitan
Dublin can be the most
challenging part of Ireland in
which to find suitable
accommodation for the traveller on a
budget. Staying outside the city
centre, perhaps in Malahide or
Portmarnock (all of the great links are
located on the north side of the city,
with the exception of the European
Club) can be an option, but on the
other hand the attractions of a central
location in one of Europe's most
vibrant capitals can be considerable.

Tullyesker House, Monasterboice,
Drogheda
(041) 983-0430
Terrific B&B with one-of-a-kind
proprietor, very convenient for
Baltray, Seapoint and Bettystown
links; *moderate*.

South Lodge B&B, Portmarnock
(01) 846-1356
www.southlodgebb.com
Built in 1873, the lodge was originally
one of two gatelodges on the Jameson
family estate, very convenient to
Portmarnock and The Island;
inexpensive to *moderate*.

Howth View, Portmarnock
(01) 846-0665
www.howthview.com
B&B with friendly and helpful
proprietor just two minutes from the
Portmarnock links and convenient for
the others on Dublin's north side;
inexpensive.

ACCOMMODATION

Browne's Hotel, Dublin
(01) 638-3939
www.brownesdublin.com
Georgian townhouse boutique hotel in St Stephen's Green, central Dublin's most desirable location; *very expensive.*

The Clarence, Dublin
(01) 407-0800
www.theclarence.ie
Perhaps the most visible symbol of Dublin's renaissance, this is the Temple Bar hotel owned by Bono and The Edge of U2, with every possible amenity of a luxury hotel and a terrific location; *very expensive.*

Kilronan House, Dublin
(01) 475-5266
www.dublinn.com
Elegant guesthouse in a Georgian terrace just five minutes from St Stephen's Green which dates from 1834; *moderate.*

Hazelbrook House, Dublin
(01) 836-5003
www.hazelbrookhouse.ie
Guesthouse established in 1997 and located in a listed Georgian terrace in central Dublin; *inexpensive.*

Kelly's Resort Hotel, Rosslare
(053) 913-2114
www.kellys.ie
Venerable family-owned and operated hotel is truly an integral part of the Rosslare golfing community, and not to be missed; *expensive.*

Northern Ireland

Northern Ireland is in some ways the most accessible of the principal golfing regions. Distances are short, the roads are better, and the major links courses are clustered around Portrush and Newcastle. Meanwhile, Belfast and its environs have a group of parkland courses that are worthy in their own right.

Bushmill's Inn, Bushmills
(028) 2073-3000 www.bushmillsinn.com
Former coaching inn located in the village which is also home to the famous distillery, very atmospheric with turf fires and gas-lit Victorian bar; *expensive.*

Bayview Hotel, Portballintrae
(028) 2073-4100
www.bayviewhotelni.com
Centrally located for the great links from Castlerock to Ballycastle, classic seafront hotel with outstanding views over the bay, just three miles from Portrush; *moderate.*

Brown Trout Golf & Country Inn, Aghadowey
(028) 7086-8209
www.browntroutinn.com
Upscale old inn which caters to golfers and has its own nine-hole course; *moderate.*

Malone Lodge, Belfast
(028) 9038-8000
www.malonelodgehotel.com
Victorian terrace hotel in south Belfast, the most attractive area of the city, and convenient to many of the

best pubs and restaurants around
Queen's University; *moderate*.

The Briers Country Guesthouse, Newcastle
(028) 4372-4347
www.thebriers.co.uk
Elegant and spacious guesthouse just
one mile from Royal County Down;
inexpensive to moderate.

Burrendale Hotel, Newcastle
(028) 4372-2599
www.burrendale.com
Located five minutes from town
centre and the Royal County Down
links, with fine views of the
Mountains of Mourne and lively
public bar and restaurant; *moderate.*

ONE HUNDRED AND FIFTY MORE GOLF COURSES

THE COURSES DESCRIBED in the previous chapters are the ones that set Ireland apart as a golfing destination, in our opinion. However, Ireland has many other courses that are certainly worth playing if you find yourself in the area, or if you can't get on one of the more highly recommended courses. Here is a list of noteworthy layouts. Those of particular quality are designated with an asterisk (*).

Monaghan, Meath and Louth

* Greenore Golf Club
Greenore, Dundalk, Co. Louth
tel: (042) 937-3212; **e-mail:**
greenoregolfclub@eircom.net
Course dating from 1897 with some
links holes overlooking Carlingford
Lough; a spacious new clubhouse was
built in 1994.

Ashbourne Golf Club
Ashbourne, Co. Meath
tel: (01) 835-2005; **fax:** (01) 835-2561;
e-mail: ashgc@iol.ie
Parkland course with its own version
of Amen Corner, though Ashbourne's
runs from holes eleven through
fourteen, one longer than the Augusta
original.

Bellewstown Golf Course
Bellewstown, Co. Meath
tel: (041) 988-2757;
fax: (041) 841-2622;
e-mail: bellewstowngolf@eircom.net
Pay-and-play facility opened in 2004
that runs along the Hill of
Crockafotha and affords some fine
views toward the Mountains of
Mourne and the sea.

Black Bush Golf Club
Dunshaughlin, Co. Meath
tel: (01) 825-0021; **fax:** (01) 825-0040;
e-mail: info@blackbushgolfclub.ie
Member-owned, twenty-seven-hole
complex by R.J. Browne dates from
1987.

Co. Meath Golf Club
Newtownmoynagh, Trim, Co. Meath

tel: (046) 943-7554;
fax: (046) 943-1463;
e-mail: sec@trimgolf.net
Gently rolling course revised by
Eddie Hackett and Tom Craddock
presents abundant hazards.

Dundalk Golf Club
Blackrock, Dundalk, Co. Louth
tel: (042) 932-1731;
fax: (042) 932-2022;
e-mail: manager@dundalkgolfclub.ie
Mid-1990s renovation of the original
Braid layout was undertaken by Peter
Alliss and Dave Thomas, with
excellent views of Dundalk Bay and
the Mountains of Mourne.

Headfort Golf Club
Kells, Co. Meath
tel: (046) 924-0146
fax: (046) 924-9282;
e-mail: info@headfortgolfclub.ie
Thirty-six-hole complex with Old
course dating from the early twentieth
century and New course designed by
Christy O'Connor Jr in 2000, with the
River Blackwater in play on thirteen
holes.

Nuremore Hotel & Country Club
Carrickmacross, Co. Monaghan
tel: (042) 966-4016;
fax: (042) 966-1855;
e-mail: nuremore@eircom.net
Hilly parkland resort course featuring
water on many holes and views of five
different counties.

Royal Tara Golf Club
Bellinteer, Navan, Co. Meath
tel: (046) 225508;
e-mail: info@royaltaragolfclub.com

Twenty-seven-hole complex, mostly by Des Smyth, adjacent to Hill of Tara and River Skane. The Red and Blue nines form the main course.

Dublin and Environs

* Corballis Golf Links
Corballis, Donabate, Co. Dublin
tel: (01) 843-6583; **fax:** (01) 822-6668;
e-mail: corballislinks@golfdublin.com
Delightful true links bordering on The Island that has been a public facility since 1971. The course is 5,000 yards, par 65, with eight par 3s and one par 5. Usually in excellent condition, and excellent value.

* Rush Golf Club
Corr's Lane, Rush, Co. Dublin
tel: (01) 843-8177;
e-mail: info@rushgolfclub.com
Relatively spacious, yet quaint and charming, nine-hole links that dates from 1943, well-hidden in the village of Rush.

* St Margaret's Golf & Country Club
St Margaret's, Co. Dublin
tel: (01) 864-0400; **fax:** (01) 864-0289;
e-mail:
reservations@stmargaretsgolf.com
Well-designed and well-conditioned parkland course, three miles from the airport. Designed by Pat Ruddy and Tom Craddock. Hosted the 1994 and 1995 Women's Irish Opens.

* Sutton Golf Club
Burrow Rd, Sutton, Dublin 13
tel: (01) 832-3013;
e-mail: info@suttongolfclub.org
Nine-hole links located near

Portmarnock. Its new clubhouse opened in 2001 and has a Joe Carr Room in tribute to the giant of Irish golf, who was a life-long club member.

Balcarrick Golf Club
Corballis, Donabate, Co. Dublin
tel: (01) 843-6957; **fax:** (01) 843-6228;
e-mail: balcar@iol.ie
Opened in the early 1990s across the road from Corballis public links. The club originated as 'The Homeless Golfers' society, who were recognized by the Golfing Union of Ireland as the Dublin & County club (playing over Corballis links until Balcarrick was completed). The parkland course has water in play on ten holes, and can be stretched to 6,900 yards from the tips.

Beaverstown Golf Club
Beaverstown, Donabate, Co. Dublin
tel: (01) 843-6439; **fax:** (01) 843-5059;
e-mail: manager@beaverstown.com
Eddie Hackett design, subsequently revised by Peter McEvoy, in former orchard near The Island.

Castle Golf Club
Woodside Drive, Rathfarnham, Dublin 14
tel: (01) 490-4207; **fax:** (01) 492-0264;
e-mail: info@castlegc.ie
Undulating, tree-lined south-side course designed by H.S. Colt.

Castleknock Golf Club
Porterstown Rd, Castleknock,
Dublin 15
tel: (01) 640-8736; **fax:** (01) 640-8735;
e-mail: info@castleknockgolfclub.ie
Enjoyable new course which opened
in 2005 in the Dublin suburbs, with
large, undulating greens and an
excellent set of par 3s, attached to
luxury hotel complex which also
opened in 2005.

City West Golf Course
Saggart, Co. Dublin
tel: (01) 401-0500; **fax:** (01) 401-0945;
e-mail: golf@citywesthotel.com
Resort course designed by Christy
O'Connor Jr, with views of Dublin
mountains. Hosted 1996 Women's
Irish Open. A second, par-65 course
was opened in 2001.

Deer Park Hotel & Golf Courses
Howth, Dublin
tel: (01) 832-2624; **fax:** (01) 839-2405;
e-mail: sales@deerpark.iol.ie
This public complex on the Howth
Peninsula comprises an eighteen-hole
course, another nine, a twelve-hole
short course and a pitch-and-putt.

Forrest Little Golf Club
Cloghean, Swords, Co. Dublin
tel: (01) 840-1763; **fax:** (01) 840-1000;
e-mail: shirley@forrestlittlc.ic
Mature, tree-lined course
exceptionally close to Dublin airport;
the greens were remodelled and water
hazards extended earlier this decade.

Grange Golf Club
Whitechurch Rd, Rathfarnham,
Dublin 16

tel: (01) 493-2889; **fax:** (01) 493-9490;
e-mail:
administration@grangegolfclub.ie
Designed by James Braid, and home
club of Ryder Cup hero Paul
McGinley, the course opens with back-
to-back par 3s.

Hermitage Golf Club
Ballydowd, Lucan, Co. Dublin
tel: (01) 626-8491; **fax:** (01) 623-8881;
e-mail: hermitagegolf@eircom.net
Fine old course bordered by majestic
trees; River Liffey is in play on tenth
and eleventh holes, which are the best
on the course.

Hollystown Golf Club
Hollystown, Dublin 15
tel: (01) 820-7444; **fax:** (01) 820-7447;
e-mail: info@hollystown.com
Public, twenty-seven-hole complex
twenty minutes from Dublin City
Centre.

Hollywood Lakes Golf Club
Ballyboughal, Co. Dublin
tel: (01) 843-3406; **fax:** (01) 843-3002;
e-mail:
secretary@hollywoodlakesgolfclub.com
Course located about twenty minutes
north of the airport, with water in play
on nine of the eighteen holes.

Howth Golf Club
Carrickbrack Rd, Sutton, Dublin 13
tel: (01) 832-3055; **fax:** (01) 832-1793
e-mail: manager@howthgolfclub.ie.
Very hilly course on Howth Peninsula
with fine views of Dublin Bay and
Ireland's Eye.

Luttrellstown Castle Golf & Country Club
Clonsilla, Dublin
tel: (01) 808-9988;
fax: (01) 808-9989;
e-mail: golf@luttrellstown.ie
Parkland course set in 560-acre estate that hosted the 1997 Women's Irish Open, with a unique, log-cabin-style clubhouse.

Malahide Golf Club
Beechwood, The Grange, Malahide, Co. Dublin
tel: (01) 846-1611;
fax: (01) 846-1270;
e-mail: manager@malahidegolfclub.ie
Venerable Dublin club that moved to its present location, a twenty-seven-hole Eddie Hackett parkland layout, in 1990.

Stackstown Golf Club
Kellystown Rd, Rathfarnham, Dublin 16
tel: (01) 494-1993; **fax:** (01) 493-3934
Home course of Padraig Harrington in the foothills of the Dublin Mountains has fine views over the city.

Kildare, Westmeath and Offaly

* Carton House Golf Club
Maynooth, Co. Kildare
tel: (01) 505-2000; **fax:** (01) 628-6555; **e-mail:** reservations@carton.ie
Thirty-six-hole development built in a thousand-acre walled country estate by European Course Design, a joint venture between the European Tour and IMG. The Mark O'Meara Course opened in July 2002, and the Colin Montgomerie Course opened in June 2003. The O'Meara is 'tranquil parkland', with the river Rye in play on the three signature holes – 13, 14, and 15 – another contender for Ireland's 'Amen Corner'. The Montgomerie (designed with Stan Eby) is an exposed 'inland links', with deep pot bunkers and undulating fairways and greens, and hosted the 2005 and 2006 Irish Opens. Thirty minutes from Dublin.

* Glasson Golf & Country Club
Glasson, Athlone, Co. Westmeath
tel: (090) 648-5120;
fax: (090) 648-5444;
e-mail: info@glassongolf.ie
This parkland resort course designed by Christy O'Connor Jr on shore of Lough Ree, where the water is visible from every hole, is one of O'Connor's best.

* PGA National Ireland
Palmerstown House, Johnstown, Co. Kildare
tel: (045) 906901; **fax:** (045) 871377;
e-mail: pganational@palmerstownhouse.com
Christy O'Connor Jr design on which no expense was spared is now home to the European PGA in Ireland. Likely has more water in play than any other course in the country.

Ballinlough Castle Golf Club
Clonmellon, Co. Westmeath
tel: (044) 966-4544;
e-mail: golf@ballinloughcastle.com
New course being developed in
Westmeath's rich pasture land,
designed by Pat Ruddy.

Castle Barna Golf Club
Daingean, Co. Offaly
tel: (057) 935-3384;
fax: (057) 935-3077;
e-mail: info@castlebarna.ie
Peaceful and inexpensive parkland
course in the heart of Ireland, about
fifty miles west of Dublin.

Curragh Golf Club
Curragh, Co. Kildare
tel: (045) 441714; **fax:** (045) 442476;
e-mail: curraghgolf@eircom.net
Oldest golf club in the Republic,
dating from 1883 (with the oldest golf
course in all of Ireland, dating from
1852). The course is heathland in
character and presents some fine
scenery. Technically still a 'Royal'
club, though it has dropped the
adjective.

Esker Hills Golf & Country Club
Tullamore, Co. Offaly
tel: (050) 655999; **fax:** (050) 655021;
e-mail: info@eskerhillsgolf.com
Christy O'Connor Jr course built
amid drumlins and eskers, relatively
open but hilly, with undulating
fairways and greens.

Kilkea Castle Golf Club
Castledermot, Co. Kildare
tel: (050) 345555; **fax:** (050) 345505;
e-mail: kilkeagolfclub@eircom.net

Relatively flat and open course
designed around castle which was
built in 1180, making it the oldest
continuously inhabited castle in
Ireland. River Greese in play on ten
holes.

Mount Temple Golf & Country Club
Mount Temple, Moate, Co.
Westmeath
tel: (090) 648-1841;
fax: (090) 648-1957;
e-mail: mttemple@iol.ie
Home-made course on former estate
grounds is pleasant, natural and
quaint.

Mullingar Golf Club
Mullingar, Co. Westmeath
tel: (044) 934-8629;
fax: (044) 934-1499
Lush inland course which is one of
James Braid's better designs, and is
relatively unaltered.

Tullamore Golf Club
Brookfield, Tullamore, Co. Offaly
tel: (057) 932-1439;
e-mail: tullamoregolfclub@eircom.net
One of the country's leading inland
layouts (at least until the recent
explosion of new developments),
course dates from 1926 and was
designed by James Braid, with recent
revisions by Paddy Merrigan,
including the inclusion of three new
lakes.

Wicklow

* Arklow Golf Club
Abbeylands, Arklow, Co. Wicklow
tel: (040) 232492; **fax:** (040) 291604

Sporty, if short (par 68), true links on the shores of Arklow Bay. The original nine holes were laid out by J.H. Taylor, and the course was extended to eighteen holes by Eddie Hackett in the 1970s. The first hole is one of the better openers in links golf.

*Woodbrook Golf Club
Bray, Co. Wicklow
tel: (01) 282-4799; **fax:** (01) 282-1750;
e-mail: golf@woodbrook.ie
Venerable parkland course, which sits along the sea atop hundred-foot cliffs, hosted the Carroll's International tournament nine times between 1964 and 1974, as well as the 1998 Irish Senior Open; it was redesigned by Peter McEvoy in the late 1990s. In the good old days Bing Crosby sang from the clubhouse balcony.

*Woodenbridge Golf Club
Vale of Avoca, Arklow, Co. Wicklow
tel: (040) 235202; **fax:** (040) 235754;
e-mail: wgc@eircom.net
Tranquil and mature course set in the lovely Vale of Avoca, with River Avoca meandering throughout as the principal hazard. Designed by Paddy Merrigan.

Blainroe Golf Club
Blainroe, Co. Wicklow
tel: (040) 468168; **fax:** (040) 469369;
e-mail: info@blainroe.com
Pleasant parkland course along the Wicklow coastline. Front nine plays over a steep hill and provides fine views of the Irish Sea, while the back brings the sea into play at the fourteenth.

Charlesland Golf & Country Club
Greystones, Co. Wicklow
tel: (01) 287-8200; **fax:** (01) 287-8136;
e-mail: teetimes@charlesland.com
Located twenty miles south of Dublin, seaside parkland course with views of Wicklow hills, designed by Eddie Hackett.

Delgany Golf Club
Delgany, Co. Wicklow
tel: (01) 287-4536; **fax:** (01) 287-3977;
e-mail: delganygolf@eircom.net
Hilly course with fine views of mountain and sea. The legendary Harry Bradshaw was an assistant pro from 1933 to 1940, and Ryder Cupper John O'Leary was also a member.

Old Conna Golf Club
Ferndale Rd, Bray, Co. Wicklow
tel: (01) 282-6055; **fax:** (01) 282-5611;
e-mail: info@oldconna.com
Hilly Eddie Hackett design amidst the Wicklow Mountains features natural use of the terrain in typical Hackett fashion.

Rathsallagh Golf Club
Dunlavin, Co. Wicklow
tel: (045) 403316; **fax:** (045) 403295;
e-mail: info@rathsallagh.com
Wooded, rolling parkland course with several streams and lakes, attached to Rathsallagh House hotel, designed by Christy O'Connor Jr and Peter McEvoy, and located on the western side of the Wicklow Mountains.

Roundwood Golf Club
Newtownmountkennedy, Co. Wicklow
tel: (01) 281-8488; **fax:** (01) 284-3642;
e-mail: rwood@indigo.ie
Rolling, gorse- and heather-lined course that doubled as 'Knockbeg Golf Club' on the popular television series *Ballykissangel*.

Tulfarris Golf Club
Blessington, Co. Wicklow
tel: (045) 867633; **fax:** (045) 867561;
e-mail: info@tulfarris.com
A Paddy Merrigan design in scenic lakeside setting on Poulaphuca Lake. Hosted the 2000 Irish Senior Open.

Wicklow Golf Club
Dunbur Rd, Wicklow, Co. Wicklow
tel: (040) 467379; **fax:** (040) 464756;
e-mail: info@wicklowgolfclub.ie
Relatively short cliffside course which plays over very hilly terrain, giving panoramic views of Wicklow Bay; extended to eighteen holes by Pat Ruddy and Tom Craddock in 1994.

Laois, Carlow and Kilkenny

* Carlow Golf Club
Deerpark, Carlow, Co. Carlow
tel: (059) 913-1695;
fax: (059) 914-0065;
e-mail: carlowgolfclub@eircom.net
Prior to the new wave of upscale parkland layouts, Carlow was often referred to as Ireland's finest inland course. It is a testing, gorse- and tree-lined layout revised by Tom Simpson of Baltray fame.

* The Heritage at Killenard
Killenard, Co. Laois
tel: (050) 245994; **fax:** (050) 242393;
e-mail: info@theheritage.com
This very upscale course, opened in 2004 and co-designed by Seve Ballesteros and Jeff Howes, is Ballesteros's first venture in Ireland. A 'world class luxury hotel', coupled with leisure centre and spa, is now open on the property, as is the Seve Ballesteros Golf School.

The Heath Golf Club
Portlaoise, Co. Laois
tel: (057) 864-6533;
fax: (057) 864-6866;
e-mail: info@theheathgc.ie
The club was founded in 1890, making it Ireland's seventh oldest, and plays over a course built on a commonage which golfers share with grazing sheep.

Kilkenny Golf Club
Glendine, Co. Kilkenny
tel: (056) 776-5400;
fax: (056) 772-3593
e-mail: enquiries@kilkennygolfclub.com
Pleasant, gently rolling course which is undemanding until final four holes.

Killerig Castle Golf Club
Killerig Cross, Carlow, Co. Carlow
tel: (059) 916-3000;
fax: (059) 916-3005;
e-mail: info@killerig.com
Opened for play in 2000, giving a second championship option in Co. Carlow. Designed by Des Smyth and Declan Branigan.

Mount Wolseley Hotel Spa, Golf & Country Club

Tullow, Co. Carlow
tel: (059) 915-1674;
fax: (059) 915-2123;
e-mail: bmurray@mountwolseley.ie
Christy O'Connor Jr estate course which opened in 1996 is long and testing, with water in play on eleven holes.

Wexford

Courtown Golf Club

Gorey, Co. Wexford
tel: (053) 942-5166;
fax: (053) 942-5553;
e-mail: info@courtowngolfclub.com.
Relatively straightforward parkland course (though very close to the sea) dating from the 1930s.

St Helen's Bay Golf & Country Club

Kilrane, Rosslare, Co. Wexford
tel: (053) 913-3234;
fax: (053) 913-3803;
e-mail: info@sthelensbay.com
Despite being a seaside course, only the final five holes of this popular Philip Walton design are of true links character, the rest being relatively open parkland. Many palm trees throughout.

Seafield Golf and Country Club

Ballymoney, Gorey, Co. Wexford
tel: (053) 942-4777;
fax: (053) 942-4837;
e-mail: info@seafieldgolf.com
Upscale Peter McEvoy design which opened in 2002, featuring course divided into roughly equal thirds of parkland, heathland and seaside holes. Very much the centrepiece of a property development scheme, with houses bordering some of the holes on the front nine.

Waterford

*Waterford Castle Golf Club

The Island, Ballinakill, Co. Waterford
tel: (051) 871633; **fax:** (051) 871634
e-mail: golf@waterfordcastle.com
Situated on a private island accessible only by ferry, a five-star castle hotel with course attached, designed by Des Smyth.

Dungarvan Golf Club

Knocknagranagh, Dungarvan, Co. Waterford
tel: (058) 43310; **fax:** (058) 44113;
e-mail: dungarvangc@eircom.net
Rolling parkland course with views of Comeragh Mountains and Dungarvan Bay includes seven lakes; moved to its present location in 1993.

Dunmore East Golf Club

Dunmore East, Co. Waterford
tel: (051) 383151;
e-mail: info@dunmoreeastgolfclub.ie
Parkland course with fine views of Dunmore Village, on which five holes, including the spectacular fourteenth, play along the Harbour.

Faithlegg Golf Club

Faithlegg House, Co. Waterford
tel: (051) 382000; **fax:** (051) 382010;
e-mail: golf@faithlegg.com
Resort course designed by Paddy Merrigan, which features some very undulating greens, has hosted Women's Irish Open.

Gold Coast Golf Resort
Ballinacourty, Dungarvan, Co.
Waterford
tel: (058) 45555; **fax:** (058) 42880;
e-mail: info@clonea.com
Front nine is the original Dungarvan
club; the second nine was added in
1996 at this resort course bordered by
water on three sides.

Tramore Golf Club
Newtown Hill, Tramore, Co.
Waterford
tel: (051) 386170; **fax:** (051) 390961;
e-mail: tragolf@iol.ie
Mature, hilly course designed by
Captain H. Tippett of Walton Heath
in 1936.

Waterford Golf Club
Newrath, Waterford
tel: (051) 876748; **fax:** (051) 853405;
e-mail: info@waterfordgolfclub.com
Venerable course with rolling terrain,
blind shots and gorse, designed by
Willie Park Jr in 1913 and extended
by James Braid in 1934.

West Waterford Golf Club
Coolcormack, Dungarvan, Co.
Waterford
tel: (058) 43216; **fax:** (058) 44343;
e-mail: info@westwaterfordgolf.com.
Eddie Hackett design on banks of
River Brickey with lovely backdrop of
Comeragh and Knockmealdown
mountains.

Tipperary

Ballykisteen Golf & Country Club
Monard, Co. Tipperary
tel: (062) 33333; **fax:** (062) 82587;
e-mail:
golf.ballykisteen@ramadaireland.com
Des Smyth course associated with
Ramada Hotels plays over former
stud farm, with mansion-style
clubhouse.

Clonmel Golf Club
Lyreanearla, Clonmel, Co. Tipperary
tel: (052) 21138; **fax:** (052) 24050;
e-mail: cgc@indigo.ie.
Hilly course founded in 1911 and
extended to eighteen holes in 1973 by
Eddie Hackett.

Co. Tipperary Golf & Country Club
Dundrum, Co. Tipperary
tel: (062) 71717; **fax:** (062) 71718;
e-mail: dundrumgolf@eircom.net
Course attached to the Dundrum
House Hotel, designed by Philip
Walton.

Cork

* Coosheen Golf Club
Coosheen, Schull, Co. Cork
tel: (028) 27758;
e-mail: coosheengolfclub@eircom.net
Spectacular and unique ten-hole
course in remote West Cork, with
views of Carbery's Hundred Isles,
Cape Clear Island and Mt. Gaberial.

* Fota Island Golf Club
Carrigtwohill, Co. Cork
tel: (021) 488-3700;
fax: (021) 453-2047;

e-mail: reservations@fotaisland.ie
Course originally designed by Christy
O'Connor Jr was substantially
revamped in 1999 by Jeff Howes
(Mount Juliet), with all eighteen tees
and greens rebuilt and eight holes rerouted. It hosted the 2001 and 2002
Irish Open, marking the first time the
national championship was played in
Co. Cork. A luxury hotel and nine
additional holes opened in 2006.

Blarney Golf Resort
Tower, Blarney, Co. Cork
tel: (021) 438-4472;
fax: (021) 438-4599;
e-mail: info@blarneygolfresort.com
John Daly's first venture in Ireland is
set in the Shournagh Valley, three
miles from Blarney village.

Charleville Golf Club
Smiths Rd, Ardmore, Charleville, Co.
Cork
tel: (063) 81257; **fax:** (063) 81274;
e-mail: charlevillegolf@eircom.net
Attractive twenty-seven-hole parkland
course that has been on its present
site since 1941.

Douglas Golf Club
Douglas, Cork, Co. Cork
tel: (021) 489-1086;
fax: (021) 436-7200;
e-mail: admin@douglasgolfclub.ie
Well-maintained parkland course
which is easy to walk, three miles
from city centre.

Fernhill Golf Club
Fernhill, Carrigaline, Cork
tel: (021) 437-2226;
fax: (021) 437-1011;

e-mail: fernhill@iol.ie
Course overlooking Owenabwee
valley, affiliated with Fernhill Country
House hotel.

Harbour Point Golf Complex
Clash, Little Island, Co. Cork
tel: (021) 435-3094;
fax: (021) 435-4408;
e-mail: hpoint@iol.ie
Spacious course with modern driving
range on banks of River Lee.

Lee Valley Golf Club
Clashenure, Ovens, Co. Cork
tel: (021) 733-1721;
fax: (021) 733-1695;
e-mail: leevalleygolfclub@eircom.net
Hilltop Christy O'Connor Jr course
from 1993, with large clubhouse and
floodlit, fifty-bay driving range.

Macroom Golf Club
Lackaduv, Macroom, Co. Cork
tel: (026) 41072: **fax:** (026) 41391;
e-mail: mcroomgc@iol.ie
Scenic estate course with first nine
designed by Eddie Hackett, extended
to eighteen holes in 1992. Hilly front
side is followed by flatter back nine
which plays along River Sullane.

Mallow Golf Club
Ballyellis, Mallow, Co. Cork
tel: (022) 21145; **fax:** (022) 42501
Hilly and wooded parkland course
overlooking the Blackwater Valley
which dates from the 1940s and was
updated in the 1990s.

Monkstown Golf Club
Monkstown, Co. Cork
tel: (021) 484-1376;
fax: (021) 484-1722;
e-mail:
office@monkstowngolfclub.com
Well-bunkered course with very
difficult closing stretch and some fine
views of Cork Harbour.

Muskerry Golf Club
Carrigrohane, Co. Cork
tel: (021) 438-5297;
fax: (021) 451-6860
Undulating course northwest of Cork
with River Shournadh much in play.
Dr Alister Mackenzie contributed to
the design.

**Skibbereen & West Carbery Golf
Club**
Licknavar, Skibbereen, Co. Cork
tel: (028) 21227;
fax: (028) 22994;
e-mail: info@skibbgolf.com
Rolling and open parkland course in
the Mount Gabriel hills of West Cork.

Water Rock Golf Course
Midleton, Co. Cork
tel: (021) 461-3499;
fax: (021) 463-3150;
e-mail: waterrock@eircom.net
Pay-as-you-play facility featuring
fearsome 240-yard par 3 over a swan-
filled lake.

Youghal Golf Club
Youghal, Co. Cork
tel: (024) 92787;
fax: (024) 92641;
e-mail: youghalgolfclub@eircom.net
Founded in 1898, the course presents
commanding views of the town and
the sea.

Kerry

* Castlegregory Golf & Fishing Club
Stradbally, Castlegregory
tel: (066) 713-9444;
fax: (066) 713-9958;
e-mail:
info@castlegregorygolflinks.com
Nine-hole links in spectacular
location, designed by Dr Arthur
Spring in 1989, was the course which
inspired him to move from medicine
to course design, like Dr Mackenzie
before him. An eighteen-hole course
was first built on the site in 1896, but
was subsequently abandoned due to
the difficulty of access from Tralee.

* Skellig Bay Golf Club
Waterville, Co. Kerry
tel: (066) 947-4133;
fax: (066) 947-4608;
e-mail: info@skelligbay.com
Ron Kirby (Old Head) has fashioned
a rugged and beautiful new clifftop
course just minutes from Waterville.
Nine holes play along the cliffs, while
nine are slightly more inland and run
along the River Fionnglassa. Over two
miles of stone walls are often in play,
and beware the fairie fort near the
sixth tee.

Beaufort Golf Club
Churchtown, Beaufort, Killarney, Co.
Kerry
tel: (064) 44440; **fax:** (064) 44752;
e-mail: beaufortgc@eircom.net
Course set in a beautiful estate just
west of Killarney, opened September

1994, designed by Dr Arthur Spring. Ruins of an eleventh-century castle feature on the back nine.

Castleisland Golf Club

Doneen, Castleisland, Co. Kerry
tel: (066) 714-1709;
fax: (066) 714-2090; **e-mail:** managercastleislandgolfclub@eircom.net
New parkland course by Dr Arthur Spring which has some fine views of the Macgillycuddy's Reeks and surrounding Co. Kerry scenery.

Castlerosse Hotel & Golf Resort

Castlerosse, Killarney, Co. Kerry
tel: (064) 31144; **fax:** (064) 31031
Nine-hole course opened in 2000 with lovely views of Lough Leane and the Macgillycuddy's Reeks.

Kenmare Golf Club

Killowen Rd, Kenmare, Co. Kerry
tel: (064) 41291; **fax:** (064) 42061;
e-mail: info@kenmaregolfclub.com
Very hilly course with beautiful vistas of Kenmare Bay and village of Kenmare. New nine is some distance from the original nine holes.

Killorglin Golf Course

Stealroe, Killorglin, Co. Kerry
tel: (066) 976-1979;
fax: (066) 976-1437;
e-mail: play@killorglingolf.ie
Eddie Hackett parkland layout overlooking Dingle Bay, very close to Dooks, with views of the Macgillycuddy's Reeks from every fairway.

Limerick

Castletroy Golf Club

Golf Links Rd, Castletroy, Limerick
tel: (061) 335753; **fax:** (061) 335373;
e-mail: cgc@iol.ie
Mature, tree-lined parkland course three miles from town, which was upgraded in 2005.

Limerick Golf Club

Ballyclough, Limerick
tel: (061) 415416; **fax:** (061) 319219;
e-mail: pat.murray@limerickgc.com
Parkland course just south of town, founded in 1891, designed at least in part by Dr Alister Mackenzie.

Limerick County Golf & Country Club

Ballyneety, Limerick
tel: (061) 351881; **fax:** (061) 351384;
e-mail: lcgolf@iol.ie
Course designed by Des Smyth in 1993 is fairly open, with large, undulating greens.

Clare

* Lahinch Golf Club (Castle Course)

Lahinch, Co. Clare
tel: (065) 708-1003;
fax: (065) 708-1592;
e-mail: info@lahinchgolf.com
Little brother to the majestic Lahinch links plays 5,500 yards over relatively flat links terrain. Nine of its holes were part of the original Lahinch eighteen laid out by Old Tom Morris, but were abandoned for some years before being revived in the 1960s. The famous castle ruins are at the eighth tee.

Dromoland Castle Golf Club

Newmarket-on-Fergus, Co. Clare
tel: (061) 368444; **fax:** (061) 368498;
e-mail: golf@dromoland.ie
Course set in grounds of magnificent castle hotel circles Dromoland Lough and was completely revised by Ron Kirby (principal designer of Old Head) and the late, great Joe Carr. The new course opened for play in April, 2004.

East Clare Golf Club

Bodyke, Co. Clare
tel: (061) 921322; **fax:** (061) 921717;
e-mail: info@eastclare.com
Course owned and operated by its members on a pay-as-you-play basis has been a full eighteen holes since 1997. Hosted the 1998 West of Ireland Senior Classic on the European Senior Tour.

Ennis Golf Club

Drumbiggle Rd, Ennis, Co. Clare
tel: (065) 682-4074; **fax:** (065) 684-1848; **e-mail:** info@ennisgolfclub.com
Short but picturesque course with tree-lined front nine and open, hilly back.

Kilkee Golf Club

East End, Kilkee, Co. Clare
tel: (065) 905-6048;
fax: (065) 905-6977;
e-mail: kilkeegolfclub@eircom.net
Mostly parkland course dating from the late nineteenth century, has a few clifftop holes with spectacular Atlantic views. More recently extended to eighteen holes, but the back nine is rather pedestrian and ultimately a disappointment.

Kilrush Golf Club

Parknamoney, Kilrush, Co. Clare
tel: (065) 905-1138;
fax: (065) 905-2633;
e-mail: info@kilrushgolfclub.com
Course overlooking the Shannon and just minutes from the ferry, extended to eighteen holes in 1994 by Dr Arthur Spring.

Shannon Golf Club

Shannon Airport, Shannon, Co. Clare
tel: (061) 471849; **fax:** (061) 471507
e-mail: info@shannongolfclub.ie
Parkland course built in 1966 and squeezed between the River Shannon and the airport.

Woodstock House Golf & Country Club

Shanaway Rd, Ennis, Co. Clare
tel: (065) 682-9463;
fax: (065) 682-0304;
e-mail: woodstock.ennis@eircom.net
Undulating parkland course built in 1993 by Dr Arthur Spring features a large lake, as well as the River Inch in play on several holes. A sixty-seven-bedroom four-star hotel opened on the property in 2000.

Galway

* Bearna Golf & Country Club

Corboley, Bearna, Co. Galway
tel: (091) 592677; **fax:** (091) 592674;
e-mail: info@bearnagolfclub.com
Course laid out by R.J. Browne over Connemara moorlands with excellent views over Galway Bay. Water in play on thirteen holes and gorse, heather and rock outcroppings also play a role. Just west of Galway town.

* Connemara Isles Golf & Sea Sports Club

Lettermore, Co. Galway
tel: (091) 572498
Nine-hole course in splendid setting on Galway Bay, with ocean inlets and rocky shoreline in play on some holes, was designed by Tom Craddock and Pat Ruddy and opened in 1993. Only thatched-roof clubhouse in Ireland.

Athenry Golf Club

Palmerstown, Oranmore, Co. Galway
tel: (091) 794466; fax: (091) 794971;
e-mail: athenrygc@eircom.net
Mixed parkland and heathland course which was extended to eighteen holes in 1991 by Eddie Hackett is adjacent to the 'Fields of Athenry' immortalized in the Irish ballad.

Galway Golf Club

Blackrock, Salthill, Galway
tel: (091) 522033; fax: (091) 529783;
e-mail: galwaygolf@eircom.net
Alister Mackenzie-designed course, but not his most interesting work; first four holes are near the water, then course moves inland.

Galway Bay Golf & Country Club

Renville, Oranmore, Co. Galway
tel: (091) 790711; fax: (091) 792510;
e-mail: info@galwaybaygolfresort.com
Christy O'Connor Jr course on the Renville Peninsula is surrounded on three sides by the Atlantic but is inland in character. Ireland's first golf course to be surrounded by a Florida-style real-estate development.

Gort Golf Club

Castlequarter, Gort, Co. Galway
tel: (091) 632244; fax: (091) 632387;
e-mail: info@gortgolf.com
Splendidly isolated course on the edge of the Burren, re-designed by Christy O'Connor Jr in 1996.

Oughterard Golf Club

Oughterard, Co. Galway
tel: (091) 552131; fax: (091) 552733
Mature parkland design by Christy O'Connor Jr on road to Connemara, extended to eighteen holes in 1985 and revised by Paddy Merrigan in 1999.

Tuam Golf Club

Barnacurragh, Tuam, Co. Galway
tel: (093) 28993; fax: (093) 26003;
e-mail: tuamgolfclub@eircom.net
Another of the many courses designed by Irish golf's patron saint, Eddie Hackett. This one was built in the early 1970s, for the sum of 250 punts plus a week's hotel lodging and train fare from Dublin; Eddie bicycled to the course each day during his stay to do the design work.

Mayo, Roscommon and Leitrim

* Achill Island Golf Club

The Sandybanks, Keel, Achill Island, Co. Mayo
tel: (098) 43456;
e-mail: achillgolfclub@eircom.net
Flat links course in outstanding setting along the Keel sandybanks on remote Achill Island.

* Mulranny Golf Club

Mulranny, Westport, Co. Mayo
tel: (098) 36262
Charming nine-hole links course in
spectacular setting on Clew Bay, with
undulating fairways and barbed-wire
fences to protect the greens from
grazing sheep. A caravan houses the
tiny clubhouse (no bar), but there are
sufficient amenities in town, just a few
minutes away.

* Westport Golf Club

Carrowholly, Westport, Co. Mayo
tel: (098) 982-8262;
fax: (098) 982-7217;
e-mail: wpgolf@eircom.net
Very long, testing, Fred Hawtree
design in magnificent isolation of
Clew Bay, has hosted Irish Amateur;
there are spectacular vistas of the Bay
and Croagh Patrick on the back nine.

Athlone Golf Club

Hodson Bay, Athlone, Co.
Roscommon
tel: (090) 649-2073;
fax: (090) 649-4080;
e-mail: athlonegolfclub@eircom.net
Parkland course in magnificent
setting on peninsula jutting into
Lough Ree; slicers beware of OB right
on ten holes.

Ballinrobe Golf Club

Cloonacastle, Ballinrobe, Co. Mayo
tel: (094) 954-1118;
fax: (094) 944-1889;
e-mail: info@ballinrobegolfclub.com
Classic, open, estate parkland layout
designed by Eddie Hackett near the
end of his career.

Carrick-on-Shannon Golf Club

Woodbrook, Carrick-on-Shannon,
Co. Leitrim
tel: (071) 966-7015;
e-mail: ckgc3@eircom.net
Course extended to eighteen holes in
2003 by Martin Hawtree, with new
nine that sweeps down toward
Drumharlow Lake and the River
Boyle, and has marshland much in
play. Original nine has the character
of more mature parkland.

Roscommon Golf Club

Mote Park, Roscommon, Co.
Roscommon
tel: (090) 662-6382;
fax: (090) 662-6043;
e-mail: rosgolfclub@eircom.net
The original nine-hole course at Mote
Park, founded in 1904, was extended
to eighteen holes in the 1990s, and a
new clubhouse was added in 1996.

Cavan and Longford

* Slieve Russell Hotel Golf & Country Club

Ballyconnell, Co. Cavan
tel: (049) 952-5090;
fax: (049) 952-6640;
e-mail: slieve-russell@quinn-hotels.com
Splendidly conditioned parkland
course opened in 1992, midway
between Dublin and Sligo, Paddy
Merrigan design.

Co. Cavan Golf Club

Arnmore House, Drumells, Co.
Cavan
tel: (049) 433-1541;
e-mail: cavangc@iol.ie

Hilly and tree-lined course with a few severely sloping greens. The new back nine, designed by Dr Arthur Spring, opened in 2006.

Co. Longford Golf Club

Glack, Longford
tel: (043) 46310; fax: (043) 47082;
e-mail: colongolf@eircom.net
Course extended to eighteen holes in 1971 plays over high ground with fine views of Longford Town; greens were redesigned in 1999 by Declan Branigan.

Donegal

* Bundoran Golf Club

Bundoran, Co. Donegal
tel: (071) 984-1302;
fax: (071) 984-2014;
e-mail: bundorangolfclub@eircom.net
Seaside course with links qualities dating from 1894 which is wedged into the grounds of the Great Northern Hotel. The course is nevertheless of significant historic interest – the present layout by Harry Vardon dates from 1927, and 'Himself', Christy O'Connor Sr, served as professional from 1951 to 1957. O'Connor is said to have perfected his wind-cheating irons on the very exposed Bundoran course.

Ballybofey & Stranorlar Golf Club

The Glebe, Stranorlar, Co. Donegal
tel: (074) 913-1093;
fax: (074) 913-1058
Parkland course in northeastern Donegal with outstanding views of River Finn and Lough Aran.

Greencastle Golf Club

Greencastle, Co. Donegal
tel: (074) 938-1015;
fax: (074) 938-1858
Remote, mixed parkland/links course located in northeast of Inishowen Peninsula which was extended to eighteen holes in 1992, its centenary year.

Gweedore Golf Club

Magheragallon, Derrybeg, Co. Donegal
tel: (074) 953-1140
Unprepossessing and hospitable seaside nine-hole club in remotest Donegal. The course has some fine views but does not live up to expectations, as much of it plays across a hill on non-links terrain. Nevertheless, a very active and friendly club which may some day expand the course to eighteen holes on more suitable golfing ground.

Letterkenny Golf Club

Barnhill, Letterkenny, Co. Donegal
tel: (074) 912-1150;
fax: (074) 912-1175;
e-mail: letterkennygc@eircom.net
A parkland layout on the shores of Lough Swilly, this was Eddie Hackett's first full-length design (in 1968), and features wide fairways and easily walkable terrain.

Redcastle Golf Club

Moville, Co. Donegal
tel: (074) 938-5555;
e-mail: info@carltonredcastle.ie
Nine-hole seaside parkland course within grounds of the Carlton Redcastle Hotel and Spa, just ten

minutes from Lough Foyle car ferry, makes a convenient base for those seeking upscale accommodation.

Londonderry, Tyrone and Fermanagh

Brown Trout Golf & Country Inn
209 Agivey Rd, Aghadowey, Coleraine, Co. Londonderry
tel: (028) 7086-8209;
fax: (028) 7086-8878;
e-mail: bill@browntroutinn.com
Short but challenging nine-hole course which is tree lined, with water in play on seven occasions, and is owned by the Brown Trout Inn.

Castle Hume Golf Club
Enniskillen, Co. Fermanagh
tel: (028) 6632-7077;
fax: (028) 6632-7076;
e-mail: info@castlehumegolf.com
Estate course built in a lovely setting on the banks of Lough Erne, with water in play on nine holes.

Enniskillen Golf Club
Castlecoole Rd, Enniskillen, Co. Fermanagh
tel: (028) 6632-5250;
fax: (028) 6632-9269;
e-mail: enniskillengolfclub@mail.com
Parkland course on which the much newer, spacious front nine contrasts with the original and old-fashioned back.

Moyola Park Golf Club
15 Curran Rd, Castledawson, Co. Londonderry
tel: (028) 7946-8468;
fax: (028) 7946-8626;
e-mail: moyolapark@btconnect.com
Thirty-year-old rolling, tree-lined parkland course bisected by River Moyola.

Strabane Golf Club
33 Ballycolman Rd, Strabane, Co. Tyrone
tel: (028) 7138-2271;
fax: (028) 7188-6514;
e-mail: strabane@aol.com
A 1974 Eddie Hackett redesign that plays along the River Mourne near the Sperrin Mountains.

Antrim

* Bushfoot Golf Club
50 Bushfoot Rd, Portballintrae, Co. Antrim
tel: (028) 2073-1317;
fax: (028) 2073-1852;
e-mail:
bushfootgolfclub@btconnect.com
Delightful nine-hole true links along the River Bush and within sight of Portballantrae beach.

* Larne Golf Club
54 Ferris Bay Rd, Islandmagee, Larne, Co. Antrim
tel: (028) 9338-2228;
fax: (028) 9338-2088;
e-mail: info@larnegolfclub.co.uk
Clifftop nine-hole course, part links in character, in spectacular setting on the southern tip of Islandmagee.

Ballyclare Golf Club
25 Springvale Rd, Ballyclare, Co. Antrim
tel: (028) 9332-2696;
e-mail: info@ballyclaregolfclub.net

Mature parkland course in the Antrim hills with water in play on several occasions.

Cairndhu Golf Club
192 Coast Rd, Ballygally, Larne, Co. Antrim
tel: (028) 2858-3324;
e-mail: cairndhugc@btconnect.com
Very hilly course which rewards with some spectacular views of the Antrim coast.

Lisburn Golf Club
68 Eglantine Rd, Lisburn, Co. Antrim
tel: (028) 9267-7216;
fax: (028) 9260-3608;
e-mail: info@lisburngolfclub.com
Attractive and mature Hawtree & Sons parkland design ten miles southwest of Belfast, the club dates from 1905, and the course at the present Blaris Lodge location dates from 1973.

Massereene Golf Club
Antrim, Co. Antrim
tel: (028) 9442-8096;
fax: (028) 9442-7661;
e-mail: info@massereene.com
Hawtree parkland layout which dates from 1961 and is set along the shore of Lough Neagh.

Whitehead Golf Club
McRae's Brea, Whitehead, Carrickfergus, Co. Antrim
tel: (028) 9337-0820;
fax: (028) 9337-0825;
e-mail: info@whiteheadgolfclub.com
Undulating course with exceptional views across Islandmagee and of the Antrim coast.

Belfast and Environs

* Balmoral Golf Club
518 Lisburn Rd, Belfast
tel: (028) 9038-1514;
fax: (028) 9038-6759;
e-mail: enquiries@balmoralgolf.com
A flat and tree-lined course dating from 1914, very close to Belfast city centre, was home to the great Irish player Fred Daly for more than forty years.

Holywood Golf Club
Nun's Walk, 76 Demesne Rd, Holywood, Co. Down
tel: (028) 9042-3135;
fax: (028) 9042-5040;
e-mail: mail@holywoodgolfclub.co.uk
Hilly course neighbouring Royal Belfast, with fine views over Belfast Lough.

The Knock Golf Club
Summerfield, Dundonald, Belfast
tel: (028) 9048-3251
Tree-lined, heavily bunkered course designed by H.S. Colt.

Down and Armagh

* Kirkistown Castle Golf Club
142 Main Rd, Cloughey, Newtonards, Co. Down
tel: (028) 4277-1233;
fax: (028) 4277-1699;
e-mail: info@linksgolfkirkistown.com
James Braid designed this flat, windswept moorland links overlooking the Irish Sea. The course has existed in the same location for over one hundred years, making it one of the oldest in Ireland.

Bangor Golf Club
Broadway, Bangor, Co. Down
tel: (028) 9127-0922;
fax: (028) 9145-3394;
e-mail:
secretary@bangorgolfclub.co.uk
James Braid designed, tree-lined
parkland course near Bangor town-
centre with views over Ballyholme
Bay. Home of David Feherty.

Bright Castle Golf Club
14 Coniamstown Rd, Bright,
Downpatrick, Co. Down
tel: (028) 4484-1319
Long and wide-open course (7,300
yards from the tips) which features a
735-yard par-6 hole; also has pitch-
and-putt course.

Co. Armagh Golf Club
Newry Rd, Armagh, Co. Armagh
tel: (028) 3752-5861;
e-mail: info@golfarmagh.co.uk
Tree-lined city centre course within
the walled demesne of the former
palace of the Archbishop of Armagh,
with distinctive limestone obelisk at
its highest point.

Donaghadee Golf Club
84 Warren Rd, Donaghadee, Co.
Down
tel: (028) 9188-3624;
fax: (028) 9188-8891
Part links, part parkland layout with
fine views over the Irish Sea. Recently
upgraded and hosted the 2001 Irish
Boys Championship.

Downpatrick Golf Club
43 Saul Rd, Downpatrick, Co. Down
tel: (028) 4461-5947;
fax: (028) 4461-7502
Undulating parkland course,
exceptional views from the seventh
fairway can extend to the Isle of Man.

Spa Golf Club
Grove Rd, Ballynahinch, Co. Down
tel: (028) 9756-2365;
fax: (028) 9756-4158;
e-mail: spagolfclub@btconnect.com
Parkland course situated amongst
drumlins with fine views of
Mountains of Mourne. The club
celebrates its centenary in 2007.

Warrenpoint Golf Club
Warrenpoint, Co. Down
tel: (028) 4175-3695;
fax: (028) 4175-2918;
e-mail: office@warrenpointgolf.com
Scenic course in tight location
nevertheless has views of Mountains
of Mourne and the Republic across
Carlingford Lough. Produced Ryder
Cup player Ronan Rafferty.

Index

Principal entries for featured golf courses are in **bold**

INDEX

INDEX